D0787021

Environmental Economics in Practice

Environmental Economics
in Practice
Case Studies from India

Edited
by
GOPAL K. KADEKODI

OXFORD
UNIVERSITY PRESS

OXFORD

UNIVERSITY PRESS

YMCA Library Building, Jai Singh Road, New Delhi 110001

Oxford University Press is a department of the University of Oxford. It furthers the University's objective of excellence in research, scholarship, and education by publishing worldwide in

Oxford   New York

Auckland   Bangkok   Buenos Aires   Cape Town   Chennai
Dar es Salaam   Delhi   Hong Kong   Istanbul   Karachi   Kolkata
Kuala Lumpur   Madrid   Melbourne   Mexico City   Mumbai   Nairobi
São Paulo   Shanghai   Taipei   Tokyo   Toronto

Oxford is a registered trade mark of Oxford University Press
in the UK and in certain other countries

Published in India
By Oxford University Press, New Delhi

© Oxford University Press 2004

ISBN 0 19 566617 8

Typeset in GaryOwen by Jojy Philip, Delhi 110 027
Printed at Pauls Press, New Delhi 110 020
Published by Manzar Khan, Oxford University Press
YMCA Library Building, Jai Singh Road, New Delhi 110 001

'When Heaven sends down calamities,
Man may escape from them,
If a man occasions calamities himself,
He will no longer be able to live.'

Mencius (Meng Tzu),
Third Century BC.

Contents

Preface

Capacity building in the use and application of environmental economics at policy and project design levels has been on the cards in India ever since the Rio declaration of the United Nations Conference on Environment and Development that took place in 1992. One of the most felt needs was developing practical case studies demonstrating the methods of economic analysis, as relevant to the problems of environmental management in India. Keeping this objective in perspective, this book is developed under the World Bank-supported programme on capacity building in environmental economics in India. It is hoped that it will meet the needs of policy-makers, practising economists, officers of state and central governments handling environmentally-sensitive projects, NGOs, and action researchers.

This is a book of case studies covering various aspects of environmental issues, and introducing appropriate economic, statistical, and sociological tools and methods. The focus of the book is on demonstrating the usefulness of environmental economics in practical applications to policy and action works. Each of the chapters is carefully chosen to meet this objective. The range of environmental issues is fairly exhaustive, covering land, forest, biodiversity and soil degradation to air and water pollution; urban issues such as solid waste management to national environmental accounting (popularly known as Green GDP Accounting); issues related to exhausting natural resources and many more. A host of economic methods and tools are available to deal with such issues. Broadly they fall within the purview of Public Economics, Micro and Macroeconomics, and Development Economics. A number of statistical and other tools are currently available to analyse the problems and also to suggest methods to deal with them. The case studies, in a way, are illustrating combinations of such economic and statistical methods, tools and policy approaches.

The book is targeted at meeting the requirements of policy-makers, managers of environmentally-relevant projects and programmes, and practising economists. While keeping this as the main objective, it is felt that there is a need to introduce some basic elements of environmental economics to the readers. Accordingly, a chapter on 'Environmental Economics through Case Studies' is developed in a somewhat unconventional way. It covers some of the major themes and topics in environmental economics, as introductory. The purpose is not to provide any textbook level discussion on the various theories and topics, but to enable policy-makers and action researchers to get familiar with available economic methods. The selected references at the end of different chapters provide many more readings and references to serve the same purpose.

In developing this book, I had the benefits of advice and guidance from a large number of scholars, researchers, practising economists and policy-makers. Kanchan Chopra, chairperson of the EETCPN sub-programme of the World Bank Aided India: Environmental Management Capacity Building Technical Assistance Project, has been a constant source of encouragement for this book. Without her generous help, it would have been very difficult to bring this book on time. I am extremely grateful to her. I also benefited from the generous support of P.R. Panchamukhi, director of CMDR, who also provided valuable comments and suggestions to make this book more purposive. I am thankful to all the contributors to this book, who had to bear with me in making this venture on time and also to have met the requirements in their respective chapters as per the agenda of the book. A large number of academic scholars provided data, information, and feedback on earlier drafts of the various chapters. I would like to express my sincere thanks to all of them. Finally, the 'page by page' work, and doing 'little by little' was handled by two of my efficient assistants. I am very thankful tò Rajeshwari Mathad and Seema Hegde for this. Ganesh Naik and Gururaj Haribhat provided the skilful support in processing the manuscripts on the computer. I am grateful to them.

At the end, it is hoped that this book will bridge the knowledge gaps between the economic researchers and practising policy-makers and the people, to whom environmental management has come as the greatest challenge of this century.

Dharwad
March 2003

Gopal K. Kadekodi

Contributors

P.A. Appasamy, Madras School of Economics, Chennai.

Kanchan Chopra, Institute of Economic Growth, Delhi.

Meghan Dunleavy, MCP Hahnemann School of Medicine and World Bank, Washington, D.C.

Ravi Hegde, TERI, New Delhi.

Gordon Hughes, The World Bank, Washington D.C., and NERA Ltd., and University of Edinburgh.

S. Jyothis, Ecological Economic Unit, Institute for Social and Economic Change, Bangalore.

Gopal K. Kadekodi, Institute for Social and Economic Change, Bangalore. Formerly with Centre for Multi-Disciplinary Development Research, Dharwad.

Kseniya Lvovsky, The World Bank, Washington, D.C.

M.N. Murty, Institute of Economic Growth, Delhi.

K.N. Ninan, Institute for Social and Economic Change, Bangalore.

Jyoti Parikh, Indira Gandhi Institute for Development Research, Mumbai.

P. Ram Babu, PricewaterhouseCoopers Ltd., Mumbai.

U. Sankar, Madras School of Economics, Chennai.

T.P. Singh, TERI, New Delhi.

List of Tables

List of Boxes

List of Figures

Glossary

Autecology
: The ecology of the whole, individual, or species, as distinct from that of a whole community.

Biodiversity
: The degree of nature's variety, including both the number and frequency of ecosystems, species and genes in a given assemblage.

Biomass
: The weight of living material, usually expressed as weight of dry matter per unit area, for example gm/m^2.

Biome
: A climatic region, characterized by its dominant vegetation.

Biotic
: Pertaining to life.

BOD
: Biological Oxygen Demand, the dissolved oxygen required by organisms for the aerobic decomposition of organic matter present in water. Used as a measure in determining the efficiency of a sewage treatment plant.

Carrying Capacity
: The maximum number of organisms or biomass which can be supported in a given area under defined circumstances.

Cladistics
: An evolutionary classification method which is based on phylogenetic hypotheses and recent common ancestries rather than on phenetic similarity.

Community
: Populations of different species inhabiting the same area or habitat bound together by their biotic interrelationships.

Concept of Irreversibility
: Implies a change in a natural resource which can not be reversed; the resource is not replaceable.

Consumer Surplus	The difference between total willingness to pay, as measured by area under the demand curve and amount actually paid.
Contingent Valuation	Valuation based on the creation of hypothetical markets, in which preferences are stated by the consumers.
Cost Benefit Analysis (CBA)	The appraisal of an investment project which includes all social and\or financial costs and benefits using a prestated decision criteria.
Demand Curve Function	A function expressing units of a commodity demanded as dependent on price, income and other relevant variables.
Direct Use Value	Economic values derived from direct use or interaction with a biological resource or resource system.
Demand Elasticity	Percentage change in quantity demanded of a commodity divided by percentage change in price of the product.
Diversity Index	As in a community, the ratio between the number of species and number of individuals.
Ecosystem/ Ecological Resilience	A measure of the magnitude of disturbance that can be absorbed before the system changes its structure by changing the variables and processes that control behaviour. Or the measure of resistance to disturbance and the speed of return to the equilibrium state of an ecosystem.
Ecosystem Services	Ecological processes or functions which have value to individuals or society.
Ecotone	A transition zone between adjacent ecosystems, which contains some organisms and characteristics of both adjacent systems plus some restricted to the zone itself.
Endemic	An organism which is only found in the area being considered.
Eutrophication	The nutrient enrichment of bodies of water caused by organic enrichment. Although a natural process, rapid eutrophication can drain oxygen levels and thus result in mortality of aquatic organisms.
Exsitu Conservation	Keeping components of biodiversity alive away from their original habitat or natural environment.

Existence Value	The value of knowing that a particular species, habitat or ecosystem does and will continue to exist. It is independent of any use that the valuer may make of the resource.
Exotics	Species introduced from another region.
Externalities	Unexpected or unaccounted for side effects of an event, either favourable or unfavourable.
Extinction	A species becomes extinct when there are no longer any living representatives.
Genetic Diversity	Variation in the genetic composition of individuals within or among species, the heritable genetic variation within and among populations.
Genome	All the genes of a particular organism or species.
Genotype	The entire genetic constitution of an organism, or the genetic composition at a specific gene locus or set of loci.
Habitat	The locality or area used by a population of organisms and the place where they live.
Insitu Conservation	Conservation of biodiversity within the evolutionary dynamic ecosystems of the original habitat or natural environment.
Joint Product	Two or more products that are consumed jointly at the same or almost the same cost.
Keystone Species	A species whose loss from an ecosystem would cause a greater than average change in other species populations or ecosystems processes.
Kharif Season	The monsoon season crop, sown in late June\July and harvested in October/November.
Marginal Value	The change in the value of a resource that is due to an incremental change in its quantity.
Market Value	Price of a produce expressed in money/barter terms in a market.
Market Failure	This occurs when market prices are not equal to the social opportunity cost of resources. External effects or externalities are evidence of market failure.
Monotypic	Taxonomic group with a single component such as a

family or genus composed of a single genus or species respectively.

Multi-criteria Analysis (MCA)	A technique of analysis which incorporates a range of decision criteria.
Neoclassical	Dominant tradition in Economics assuming cardinality of utility and using techniques of marginal analysis to analyse utility maximizing behaviour of individuals.
Net Present Social Benefit (NPSB)	Excess of the discounted present value of benefits over the discounted present value of costs, measured at social prices.
Net Present Value (NPV)	The discounted value of the net benefits of the use of a resource.
Niche	The 'space' occupied by and the resources used by a species. Conceptually the niche has many dimensions and each resource used by the species can be considered as a dimension.
Non-use Value	Value accruing out of the knowledge of existence of a resource, without any present or future intention to use it.
Opportunity Cost	The value of the best alternative use of a resource. This consists of the maximum value of other outputs we could and would have produced had we not used the resource to produce the item in question.
Phenetic	Similarity based on characters selected without regard to evolutionary history and including characters arising from common ancestry.
Phenotype	The observed traits of an organism, resulting from an interaction of its genotype and its environment.
Preference Function	A function defining individual preferences over a given utility space.
Primary Productivity	The rate at which energy from the sun is absorbed by plants in the production of organic matter.
Quasi-option Value	The value of future information made available through the preservation of a resource.
Rabi Season	Winter cropping season, usually from November to April.

Sensitivity Analysis	An analysis of a project with changing values of different parameters defining constraints.
Social Welfare Function	Function defining welfare of society as a summation of individual welfare.
Species richness	The number of species present in an area.
Species diversity	The variety and number of species in an area (c/f species richness).
Species	A group of organisms of the same kind that can reproduce sexually among themselves but are reproductively isolated from other organisms. The basic unit in a classification.
Stakeholders	A group or individual with any interest or stake in a resource or habitat.
Surrogate markets	Markets used in place of the missing markets for environmental resources. Surrogate markets are at least existing markets for resources with some of the properties of the non-marketed resource being valued.
Threatened Species	Species that are often genetically impoverished, of low fecundity, dependent on patchy or unpredictable resources, extremely variable in population density, persecuted or otherwise prone to extinction in human-dominated landscapes.
Time Horizon	The period of time taken into account.
Total Economic Value	The sum of use and non-use values with due consideration of any trade-offs or mutually exclusive uses or functions of the resource/habitat in question.
Travel Cost Method (TCM)	A method which uses the travel costs incurred by an individual to reach the site as a surrogate for the price of the site. Since the travel costs will vary across individuals living at different distances from the site, this data can be used to derive a demand curve for the site services.
Use Value	Values obtained through the use of a resource. This includes direct and indirect use values. Preservation in this sense is as much a use as development.
Valuation	A method for determining environmental consequences

of economic activity that are not taken into account in market transactions.

Weights	The significance attached to groups or individuals.
Willingness to Accept (WTA)	The amount of compensation an individual is willing to take in exchange for giving up some good or service. This may be elicited from stated or revealed preference approaches.
Willingness to Pay (WTP)	The amount an individual is willing to pay to acquire some good or service. This may be elicited from stated or revealed preference approaches.

Environmental Economics
Through Case Studies

Gopal K. Kadekodi

WHY DO WE NEED A BOOK OF CASE STUDIES IN ENVIRONMENTAL ECONOMICS ?

This book is intended to enthuse practising economists and policy makers, who have to deal with environmental matters on a day-to-day basis. Elements of environmental economics deal with best methods of application of environmental regulations and laws to deal with environmental problems and management in various sectors of the economy on implementability and monitoring. A lot of thinking will have gone into their logic, practicality, and applicability. In all such situations, apart from economics, elements of sociology, history, law, and anthropology are to be employed to make environmental management a reality. Therefore, even a cursory exposure to such social scientific tools and methods can make the practitioners appreciate the thinking behind such regulations and laws. In this book, therefore, the economic, sociological, statistical and other tools are demonstrated through various case studies as are relevant for policy makers, practising economists and NGOs. Since environmental issues are not only restricted to water or air pollution, ten different environmentally-relevant themes and issues have been selected as case studies for the book which are briefly described in this chapter.

Rapid growth of industrialization within the country, liberalization of the external sector, globalization in terms of flow of direct foreign investments and privatization, together with increasing population pressures have been witnessed in India in the last decades of the twentieth century. The process of restructuring the Indian economy has, however, paved the growth path of the country at a pace much higher than the 'new Hindu growth rate of 5 per cent', a phrase borrowed from Parikh (1999). Is this new growth paradigm without any costs? Among many questions that come to our mind is the fundamental issue of increasing demands made on natural and environmental resources of the country in a globalized world economy. India is very rich in a number of natural resources. It is a land of the great Himalayan mountains, vast Western and Eastern Ghats, major rivers such as Ganga, Brahmaputra, Narmada, Krishna, and Godavari, forests spread all over India covering about 20 per cent of the geographical area, rich biodiversity in plant and animal life, areas rich in fossil and solid fuels, ferrous and non-ferrous minerals, vast coastal and marine ecosystems, backwaters, large lakes such as Chilka (covering an area about 1200 sq km) and Loktal, mangroves such as Sundarbans and many more[1]. Being a tropical country, diverse environmental resources are also visible such as diverse soil types (differing in soil texture, colour, depth, salinity, drainage and water percolation level), temperature zones (from hot Rajasthan deserts, temperate main lands, to cold sub-zero Himalayan high-altitude zones), air (varying from fresh ocean blows to polluted and clogged and smoggy levels in urban areas), water quality (varying in its mineral contents and hazardous chemicals), rainfall (varying from no rain in parts of Rajasthan to high of 500 m.m. in Chirapunji) and so on. All these attributes directly and indirectly contribute to the development process of the country, some positively and some negatively. In turn, they raise the issue of their sustainable management. The management of all such resources is a joint responsibility of the government, citizens, scientists and NGOs.

The starting point to be understood is that management of natural and environmental resources requires scientific and technological methods going hand-in-hand with a socio-economic approach. After all, nature belongs to all. Environment is a public good. Though a gift of God, natural resources are the inheritance of all societies. Hence, its use in the current spaceship of development has to be carefully monitored and managed with a social outlook (Boulding, 1966). It is with this in view that a concept of sustainable development is being talked about. By sustainable development, we mean attaining a sustainable resource management while attaining sustainable level of

---

[1] Interested reader can have a summary account of all these from Annex A.1.

living. Therefore, methods of sustainable development require an interdisciplinary and unified approach encompassing natural and social sciences.

Talking about an interdisciplinary approach, a number of methods and tools, out of the foundations of economic and sociological theories, have been found to be relevant to look at the management of natural and environmental resources. The major ones are: theory of public finance and public choice, economics of trade and development, micro theories of production, investment and consumption decision-making, theory of value, valuation and accounting, theory of evaluation of resource use, political economy of property rights, theory of institutions, theory of sustainable development and several other branches of social sciences.

How far are these theoretical foundations relevant and practical in the management of natural and environmental resources in India? To what extent are the economic and sociological methods and tools to be designed to suit the Indian socio-economic, cultural, anthropological, historical and ecological conditions and situations? How does a development administrator use the economic methods and tools in policy making towards the goal of sustainable use of natural resources? How to build institutions to manage natural resources and the environment in the best interests of the present and future generations?

The answers to these questions are not easy. But, ever since the 1972 Stockholm conference of the Heads of Nations and subsequently the UN Conference of Environment and Development (UNCED) held in Rio de Janeiro in 1992, followed by the Johannesburg Conference on Sustainable Development in 2002, the concerns of all nations including India have been increasingly aired to conserve, preserve, and protect our natural resources on a sustainable basis in the best interests of the people. Governments are to act as enablers and not masters. A number of countries, including India, have committed to implement several measures to protect and preserve the natural and environmental resources. For instance, among many declarations of the Rio Conference under Agenda 21, some of the major ones are:

- encouraging macroeconomic policies conducive to environment and development;
- reducing health risk from environmental pollution and hazards;
- promoting sustainable development through trade liberalization;
- making trade and environment mutually supportive;

- promoting patterns of consumption and production that reduce environmental stress and to meet the basic needs of humanity;
- assessing human vulnerability in ecologically-sensitive areas and centres of population to determine the priorities for action at all levels, taking full account of community-defined needs;
- integrating environment and development at the policy, planning and management levels;
- establishing a system for integrated environment and economic accounting.

When it comes to environmental management, therefore, there is a huge agenda of planning, policy and action needed at all levels. Environmental economics, enters in all these spheres. With such an objective, a number of studies and researches have been specifically carried out in India during the last 30 years, so as to develop appropriate economic and sociological tools and methods to aid the management of our natural resources and policy making.

A number of studies are carried out across the country on a variety of environmental issues. Each study refers to a specific situation, a specific environmental problem, or even specifically relevant policy options. Exposure to the major economic, sociological and statistical methods through selected case studies is one of the best ways to understand their relevance for policy planning and design of institutions to protect and preserve environmental resources.

This book is a compendium of case studies in environmental economics based on a large number of research projects where basic economic, sociological and statistical methods and tools have been applied in the Indian context towards better policy structuring. The relevance of the basic economic theory and tools is better understood only when they are put to actual practice at the policy and action levels. The case studies presented in this book are aimed at bridging this knowledge gap between the theory of environmental economics, its practicability and policy relevance. Using environment- ecology-economy-linked approaches, effective natural resource management is proposed.

The case studies are selected based strictly on three criteria. Firstly, the case studies demonstrate the usefulness and applicability of different economic models and approaches (without replicating them). Examples are theory of public finance and welfare economics, theory of institutions and societal behaviour, and micro and macro-economic theories of price, value and income etc. Secondly, they demonstrate different statistical and mathematical tools that are commonly used in environmental economics. Examples are statistical regression theory, cost–benefit analysis etc. Thirdly, care is taken to cover different aspects of environmental issues. The notable ones are pollution abatement, health hazards and costs of environmental degradation, solid waste management, accounting for natural resources such as biodiversity and forests etc.

WHAT ECONOMICS HAS TO OFFER IN ENVIRONMENTAL MANAGEMENT?

Most people dealing with environmental management (e.g., pollution control boards, foresters, mining engineers, irrigation engineers, soil scientists, NGOs and the like) ask one basic question. What has economics got to do with environmental management? Looking at the Agenda 21 of the Rio Declaration or otherwise, environmental economics enters as an important tool in many aspects of environmental management. It is useful to take a look at one possible definition of environmental economics.

Economics is the science of explaining the behaviour of different agents who take part in production, consumption and distribution activities in the economy and make decisions regarding the use of resources. By agents we mean, the households (men, women, children, elders and so on), traders, producers, government, scientists, NGOs and many more. Market is considered as one among the many institutions around which this behavioural science is developed. Natural and environmental resources are very much a part of the set of resources that economic science explores for their sustainable use and development, but with three major differences. First, environmental and many natural resources do not always have a market. That leads to several problems of externality associated with such resources (hence a gap between the value and notional price, or between equilibrium and the actual rates of use). Second, they have the peculiarity of inter-generational use. Because of this, standard static (that is, without a time dimension) economic models do not serve the whole process of decision-making on production, pricing and distribution. There is also the question of appropriate discount rate. Third, they are subjected to a variety of property rights systems different from individual or private property rights' (open access, public goods, common property resources, common pool resources etc.). Therefore, management of such resources makes it necessary to go beyond the conventional economic theories. That is what makes environmental economics as a branch of economics. Environmental economics focuses on market and non-market behaviour of different agents in the society regarding natural and environmental resources, viewed from inter-generational, inter-temporal and different institutional frameworks.

Before viewing the applications of environmental economics, as seen through various case studies presented as separate chapters, it is important to briefly understand the various economic and sociological theories, tools and methods that are directly relevant for improving the management of environmental resources. However, in this brief introductory chapter only selected topics or methods will be summarily dealt with (Hanley et al., 1997; Pearce and Turner, 1990). The case-study chapters following this chapter provide more details on the kinds of economic methods specifically applied for the particular natural-resource situation.

Among the many aspects of environmental economics in theory, the following are specifically dealt with here so as to give a flavour of them, before dealing with the case studies. They are: Welfare Economics, Public Economics, Theory of Valuation, Linkage between Environment and Development, Theory of Sustainable Development and Theory of Property Rights and Institutions (Bhattacharya, 2001).

Welfare Economics

Welfare economics is an important branch of economic theory. It aims to evaluate economic policies, for the common good, in terms of their effects on the well-being of individuals and the community as a whole. It is a branch of economics that goes beyond an analysis of individual behaviour (e.g., as a consumer or as a firm). It deals with the society as a whole in respect of decision making with reference to the management of resources, production and consumption activities. The community behaviour in the management of natural and environmental resources is different from the individual behaviour. Therefore, there can be conflicts between the private interests, rationality or objectives and public or social objectives. For instance, to litter a road with garbage may be perfectly rational for any individual (in the absence of any collective responsibility), as it does not cost anything, but not one's own house (as it adds to one's own cost of cleaning the floor or house). Most issues relating to environmental and natural resources have some relevance in a societal sense. That is what makes welfare economics relevant for Environmental Economics. The theoretical foundation for this branch of economics is a concept of competition and individual rationality. Under individual rationality, it is assumed that individuals, firms or even government (in some instances) are free to choose out of a variety of alternative options regarding consumption, production, marketing, distribution etc., in a competitive situation without being influenced by each other, but dictated by one's own ability, capability and preferences.[2] Competitive conditions make all the individuals and firms to be price takers and not dictators. There is a concept of 'Pareto optimal solution' which means that no alternative situation or solution can make all other members of the society better off without making at least one of them worse-off. Individual rationality with competitive conditions then makes the society reach the Pareto optimum.[3]

But, when it comes to natural and environmental resources, many of these assumptions do not hold good. The resources are not necessarily privately-owned. Many of them are public goods, e.g., a wildlife sanctuary. Because of the 'open access' nature of several natural and environmental resources, there is a problem commonly known as 'tragedy of the commons' (or some kinds of externalities). Examples of open-access grazing is common in India. When it comes to natural common resources, individuals are not independent in their choices as regards their uses. In many parts of the country, there are customary (including religious) laws and norms on the use of natural resources such as protecting sacred groves. Apart from being interdependent, they may have to give some weight to equity and interpersonal comparisons. Many natural resources do not have markets; and even if they have, they are not competitive. An example of market for fuelwood can be given here. Therefore, only under very ideal (so called laissez-faire) conditions, such individual rationality can also

---

[2] More fundamentally, the individuals are assumed to be utility maximizers and firms are to maximize profits, or a revenue-maximizing government may be maximizing tax earnings.

[3] A well-known criticism of this Pareto optimality condition is about its inability to guarantee any equitable distribution of gains (or losses), from the use of resources in production or consumption.

lead to a common good (Pigou, 1952; Little, 1960; Arrow, 1951; Sen, 1970). How to get to the common good under the circumstances in which natural resources are to be managed? This is the basic question posed in welfare economics, essentially as a search for a social welfare function having certain acceptable properties. This is not only an economic question but also a political one, in the sense that community as a whole has to come to an understanding of what is best for them. Given the real-life situation, the social welfare can not be a sum of individual welfare (unless all the assumptions for Pareto optimality are met). Is there a possibility of a social-welfare function, that can guide decisions regarding the use of resources?

Regarding this question, starting from the early works of Bergson (1938) and Arrow (1951), developments in Welfare Economics have reached very little beyond saying that under conditions normally expected of the society, such a group rationality or social welfare does not exist (Arrow, 1951; Sen, 1977). The normal social conditions or behaviour expected are: (i) unanimity in the decision making process, (ii) existence of non-dictatorship among the members of the society, (iii) existence of transitivity in individual's preferences and choices, (iv) possibility of a wide range of alternatives to choose from and (v) the alternatives to be independent (Sen, 1977). All these conditions are extremely difficult to maintain or fulfil in a real-life situation. A possible practical approach, based on recent experiments in 'stakeholder analysis' is to bring together all the major agents or parties involved (or associated) with the natural and environmental resource under question, and evolve such solutions that are most 'conflict resolving'. The chapter 'Stakeholder Analysis in Joint Forest Management' by T.P. Singh and Ravi Hegde develops one such approach in the management of forest resources.

The distribution or sharing the gains from the use of natural and environmental resources is as important as the welfare of all the members of community. This is a standard question in Economics, as part of the theory of distribution. In the absence of markets, as the case may be with common-property resources, or open-access resources, before launching any environmental and natural resource-based programmes (e.g., afforestation, watershed development etc.), there is a need to design the sharing rules, well in advance, in a transparent way (Olson, 1965; Ostrom, 1990; Chopra et al., 1990).

On Public Economics

In a way, Public Economics can be considered as an extension of Welfare Economics. It is the 'study of public economy or economy at large, of economic questions requiring public interventions on individual (or firm) behaviour or market economy through taxes and subsidies, and relating to issues arising from market failures'. The starting point is the failure of the market-based instruments to handle the problems of resource management. The 'common good' (referred in 'Welfare Economics') to be attained by the society often requires some interventions by the 'state'. The 'state' can be in the forms of central or state governments, municipal corporations and such other bodies (including Zilla Panchayats). The interventions can be in the forms of taxes, subsidies, quota, sanctions and zoning, rules and regulations etc.[4] Among many, there are two major reasons for such interventions. First, a large number of environmental and natural-resource linked goods and services are 'public good' in character. They are often subjected to open access, due to ill-defined or less-understood property rights, conventions and traditional rights. Second, externalities (in production, consumption and distribution) arise in the management of such resources.

Accordingly, there are three broad areas of natural resource economics that require the treatment of public economics. They are: i) theory of public goods as applied to resource economics, ii) theory of production and consumption externality, and iii) theory of collective action.

Public goods are those resources, that are not owned by any one individual (or firm), the use of it by one individual or firm (with or without payment) does not exclude others from using or enjoying it (or the users or consumers of it do not have any rivalry among them). It entitles for collective use or consumption and often they are indivisible (because of which, no individual may be capable of appropriating it).[5] Example of public-good natural and environmental resources are

---

[4] Examples of these are: taxes on petrol, subsidy on kerosene, quota on exporting timber, zoning for sugar trade, rules and regulations regarding environmental waste discharge (of polluted water), water charges and so on.

[5] A more rigorous definition of public good requires an added condition that it is available at zero marginal cost to the user. It may also be owned by single individual, firm or the 'state', but the owner can not exclude one or the other from using such a resource. For instance, a patent holder owns a technology, receives royalty from the

public parks or wildlife sanctuaries, oceans, waterways (with or without toll fee) and so on. In the management of such public goods, apart from applying the modified Pareto optimality condition that 'sum of all the individual marginal rates of substitution to be equal to the marginal rate of transformation', policy tools of taxes, subsidies and several rules can be suitably designed to regulate the use of such resources. Several other allocative rules and policy imperatives drawn from the economics of public goods should be followed. For instance, in the case of public parks, there can be entry fees, time restrictions, security restrictions and so on (Buchanan, 1968; Atkinson and Stiglitz, 1980).

Public economics can be applied for problems of managing ocean fishing, forest and game sanctuary, water bodies and such other natural resources. Fixing an entry fee for a national park such as Keoladeo Bird Sanctuary dealt as a case study, by Kanchan Chopra. The chapter gives some practical insights into estimating the value of the park and designing appropriate entry fees.

Secondly, recognizing that natural resources have inter-generational values, their rates of extraction and use and price are matters of Resource Economics. This is particularly relevant for both non-renewable and renewable resources. In particular, some of the tools of Resource Economics, with or without public-good characterizations are using methods such as consumer surplus theory, willingness to pay, willingness to accept, and user costs, the inter-generationally consistent welfare models for optimal rates of extraction and prices (Hotelling, 1931; El Serafy, 1989). The case studies by M.N. Murty, U. Sankar, and Kanchan Chopra amply demonstrate the use of these concepts.

As stated in the beginning of this section, design of intervention strategies by the 'state' is very much a part of the theory of Public Economics. Consider the example of abating pollution. In the absence of economic instruments (such as pricing or taxing), various countries have adopted 'command and control' strategies of pollution reduction. Recent theories and experimentations with economic instruments

---

users of it, but can not restrict entry of others from using it. Once a royalty is paid, the repeated use by the individual does not attract additional royalty. Similarly, once an entrance fee is paid, enjoying a public park over hours and hours does not ask for additional fee.

have shown that a combination of tax and subsidy measures that are regulatory in nature show better results. These are inherently based on the notion of defining a socially acceptable (or scientifically tolerable) level of pollution to be regulated through a fiscal regime. The idea behind any fiscal measure and incentives is to reduce the environmental damage to a particular level and not necessarily aim at reducing it to zero. Assuming that the 'principle of polluter pays' is an implementable policy, it is possible to arrive at optimum tax and subsidy rates to manage the environmental degradation. For reasons beyond economics, however, it may not be feasible to introduce such optimum tax or subsidy rates. Then, the fiscal method does not guarantee attaining environmental standards based on technical and consumers' tolerance evaluations. Therefore, a combination of fiscal methods and standards may be necessary to arrive at the most acceptable policies. M.N. Murty goes into the relevance of such a 'tax-standard' approach the Indian context. After reviewing the present practice of regulatory mechanisms through the Pollution Control Boards, he presents a case study of water pollution to which the 'tax-standards' approach has been applied and demonstrated. Murty also goes one step ahead by spelling out the various stages and steps involved in estimating the tax-standard-based fiscal instrument for introducing Combined Effluent Treatment Plants (CETPs) in India.

The tax principle, first developed systematically by A.C. Pigou (1952) accounts for pollution damage as a social cost and the net benefit from production activities as a private gain to the polluter, who creates the pollution externalities. Assuming that a polluter finds it worth paying pollution tax up to a level when the marginal net benefit (profits) from production activities is greater than the marginal tax to be paid, it is possible to derive the optimum pollution damage and the corresponding tax rate. However, in practice, it will be extremely difficult to identify and estimate the marginal damage due to pollution activities and, hence, to arrive at precise optimum tax rates. To the extent that marginal gains from production activities are difficult to identify and estimate, the tax principles are often misused and cursed.

Alternatively, the social optimum damages may be defined as an absolute maximum standard of acceptable pollution level arrived at on the basis of health or any other standard, defined exogeneously. Acceptable environmental concentration (for example, x micrograms per m³ of air, or levels of contamination in drinking water) are decided by Pollution Control Boards that have the power to impose penalty in case of violation of standards. The setting of standards may further be complemented by a host of incentive policies, the likes of which are listed in Table 1.1.

TABLE 1.1
Typology of Economic-Incentive Pollution Control Instruments

Type of instrument	General description
Effluent charges	Paid on 'discharges into the environment' and are based on the quantity and /or quality of the effluent.
Incentive effluent charges	Revenue collected via the charge; it is not returned to the polluter.
Distribute effluent charges	Revenue collected via the charge; part of it is returned to the polluter, in the form of subsidies on abatement equipment.
User charges	Payments for the cost of collective or public treatment of effluents.
Product charges/tax differentiation	Additions to the price of products that are polluting or are difficult to dispose of; the former have a revenue-raising feature.
Administrative charges	Control and authorization fees.
Subsidies/Grants	Non-repayable forms of financial assistance, contingent on the adoption of pollution-abatement measures.
Soft loans	Loans linked to abatement measures and carrying below-market rates of interest.
Tax allowances	Allows accelerated depreciation, tax or charge exemptions or rebates if certain pollution-abatement measures are adopted.
Deposit-refund system	Systems in which surcharges are laid on the price of potentially-polluting; refund of the surcharge is given on the return of the product or its residuals.
Market creation	Artificial markets in which actors can buy and sell 'rights' for actual or potential pollution.

Type of instrument	General description
Emissions trading (bubbles, offsets, netting and banking)	Within a plant, within a firm or among different firms.
Market intervention	Price intervention to stabilize markets, typically secondary materials' (recycled) markets.
Liability insurance	Polluter liability leading to the insurance market.

Source: Pearce and Turner (1990)

Some of the options shown in Table 1.1 are based on the 'polluter-pays' principle. For practical reasons the choice of these methods is often guided by 'revenue raising' and 'bureaucratic compatibility' criterion. Usually a combination of regulation and incentive instruments serve the objective of pollution control quite well, as long as maintaining economic efficiency is not the primary goal. A combination of 'standards' and tax policy will generally be preferable to the imposition of standards alone, unless the latter recommends outright prohibition.

The second major application of Public Economics is the problem of externality. To the extent environmental resources are not privately owned, there is every possibility that their care and concern is minimal in the eyes of the people and the public at large. Buffer areas of forests can be one such example, when the neighbourhood villagers do not take good care of those forest areas. In an economic language, this is termed as a problem of externality. Externality in Economics is defined as 'a situation when there are unpaid (or uncompensated) side effects or free benefits of production or consumption suffered or enjoyed by other producers or consumers'. A situation in which no single individual feels responsible to bear the cost of the damages done to the environment due to her or his actions in production or in consumption is called negative externality. Externality can also be positive. An example of positive externality is a resident enjoying fresh air coming from a nearby public green patch or park. On the other hand, an open drainage in a neighbourhood that increases one's health problem is a case of negative externality. In a sense, externality is a public 'bad' or 'good' depending upon whether there is negative or positive externality.

Again, externality can be at the stage of production or consumption.

Industries dumping polluted water in the rivers without treating the effluents 'at least to a level of bathing quality' is a case of production externality; urban households dumping kitchen waste on the roads is that of consumption externality. Talking in economic terms, essentially, externality can bring in a divergence between the social costs and private costs, and/or social benefits and private benefits. In such a situation, the equilibrium solution by equating private marginal costs and private marginal benefits does not yield a social optimum of costs and benefits (rather they yield sub-optimum), as can be seen from Figures 1.1a and 1.1b. In the presence of any negative externality, the social marginal costs are higher than the private marginal costs. Then, as compared to private optimization (when marginal benefits (MB) equal private marginal cost (PMC)), the social optimization (when marginal benefits equal to social marginal cost (SMC)) leads to a lower level of production and a higher social value or price. In other words, some one will have to bear the social costs, anyway. Social Benefit-Cost models (referred in 'Tools and Methods of Economic Analysis') are designed to arrive at the corresponding rules for decision-making. Likewise, if there is any positive externality, the social marginal

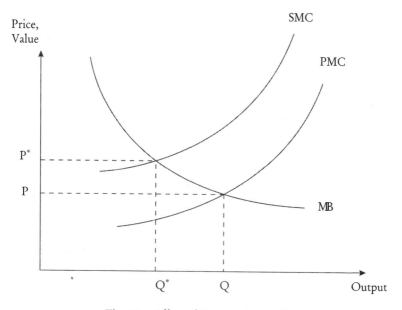

Fig. 1.1a: Effect of Negative Externality

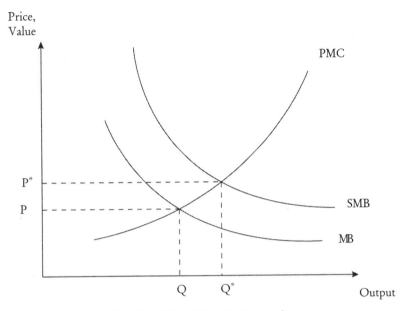

Fig. 1.1b: Effect of Positive Externality

benefits (SMB) would be higher; but the additional benefits will have to be paid (as socially-optimum value or price P^* is higher than private price or value P).

Public economics and public finance theories can provide methods to deal with the problems of externalities emerging out of using natural and environmental resources. 'Fiscal and Institutional Approaches to Pollution Abatement' by M.N. Murty and 'Pollution Control in Tanneries' by U. Sankar go substantially into such externality problems associated with industrial water pollution and demonstrate the possibility of designing appropriate interventions such as setting up of CETPs. Paul Appasamy in his chapter 'Economic Benefit-Cost Analysis of a Proposed Solid Waste Resource Recovery Plant' highlights the externality problem of solid waste in the urban city of Lucknow. While these are demonstrations of production externalities, the chapter 'The Health Benefits of Improving the Household Enviroment' by Hughes, Dunleavy and Lvovsky provides a case of consumption externality. They estimate the cost of improving household or indoor environment by minimizing pollution and link it to health benefits. In doing so, they also demonstrate the method of estimation and use of 'disability-adjusted life years (DALY)', as against the commonly used 'expectation of life at birth' as an indicator of health status.

The major relevant economic instruments emerging out of the theory of public finance are taxes, cess, surcharge or subsidy to be considered in determining the price or cost of producing goods and services, using environmental goods and services or creating environmental externalities. When it comes to environmental degradation, a principle of 'polluter pays' is generally propagated to determine pollution taxes consistent with optimum abatement levels (Pigou,1952).

Now we come to the theory of collective action. In fact, this was first talked about by Adam Smith in 1776 when he showed interest in the concept, that urban population need to be motivated to act collectively as a possibility to protect and preserve the capital resources of their areas. The concept grew later when it came to the management of natural resources which are either under the custody of the 'state' or common-property resources (also sometimes as open access resources). Essentially collective action is a new institutional arrangement in which individuals (producers or consumers) form a group, share a collective responsibility, frame rules, conduct procedures, institute rewards and penalties and manage the resources through a process of collective decision. The three broad reasons which call for collective actions are i) tragedy of the commons (e.g., over grazing in common lands) ii) failure of the market (e.g., industrial pollution as an externality) iii) government acting more for policing or revenue earning than as a benevolent state (e.g., forests managed by the governments for revenue purposes, but the cost of policing exceeding the revenues).

In the first instance, because of the open access nature of a resource such as a grazing land, individuals may not feel responsible to maintain their cattle stock within a manageable size (commonly referred to as 'carrying capacity'). 'After all it does not cost anything extra to graze one more cattle' can become the logic of livestock management. The end result is the degradation of land for grazing that is unfit to maintain even a single cattle head. Such examples are plenty in the rural Indian context having a variety of environmental resources. Extracting water from open access ponds, camping on sea beaches, or free fishing in lakes, free grazing in villages forest buffer areas are some of the examples. No single individual feels responsible for the act of over exploiting or damaging the resource. Yet, all of them may feel that the resource is getting degraded or depleted. Collective action may emerge as one possible solution to protect and preserve the resource on a sustainable basis.

The case of market failure is quite well-known to most officials working as practising economists. The basic point is that a large number of natural resources do not have prices. For instance, people in the villages do not think that there can be a price for water. Often, many such resources are controlled by certain groups (either traditionally or with some monopoly power, or some imperfections such as social inequity). Forests are under state monopoly. For all practical purposes, there is no land market in rural India, in the sense that selling land is considered to be only a distress option rather than an economic option. Otherwise, it is prestigious to own land (and also cattle). In the absence of any market situation, resources may be over exploited or neglected. Either way, they may get depleted or degraded.[6] Once again, the management of many of those resources through collective action can make the difference. Finally, in many countries, the governments treat forests as a revenue-earning asset, rather than a common property of the people. That may lead to over exploitation of forests. It is only a benevolent government that can give the management of such natural resources to the people.

Olson (1965) presented a systematic account of a new institutional arrangement called 'collective action'. Collective action can emerge either in an evolutionary way or through external interventions. In the event that people do not realize the importance of collective action, he proposed an external coercive method to initially bring about collective action. A living example of the emergence of such a collective action can be seen in the village Ralegan-Siddhi in Maharashtra. Initially, the people of the village did not agree to cooperate and come together to protect their water, forest and grazing lands, till such time when Kishan Baburao Hazare, affectionately known as Anna Hazare arrived in the village and used several coercive methods to make the people realize the importance of coming together (Antia and Kadekodi, 2002).[7]

---

[6] Though the estimates differ from source to source, almost 35–45 per cent of non-forest lands in India are either degraded or categorized as wastelands.

[7] Later, he converted the will of the people in to an evolutionary process of collective action.

Ostrom (1990) develops a Design Principle based on an evolutionary process to manage such resources. Such design principles are found to be practical in the management of water, common lands and common fishing areas. The collective action approaches are found to be very useful and relevant particularly in watershed management (Chopra et al, 1990, Sengupta; 1991, Ostrom et al., 1994).[8] 'A Case Study of Haryana Shivaliks' by T.P. Singh and Ravi Hegde is an example of conflict resolution by the stakeholders using some methods of majority voting and following the principles of collective action.

Recent developments in the theory of public economics also propagated the use of this collective action as an instrument to manage industrial pollution problems. Examples are Combined Effluent Treatment Plants (CETP), as dealt by M.N. Murty and U. Sankar in their Chapters in this book, and even in joint implementation projects to abate climatic change and global warming problems. Specifically, in the Chapter by Sankar, estimates of the cost of sharing the management of CETP in the case of the tannery industry in Tamil Nadu are arrived at. Although the details of the steps involved may look remote, they have the stamp of economic viability and social acceptability by the small-and medium-scale polluting units in India.

Theory of Valuation

One of the major branches of economic theory is the 'Theory of Value'. Economic theory always makes a distinction between value and price. Value of a commodity is based on a theory of utility. Demand for a commodity is based on this utility value. On the other hand, price for a commodity (or service) emerges with the interplay of the demand and supply factors. This can happen only if there is a market. It reflects a balance between what a buyer or a consumer is 'willing to pay' (WTP) and a seller is 'willing to accept' (WTA). But the commodity may or may not have a market. Hence, its value is not always revealed. But the value for a commodity may exist even if there is no market to express it. A typical example of this dilemma is that of water in a rural setting. The people would know its value, but do not know if they have to pay for it, as there may not be any water market in the village. Second, even if a market exists, the commodity may have been under an administered pricing system (as it happens with

[8] See Annexure 2 for a list of principles suggested by Elinor Ostrom.

urban water supply). Then its price may not reflect its true value. Most urban municipalities claim that the cost of urban drinking water is at least three times higher than the administratively fixed rates. Third, under imperfect market conditions the value which the consumer is willing to pay and the price as determined by the market conditions may differ.[9] Therefore, in practice, value and price of a commodity may or may not be the same. This can happen to natural resources such as water (not a well-defined market), minerals (under monopolistic conditions), forests products (with externality benefits and costs which are not internalized in pricing), things of beauty such as a tiger in a wildlife sanctuary (not having a market) or an architectural monument (being a public good) and so on.

Generally, the value of any resource can be assessed through the demand behaviour. As long as the market for any resource exists, this information can be obtained by appropriately designing consumer surveys to capture the demand behaviour. The method of valuation is based on a concept of 'willingness to pay' by consumers who reveal their preferences based on their income, family size and other considerations (Samuelson, 1948). Examples are timber prices, mineral prices or water prices (wherever the water market exists). 'Willingness to pay' does not necessarily mean the actual price, that an individual (or a society with some special characteristics) will be willing to pay for the current rate of its purchase. It all depends upon the shape of the demand curve (or the preferences).[10]

In order to add more clarity to the issue, it may be useful to introduce the economic concept of 'willingness to pay'. As shown in Figure 1.2, the amount of money income BC (i.e., willing to give up an income from M_0 to M_1), which an individual is willing to pay in order to enjoy $E_0 - E_1$ of an environmental good or facility, but staying at the same old preference curve U_0 is the estimate of maximum marginal 'willingness to pay' for a marginal environmental gain.[11] Similarly, GF can be argued to be the estimate of 'willingness to accept' a marginally lower environmental good or service. It can be further shown that only under a perfect substitution situation between income

---

[9] Only under a competitive economic condition, the price and value would be the same.

[10] Only if the demand curve were horizontal, the value and price would be the same.

[11] Incidentally, this is the Hicksian compensated consumer surplus.

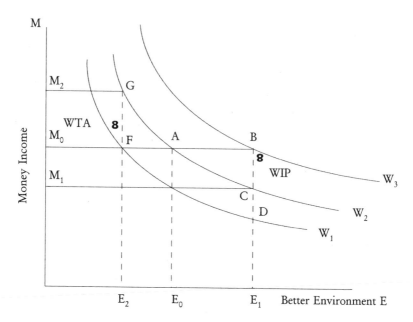

Fig. 1.2: Economic Rationale for Willingness to Pay and Accept

and environmental good, the WTP and WTA would be equal for the same level of marginal environmental change. With a lesser and lesser degree of substitution, the two would differ, which is perhaps is the real life situation in India and elsewhere.[12]

Why Value Natural Resources Specifically?

This is one of the most commonly asked questions in any debate on natural resource management. There are at least six reasons for this. First, there is the situation of the 'missing market'. In the absence of such a market, values of goods and services are not revealed. For instance, there are no markets for ecosystem services such as nutritional cycle, carbon sequestration, watershed functions, temperature control, soil conservation etc. Secondly, even if there are markets, they do not do their job well. For instance, the market may be a regulated one. There may be restrictions on one's entry into it—either to buy or sell. Good examples are licensing or rationing introduced by

[12] With different marginal utility of money income, different societies and sections of societies may be willing to pay differently from willingness to accept.

the government. An example of an entry barrier is the 'State Forest Trading Corporations' having the exclusive rights to sell forest products. An example of a regulated market is for *kendu* leaves' price fixation by the cooperatives in Madhya Pradesh. Going by the debate on global climate change, one may say that there is a market for carbon sequestration. But the so-called 'market for carbon trading' is restricted and regulated by international politics and relations. Thirdly, for most goods and services, it is essential to understand and appreciate their alternatives and alternative uses. For instance, an alternative to fuelwood can be kerosene. Alternative uses of electricity can be for cooking, lighting, as much as space heating. Alternative uses of *bhabbar* grass can be for making ropes, or pulp making in a paper mill. Because of this, the alternative value or opportunity costs are also relevant. Fourthly, uncertainty involving the demand and supply of natural resources exists, especially in the future. Most economic markets capture, at best, the current preferences of the buyers and sellers. But when it comes to natural resources, there are several types of uncertainties about the future demands and supplies. Therefore, valuation beyond the present is also necessary as an option. Fifthly, the government may like to use the valuation as against the restricted, administered or operating market prices for designing resource conservation programmes (including inviting external donor agencies and corporate sectors, and for negotiating carbon credits and so on). Finally, in order to arrive at natural-resource accounting, for methods such as 'Net Present Value' methods, resource valuation is a must. Some more details of the rationale for valuation of natural resources such as biodiversity is given by Kanchan Chopra in 'Economic Valuation of Biodiversity', and an application of valuation in natural-resource accounting is given in 'Approaches to Natural Resources Accounting in the Indian Context' by Gopal K. Kadekodi.

Concept of Total Economic Value

In the case of natural and environmental resources a concept of Total Economic Value (TEV) is considered as the best measure to express the full range of value or benefits—both tangible and intangible. Basically, it is understood that natural and environmental resources provide several 'use values' and 'non-use values' to enhance human welfare and provide sustainability to all lives (often termed as anthropogenic values). Conceptually, it is the sum of use values (UV) and non-use values (NUV) which constitutes the TEV. Some further elaboration of these are given below.

Use Values (UV)

Natural resources provide a variety of goods and services to the users for their current or future benefits or welfare. Hence, they are said to have use values. Examples are use of fuelwood from forests, water from rivers or from underground, coal from fossilized earth and so on. The current use (consumption) of these goods and services can be either direct or indirect. Accordingly, the use values can be further broadly classified into three groups: direct, indirect and option values.

Direct Use Values (DUV): Direct use values refer to the current use (consumption) of the resources and services provided, directly by natural and environmental resources. Examples are the use of timber and non-timber forest products (NTFPs) and services. Direct use value can be either consumptive or non-consumptive. Forests provide fuelwood, fodder, medicinal plants, fruits, poles, etc., to the people, particularly the local communities, and thereby generate direct consumptive use values. Recreation (e.g., tourism to wildlife sanctuaries or Himalayan glaciers, mountains), education, research etc., are examples of direct non-consumptive use values, i.e., pertaining to those outside of the locals population. While seeing elephants in the wild is the best example of direct non-consumptive use, hunting elephants for ivory is, on the other hand, a direct consumptive use.

Indirect Use Values (IUV): Indirect use values generally, are referred to the ecological functions that natural resource environments provide. It can be broadly classified into three groups: watershed values, ecosystem services and evolutionary processes. Watershed values include flood control, regulation of stream flows, recharging of ground water, effect of upstream or downstream etc.; the ecosystem services include fixing of nitrogen, assimilation of waste, carbon sequestration, gene pool etc.; and evolutionary processes include global life support, cultural and aesthetic concerns, biodiversity preservation etc.

Option Value (OV)

Option value (OV) is associated with the benefits received by retaining the option of using a resource (say a river basin) in the future by protecting or preserving it today, when its future demand and supply is uncertain. Take the example of the Narmada river basin. The option value here is the amount that individuals would be willing to pay to postpone the decision on building a dam on the river, or any other future use. Here, people do not have the intention to use the dam in the present but the same use may emerge in the future.

Non-use Values (NUV)

Non-use values are entirely different from use values and are generated without any direct link with the use of natural resource under question. An example can be the kinds of values people of a southern state, say Kerala, will put for the Himalayan mountains. These values are often revealed through people's perceptions and concerns towards conservation, culture, aesthetics and so on. For instance, existence values (EV) and bequest values (BV) are the two significant non-use values of forests. Option value and quasi-option value are generally considered as future use values (Dixon and Sherman, 1999).

Bequest Value (BV)

The bequest value originates when people are willing to pay to conserve a resource for the use of future generations. By doing so, these people do not have the intention to 'use' the benefits during their own life span, but are bequesting those benefits to the future generations (Swanson and Barbier, 1992).

Existence Value (EV)

Existence value is a concept associated with people's willingness to pay simply for the pleasure they derive from knowing that a natural area or particular species or characteristic exists irrespective of any plans they may have to hunt, observe or otherwise use these resources (Swanson and Barbier, 1992). People's willingness to pay for the preservation of endangered species is an example of existence value.

With these definitions, therefore, the Total Economic Value can be expressed as:

$$\text{TEV} = \text{UV} + \text{NUV} = (\text{DUV} + \text{IUV} + \text{OV}) + (\text{BV} + \text{EV}) \qquad (1.1)$$

The above classification helps the analyst to estimate the total economic value of natural and environmental resources. However, when some of the goods and services may fall in more than one category, attention is required to avoid double counting. Therefore,

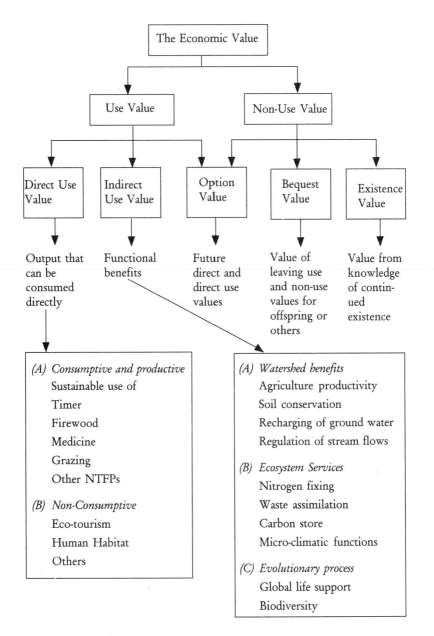

Fig. 1.3: Total Economic Value of Forests

classification of goods and services into the above framework is an important aspect in estimating TEV. In Figure 1.3, an example of this is shown, using forest resources.

On Actual Methods of Estimating Values

The actual methods of estimating values will have to follow the above-mentioned conceptual framework, as well as the empirical feasibility. Several different approaches and methods however, can be mentioned here.

1. Market approach: Productivity change, opportunity cost, replacement cost, shadow price etc.

2. Surrogate market approach: Property value or hedonic prices, travel cost method, etc.

3. Artificial market or stated preference approach: Contingent value method, bidding games etc.

Whenever a market exists for any natural or environmental resource, the prices as revealed from the market can be an indicator of the value of those resources. Examples are timber prices, mineral prices or water prices (wherever a water market exists).

What does one do if there is no market for a particular use of the resource under question? But the resource may have alternative uses with revealed market prices or may have alternative substitute resources. For example, the market for fuelwood may not exist for household consumption, but it exists for industrial uses. Or, there are substitutes such as kerosene for fuelwood in household uses. Other methods are also possible. Methods such as opportunity or replacement costs basically draw upon market data and information on prices and values for such alternative, replacement or substitute. Surrogate prices are hypothetical market prices taken from such goods and services, that are close substitutes for those resources. A good example can be the value of herbal medicinal plants as compared to the price of non-herbal chemical-based products such as synthetic creams or perfumes.

What if there are many possibilities of substitutes, or replacements? Economic theory can also provide information on values for resources having many alternatives or substitutes. The shadow prices are supposed to reflect the optimal values of resources, by taking into account all those alternatives and their combinations. These can be derived only from an empirical model of optimization of consumption or welfare, in which the resources enter as inputs. It may be possible to derive the shadow price of water or minerals in a model of production based on such resources.

How to go about valuing resources for which there are neither markets nor surrogates? It is here that alternative user or non-user based methods are to be devised. The users or non-users of such resources may have to be brought to a homogeneous psychological situation in which they may agree to pay for the use or existence of the resource. Or at least, state or reveal the preferences on such natural resources assuming artificially created market situation. If an individual is then made to state her or his preferences, it only reflects a statement of value. Hence it is called a 'stated preference' method. Contingent valuation method is one such method (Kadekodi 2000b; Murty and Markandya 2000). With all the developments in valuation methods, it is still not easy to assign values to environmental resources especially in terms of monetary values as the role played by the various species are many, complex, and often hidden or insufficiently understood by humans.

Many of these techniques are demonstrated in different chapters in this book. The chapter 'Economic Valuation of Biodiversity' on valuation of Keoladeo National Park by Kanchan Chopra is a case demonstrating the travel cost method. Apart from demonstrating the use of this method, she presents the various steps involved in applying the method. In 'Valuing the Health Impact of Air Pollution' by Jyoti Parikh the method of social opportunity cost of health is demonstrated, to value the health impacts of air pollution in a city like Mumbai. In it she develops a 'dose response' approach, that is commonly used in identifying environmental damages to estimate the cost of air-pollution-related morbidity. Gopal K. Kadekodi in 'Approaches to Natural Resource Accounting in the Indian Context' presents several case studies covering various other methods of valuation, as well as deriving natural resources accounts.

Economics of Environment and Development Linkages

There are two major aspects of linkages between economy and environment that are of policy relevance to any student of environmental economics. They are: (i) direct linkage between the process of economic development and the state of environment and (ii) the opening of an economy to international trade (i.e., importing and exporting)

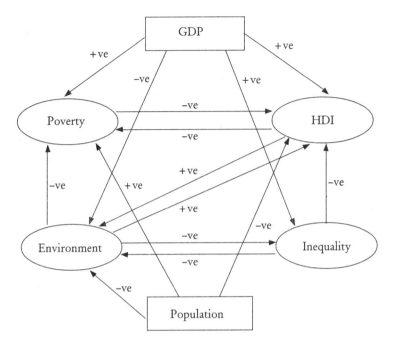

Fig. 1.4: Environmental and Quality of Life Linkages

and its links with environment. As far as the economy-environment (or ecology) linkages are concerned, the major attributes to be linked are:

- Level of economic development (as measured by, say per capita gross domestic product [GDP]),
- Level of environmental quality (say, degree of deforestation or suspended particulate matter [SPM] emissions), (poverty [say, head-count ratio], income inequality [say, Gini coefficient] and population pressure [say, density of population]).
- Social dimensions

As can be seen from Figure 1.4, the various attributes listed above are linked via environmental considerations. It is not difficult to visualize the various possible linkages between them. As far as the environment is concerned, three of the most talked about linkages are between environmental quality (or level or both) and poverty, between environment and income and between environment and population. For a country such as India, based on available case studies

(Kadekodi, 2000a, not presented in this book) the following views can be made:

1. One does not see any negative relation between the level of income and environmental quality in general. With over 50 per cent of the population below the poverty line, sometimes it is difficult to segregate negative environmental effects of low income levels and the quality of life. This negates the Environmental Kuznets hypothesis (Munasinghe, 1999; Kadekodi and Agarwal, 2000) which suggests that environmental quality declines in the initial phase of economic development, to be corrected in the latter phase of development.

2. Also one does not see much evidence on the causality of poverty upon the environmental quality deterioration. But certainly, there are some evidences that show that degrading environment hurts the poor.

3. Population growth seems to affect environmental conditions adversely.

With regard to international trade and environment, three distinct linkages are recognizable. They are: i) Trade flows affecting environments and environmental policies; ii) Environmental policies affecting trade flows; and iii) Trans-boundary environmental externalities.

As far as India is concerned, all the three aspects of these linkages are important. Examples of environmental dumping, relaxation of environmental regulations for the sake of reaching out through exporting and importing and environmental regulations acting as non-tariff barriers are important policy-related issues taken up by the World Trade Organization (WTO) and General Agreement on Trade and Tariff (GATT) (Uimonen and Whalley, 1997). Though there is a general feeling that environmental regulations reduce the prospects of exports from developing countries such as India, there are no clearly visible empirical case studies or evidences on this postulate. Rather, Porter and Linde (1995) and several others have argued that environmental regulations have in fact encouraged innovations, improvements in process technologies and made international trade very competitive.

Study of macroeconomic or trade linkages with environment can be analysed using the economic theory of welfare or public economics. Some of the statistical tools normally used are estimating welfare losses and gains using regression techniques (say, trade surplus or deficit regressed on a large number of macro-micro variables including tariff and non-tariff barriers), studying the effects of tariff and non-tariff instruments by Cost-Benefit models or estimating general equilibrium models of population, production, consumption, resource use and trade etc. All these are very important policy questions. In most of the cases, they can be answered only with a series of data over a long time period.

Apart from the trade linkages, in the context of environment, another important global link issue is about climate change. The emission of methane, CFL and such other greenhouse gases lead to global warming. Among the many sources contributing to global warming, methane and carbon dioxide emissions from urban and solid industrial waste also count. Paul Appasamy in 'Economic Benefit-Cost Analysis of a Proposed Solid Waste Recovery Plant' takes a look at the contribution of solid waste to this climate change problem in the urban city of Lucknow, and also estimates the gain from reversing it by biomethanation processes. Urban sanitary and pollution control boards are aware of commonly known methods of managing or mitigating solid waste problems. The notable ones are land filling, setting up of incineration plants, composting and many others.

Theory of Property Rights and New Institutional Economics

Most fundamental to understand the resource management systems is to take note of the institutional framework in which the resources are used or allocated for production or consumption. Economic theory normally talks about different forms of ownerships and use of the resources. The ownership of resources can be private (or individual), state, collective or common and several other variants. Normally two different sets of agents are involved in the process of resource management. They are loosely termed as producers and consumers. The 'state' or the government can also be added as a third agent as the custodian of resources (e.g., forests). All of them are responsible for formulating the kinds of institutions needed to manage or govern the resources. The ownership rights set out different types of rules to manage the resources. Some of the major rules are: User rights, rights to prevent or admit others to use the resource, rights to sell or not to sell and customary laws.

It is the interplay between the above-mentioned agents and the ownership types and rights that establishes the economic and societal behaviour with respect to production and consumption, pricing, and exchange for the resources. The study of this is sometimes termed as 'Institutional Economics'. The pattern of ownership and rights are commonly known as property rights. Property right is an institutional system in which the ownership and management of resources are well-specified and well-prescribed. Resources classified accordingly are private goods, public goods, state-owned goods, common property resources, and open access resources. An application of this concept of property rights in policy making (such as community participation) is available in 'Fiscal and Institutional Approaches to Pollution Abatement' chapter by M.N. Murty.

When it comes to the management of environmental and natural resources, the common property resources and open access resources emerge as two important property rights' systems that are directly relevant. A common property resource is defined as 'a property on which well-defined collective claims by an exclusive group are established, the use of the resource is subtractive, having the characteristic of a public good such as indivisibility'. If the identification of an 'exclusive group' is absent, the resource can be called as an 'open access resource'.

Common property resources are often complementary to private resources. For instance, livestock rearing (an activity linked with private property) requires a good amount of common grazing grounds (though some fodder can always come from private lands). Similarly, underground or surface water (a common property resource) is essential for good land cultivation (a private resource-based activity). Fishing in an open sea or pond, collection of NTFP from forests are other examples of such links between common and private property resources.

Numerous case studies from India already exist on the collective action-oriented common and even open access resources (Chopra et al., 1990; Singh and Ballabh, 1996). M.N. Murty in 'Fiscal and Institutional Approaches to Pollution Abatement' and U. Sankar in 'Pollution Control in Tanneries' present case studies of CETPs maintained by polluting units and the affected parties. They are illustrations of collective action. Essentially, the gains from community management can be assessed in comparison to open access or state-managed institutional mechanisms. The case study of 'social forestry' in Karnataka by

K.N. Ninan and Jyotis evaluates the management of such a common property forest resource. In doing this, they first give a comprehensive picture of social forestry in India, followed by a cost-benefit analysis of a particular case study from Karnataka. Joint Forest Management as illustrated in 'Stakeholder Analyis in Joint Forest Management' by T.P. Singh and Ravi Hegde is an example of such a collective action-oriented programme. Both stakeholder analysis and cost-benefit analysis can be useful as relevant evaluation techniques for such collective action programmes.

Incidentally, out of about 328 million hectares of geographical land area in India, the common property land resources are estimated to be about 74.6 million hectares (Kadekodi, 2000a), for which many more action programmes are needed. Therefore, understanding of such alternative methods and techniques to evaluate them is called for.

Theory of Sustainable Development

Economists like J.S. Mill, David Ricardo and T.R. Malthus (all in the nineteenth century) talked about sustainability much before the present generation started evolving a conscientious definition of sustainable development. The most widely quoted definition of sustainable development is from the World Commission on Environment and Development in 1987. They have defined it as: 'Sustainable development is development that meets the needs of the present without compromising the ability of future generations to meet their own needs'.

In essence, we are talking about production and consumption patterns with a concern about the use of natural and environmental resources for the present and the future. In essence, the concern is about both the levels of living and maintenance of natural resources, both over time. Such an objective calls for a design of policies that can maintain the streams of benefits from natural resources constantly over a long horizon of time. Hartwick (1977) provided a possible rule for such a developmental process, saying that 'as long as all profits (rents) from the use of extracted non-renewable resources are reinvested on either man-made capital or on regenerating renewable resources, the stream of consumption flows remains constant over generations'. The usefulness of such economic rules and findings can be put to practice by instituting proper tax, cess and fixing extraction rates and so on. This is where policy making and practice of economic thinking can go hand in hand.

When it comes to projects based on environmental and natural resources, there is an added problem of 'irreversibility'. For instance, land mined for coal or iron cannot be easily returned to the nature. Dams and reservoirs change the landscape to an irreversible stage.[13] Hence, there is always a 'choice between development and preservation'. This requires, methods and designs to use such resources, keeping in mind the exhaustibility of the resources, irreversibility of environmental damages and degradations, species' extinction and so on. The choice of action can be taken care of by experimenting with alternate streams of benefits from preservation and development. Assuming that all natural resources have some preservation value in a finite time horizon but will have developmental value in infinite time horizon planning, the irreversibility cost can be accounted by comparing the current rate of using the natural resource versus its infinite time use. El Serafy (1989) proposed a method to estimate the premium called 'use cost' to be charged on the developmental use of natural resources such as minerals, so as to arrive at its estimate of preservation losses. Gopal K. Kadekodi in 'Approaches to Natural Resource Accounting in the Indian Context' illustrates this way of accounting for developmental use of exhaustible resources with an example of iron ore from the state of Goa.[14]

One final and most important question commonly asked by policy makers, practitioners and implementers of environmental policies is about the measurability of sustainable development. One can specify three types of indicators to monitor the process of sustainable development. They are pressure indicators, impact indicators, and sustainability indicators.

Pressure indicators are indicators that refer to flows or changes in environmental, ecological and many other attributes that bring about some pressures on the state of environment. They express the burden placed on the stocks of environmental goods and services. Pressures can emerge from the same geographical region or outside of it. Examples of pressure indicators are: CO_2 emissions, population growth, forest degradation etc.

Impact indicators represent the effects of pressures. They are the

[13] Sometimes such decisions can add to the problems in the future. Examples of big dams in seismically-sensitive regions enhance the danger of earthquakes.

[14] Apart from the Brundtland Commission report of 1987, writings of Pearce and Warford (1993) may be useful as additional readings.

receptors. Examples are rise in morbidity and mortality, increase in hedonic prices of real estate (particularly around lakes and parks), water and air pollution and so on. The net result of pressures and impacts of environmental changes is the state of development. These are measured by sustainability indicators. Carrying capacity, quality of life, human development index (HDI), life expectancy etc., can be cited as examples.

Such indicators can be estimated for specific resources (e.g., mining, industrial pollution), specific region (e.g., coastal zone, Ganga basin, city of Mumbai), and for specific time zones (if they are relevant, e.g., midday air pollution, monsoon water-logging etc.). Case studies putting such estimated indicators can become useful in project monitoring and evaluation and design of economic instruments. Data from Pollution Control Boards, Flood Control Boards, Municipal Corporations etc. can be used to construct such indicators.

Closely associated with this concept of sustainability is a definition of 'carrying capacity', that has more direct relevance in development planning. It is an indication of the level of human and animal population that can be sustained on a 'no hardship basis'. A number of case studies indicating the criticality of carrying capacities are now available in India. For instance, carrying capacity of livestock rearing (0.16 livestock per hectare in Uttaranchal hills as against which the actual cattle population in Kumaon hills ranges from 1.6 to 3.3; in UP hills, in general, it is about 3), forest lands for agricultural use (15 hectares for one hectare of cultivated lands in Uttachanchal, whereas it is just about 2 hectares now), water supply system for National Capital Region (NCR), maximum sustainable yield of river or coastal sea fishing (10 tons per square kilometre per year in coastal Kerala), etc., are some examples. There are a number of carrying-capacity studies carried out for Ministry of Environment and Forests. Some major ones are on Doon valley, Damodar basin and NCR (for Delhi).

Tools and Methods of Economic Analysis

When it comes to applying Environmental Economics to policy planning (e.g., designing tax and subsidy policies, various other economic instruments listed in Table 1.1), instituting environmental regulations (e.g., standards), monitoring performances (e.g., that of CETP), decision making on environmentally-sensitive projects (e.g., hydroelectricity power projects, passing a national highway through a wildlife sanctuary, cases of big dams etc.) and in many other instances, a common question is asked. What are the tools, techniques, and methods to be used to understand the problem, analyse them and to arrive at plausible solutions? The case studies presented in this book use a large number of such tools, techniques and methods. A number of statistical, mathematical and economic tools and techniques have been found to be useful to resolve environmental problems and policy making. Some of the major ones are:

- Environmental data base
- Statistics and econometrics
- Material balance approach
- Optimization and computer models
- Methods of evaluation
- Energy and environmental budgeting
- Simulation techniques
- Game theoretic and other approaches

At this stage, it may be useful to briefly review some of them, by way of introduction and exposure to the policy makers and decision makers.

Data Base, Statistics and Models

At present, the Indian statistical system does not provide sufficient database on environmental statistics. However, Central Statistical Organization (CSO), Ministry of Environment and Forests (MoEF), Tata Energy Research Institute (TERI), Centre for Science and Environment (CSE), Centre for Monitoring Indian Economy (CMIE), National Sample Surveys (NSS) and several other organizations provide different aspects of this database. Some of the prominent database-related publications from within India on a regular basis are:

- Compendium of Environmental Statistics (CSO; occasionally)
- Tata Energy Data Directory Yearbook (TEDDY, and also on web as TEDDY ONLINE, by TERI, annually)
- Wastelands Atlas of India (NRSA, regularly)
- State of Forest Report (Forest Survey of India, regularly)
- Forestry Statistics of India (MoEF/FRI , regularly)
- The State of India's Environment: The Citizen's Report (CSE, regularly)
- Various reports of Central Pollution Control Boards

- Sarvekshana issues of National Sample Survey Organization (NSSO)

Apart from these, there are several commissioned reports, annual reports and documents that come from various ministries of central and state governments. Some of the notable ones are: Human Development Reports (currently available for two states in India namely, Madhya Pradesh and Karnataka, and at the all-India level by NCAER) and National Income Accounts (both at the central and state levels). An all-India level data on common property resources has been collected on a sampling basis by the National Sample Survey Organisation in 1998 (54th Round), which is also available on CD.

Most of the information on environmental status and its impact on welfare etc., can also be got from actual field level data. But collection of this information has to be based on specially designed questionnaires or interviews with the concerned individuals and groups, focus-group discussions, PRA/RRA exercises, and scientific experiments. Particular mention may be made about the 'Contingent Valuation Method'. In this method, basically, the individuals or household are asked as to how they are willing to pay for any improvement in environmental status or quality (in a situation in which there is no market to determine this). For this, the respondent will have to be made fully aware of the implications of such an improvement. In some way, the respondents will have to be homogenized in their knowledge about the implications and the relevance of the environmental quality (Grosh and Glewwe 2000).

In so far as analyses of data on environmental and natural resources are concerned, starting from simple statistical techniques of averages to regression analysis have been found to be useful. For instance, the rainfall cycles can be modelled using non-linear regression models or even the more sophisticated techniques such as the stochastic processes. Time-series data on demands for various natural resources can be analysed using regression and other methods such as trend analysis. Statistical techniques can also be used to estimate dose-response coefficients. An example can be the elasticity of expenses on health on account of increasing water and air pollution. U. Sankar in 'Pollution Control in Tanneries' on water pollution from tanneries demonstrates the use of such a regression technique for estimating the capital cost for setting up of CETP using the data on waste water and number of tanneries. Using a regression technique, Kanchan Chopra estimates the travel cost (as an indicator of value of biodiversity) to derive the 'willingness to pay' to visit a national park. Similarly Jyoti Parikh uses a Logit econometric model to estimate the incidence of respiratory diseases and other health effects. M.N. Murty uses this technique for estimating the water pollution taxes. Commonly used statistical software packages for such regression studies are LIMDEP, SPSS, SAS and MFIT.

'Material Balance' approach is another technique that is quite commonly used by the Central and State Statistical Organizations to compile the data on flow of goods and services in the economy in the form of an Input-Output Table. This technique can also be used at a sectoral level, at least for major sectors such as energy (see TEDDY), steel, and so on. A similar approach can be developed for the relevant sectors, such as forestry. A further development in the 'material balance approach' is construction of Social Accounting Matrix (SAM) and System of Environmental and Economic Accounting (SEEA). Natural Resource Accounting (NRA) is a specific case of such accountings addressed to accounting for the use and abuse of natural and environmental resources. In the final chapter 'Approaches to Natural Resources Accounting in the Indian Context', Gopal K. Kadekodi goes into the logic, methods on this, and presents selected case studies in this direction from among the studies carried out in India.

It may be possible to formulate consistency or optimization models for energy use, environmental flows or solid waste management, and other such environmental problems. A linear programming model of solid waste management, exploring alternative methods of collecting and disposing the urban waste is an example (Reyer, et al., 1999). Various computer softwares such as SENECA (A Simulation Environment for Ecological Application), STELLA, DEFINITE (Decisions on a FINITE set of alternative), GAMS (General Algebraic Modelling System) are available. These ecology-economy interactive models (Fig. 1.4) help in estimating and understanding the interactions between environment and economy. Simulation techniques are used to project the scenarios, distinct from base-line scenarios (Kadekodi and Nayampalli, 2003). They are used to deduce policy-oriented decision rules and advance warning systems.

Methods of Evaluation

As part of public investment decision making, one may have to compare various development projects. A number of them require, directly and indirectly, natural and environmental resources. How to go about taking decisions on such projects, having implications on such resources? There are three distinct issues here. First, the rate and use of the resource may have to be 'valued' properly. Second, the use of natural and other resources may create externalities in terms of pollution, waste and so on. Third, there are the issues of appropriate discount rate to evaluate the project performance, and tax and subsidy provisions at the time of project clearance. The theory of valuation comes very handy in valuing the use and abuse of natural resources in projects.

In the design of environmentally-relevant projects, there are a number of options to choose from. Firstly, there is always a choice between development and preservation. An example is that of a hydroelectricity power station or preservation of a natural forest such as the Silent valley in Kerala. Secondly, there are choices between benefits to different stakeholders. Examples of paper mills taking away the forest resources away from local habitants is quite well known. Thirdly, there may be a choice between different techniques of project designs (e.g., big versus small dams), different input mix (e.g., use of organic versus chemical fertilizer), and even species choices (e.g., monoculture versus multifarious plantation) and many such choices. How to go about making decisions on such choices?[15]

Four major techniques of evaluation are normally used in Environmental Economics. They are:

- Cost-Benefit Analysis
- Multi-criterion Approach
- Stakeholders Analysis
- Environmental Impact Assessment

It may not be easy to completely describe the cost-benefit analysis here. K.N. Ninan and Jyotis in 'Social Forestry' present the method and demonstrate the use of this technique. Ninan and Jyotis also give a number of tables showing the steps involved in the computations as well as several exercises. In 'Economic Benefit-Cost Analysis of a Proposed Solid Waste Resource Recovery Plant' Paul Appasamy covers an important aspect of environmental degradation due to solid waste accumulation and free disposal in an urban city, and externality

[15] Apart from the standard problem of not having a social welfare function to rank the projects, there are problems of multiple objectives.

benefits (contributing positively to climate change) through the installation of a methanisation plant. He uses the cost-benefit analysis to evaluate alternative disposal-and-use techniques (including land filling, as an example). Then we have a chapter 'The Health Benefits of Improving the Household Environment' by Lvovsky and her colleagues showing the methods and estimates of benefits and costs of improving household environment.

Talking of natural resources and decision making over time, two important considerations must be mentioned. Firstly, a number of natural resources are inter-generationally relevant. They may have to be viewed from a long-run sustainability point of view. Hence, there is a question of the appropriate discount rate. In so far as a large component of inputs are natural and environmental resources, it is suggested to use a lower discount rate (estimated for the Indian situation to be around 6 per cent). The second consideration is about the rate of using natural resources. Whenever the use of natural resources, particularly the exhaustible ones are involved, appropriate user costs (El Serafy, 1989) or shadow price for the over extraction be imputed as costs to the projects. The valuation methods referred in the section 'What Economics has to offer in Environmental Management?' are relevant here.

A related problem in policy design and decision making is about multiple objectives, and some of them are only ordinal (i.e., not measurable on any cardinals scale such as rupees, or tonne). The multi-criterion approach is a method to incorporate both tangible and non-tangible multiple attributes of natural and environmental resources in decision making. The basic issue then is how to consider a multitude of benefits and costs involving both tangible and non-tangible attributes? For instance, in evaluating a road project to be built in a forest area, the tangible benefits foregone are the timber line losses. But non-tangible costs involved are hardship to local communities and wildlife, soil losses, loss of biodiversity and existence values etc. If information on such non-tangible attributes are obtained on a sample basis on an ordinal scale, they can also be utilized in arriving at some kind of rankings or scores on project or technological alternatives. Generally, in designing environmentally-sensitive projects, a large number of conflicting socio-economic factors and variables emerge. There are well-developed techniques to take into account such a mixed information base in decision making about projects (Janssen,

1994; Munda and Nijkamp, 1994). Kanchan Chopra demonstrates this technique of 'Multi-criteria Analysis' to estimate the rankings of perceptions of scientists, tourists and local residents on biodiversity preservation.

The stakeholder analysis is one of the more recent techniques to incorporate the views and knowledge of all the stakeholders in a project. For instance, the various stakeholders in designing Joint Forest Management projects are the forest department, local communities, women, NGOs, other line departments (such as irrigation, soil conservation), private industries (buyers of forest products), social activists and so on. Once again, priorities may have to be assigned to rank the stakeholders' preferences, losses and gains. The distributional aspects of gains and costs to various stakeholders is a very important consideration in taking decisions regarding forest-related projects. This cannot be easily done by applying the usual cost-benefit analysis. 'Stakeholder Analysis in Joint Forest Management in India' by T.P. Singh and Ravi Hegde demonstrates this technique more elaborately, as applied for a joint forest management project.

Environmental Impact Analysis (EIA) is yet another technique to design a project and to monitor the performance during its lifetime. As stated earlier, at the time of project designing, not all the information on externalities or implications of using natural resources on future generation etc., is known. Basically, in designing and monitoring, the values of various environmental impacts will have to be taken note of. When all such information is not available at the start of the project, a technique known as 'Benefits Transfer' can be used. Here, essentially, the experience and information from a similar project or previously conducted research estimate can be used to assign values at the time of designing the project. During the course of the project, a method known as 'Rapid Analytic Method' can be used to improve the impact-value estimates. EIA is also a method designed to provide dose-response information flows so as to monitor the projects. Good examples of applying EIA are in the assessment of health impacts from air pollution control projects (ADB, 1996). P. Ram Babu in 'Environmental Impact Assessment Process in India and Air Quality Management' uses the EIA technique to make an assessment of air quality in the city of Mumbai.

It should be recognized that energy and environmental resources are always scarce (though they may be gift of nature). Therefore, their

Box 1.1
The Framework for the Case Studies

Chapter 1 by Gopal K. Kadekodi introduces the basics of environmental economics justifiably meant for practising economists in the governments, NGOs, Scientists, Corporate planners and financial institutions.

Author (s)	Environmental Theme	Chap. No.	Economic Theory	Statistical and Economic Tools and Techniques	Comments
U. Sankar	Water Pollution	2	Command and Controls Methods versus Collective Action	Regression Techniques	Problems of water pollution in leather tanneries
K. Chopra	Valuation of a National Park	3	Theory of Valuation	Multi-Criterion Analysis, Travel Cost Method	Tourism value and designing entry fees to Keoladeo National Park
Hughes et al.	Household Environment	4	Health Economics, externality	Cost-Benefit Analysis, Dose-Response Analysis	Case study from rural Andhra Pradesh
P. Ram Babu	Project formulation	5	Public Finance, Valuation	EIA Techniques	Project Design with instruments for abating air pollution
K.N. Ninan	Social Forestry	6	Public Finance, Sustainable development, Externality	Cost-Benefit Analysis	Case study from Karnataka, sensitivity to discount rate, and alternative schemes

Author (s)	Environmental Theme	Chap. No.	Economic Theory	Statistical and Economic Tools and Techniques	Comments
T.P. Singh and R. Hegde	Joint Forest Management	7	Welfare Economics, Collective action	Stakeholder Analysis	Case study from Haryana state
Jyoti Parikh	Air Pollution	8	Public Finance, valuation of health impacts	Regression Techniques; Dose-Response Analysis	Case study from Mumbai city
Paul Appasamy	Solid Waste Management	9	Externality benefits due to climate change abatement	Cost-Benefit Analysis	Case study from Lucknow city, on establishing methanation plant
M.N. Murty	Industrial Water Pollution	10	Demonstration of Fiscal Instruments	Market-based Instruments; Regression Techniques	New economic methods like Output Distance demonstrated with data from a large number of water intensive industries.
Gopal K. Kadekodi	Natural Resource Accounting	11	Environment and Development Linkages	Green accounting, satellite accounting and methods of integrating with national income accountings	Case studies from Yamuna basin, accounting for iron ore exhaustion, industrial and air pollution

41

use and allocation at present, and also over generations, requires some elements of budgeting. While making such assessments, priorities may have to be assigned to local users (and also local protectors), long-term users and gainers, and societies and users having no alternatives. Such an allocative design falls in the methodology of environmental budgeting (Shekhar Singh et al., 1999).

Finally, the use of 'game' theory in environmental economics may be mentioned. In many natural resource and environmental situations, there are a number of stakeholders (and agents) who have different objectives. An example can be cited from the forestry situation. The different stakeholders here are the forest department, local communities, women, tourists and scientists. The objective of the forest department may be maximizing revenue from the sale of timber and fodder, that of the locals can be maximizing fuelwood collection, of women it can be water, of scientists it may be micro-organisms and flora and fauna, of tourists it can be recreation and so on. Then, each of them may be following different strategies. Any strategy by one agent (say forest department) will have some pay-off to himself, and different pay-offs to others. It may even happen that a positive pay-off to one agent may install a negative pay-off to another. The game that goes on in such a situation of diverse strategies and stakes can be conflicting, cooperating or even a 'tit-for-tat'. Game theory is a branch of mathematics which offers to model such a behavioural situation and predict the outcomes (both in a static and a dynamic situation). Cooperative and non-cooperative games are normally talked about. For a flavour of such a 'game theoretic approach' as applied to a bargaining problem between the village communities and the forest departments, see Chopra et al., (1990) and Lise (1997).

Introducing the Chapters

The various chapters that now follow in this book put forward the application of one or the other economic theories and methods, and also demonstrate the use of various statistical and mathematical methods and tools in addressing the problems of environmental management and policy making. All the case studies chosen for this book are taken from various studies carried in India, with Indian data. Secondly, only the most appropriate branches of environmental economics and the necessary tools are used here.

Undoubtedly, valuation is one of the most important stage in Environmental Economics. With growing industrialization and demand on natural resources, abatement of pollution and design of policies and strategies is the next most important branch of enquiry. Decision making regarding project selection and implementation is yet another aspect of applied Environmental Economics in India today. Finally, one cannot ignore the role of institutions, and relevance of resources to the local communities Inter-generational use of resources is to be kept in mind in developing the use of environmental and natural resources in India.

In the earlier sections, the chapters have been referred while introducing and describing relevant elements of environmental economics. The case study chapters, however, do not cover all the major environmental themes and elements of environmental economics either. Box 1.1 may help the reader to organize to pick and choose the different economic and statistical tools and methods and the relevant chapter of their interest and concern.

REFERENCES

Antia, N.H. and Gopal K. Kadekodi (2002): *Dynamics of Rural Development: Lessons from Ralegan Siddhi*, Monograph, Ministry of Rural Development, Government of India. New Delhi.

Arrow, Kenneth (1951): *Social Choice and Individual Value*, Wiley, New York.

Asian Development Bank (ADB), (1996): *Economic Evaluation of Environmental Impacts: A Workbook*, Environment Division, ADB, Manila.

Atkinson, A.B. and J.E. Stiglitz (1980): *Lectures on Public Economics*, McGraw Hill International, Singapore.

Bergson, A. (1938); 'A reflection of certain aspects of welfare economics', *Quality Journal of Economics*, 52: 310–34.

Bhattacharya, R.N. (2001): *Environmental Economics: An Indian Perspective*, Oxford University Press, New Delhi.

Boulding, Kenneth E. (1966): 'The economics of the coming spaceship earth', in Henry Jarret (ed.), *Environmental Quality in a Growing Economy*, John Hopkins Press, Baltimore.

Buchanan, J.M. (1968): *The Demand and Supply of Public Goods*, Rand-Mcnally, Chicago.

Chopra, Kanchan, Gopal Kadekodi, and M.N. Murty (1990): *Participatory Development: People and Common Property Resources*, Sage Publications, New Delhi.

Dixon, A.J. and P.B. Sherman (1999): *Economics of Protected Areas: A New Look of Benefits and Costs*, Earthscan Publication, London.

El Serafy, S. (1989): 'The proper calculation of income from depletable natural resources', in Y.J. Ahmed et al., (eds.), *Environmental Accounting for Sustainable Development*, World Bank, Washington. D.C.

Folmer, Henk and H.L. Gabel (eds.) (2000): *Principles of Environmental and Resource Economics*, Edward Elgar Publications, Cheltanham.

Grosh, Margaret and Paul Glewwe (2000): *Designing Household Survey: Questionnaires for Developing Countries*, The World Bank, Washington, D.C.

Hanley, Nick, J.A. Shogren and Ben White (1997): *Environmental Economics in Theory and Practice*, Macmillan Press, Delhi.

Hartwick, John (1977): 'Inter-generational equity and the investing of rents from exhaustible resources', *American Economic Review*, 67(5): 972–4.

Hotelling, Harold (1931): 'The economics of exhaustible resources', *Journal of Political Economy*, 39: 137–75.

Janssen, Ron (1994): *Multi-objective Decision Support for Environmental Management*, Kluwer Academic Press, Dordrecht.

Kadekodi, Gopal K. (2000a): 'Environment and Development', in R.N. Bhattacharya (ed.), *Undergraduate Textbook in Environmental Economics*, Oxford University Press, New Delhi.

—— (2000b): *Water in Kumaon: Ecology, Value and Rights*, Gyanodaya Publications, Nainital.

Kadekodi Gopal K. and M.M. Agarwal (2000): 'Why an inverted U-shaped Environmental Kuznet's Curve may not exist', in Mohan Munasinghe, O. Sunkel and Carlos de Miguel (eds.), *The Sustainability of Long Term Growth*, Edward Elgar Publications, London.

Kadekodi, Gopal K. and Aparna Nayampalli (2003): 'Towards Sustainability: Reversing Biodiversity Losses of Chilika Lake in India', forthcoming in *Pacific and Asian Journal of Energy*.

Little, I.M.D. (1960): *A Critique of Welfare Economics*, Oxford University Press, London.

Lise, Wietze (1997): An Econometric and Game Theoretic Approach to Common Pool Resource Management: Case Studies in Rural India, Unpublished Ph.D. Monograph, Institute of Economic Growth, New Delhi.

Munasinghe, M. (1999): 'Is environmental degradation an inevitable consequence of economic growth? Tunneling through the environmental Kuznet's curve', *Ecological Economics*, 29(1): 89–109.

Munda, G. and P. Nijkamp (1994): 'Multi-criteria evaluation in environmental management: Why and how?', in M. Paruccini (ed.), *Applying Multiple Criteria Aid for Decision to Environmental Management*, ECSC, EEC, EAEC, Brussels.

Murty, M.N. and A. Markandya (2000): *Cleaning of Ganges: A Cost-Benefit Analysis*, Oxford University Press, New Delhi.

Olson, M. (1965): *The Logic of Collective Action*, Harvard University Press, Cambridge, Mass.

Ostrom, E.(1990): *Governing the Commons: The Evolution of Collective Action*, Cambridge University Press, New York.

Ostrom, E., R. Gardner and J. Walker (1994): *Rules, Games and Common-Pool Resources*, University of Michigan Press, Ann Arbor.

Parikh, K.S. (1999): *India Development Report: 1999–2000*, Oxford University Press, New Delhi, India

Pearce, David (1976): 'The limits to cost-benefit analysis as a guide to environmental policy', *Kyklos*, 29, fasc. 1, pp. 97–112.

Pearce, D. and R.K. Turner (1990): *Economics of Natural Resources and the Environment*, Hemel-Hamstead, Harvester-Wheatsheaf.

Pearce, D.W., and J.J. Warford (1993): *Economics, Environment and Sustainable Development*, Oxford University Press, Oxford.

Pigou, A.C. (1952): *The Economics of Welfare*, 4th edition, MacMillan Press, London.

Porter, M.E. and C. van der Linde (1995): 'Towards a new conception of the environmental competitiveness relationship', *Journal of Economic Perspectives*, 9(4): 97–118.

Reyer Gerlagh, Pieter van Beukering, Madhu Verma, P.P. Yadav and Preeti Pande (1999): *Integrated Modelling of Solid Waste in India*, CREED Working Paper No. 26, IIED, London.

Samuelson, P.A. (1948): 'Consumption theory in terms of revealed preference', *Economica*, XV, pp. 243–53.

—— (1963): *Foundation of Economic Analysis*, Cambridge University Press, Harvard.

Sen, A.K. (1970): *Collective Choice and Social Welfare*, Holden-Day, San Francisco.

—— (1977): 'Social choice theory: A re-examination', *Econometrica*, 45: 53–89.

Serafy, El Salah (1989): 'The proper calculation of income from depletable natural resources', in *Environemnal Accounting for Sustainable Development*, Y.J. Ahmed El Serafy, and Ernst Lutz, World Bank, Washington D.C.

Sengupta, Nirmal (1991): *Managing Common Property: Irrigation in India, and the Philippines*, Sage Publications, New Delhi.

Singh, Katar and V. Ballabh (1996): *Cooperative Management of Natural Resources*, Sage Publications, New Delhi.

Singh, Shekhar, V. Sankaran, P. Rao and R. Mehta (1999): *Natural Resource Accounting and Budgeting: An alternative methodology*, Monograph, Indian Institute of Public Administration, New Delhi.

Swanson, T.M. and E.B. Barbier (eds.), (1992): *Economics for the Wilds: Wildlife, Wild lands, Diversity and Development*, Earthscan Publication, London.

Uimonen, Peter and J. Whalley (1997): *Environmental Issues in the New World Trading System*, MacMillan Press, London.

ANNEXURE A.1.1

A GLIMPSE OF NATURAL RESOURCE ENDOWMENTS IN INDIA

Description	Unit & Year	Extent
Exhaustible Resources		
A) Proven and balance recoverable reserves of Oil and Natural Gas		
i) Offshore crude oil	Million tonnes (1997)	320.0
ii) Onshore crude oil	Million tonnes (1997)	426.0
iii) Offshore natural gas	Billion cubic metres (1997)	274.0
iv) Onshore natural gas	Billion cubic metres (1997)	418.0
B) Proven resources of Coal	Million tonnes (1999)	79,106.19
C) Recoverable Reserves of select minerals		
i) Iron ore	Million tonnes (1998)	9602
ii) Copper	Million tonnes (1998)	431.04
iii) Manganese	Million tonnes (1998)	176.50
iv) Bauxite	Million tonnes (1998)	2525
Flora and Fauna		
A) Total Biological Diversity in India	Number in '000s (1998)	126.67
B) Flora		
i) Total plant species	Number in '000s (1997)	45
ii) Total threatened species	Number (1997)	583
C) Fauna		
i) Total animal species	Number in '000s (1998)	81

Description	Unit & Year	Extent
ii) Total threatened vertebrates	Number (1997)	158
iii) Tiger population	Number (1993)	3750
iv) Fish production		
a) Inland	Lakh tonnes (1996–7)	28.57
b) Marine	Lakh tonnes (1996–7)	22.83
D) Area under Tiger Reserves	Thousand Sq Km (1998)	33.05
Inexhaustible Resources		
A) Water Bodies		
i) Area under lakes/reservoirs/canals	Hectares (1988–9)	2,195,968
ii) Area under rivers/streams	Hectares (1988–9)	8,414,852
iii) Length of select major rivers		
a) Ganga	Km	2525
b) Indus	Km	1114
c) Brahmaputra	Km	916
d) Krishna	Km	1401
e) Cauvery	Km	800
Forests		
i) Total forest cover area	Sq Km (1997)	3287263
ii) Dense forest area	Sq Km (1997)	367130
iii) Open forest area	Sq Km (1997)	261310
iv) Mangroves	Sq Km (1997)	4827
v) Scrub area	Sq Km (1997)	57211
Other Resources		
i) Total Coast length	Km	7515
ii) Total Sandy area	Hectares (1988–9)	55,720,861
iii) No. of Biosphere Reserves	Number (1998)	10

Sources: 1. Compendium of Environment Statistics, 1997; 2. India 1998, GOI Publication; 3. State of Forest Report, 1997; 4. NRSA Land Use/Land Cover Area Statistics, 1995; 5. Tata Energy Data Directory and Yearbook, 1999/2000; 6. Implementation of Article 6 of CBD in India: National Report, GOI,1998

ANNEXURE 2
DESIGN PRINCIPLE FOR POOLED COMMON RESOURCES

1. Clearly Defined Boundaries: Individuals or households with rights to withdraw resources from the common pool resource and the boundaries of the common-pool resource itself are clearly defined.

2. Congruence: A. The distribution of benefits from appropriation rules is roughly proportionate to the costs imposed by provision rules; B. Appropriation rules restricting time, place, technology and/ or quantity of resources are related to local conditions.

3. Collective-Choice Arrangements: Most individuals affected by operational rules can participate in modifying operational rules.

4. Monitoring: Monitors, who actively audit common-pool resource conditions and appropriator behaviour, are accountable to the appropriators and /or are the appropriators themselves.

5. Graduated Sanctions: Appropriators who violate operational rules are likely to receive graduated sanctions (depending on the seriousness and context of the offence) from other appropriators, from officials accountable to these appropriators, or from both.

6. Conflict-Resolution Mechanisms: Appropriators and their officials have rapid access to low-cost, local arenas to resolve conflict among appropriators or between appropriators and officials.

7. Minimal Recognition of Rights to Organize: The rights of appropriators to devise their own institutions are not challenged by external governmental authorities.

8. Nested Enterprises: Appropriation, provision, monitoring, enforcement, conflict resolution and governance activities are organized in multiple layers of nested enterprises.

Source: Ostrom et al., 1994.

Pollution Control in Tanneries*

U. Sankar

INTRODUCTION

Tanneries come under the category 'Red'—highly polluting industry. Most of the tanning units are in the small-scale sector and are located in clusters in river basins. They face both internal and external pressures for compliance with the standards prescribed by the Pollution Control Boards. A techno-economic study of tanneries in the Vellore District of Tamil Nadu during 1996–8 is used (i) to understand the sources and magnitudes of pollution in the tanning processes, (ii) to assess the impact of pollution on water, soil and people, (iii) to study the problems in establishing and operating the common effluent treatment plants (CETPs) as an institutional arrangement for collective action, (iv) to estimate the costs of compliance with the standards for members of the CETPs and the resulting abatement burden and compare them with the costs of units having individual effluent treatment plants and (v) to offer suggestions to make CETPs an effective institutional mechanism for pollution prevention and control in tanneries.

The Water (Prevention and Control of Pollution) Act 1974, the Environment (Protection) Act 1986 and the rules issued under these Acts provide the legal framework for prevention and control of

* This chapter is based on the project report, Economic Analysis of Environmental Problems in Tanneries and Textile Bleaching and Dyeing Units and Suggestions for Policy Action, funded by the UNDP and completed in 1998. See Sankar (1998/2000). The author is grateful to M. Mariappan, Central Leather Reaserch Institute (CLRI) for technical advice and to V. Kannan, J.K. Jawahar, V. Anuradha and the project staff for research support. He thanks Gopal Kadekodi for comments and suggestions on the first draft.

environmental pollution. The Central Pollution Control Board (CPCB) has prescribed concentration-based source-specific standards for different pollution parameters that vary depending on the medium of discharge of the effluents. The tanning units are required to obtain consent certificates from their respective State Pollution Control Boards (SPCBs) for establishing tanneries and continuing their tanning operations. The laws prescribe penalties for non-compliance with the standards and other provisions of the Acts. Despite the establishment of the legal and administrative system for pollution control, the enforcement of the standards for the small-scale industry has been poor. The public interest litigations culminating in the Supreme Court judgements during the mid-1990s triggered administrative action for pollution control and also awakened public awareness of the impact of water pollution. For some details regarding laws and institutions relating to environmental protection in India see 'Fiscal and Institutional Approaches to Pollution Abatement' by Murty in this book, and Sankar (1998).

Tanneries form an intermediate segment of the leather industry. The basic raw materials for tanneries, namely hides and skins, come from the animal husbandry sector. The tanned leather is used for the manufacture of leather products. Leather industry is an important foreign exchange earner for the country via its exports. In recent years, its export prospects are being affected by two external factors: (i) growing competition from China and East Asian countries and (ii) the attempts by developed countries either to ban leather imports or to impose countervailing duty on the ground that the production of leather products in India and a few other developing countries do not meet their tight environmental standards.

Thus, the tanning units face internal and external pressures for compliance with the standards. There are four options to tanners: (i) become a member of a common effluent treatment plant (CETP), (ii) erect and operate an individual effluent treatment plant (IETP), (iii) relocation and (iv) closure. Each option involves extra cost. The best option is to become a member of a CETP but this option is feasible only for a unit in an industrial cluster. For an isolated unit the choice is among the remaining three options.

The objectives of this chapter are to demonstrate the relevance and applications of some basic economic concepts as applicable to a polluting industry such as tanning. The various steps involved are: (1) to understand the sources and magnitudes of pollution at different stages for different types of tanning processes; (2) to assess the impact of pollution on water, soil and the people; (3) to consider the rationale for and problems in establishing and operating the CETPs in tannery clusters; (4) to estimate the costs of compliance with the standards and their impact on the production costs, sales and value added for units belonging to the CETPs; (5) to offer suggestions for policy action.

As part of demonstrating a techno-economic study of tanneries, data from CETPs and IETPs from Vellore District of Tamil Nadu operating during 1996–8 are used here. Several studies assessing the impact of tannery pollution on the ecology are also cited. The estimation of pollution abatement cost is based on the economic costing method (Mehta, et al., 1997; Murty et al., 1998). Wherever necessary, the private production costs of the products and the actual compliance costs are estimated. This case study is presented in the form of a dialogue.

The plan of the case study is as follows. The section 'Leather Industry: Development and Environment' deals with the importance of leather industry in Indian economy, assesses the trade-off between environment and development, and argues the need for development of the industry with environmental safeguards. 'Tanning Processes and Pollution Generation' describes the different stages of tanning processes and water and other input usages, and gives estimates of volumes and concentrations of pollutants in the untreated effluents and solid wastes. 'Impact of Untreated Tannery Effluent on Water Quality, Soil and Human Health' provides an assessment of the impact of pollution in the case study area. This is based both on secondary data and a survey of perceptions of the affected people on tannery pollution. 'Economics of Common Effluent Treatment Plants' covers the rationale of CETP, designs of CETPs, and costs and performance of CETPs. It also gives the estimates of add-on costs required for full compliance with the standards and gives estimates of the abatement burden. The abatement costs and abatement burden for CETP members are compared with the abatement costs and burden for units with IETPs. The section 'CETP as a Social and Economic Organization' suggests a number of measures to make CETP an effective institutional mechanism for pollution prevention and control. Finally we have the 'Concluding Remarks'.

LEATHER INDUSTRY: DEVELOPMENT AND ENVIRONMENT

Growth of the Leather Industry

Until 1845, the Indian leather industry remained a rural cottage industry. The activities ranged from carcass collection, flaying and curing of hides and skins, to the production of leather goods such as chappals, shoes, drumheads and irrigation buckets. The village artisans utilized locally available raw materials and produced leather products to primarily meet the local demands.

The first modern tanning unit was established at Madras (now Chennai) in 1845. The development of railway network provided increased access to hides and skins from the hinterland for the tanning units and the existence of port facility made exports of tanned hides and skins to Great Britain possible. The 1857 uprising disrupted the system of obtaining boots, harness and saddlery for the Indian army from the Indian contractors. The Government Harness and Saddlery Factory was established at Kanpur in 1867 to meet this need.

After the independence, the government's industrial policies facilitated the establishment of tanneries in the small-scale sector. In the early 1970s, both external and internal factors were ripe for the rapid growth of the industry. In USA, UK, and Germany rising real wages as well as public concern about environmental damages from the tanneries resulted in a gradual shift of the industry to relatively low wage and less pollution-conscious countries. In India, the chrome tanning process was introduced for the first time. Its speed of production combined with the myriad applications made this method popular. Also, the basic chemicals (salt, sodium compounds, sulphuric acid), minerals, vegetable and synthetic agents, fat liquors, dyeing and tanning auxiliaries were available in India.

In the mid-1970s, based on the recommendations of the Seetharamiah Committee, the government announced a policy package consisting of a ban on export of raw hides and skins, quota restrictions on export of semi-finished leather, increase in leather manufacturing capacity and many fiscal concessions to encourage value-added leather exports.

Leather tanning up to wet blue (semi-finished) stage is reserved for the small-scale industry. Production of footwear and components are also reserved for small enterprises. The investment ceiling on plant and equipment for qualifying and classification under small-scale enterprises which was Rs 65 lakh has now been raised to Rs 100 lakh.

Under the new economic policy licenses are issued to large units provided they undertake to export 75 per cent of their production. Approval of foreign holding up to 51 per cent is given on a case by case basis. In 1998, the Commerce Ministry identified 11 specific products including leather and leather products for export promotion. The goal is to increase the value share of Indian leather exports in world export, from 4 per cent in 1995–6 to 10 per cent by 2005–6.

What is the Present Status of the Leather Industry?

India has a comparative advantage in the production of leather products. This advantage arises from its strong raw material base, long and rich tradition of leather craftsmanship and availability of cheap labour. This industry has achieved a decentralized pattern of development and contributed to employment generation particularly for the weaker sections in rural areas and small towns.

Tanneries form an intermediate segment of the leather industry. They get hides and skins for tanning from the animal husbandry sector. The main sources of hides and skins are cattle, buffaloes, goats and sheep. In 1992, India accounted for 59.3 per cent of world stock of buffaloes, 15.5 per cent of cattle, 18.8 per cent of goats and 3.8 per cent

TABLE 2.1
Livestock and Production of Hides and Skins

Species	Livestock	Off-take rates		Estimates of hides and skins production		
	1992 in million	India's share in world (in %)	CLRI Survey 1987 (in %)	CLRI recommendation (in %)	1995 million pieces	1995 million pieces	1995 million pieces
Cattle	200	15.5	10.8	11.6	23.5	24.9	498
Buffaloes	84	59.3	20.7	23.3	20.7	24.4	488
Goats	112	18.8	67.9	67.8	81.1	90.9	455
Sheep	46	3.8	60.4	62.0	28.8	29.4	147

Sources: Livestock estimates are based on 1961–87 Livestock Census growth rates. World estimates from FAO: World Statistical Compendium for Raw Hide and Skins, Leather and Leather Footwear 1972–90, Rome 1992. The off-take rates for 1987 are from CLRI: Report of All India Survey on Raw Hides and Skins, 1987

of sheep (See Table 2.1). According to CLRI (1987) Survey of Hides and Skins, the off-take rates for cattle and buffaloes in India in 1987 were only 10.8 per cent and 20.7 per cent, respectively. The off-take rate for bovine (cattle and buffaloes) for the world was 20.2 per cent and 35.7 per cent for USA. The low off-take for cattle, particularly for cows in India, is due to ban on cow slaughter in some states and low collection rates in other states because of the absence of well-organized slaughter houses in many areas. It is estimated that about six lakh persons, most of them belonging to weaker sections, are engaged in collection, flaying and curing of hides and skins. Environmental problems arise at the pre-tanning stage, in slaughtering the animals, collecting the carcasses, curing and transporting the hides and skins and also leaving the carcasses on land. But as these damages are dispersed and are perhaps within the assimilative capacities of the regions, they do not yet receive the public attention.

TABLE 2.2
Tanneries in 1988

State	SSI	DGTD	Total	Percentage
Tamil Nadu	536	41	577	53.2
West Bengal	227	6	233	21.5
Uttar Pradesh	140	7	147	13.6
Maharashtra	27	3	30	2.8
Andhra Pradesh	18	5	23	2.1
Karnataka	15	1	16	1.5
Others	45	12	57	5.3
Total	1008	75	1083	100.0

Source: Report on Capacity Utilization and Scope for Modernization in Indian Tanning Industry, CLRI, Chennai 1990

Most tanneries in India are located in clusters in river basins—in the Gangetic basin in Uttar Pradesh and West Bengal and Palar and Cauvery river basins in Tamil Nadu. According to the CLRI Report (1990), in 1988 there were 1083 tanneries of which 1008 were in the small-scale sector and 75 under the Directorate General of Trade and Development (DGTD) sector. It may be seen from Table 2.2 that Tamil Nadu accounted for 53.2 per cent of the tanneries, followed by

West Bengal (21.5 per cent) and Uttar Pradesh (13.6 per cent). About 62 per cent of the tanneries in the small scale sector and 48 per cent of the tanneries in the DGTD sector were established after 1973. The total installed capacities in 1987-8 were 62 million pieces of hides and 161 million pieces of skins. At present there are 1589 tanneries in India of which 833 are in Tamil Nadu, 361 in West Bengal, 188 in Uttar Pradesh, 79 in Punjab and 33 in Maharashtra (Basu, 2000).

Data relating to exports of leather and leather products are given in Table 2.3. The compound annual growth rate (CAGR) of total value of leather exports for the period 1951-2 to 1971-2 was 5.5 per cent. With an export policy thrust, the CAGR increased to 15 per cent during 1971-2 to 1981-2 and further to 19 per cent during 1981-2 to 1991-2. The growth rate had fallen to 12 per cent during 1991-2 to 1996-7. There has been a significant change in the composition of the exports. Until 1971-2, the share of leather products in the total value of leather exports was less than 1 per cent, but the share had increased to 36.9 per cent in 1981-2, 76.4 per cent in 1991-2 and to 80.8 per cent in 1996-7. It may be noted that for hides and skins worth Rs 100, the average value additions at the finishing and leather production stages are about Rs 86 and Rs 345, respectively.

The value of leather exports reached a peak figure of US$ 1.731 billion in 1995-6 and fell to US $ 1.620 billion in 1998-9. The recent decline in exports is attributed to closure of some tanneries, recession

TABLE 2.3
Exports of Leather and Leather Products: India

(Rs lakh)

Item	1951-2	1971-2	1981-2	1991-2	1996-7
Raw hides and skins	824	66	44	—	—
Semi-tanned hides and skins	2534	8587	5352	—	—
Finished leather	—	430	22,640	72,621	1,05,941
Leather footwear	—	858	3005	43,081	1,20,802
Leather footwear components	—	15	7722	66,335	79,162
Leather goods and garments	37	232	5667	1,25,586	2,45,811
Total	3393	10,188	44,430	3,07,624	5,51,716

Source: Council for Leather Exports

in developed countries and growing competition from China, Hong Kong and Thailand. Between 1988 and 1994, the CAGRs of the values of exports of leather and leather products were 32.6 per cent for China, 27.9 per cent for Hong Kong and 21.3 per cent for Thailand. As environmental issues are being brought into the world trade agenda, India's exports to developed countries may be affected unless the industry meets the environmental standards.

Thus, there appears to be a trade-off between development of the industry and environmental quality. In the past, the policy thrust was on decentralized growth, employment generation and export growth. Now with citizens having the right to ask for clean air and clean water, and the Supreme Court enforcing the rights, the tanners are under pressure to comply with the environmental standards. The industry also faces export competition from China and East Asian Countries and ban on imports or imposition of countervailing duties by many Organization for Economic Co-operation and Development (OECD) Countries. The challenge is how to achieve a sustainable development of the leather industry.

TANNING PROCESSES AND POLLUTION GENERATION

What are the Stages and Processes in Tanning?

The process of converting hides and skins into leather—a non-putrescible product—is called tanning. The two tanning processes available are vegetable tanning and chrome tanning. Conversion of raw hides and skins to semi-finished leather by vegetable tanning is called 'Raw to East India'[1] Conversion of raw hide and skin to semi-finished leather by chrome tanning is called 'Raw to Wet Blue'. Semi-finished leather can be converted to finished leather either by vegetable tanning or chrome tanning. It is also possible to combine the two stages and convert raw hides and skins to finished leather by either vegetable tanning or chrome tanning.

What are the inputs used in tanning? How much effluents and solid wastes are generated in tanning? The sequential steps in the tanning of hides and skins along with the consumption of chemicals and water usage and waste generation for the two tanning processes are given in the form of flow charts. Figure 2.1 shows 'Raw to Wet Blue' stage by

[1] An expression nostalgic to trading through East India Co.

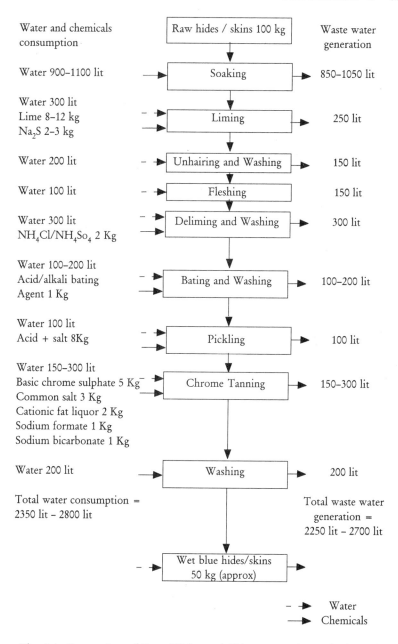

Fig. 2.1: Processing of Raw Hides and Skins to Semi-Finished Leather by Chrome Tanning (Raw to Wet Blue)

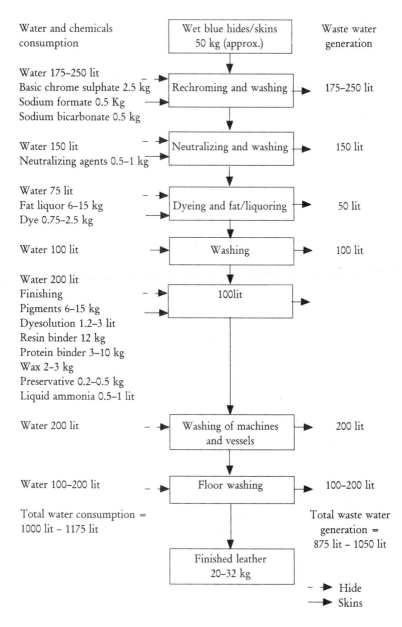

Water and chemicals consumption	Wet blue hides/skins 50 kg (approx.)	Waste water generation
Water 175–250 lit Basic chrome sulphate 2.5 kg Sodium formate 0.5 Kg Sodium bicarbonate 0.5 kg	Rechroming and washing	175–250 lit
Water 150 lit Neutralizing agents 0.5–1 kg	Neutralizing and washing	150 lit
Water 75 lit Fat liquor 6–15 kg Dye 0.75–2.5 kg	Dyeing and fat/liquoring	50 lit
Water 100 lit	Washing	100 lit
Water 200 lit Finishing Pigments 6–15 kg Dyesolution 1.2–3 lit Resin binder 12 kg Protein binder 3–10 kg Wax 2–3 kg Preservative 0.2–0.5 kg Liquid ammonia 0.5–1 lit	100lit	
Water 200 lit	Washing of machines and vessels	200 lit
Water 100–200 lit	Floor washing	100–200 lit
Total water consumption = 1000 lit – 1175 lit		Total waste water generation = 875 lit – 1050 lit
	Finished leather 20–32 kg	

- ▸ Hide
→ Skins

Fig. 2.2: Processing of Semi-Finished (Wet Blue) Hides/Skins to Finished Leather

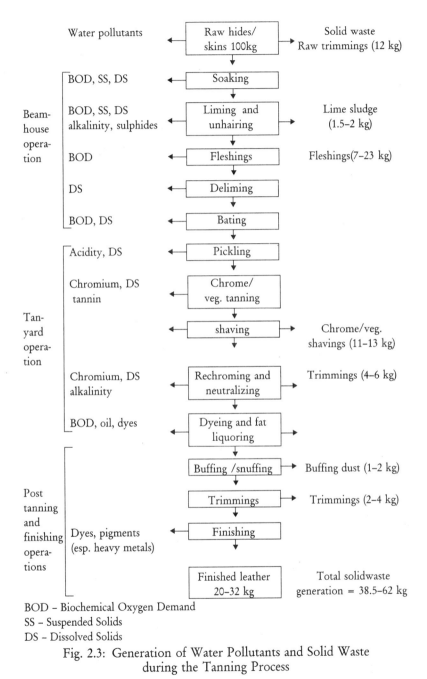

Fig. 2.3: Generation of Water Pollutants and Solid Waste
during the Tanning Process

Box 2.1

Major Water Pollutants in Tannery Sector

Biological Oxygen Demand (BOD)

BOD is the quantity of oxygen required for the biological and chemical oxidation of waterborne substances under ambient or test conditions. In leather tannery waste water, the BOD derives principally from organic materials such as hide/skin substances and from ammonia from the deliming process and from hydrolytic deamination of proteinaceous hair and hide substance. The BOD of waste water adversely affects the dissolved oxygen resources of a waterbody by reducing the oxygen available to fish, plant life and other aquatic life. The tolerance limits for BOD for discharge of trade effluents are 30 mg/l in case of inland surface water and 100 mg/l in case of main coastal areas and on land for irrigation.

Chemical Oxygen Demand (COD)

COD is a purely chemical oxidation test devised as an alternative method of estimating the total oxygen demand of a waste water. The test relies on the oxidation reduction systems of chemical analysis; it indicates the quantum of carbonaceous matters precisely. High COD contributions in tannery waste water are attributed to a wide range of complex organic and inorganic process chemicals including dyes, detergents, biocides and syntams. The tolerance limit for discharge of COD is 250 mg/l.

pH

Although not a specific pollutant, pH is related to the acidity or alkalinity of a waste water stream. It is not a direct measure of either; it may be used to control both excess acidity and excess alkalinity in water. Knowledge of the pH of waste water aids in determining measures necessary for corrosion control, pollution control and disinfection. Rapid changes in pH from acceptable limits (5.5 to 9.0) can harm some species.

Sulphides

A significant portion of sulphides contained in tannery waste water is converted to hydrogen sulphides at a pH less than 8.0. Release of this gas to the atmosphere is hazardous. This gas is odorous and can damage property by corrosion. It is lethal to operation and maintenance workers in sewers and effluent treatment plants. The tolerance limits for sulphide (as S) is 2 mg/l for inland surface water and on land for irrigation, and 5 mg/l for marine coastal areas.

Suspended Solids (SS)

SS include both organic and inorganic materials. The inorganic components include sand, silt, clay and toxic materials. The organic compounds include grease, oil, proteins and carbohydrates. SS may settle rapidly by gravity and deposit at the bottom of streams, canals, pipes etc. They may be inert, slowly biodegradable, or rapidly decomposable substances. While in suspension, they increase the turbidity of the water, reduce light penetration and impair the photosynthetic activity of aquatic plants. Solid substances leached out by water are detrimental to aquatic life by clogging of fish gills and respiratory passages, screening out light and promoting and maintaining the development of noxious conditions through oxygen depletion. The tolerance limits for SS are 100 mg/l for discharge of waste water into inland surface water and marine coastal areas, 200 mg/l on land for irrigation.

Total Dissolved Solids (TDS)

Tannery waters have high TDS, the majority of which are sodium chloride and calcium sulphate. Sodium chloride comes principally from soaking of raw hides and skins in water and washing of the raw material and from the salt added in the pickling operation. TDS have impact on stream life and water treatment processes. The tolerance limit for TDS is 2100 mg/ l.

Oil and Grease

Oil and grease result from the degreasing process used in some tanneries and from the oils used directly in leather processing especially fat liquoring. Most of these oil and grease materials are animal or vegetable based and therefore amenable to biodegradation. Oil and grease cause non-relishable taste and odour problems. Oil emulsions may adhere to the gills of fish, causing suffocation, and may taint the flesh of fish. Oil deposits in the bottom sediments of water can inhibit bottom flora and fauna. The tolerance limit for oil and grease in discharge of effluents are 10 mg/l in inland surface water and on land for irrigation and 20 mg/l for marine coastal areas.

Chromium

Disposal of sludge containing very high trivalent concentrations can potentially cause problems in uncontrolled landfills. Incineration or similar destructive oxidation processes can produce hexavalent chromium which in turn is potentially more toxic than trivalent chromium under certain circumstances. The tolerance limits for total chromium (as Cr) are 0.1 mg/l for inland surface water and 1.0 for marine coastal areas and land for irrigation.

Tannins

Tannins are derived from the barks and extracts used for vegetable tanning. It imparts colour to the receiving body of water, exerts COD and persists in the environment for long time.

chrome tanning. The tanning process uses 23.5 litre to 28 litre per kg of hide/skin processed; the waste water generated in the processing is in the range 22.5 l to 27.0 l. Many chemicals are used in the 'Raw to Wet Blue' processing. Approximately 50 per cent of the weight of raw hide/skin becomes waste.

The input usages in vegetable tanning process, 'Raw to East India' upto the pickling stage are the same as for the 'Raw to Wet Blue' process. Vegetable tanning requires lesser water; 1.0 l to 2.0 l per kg instead of 1.5 l to 3.0 l per kg, and instead of using chemicals it uses wattle extract in the range of 0.24 kg–0.45 kg and retanning agent in the range of 0.06 kg–0.14 kg per kg of hide/skin processed.

The steps and input usages in the conversion of semi-finished (wet blue) leather to finished leather are shown in Figure 2.2. This process requires 10.00 l to 11.75 l per kg of hide/skin processed of which 8.75 l to 10.50 l comes out as effluent. The steps and input usages in the conversion of semi-finished (East India) leather to finished leather are the same as for the conversion of wet blue leather to finished leather, except that the former uses larger quantity of basic chrome sulphate, that is 0.075 to -0.1 kg instead of about 0.025 kg per kg of the raw material processed.

What are the Major Water Pollutants?

There are a number of water pollutants that come under the scrutiny and purview of environmental regulations. The major water pollutants are shown in Box 2.1

Figure 2.3 provides estimates of major water pollutants and solid wastes in the tanning of hides/skins to finished leather under beam-house operation, tan-yard operation and post-tanning and finishing operations.

What are the Characteristics of the Effluents?

Characteristics of effluents are likely to vary over a wide range depending on the type and source of raw material, vintage of the plant, process used and also the nature of sampling. Soaking effluent contains dirt, dung, blood, soluble protein, proteolytic and other bacteria and high salt content. Effluent from unhairing and fleshing contains fatty and fleshy matter along with hair and sulphides. Liming and deliming effluent contains gritty material, unused salt and high organic content. Effluent from vegetable tanning is highly acidic and coloured together with high organic content. Chrome tanning is also acidic and contains trivalent chromium.

The characteristics of combined waste water in conversion of raw hide/skin to finished leather for chrome tanning and vegetable tanning

TABLE 2.4
Charateristics of Waste Water from Tanneries

Parameter	Raw to finish vegetable tanning concentration range	Raw to finish chrome tanning concentration range	Pre-scribed standards by TNPCB*
(1)	(2)	(3)	(4)
pH	8.7–9.5	7.5–8.5	5.5–9.0
Suspended solids (SS) (mg/l)	3000–5600	3000–4500	100
Totally dissolved solids (TDS)(mg/l)	8500–19,680	14,000–20,500	2100
BOD (mg/l)	2300–2650	1200–2500	30
COD (mg/l)	5320–7160	3000–6000	250
Sulphides (mg/l)	75–90	20–40	2.0
Chromium total (mg/l)	8–22	80–250	0.1
Oil and grease (mg/l)	17–43	28–55	10.0

* For effluents discharged into inland surface water
Source: Tamil Nadu Pollution Control Board

processes are given in Table 2.4. It may be observed that while the BOD, COD and sulphide values are higher in vegetable tanning effluents, TDS, chromium total and oil and grease values are higher in chrome tanning effluents. It may also be observed that the parameter values, except pH, in the untreated waste water are far above the prescribed standards.

What are BOD Pollution Loads Before and After Treatment?

The pollution load is defined as the quantity of waste water times the concentration of a pollutant in the waste water. As an example, consider the BOD loads before and after treatment as per the standard and compare them with the BOD load in municipal sewage in two tannery towns of the Vellore district of Tamil Nadu. The tanneries in Ranipet town with an installed capacity of 4000 kilolitres per day (KLD) and an average BOD of raw effluent at 2795 mg/l could generate a total BOD load of 11.180 tonnes/day which is 5.44 times the BOD load generated from the municipal sewage for a population of 45,680 in 1995–6. If all the tanneries had complied with the BOD standard, the average BOD load after treatment would be only 0.120 tonne/day which is only 5.8 per cent of the BOD load in the municipal sewage. Vaniyambadi town with an effluent capacity of 7061 KLD and an average BOD of raw effluent at 2000 mg/l could generate a BOD load of 14.122 tonnes/day, which is 3.85 times the BOD load generated from the municipal sewage for a population of 81,500 in 1995–6. With full compliance, the BOD load from tanneries would be only 0.212 tonne/day or 5.8 per cent of the BOD load from the municipal sewage. Thus, the need for compliance with the standard is obvious.

IMPACT OF UNTREATED TANNERY EFFLUENTS ON WATER QUALITY, SOIL AND HUMAN HEALTH

Some evidences about the impact of continuous discharge of untreated tannery effluents in and around the tannery towns of Ranipet and Vaniyambadi on water quality, soil and human health are provided here. It also gives perceptions of the people in the worst affected villages on the impact of the effluents.

What are the adverse effects of water pollution on ground water quality and soil? The ground water along the Palar river basin in

Tamil Nadu is used for drinking and agricultural use. With data from 12 public works departments (PWD) observation wells located in several villages within a radius of 15 km of Ranipet and Vaniyambadi towns for the period 1972–93 it is possible to study the changing quality of ground water over time.

Electrical conductivity (EC) is a measure of the capacity of a substance or solution to conduct electric current. It is measured as mS/cm. It provides a rapid and convenient way of indicating the salinity of water. In nine of the twelve villages of Palar river basin the maximum observed values exceeded the tolerance limit of 2250 mS/cm for irrigation. Only in three of the villages the estimated values were below the limit over the whole period. It was found that in eight villages the EC values increased with time. TDS indicates various kinds of minerals present in the water. The maximum observed TDS values were below the standard of 2000 mg/l in only four out of twelve villages. It was found that in eight of the 2 villages TDS values increased with time. The chloride twelve standards for drinking water and irrigation are 250 mg/l and 600 mg/l, respectively. In six villages, the average values were below the standard for drinking water. During this period the observed values of chloride exceeded the limit for irrigation at least once in nine of the twelve villages.

The CPCB Ground Water Quality Monitoring Data for eight dug wells within a radius of 15 km of Ranipet and Vaniyambadi at monthly intervals, during the calendar year 1994 reveal that, compared with the EC tolerance limit of 2250 mS/cm for irrigation, the measured values ranged from 4100 mS/cm to 17,050 mS/cm. The TDS values were all above the standard of 2100 mg/l. The MPN index of total coliforms/ E. Coli/S. fecal should be zero or 0.01 ml for drinking water, but, in the sample, the values ranged from 236 to 1413 indicating high bacterial contamination of the ground water.

A study undertaken by Tamil Nadu Agricultural University and Division of Soils, Commonwealth Scientific and Industrial Research Organization, Urrbrae, South Australia assessed the extent of contamination of soil and ground water due to chromium in a few sites in Vaniyambadi. This study reports high values for EC, NA and Cr in surface and sub-soil samples. It also reports that the chromium content in borehole water exceeded the prescribed limit.

What are the perceptions of people in the affected areas about pollution from tanneries? This analysis requires survey of village households. Analysis based on three villages, Gudimallur, Devathanam and Vannivedu in Walajah Taluk, located in the downstream of the Palar river which carries the waste water stream from tanneries in Ambur, Ranipet, Vaniyambadi and Walajapet is presented here. The Vellore Citizens Forum cites these villages as the most affected villages in support of their public litigation case filed in the Supreme Court in 1991. A random sample of 352 households was chosen to study the perceptions of the villagers on the impact of tannery effluents on water, health and agriculture.

For the question whether they faced any problem of stagnation or run-off of tannery effluents in their areas, 77 per cent responded. Of the respondents, only 7 per cent said they did not face any problems; 82 per cent cited mosquito menace as the problem and 70 per cent cited water contamination and odour as problems. As far the ground water quality, 88 per cent of the respondents said that hardness/salinity of ground water had increased during the last 20 years. More than four-fifths of the respondents cited bad taste as an indicator of poor ground water quality.

As for the impact on health, 31.5 per cent of the respondents reported that they suffered from one or more diseases during 1996. Respiratory disease was the most frequent disease followed by allergy-related sickness. About three-fourths of those suffering from an illness attributed water pollution and three-tenths air pollution as causes of their illness. Of the 63 persons who could not attend their work due to illness, seven reported number of days not worked as a week or less, 25 between a week and a month, and 11 more than three months.

Of the 80 respondents owning land, 52 cited soil or/and water pollution as the reason for leaving part or all of their land uncultivated. Except two, others reported that the yield rates had been falling over time. More than three-fourths of the owners reported that the market values of their lands had been declining over time.

A caution is warranted that the observed changes in water quality, soil quality, agricultural productivity or human illness cannot be attributed entirely to the discharge of tannery effluents on land and rivers. Also, valuation of damages poses many conceptual and measurement problems. For this type of analysis, panel data are required for many years as well as a prior knowledge of the links between discharge of the effluents and their impacts in physical and biological environments, to estimate the 'dose response functions'.

What is the Supreme Court Verdict on the Vellore Citizens Welfare Forum versus Union of India and others? The Public Interest Writ Petition (c) No. 914 of 1991 was filed by the Vellore Citizens Welfare Forum. It was 'directed against the pollution which is being caused by enormous discharge of untreated effluent by the tanneries and other industries in the State of Tamil Nadu'. In the Judgement dated 21 August 1996, Justice Kuldip Singh observed that 'though the leather industry is of vital importance to the country as it generates foreign exchange and provides employment avenues it has no right to destroy the ecology, degrade the environment and pose as a health hazard. It cannot be permitted to expand unless it tackles by itself the problem of pollution created by the said industry.'

After citing the Stockholm Declaration of 1972, the constitutional and statutory provisions, and common law to protect a person's right to fresh air and clean water and pollution free environment, the Court endorsed the 'polluter pays principle' and the 'precautionary principle'. It directed the Central Government to constitute an authority under Section 3(3) of the Environment (Protection) Act, 1986 to implement the two principles. The Court said: 'The authority shall, with the help of expert opinion and after giving opportunity to the concerned polluters, assess the loss to the ecology/environment in the affected areas and shall also identify the individuals/families who have suffered because of the pollution and shall assess the compensation to be paid to the said individuals/families. The authority shall further determine the compensation to be recovered from the polluters as the cost of reversing the damaged environment.' It imposed a fine of Rs 10,000 on each of the 700 tanneries in Tamil Nadu and asked them to install IETPs or become members of CETPs.

ECONOMICS OF COMMON EFFLUENT TREATMENT PLANTS

What is the Rationale of a CETP?

The major justification for establishing a CETP in an industrial cluster is economies of scale in waste-water treatment. As the volume of waste water treated increases the unit cost of treatment decreases. However, there is a cost involved in connecting the tanneries by a pipeline system and this cost increases with the number of tanneries connected to a CETP.

The DGTD constituted a Committee under the Development Council for Leather and Leather Goods in 1986 to prepare a Fiscal Plan for setting up CETPs for Indian tanning industry. The Committee found the feasibility of establishing 70 CETPs in 14 states with an indicative aggregate capital cost (excluding land cost) of Rs 53 crore at 1985-6 prices. Utilizing the data available for 65 tannery clusters on capital cost (C), estimated volume of waste water (F), and number of tanneries (N), the following regression equation was estimated by ordinary least squares method:

$$\text{Ln C} = -0.8690 + 0.7879 \ln F + 0.0547 \ln N \qquad (2.1)$$
$$\phantom{\text{Ln C} = } (0.0315) \quad (0.0050) \qquad (0.0099)$$
$$\bar{R}^2 = 0.9976, \text{ Degrees of freedom} = 62$$

Figure in brackets are standard errors of the regression coefficients; ln or Ln means natural logarithm.

Variations in F and N account for 99.8 per cent of the variation in the cost. The coefficient of ln F indicates that a 10 per cent increase in the volume of waste water increases the capital cost only by 7.9 per cent. This coefficient is less than one at the 5 per cent level of significance. The coefficient of ln N is positive which means that as the number of tanneries increases, given the volume of waste water, the capital cost increases, but at much lesser rate. An increase in the number of tanneries by 10 per cent can raise the total capital cost of CETP by 0.5 per cent only.

A similar exercise was carried out using the data for 28 CETPs planned in Tamil Nadu. The estimated capital cost function is:

$$\text{Ln C} = 0.9923 + 0.5100 \ln F + 0.2528 \ln N \qquad (2.2)$$
$$\phantom{\text{Ln C} = } (0.3831) \quad (0.0835) \qquad (0.0912)$$
$$\bar{R}^2 = 0.9073, \text{ Degrees of freedom} = 25$$

This equation explains 91 per cent of the variation in the capital cost. The results are qualitatively similar to the equation based on the All-India data reported above. A 10 per cent increase in the volume of waste water increases the capital cost only by 5.1 per cent. A 10 per cent increase in the number of tanneries increases the capital cost, given the volume of waste water, by 2.5 per cent. Both the economic cost models show the strength of scale economies in CETP (Misra, 1998).

Apart from the economies of scale, there are other factors which favour CETPs. They are eligible for subsidy on project costs from the central and state governments. The subsidy amount by central government is 25 per cent of the project cost subject to a maximum amount of Rs 50 lakh; the state government also provides subsidy subject to the above condition. The tanners are required to provide 20 per cent of the project cost by way of share capital. They can get the balance amount of the project cost by way of loan from financial institutions.

Common effluent treatment plant, as a cooperative venture for collective action, confers many benefits to its members and to society. Each tannery is small in size, its information base about clean technologies and waste minimization is poor and its managerial capabilities are limited. A CETP can seek technical help from technical institutions, government and international agencies such as United Nations Industrial Development Organizational (UNIDO), United Nations Development Programme (UNDP), United Nations Environment Programme (UNEP) and World Bank. It can hire technical persons for management. The society can achieve cost saving if the monitoring task by Pollution Control Boards can be shifted from individual tanneries to CETPs. The society can also benefit from improvement in environmental quality if the CETPs can meet the standards.

What are the hurdles in establishing the CETPs? Even though the rationale for CETPs is obvious, there are many hurdles in establishing and operating CETPs. First, the end-of-pipe treatment involves capital cost in the form of contribution to equity shares and recurring cost to meet interest and repayment of loan, and operating costs. As these abatement costs would affect their unit production costs and hence their international competitiveness, the tanners adopt 'wait and see' attitude. Second, the preparation of a technical and cost-effective plan for a CETP requires a good information base on spatial distribution of tanneries and volume of and concentrations of pollutants in the effluents from each source, and technical expertise for location of a site for CETP, design of conveyance system for bringing the effluents from tanneries to CETP, design of CETP, treatment processes to be followed and estimation of costs and allocation of costs among members. The third problem is getting approval of the technical plan by authorized technical experts, approval of technical and financial plan by funding agencies, and finally getting the approval of government agencies for the site, conveyance system and mode of discharge of treated effluents and solid wastes. All theses actions involve delays and transaction costs.

What are the Characteristics of the Sampled CETPs?

Particulars regarding number of beneficiaries, process capacity, volume of effluents and length of sewer are given in Table 2.5. All 5 CETPs are registered under Section 25 of the Companies Act. The size of CETP, in terms of number of members, varies from 10 to 110, and in terms of volume of effluent from 200 to 4000 m³ or kilo litres per day (KLD). The length of the sewer varies from 1.5 km to 8.00 km.

TABLE 2.5
Characteristics of CETPs in the Study Area

Name of the company	Year of CETP operation	No. of beneficiaries Exising	Proposed	Total process capacity	Volume of effluent Design m³/day	Current m³/day	Length of sewer
1. Ranitec	1995	76	0	34,000	4000	3000	7.60
2. Melvisharam	1997	22	15	82,450	3375	1200	150
3. SIDCO Phase I	1995	81	6	1,17,500	2500	1300	6.86
4. Vanitec (Udayendram)	1995	10	0	8000	200	200	2.20
5. Vanitec (Valayampet)	1991	110	0	83,600	2850	2400	8.00

Source: Primary data

The Supreme Court case brought together the All India Skin and Hide Tannery and Merchants Association, Tamil Nadu Leather Development Corporation, Central Leather Research Institute, National Environmental Engineering Institute, Tamil Nadu Pollution Control Board (TNPCB) and the affected parties in speeding up the establishment of CETPs. At least five CETPs are in operation in the tannery clusters of Ranipet and Vaniyambadi in North Arcot district of Tamil Nadu, as shown in Figure 2.4.

How are the CETPs designed? The technical design features of CETPs are given in Table 2.6. Small Industries Development Corporation (SIDCO) Phase I CETP members process semi-finished leather to finished leather. For tanneries connected to the other four

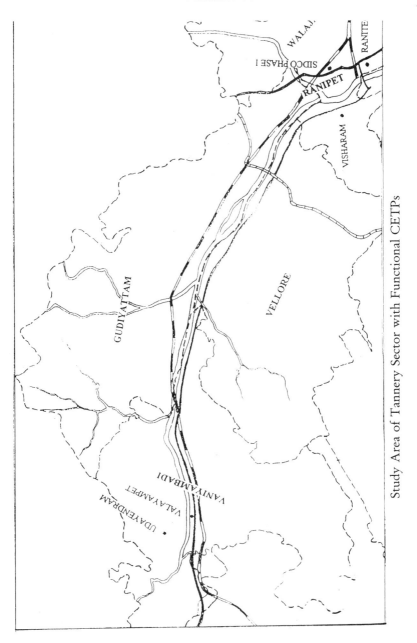

Fig. 2.4

TABLE 2.6
Waste Water Treatment: Design of CETPs

Name of the company	Processes in tanneries	Segregation of soak and pickling waste water from other effluents	Equalization and flash mixer	Primary solid separation	First stage	Second stage	Sludge treatment
					Biological treatment		
					CETP design		
1. Ranitec	Mixed	Separation & treatment at the tanneries	E FM	PC	ANL, PAT AT I	.	SDB ST
2. Melvisharam	Mainly R-F	Separation & treatment at the tanneries	E FM	C	AT I	AT II	SDB
3. SIDCO Phase I	SF-F	Not necessary	E FM	C	AT I	AT II	SDB
4. Vanitec (Udayendram)	R-F	Two separate lines to CETP	E FM	C	AT I	AT II	SDB
5. Vanitec (Valayampet)	Mainly R-F	Two separate lines to CETP	E FM	PC	ANL	AL	SDB

E: Equalization   FM: Flash Mixer   PC: Primary Clarifier   C: Clarifloculator
ANL: Anaerobic Lagoon   PAT: Pre-aeration Tank,   AT: Aeration Tank   AL: Aerated Lagoon
SDB: Sludge Drying Bed   ST: Sludge Thickener

Source: Tamil Nadu Pollution Control Board

CETPs, segregation of soak and pickling effluents from other influents is required. Members of Ranitec and Visharam CETPs do this treatment at the solar evaporation tanks in their premises whereas for the units connected to the two Vanitec CETPs there are two separate pipelines—one for soak liquours and pickling wastes and another for the other effluents—from the tanneries to the CETPs. All the five CETPs are designed to treat conventional pollutants like BOD, COD, pH and SS. Primary solid separation is done either by primary clarifier or clarifloculater. The first stage biological treatment is done using anaerobic lagoon and aeration tank or aeration tank alone. The second stage treatment requires either aerated lagoon or aeration tank. All the CETPs have sludge drying beds but only Ranitec has a sludge thickener.

How are the costs computed? The economic costs, both capital, and operating and maintenance costs, are furnished in Table 2.7. These costs are computed at 1995-6 prices. The procedure for computation of capital cost per KLD of waste water is as follows. First, all capital costs are converted to 1995-6 prices. Second, the annualized capital costs are computed using the assumptions of 20 years of plant life and cost of capital at 15 per cent per annum. Third, the capital cost per KLD is based on the assumption of full utilization of capacity for 365 days in a year. The capital cost per KLD varies from Rs 9.30 for

TABLE 2.7

Capital and Operation and Maintenance Costs per Kilolitre/Day of Waste Water Treated

(at 1995-6 prices)

Company	capacity utilization per cent	Cost (in Rs)			Government subsidy Rs
		Capital	O&M	Total	
1. Ranitec	75	9.30	7.00	16.30	2.08
2. Melvisharam	36	17.25	15.00	32.25	1.23
3. SIDCO Phase I	52	13.25	13.18	26.67	1.75
4. Vanitec (Udayendram)	100	23.58	20.00	43.58	7.65
5. Vanitec (Valayampet)	84	15.06	8.18	23.24	2.17

Source: Tamil Nadu Pollution Control Board

the CETP with maximum designed capacity to Rs 23.58 for the CETP with lowest designed capacity. The actual share of government subsidy in capital cost varies from Rs 7.00 to Rs 20.00. These estimates provide further evidence for economies of scale in waste water treatment.

What is the existing cost-sharing arrangement? Details of the cost-sharing schemes for member units in the five CETPs are given in Table 2.8. It may be observed that the basis for equity contribution as well as monthly contribution varies among the CETPs—capacity in terms of kilograms of hides and skins processed or number of pieces of hide/skin processed or volume of effluent or a flat rate.[2] The monthly contribution for operation and maintenance and improvement is based not on the volume of effluent or concentrations of pollutants. The only justification for use of such measures appears to be that they are readily observable and measurable. For the purpose of comparison, all the costs are expressed in terms of cost per kilogram of hides and skin processed. It should be noted the actual costs differ from the economic costs given above because (i) economic costing excludes government subsidy, (ii) the actual interest rates on loans differ from the assumed interest rate and (iii) the periods for repayment of loans differ from the assumed life of the CETPs.

Are the CETPs Complying with the Standards?

The pollution parameters before treatment (at inlets) and after treatment (at outlets) are given in Table 2.9. In order to assess the CETPs extent of compliance with the standards, the parameter values at the outlets should be compared with the norms of the TNPCB. All the CETPs comply with the standards for pH, sulphide and total chromium. The CETP at SIDCO phase I violates the standards for four parameters—BOD, COD, SS and TDS. Melvisharam violates the standards for COD and TDS. For all the five CETPs, the TDS values at the outlets are far above the norm of 2100 mg/l. Discussions with the designers of the CETPs reveal that CETPs were not designed to solve the TDS problem.

---

[2] The concept of installed capacity in terms of kilograms of hides and skins processed is a crude measure, as the value weights for different hides and skins differ. Even the measure of number of pieces makes some sense if it refers to a particular hide or skin, but even here there is a considerable variation in the quality in each group.

TABLE 2.8
Cost-sharing by Member Units

| Name of the company | Basis for contribution of equity | Annualized capital cost per kg of hides and skins (Rs) | Basis for monthly contribution | | | Cost per kg of raw material processed (Rs) |
			For O & M and improvement	For servicing the loan	Total	
1. Ranitec	Rs 68.66/kg of hide/skin/day	10.95	Rs 6/kg of hide/skin/day	Rs 4/kg of hide/skin/day	Rs 10/kg of hide/skin/day	0.44
2. Melvisharam	Rs 2400/m³ of effluent/day	9.57	Rs 7/kg of hide/skin/day	Rs 4/kg of hide/skin/day	Rs 11/kg of hide/skin/day	0.47
3. SIDCO Phase I	Rs 83,908/member	9.25	Rs 6321.80/member	Rs 3178/member	Rs 9498.80/member/day	0.29
4. Vanitec (Udayendram)	Rs 175/piece/day	22.33	Rs 15/piece/day	Nil	Rs 15/piece/day	0.55
1. Vanitec (Valayampet)	Rs 80.62/piece/day	10.29	Rs 10/piece/day	Rs 5/piece/day	Rs 15/piece/day	0.51

Source: Tamil Nadu Pollution Control Board

75

TABLE 2.9
Performance of CETPs (Pollution Parameter Values at Inlets and Outlets)

Parameter	Ranitec		Melvisharam		SIDCO Phase I		Vanitec (Udayendram)		Vanitec (Valayampet)	
	Inlet	Outlet	Inlet	Outlet	Inlet	Outlet	Inlet	Outlet	Inlet	Outlet
pH	8.0	6.1	7.6	7.1	6.72	8.1	8.23	5.12	6.9	7.0
Suspended Solids, mg/L	4460	87	2588	84	920	168	3660	58	3660	58
Total Dissolved Solids, mg/L	20,686[b]	15,326	16,400[b]	16,300	2926[c]	3690	6056[a]	8006	7014[a]	5674
BOD, mg/L	3016	27	1820	20	962	49	1500	22	1500	22
COD, mg/L	9728	224	3640	292	4400	520	6664	282	2320	244
Sulphide, mg/L	122	1.5	12	BDL	BDL	BDL	26.2	BDL	48	BDL
Total Chromium, mg/L	17.1	0.653	BDL	BDL	BDL	BDL	127.3	BDL	BDL	BDL
Oil & Grease, mg/L	8.6	4.9	42	BDL	6	4	5	2	12.8	9.6
Hexavalent Chromium, mg/L	BDL	BDL	BDL	BDL	BDL	BDL	BDL	BDL	BDL	BDL

Notes: BDL : Below detection limit; [a] Soak liquor segregation effective low TDS; [b] Soak liquor segregation ineffective high TDS; [c] Soak liquor segregation not necessary SF – F process low TDS

Source: Tamil Nadu Pollution Control Board

What are the Add-on Costs For TDS Reduction and Sludge Treatment?

Add-on costs: Compared with various technical options for TDS reduction, two options—membrane separation (reverse osmosis (RO) process) and high rate transpiration system (HRTS) are under experimentation. An attempt is made to estimate the tentative costs of TDS removal by both methods.

The cost estimates for adopting the RO process by four CETPs are given in Table 2.10.[3] The annualised capital cost is calculated at 1995–6 prices, assuming a 20-year plant life and cost of capital at 15 per cent. The rejection rate for RO plant is assumed to be 20 per cent. The investment requirement for treatment of the rejected water via solar evaporation plant is estimated at Rs 225/m^2 for an evaporation rate of 4.5 mm per m^2. The capital cost per KLD effluent treated works out to Rs 10.93 for all CETPs except Udayendram; for Udayendram the cost is higher, that is, Rs 13.11. The capital cost for solar evaporation plant (SEP) is taken as Rs 5.34 KLD. The market price of water in this area was Rs 30 per KL during the study period and hence at 20 per cent rejection rate, the value of water recovered per KL of effluent treated was Rs 24. As the gross operating cost is below the value of water recovered in all CETPs except Udayendram, their net operating costs are negative. The total cost per KLD effluent treated varies from Rs 4.27 to Rs 22.45.

National Environment Engineering Research Institute (NEERI) (1997) recommended the application of HRTS for solving the TDS

TABLE 2.10
Capital and Operating Costs of RO Plants

Name of CETP	Effluent volume	Installation cost			Cost per KLD effluent treated in Rs				
		Flow m^3/hr.	Cost per m^3 (Rs in lakh)	Total cost (Rs in lakh)	Capital cost		Operating cost		Total cost
					RO Plant	SEP	Gross	Net	
Ranitec	3000	150	5.00	750	10.93	5.34	12	−12	4.27
Visharam	1200	60	5.00	300	10.93	5.34	16	−8	8.27
Udayendram	200	10	6.00	60	13.11	5.34	28	4	22.45
Valayampet	2400	120	5.00	600	10.93	5.34	12	−12	4.27

Source: Tamil Nadu Pollution Control Board

[3] SIDCO Phase I is omitted as members of this CETP process leather from semi-finished stage to final stage, and hence TDS reduction is not a major problem.

problem in the effluents discharged by the Ranitec CETP. Based on certain assumptions, the tentative capital and maintenance costs per KLD of waste water treated are at Rs 0.94 and Rs 0.59, respectively. (Sankar, 1998/2000).

Comparison of the RO option with the HRTS option shows that HRTS is a low-cost option. But there are two problems with the HRTS option. First, the required land may not be available near a CETP. Second, there are many uncertainties regarding the cumulative impact of using the waste water on soil quality and products from the trees. The RO process is costlier, but it enables recovery of 80 per cent of the used water. In a water scarce region like Vellore district, the social benefit of recovering and reusing the water is high.

What are the Economic Costs of Pollution Abatement?

Now, consider the estimates of pollution abatement costs per KLD of effluent treated (Sankar 2000a). The total pollution abatement economic cost consists of (i) the existing CETP economic cost, (ii) add-on cost under RO or HRTS and (iii) sludge treatment cost. Based on NEERI's recommendation for additional investments for better utilization of Ranitec CETP which amounted to Rs 1.31 per KLD, the cost figures for the existing CETPs are adjusted. These cost details for four CETPs are given in Table 2.11. With the RO option, the abatement economic cost per KLD of waste water treated varies from Rs 20.76 for the largest CETP to Rs 66.18 for the smallest CETP; with the HRTS option the corresponding variation is from Rs 18.02 to Rs 45.26.

TABLE 2.11
*Economic Costs of Pollution Abatement (in Rs)
per KLD of Effluent Treated*

(in Rs)

Name of CETP	Existing CETP cost	Add-on cost			Total cost	
		RO	HRTS	Sludge Treatment	(2) + (3) + (5)	(2) + (4) + (5)
(1)	(2)	(3)	(4)	(5)		
Ranitec	16.30	4.27	1.53	0.19	20.76	18.02
Visharam	32.25	8.27	1.53	0.11	38.63	33.89
Udayendram	43.58	22.45	1.53	0.15	66.18	45.26
Valayampet	23.24	4.27	1.53	0.15	27.66	24.92

Source: Tamil Nadu Pollution Control Board

TABLE 2.12
*Economic Costs of Pollution Abatement per kg of
Raw Material Processed*

(at 1995–6 prices)

Name of CETP	Abatement costs (in Rs)		Shares of abatement costs in			
			Private cost		Sales	
(1)	HRTS (2)	RO (3)	HRTS (4)	RO (5)	HRTS (6)	RO (7)
Ranitec	0.57	0.65	0.41	0.46	0.29	0.33
Melvisharam	1.04	1.18	0.74	0.84	0.53	0.60
Udayendram	1.14	1.66	0.81	1.19	0.58	0.85
Valayampet	0.86	0.95	0.61	0.68	0.44	0.48

Notes: a. RO: Reverse Osmosis process, b. HRTS: High rate transpiration system
Source: Tamil Nadu Pollution Control Board

The economic costs of pollution abatement per kilogram of hides and skins processed and as per cent of sales are given in Table 2.12. The abatement cost as per cent of sales is less than 1 per cent. The conversion cost of one kilogram of raw hides and skins into finished leather is in the range Rs 28 to Rs 35 (Sankar, 1998/2000). Hence the abatement cost as per cent of the conversion cost can range from less than 1 to about 3.

Sankar (1998/2000) carries out a similar exercise for seven IETPs in the same region. The economic abatement cost per KL of waste water treated varies from Rs 74.25 to Rs 126.95, and the abatement cost per kilogram of hides and skins processed varies from Rs 2.12 to Rs 7.93. The abatement cost as per cent of sales is lowest (0.56) for an IETP with capacity of 400 KLD; for units with capacities of 60 or below these percentages are in the range 1.62 to 2.71. In fact this percentage share for the largest IETP is smaller than the share for the smallest CETP, namely 0.85. Hence, one can conclude that for plants with designed capacity of less than 400 KLD, CETP is a cost-effective option for full compliance with the standards (Misra, 1998).

The Ministry of Environment (MoEF) and Forests directed the SPCBs for mandatory intallations of CETP or IETP and Chrome Recovery Plant latest by 31 August 2000. (Sankar, 1998/2000) finds that for IETPs with production capacity 1000 kg/d or above chrome recovery is a profitable venture.

Why are the tanners reluctant to incur the expenditures? What are the reasons for the delayed responses of tanneries to establishing CETPs and their reluctance to invest on the add-on investments for TDS reduction and sludge treatment? First, even though these costs form less than 1 per cent of sales, as per cent of the conversion costs they can be as high as 3 per cent. Second, even in the case of Ranitec CETP, the largest CETP in the case study sample, the incremental capital cost for the RO plant is about 1.6 times the cost of existing CETP. For some tanners, the annualized capital cost and annual operation and maintenance (O&M) expenses they have to pay are as high as the rental price of capital for their main plant. Third, there are some uncertainties regarding the RO process. As this process is new, its financial viability is yet to be demonstrated. Further, there is no easy technical solution for treating or disposing the rejected water from the RO plant. Experts propose two options; (a) disposal of the waste water by pipeline to sea and (b) disposal in a landfill.[4] Fourth, as a highly competitive industry, its export prospects depend as external factors, such as environmental and trade policies of developed countries and world demand for leather. Internally, unless the environmental standards are enforced by all states and all tanners abide by the regulations, there is an incentive to shirk on the part of each tanner.

CETP AS A SOCIAL AND ECONOMIC ORGANIZATION

Rawls (1971) lists three desirable attributes of a social organization, namely, equity, efficiency and stability. If the establishment and management of CETP is viewed as a voluntary collective action problem, then it must practice democratic proceedures in framing rules and must have incentive and penalty structures for enforcing the rules.

As noted earlier, CETPs were created out of domestic pressures and fear of loss of exports markets. In the case study area, CETPs are non-profit companies registered under the Companies Act. The members of CETPs are the polluting units and their power in managing the CETPs are proportional to their shares, which depend on some

---

[4] These two options were explored in an International Consultation Meeting on Technology and Environmental upgradation in Leather Sector organized by the Central Leather Research Institute and the Council of Scientific and Industrial Research (CSIR), New Delhi, 29–30 November, 1999.

measure of pollution load. As the decisions are being made at the meetings of the General Body, they can communicate with each other and introduce changes in rules, programmes and policies, as and when circumstances warrant.

There is ample scope for transforming the CETPs into dynamic and efficient organizations to achieve development with improved environmental quality. This is a challenge and an opportunity. This goal can be achieved if the following changes are initiated.

An environmental management information system (EMIS) must be set up for each CETP. A necessary prerequisite for establishing the EMIS is installation of meters at the outlets of the member units. The meters should record both the volume of and concentrations of major pollutants in the waste water discharged into the conveyance system. The meters must be tamper proof and be connected to CETPs, if feasible. The advantages of installing meters at the sources are (i) generation of good data base on pollution loads on real-time basis, (ii) effective monitoring of member tanneries, and (iii) scope for introduction of economic instruments for pollution prevention and control.

An EMIS can be of great help to CETP management in carrying out its operations. The information about pollution loads will also be useful to industry organizations and to the regulators. With a reliable information system, monitoring and enforcement can be at the CETP level instead of at the firm level. This means cost-saving to Pollution Control Boards. Shifting of environmental risk from tanneries to CETPs will permit pooling of risk and sharing of costs of risk.

With an EMIS, it will be feasible to introduce a three part tariff. The first part will cover capital-related cost. The second part will be in the form of user charge based on both the volume and concentrations of pollutants in the effluent. The third part will be customer-related cost. The tariff revision can be made once a year. If a member can achieve reduction in the volume of or/and concentrations of pollutants in the effluent, the member must be given rebates on the charges. If, on the other hand, a member increases the pollution load, he should pay, in addition to the user charges, penalties on the excess loads. The cost-sharing agreements should be incentive compatible in the sense that each member's contribution should be between his incremental cost to the CETP and his stand-alone cost. Such a scheme will make CETP a stable institution.

There is scope for prevention of pollution by tanneries. Ramasami (1999) reports that by adoption of in-plant control measures, net reductions of 30–35 per cent in the levels of BOD and COD, 50–60 per cent in sulphide, 98–99 per cent in chromium and 20–25 per cent reduction in dissolved solids are feasible. The CETP, as a social organization, can create incentives for its members to adopt the in-plant control measures. Adoption of such measures will enable the tanners to expand production while containing the aggregate volume of effluent.

It is worth experimenting a tradable permit system among members of each CETP. The rationale for introducing the system is its cost effectiveness. Tanners' abilities in reducing pollution loads via adoption of pollution-prevention measures or primary treatment and their marginal costs of reducing/abating pollution differ, because they are heterogeneous in terms of size, vintage, raw material processed, process adopted and management skills. A tradable permit scheme based on the volume of effluent and concentrations of pollutants in the effluent discharged will provide an incentive to each tanner to search for the least cost-options for reduction, of pollution loads. When a firm achieves pollution reduction it can use the surplus permit for capacity expansion or sell it to another member. Hence, with the same CETP capacity, tannery production can increase.

CETP itself as a large organisation can seek technical assistance from universities, institutions and international agencies on pollution abatement, recovery and reuse of water and chemicals, and safe disposal of wastes.

CONCLUDING REMARKS

Tannery is a highly polluting industry. In the Indian context, there is a need for finding a cost-effective and sustainable solution to environmental problems caused by tanneries. About 90 per cent of the tanneries in India are in the small-scale sector and most of them are located in small towns. As an intermediate segment of the leather industry, its growth is crucial for the animal husbandry sector and for the downstream leather products sector. Most people engaged in the collection and curing of hides and skins are from the weaker sections. Leather industry's contributions to employment and exports are significant. India has a comparative advantage in leather production because of its strong raw material base, rich tradition of leather craftsmanship and availability of cheap labour. This potential is not yet fully tapped. The government can play a catalytic role in solving the environmental problem. In fact, past government policies such as reservations of products to small-scale units, ceilings on investments in plant and equipments, incentives to adopt the chrome tanning process and lax enforcement are partly responsible for the present environmental problem. At present the government role is confined to provision of subsidy, subject to a ceiling on the project cost of CETPs. There appears to be no justification for a ceiling on subsidy for CETPs. Subsidies for installation of meters to record volume of and concentration of pollutants in tannery outlets, investments in facilities for recovery and reuse of water and chemicals, and technological upgradation of tanneries are in the public interest. In industrial towns, the necessary infrastructure should be created for combined treatment of household sewage and industrial waste water. Such a facility exists in Kanpur (Pandey and Deb, 1998). There may be economies of scope in the joint wastewater treatment. The government must also take necessary steps to enable the exporters to meet the environmental standards stipulated by some developed countries.

A number of measures to make the CETPs viable social organizations for pollution prevention and control have been suggested. The government, industry associations and technical institutions should provide the necessary technical information and managerial expertise to tanners and CETPs. The tanners, CETP management and the industry associations should realize that the 'polluter pays' principle and the precautionary principle have been recognized as principles of environmental policy by the government, the courts and also international agencies. Given the domestic regulatory pressures and external pressures, the tanners must use CETP as an institutional mechanism for solving the environmental problems caused by them.

REFERENCES

Basu, S. (2000): Crackdown on Tanneries Planned, *The Hindu*, 1 July, p. 14.

Central Leather Research Institute (1987): *Report of All India Survey on Raw Hides and Skins*, prepared for the Ministry of Commerce, Government of India, Chennai.

Central Leather Research Institute (1990): *Report on Capacity Utilisation and Scope for Modernisation of Indian Tanning Industry*, prepared for Industrial Development Bank of India and State Bank of India, Chennai.

Directorate General of Technical Development (1986): *The Fiscal Plan for Setting up CETPs for Indian Tanning Industry*, New Delhi.

Food and Agricultural Organization (1992): *World Statistical Compendium for Raw Hides and Skins, Leather and Leather Footwear*, 1972-90, Rome.

Mehta, S., S. Mundle, and U. Sankar (1997): *Incentives and Regulation for Pollution Control*, Sage, New Delhi.

Misra, Smita (1998): Economies of Scale in Water Pollution Abatement: A Case Study of Small-scale Factories in an Industrial Estate in India, working paper No. 57, Centre for Development Economics, Delhi.

Murty M.N., A.J. James and S. Misra (1998): *Economics of Water Pollution; The Indian Experience*, Oxford University Press, Delhi.

National Environmental Engineering Research Institute (1997): Waste Management in Cluster of Tanneries in Tamil Nadu: TALCO-RANITEC CETP, Ranipet.

Pandey, R. and S. Deb (1998): CETPs and Pollution Abatement in SSIs, National Institute of Public Finance and Policy, New Delhi.

Ramasami, T. (1999): Upgradation of Technology and Environment in Leather Sector: A Call for Technology Policy Dialogue, Keynote Address at International Consulation meeting on Technology and Environmental Upgradation in Indian Leather Sector, India Habitat Centre, New Delhi, 29-30 November.

Rawls, J. (1971): *A Theory of Justice*, Harvard, Cambridge Mass.

Sankar, U. (1998/2000): *Economic Analysis of Environmental Problems in Tanneries and Textile Bleaching and Dyeing Industries*, UNDP Project Report, 1998, Chennai: Madras School of Economics, Allied Publishers, 2000, New Delhi.

—— (1998): Laws and Institutions Relating to Environmental Protection in India, Presented at the Conference on the 'The Role of Law and Legal Institutions in Asian Economic Development', held at the Erasmus University, Rotterdam, November 1-4, STET. MSE Occasional Paper No. 2.

—— (2000a): Environmental Policy, in U. Sankar (ed.), *Environmental Economics Reader*, Oxford University Press, New Delhi.

—— (2000b): Common Effluent Treatment Plants: An Institutional Arrangement for Pollution Control in Small Scale Tanneries in India, presented at the Second International Conference on Environment and Development, Stockholm, 6-8 September.

Supreme Court of India (1995, 1996), Judgements on the Public Interest Litigation Writ Petition filed by the Vellore Citizens Welfare Forum, 1 May 1995 and 28 August, 1996.

Economic Valuation of Biodiversity
The Case of Keoladeo National Park*

Kanchan Chopra

ASPECTS OF VALUE ACCRUING FROM BIODIVERSITY RICH ECOSYTEMS

This chapter illustrates two possible approaches to the valuation of biodiversity in a protected area using the Keoladeo National Park as an example. It maintains that comprehensive biodiversity valuation needs to be carried out both in terms of its market linkages and the existence of value outside the market as considered relevant to a set of pre-identified stakeholders. A travel-cost method is used to capture the market-linked valuation of tourism and recreation. It is found that demand for tourism services is fairly insensitive to price. An increase in entry fee and redistribution of proceeds (to enable cross subsidization of different stakeholders) can improve the financial and physical management of the park. The study also uses multi-criteria analysis to arrive at value ranking by different stakeholders. Here, a fair degree of congruence with respect to ecological function value and livelihood value is found to exist in the perceptions of diverse groups. This perceived congruence suggests, in turn, policy instruments for management and in particular, local-level committees of stakeholders.

*This chapter draws substantially from the work done at the Institute of Economic Growth, Delhi as part of the Capacity 21 project sponsored by the UNDP and the Ministry of Environment and Forests, Government of India. The author wishes to thank Malavika Chauhan, Suresh Sharma and N. Sangeeta who worked on the project during 1997–8. She also wishes to thank reviewers of the present volume for comments that helped to improve the content and presentation of the chapter.

Richness of biodiversity is as much a part of our life as linguistic, cultural and religious diversity, which we all cherish. As part of Environmental Economics, one of the first question that comes to one's mind in respect of biodiversity is 'why and how to value it?' The measurement and valuation of biodiversity of different ecosystems can raise the level of understanding of the cost that 'biodiversity loss imposes on society or the gains from its preservation'. For instance, often developmental interventions alter land, water and air use patterns. Then policy makers and the people alike need to know the opportunity cost of such changes in terms of lost values. However, value has many dimensions. While the distinction between 'value in use' and 'value in exchange' has always been a part of standard economic theory, option and existence values have, of late, entered its stock-in-trade. Further, most systems have a large number of stakeholders and policy must take account of the aspects of value that are relevant to them.

The attempt at ascribing an economic value to 'biodiversity' arises out of reasons, some of which are (i) Some components such as the existence of a large variety of species of fauna and flora possess a value expressed on the market by willingness on the part of groups such as tourists and pharmaceutical firms to pay for them: otherwise referred to as tourism or bio-prospecting value, (ii) Resources extracted from biologically-rich economic systems possess an economic value which may or may not be expressed in the market and (iii) Conservation of biodiversity-rich systems and endangered species has a future use value and/or an existence value which, though highly significant, may not find expression in market value.

The next important question is 'What kind of values?' The different components of a biodiversity system possess different kinds of values: (i) a commodity value (as for instance the value of grass in a park), (ii) an amenity value (the recreation value of the park) and/or (iii) a moral value (the right of the flora and fauna of the park to exist). Value in one or the other of the senses referred to earlier, is attributed to resources which are component parts of ecosystems. It also arises from the existence of interrelated species within geographical areas and from the characteristics of diversity possessed by ecosystems. While the first and the second sources of value are based on a utilitarian ethic, the third is based on a right-based ethic. This last locates end-values in other than human-held values. Integrating it with other kinds of values is difficult in the absence of a common denominator[1]. But human-centered valuation of a commodity or a service is relatively easy when it can be defined in relation to other resources in a market or a non-market situation characterized by trade-offs. An exchange concept of value can be relevant here. Trade-off can be identified due to the existence of substitutability between one good and another.

An ecosystem, on the other hand, is difficult to value since it possesses a large number of characteristics, more than just market-oriented ones. It represents a collection of goods and services, which possess value from more than just an exchange or a utility viewpoint. It performs significant ecological functions that arise out of interdependence between its different components. Further, an attempt at valuing biodiversity (essentially a characteristic possessed by a system) takes us into a more difficult terrain, in fact, to another level of abstraction. It can be defined in a number of ways, its dominant value arising out of ecological considerations not always reflected in market situations and the nature of the interdependence between its components is often ill-defined.

The significance of value in exchange and direct use decreases as one moves from the ordinary resources to that of the ecosystem and ecosystem services (or functions). Simultaneously, the relevance of right-based value and existence value increases. And the latter are more difficult to put a value tag on.

But then, how to go about valuing biodiversity? When it comes to biodiversity, there are a number of stakeholders who claim their due shares of benefits and rights from biodiversity. The stakeholder identification enables us to define alternative notions of value.[2] This is because stakeholders are of the essence in so far as value is defined in anthropocentric terms. There is no danger of any relevant notion of value being omitted if the sets of stakeholders are appropriately defined. A stakeholder centered approach shall therefore be followed in the valuation of biodiversity. Such an approach provides a viable expression of value, different from both primarily the market and non-market contexts.

[1] We shall not attempt to do this, adopting a somewhat uncompromisingly anthropocentric view of value.

[2] As argued by T.P. Singh and Ravi Hegde in this book in 'Stakeholder Analysis in Joint Forest Management in India', stakeholder analysis helps in designing, monitoring and implementing many land, water and forest management policies.

What follows from the above discussion is that biodiversity valuation needs to be carried out both in terms of its market linkages and the existence of value outside the market as considered relevant by a set of pre-identified stakeholders. Accordingly, two alternative methodologies are used to do this in the context of the Keoladeo National Park, a Ramsar site in Northern India. The two methodologies, a travel-cost approach (a market-related approach) and a multi-criteria analysis approach (a stakeholder, non-market approach) approximate the following aspects of biodiversity value: (i) Value expressed by one category of stakeholders i.e., tourists, reflecting a market-based situation of selecting a particular tourist place and spending time and money, and (ii) Value accruing to other identified stakeholders inside and outside of the park, highly linked to ecosystem values and functions, which is ranked ordinally.

KEOLADEO NATIONAL PARK: AN INTRODUCTION

The Keoladeo National Park located on the Indo-Gangetic Plain near the town of Bharatpur (27 13′N, 77 32′E) is at Ramsar and a designated World Heritage site since 1985. It is a resting place for many migratory birds including the Siberian crane. Due to this and the location of the park within easy access from a number of other tourist sites, it has attracted a very high rate of tourism.

The Keoladeo National Park (KNP) is a 29 sq km mosaic of monsoonal wetlands, seasonally-flooded grasslands and thorny woodlands. The wetland area of the park covers a central depression of about 8.5 sq km, that is divided by dykes into a number of compartments or blocks. These blocks are interconnected by gates or bunds. In some of the blocks, small mounds have been constructed and planted with *Acacia* trees to provide nesting and breeding sites for the heronry species. Though the maximum potential depth of water in the blocks is about 2m, the mean maximum depth is usually around 1 to 1.5 m. The variety of habitats available i.e., wetland, part grassland and part semi-arid forested grassland gives an idea of the multitude of niche present within the park area. The wetland itself is at places grassy meadows, reed beds and open water regions with submerged plants, and within the canal, free-flowing deeper water teeming with fish. A variety of organisms inhabit these niches and it is especially favoured as a waterfowl habitat.

The monsoon determines the seasonal nature of biotic life in the park. The area in which the park is situated has received an average annual rainfall of 496 mm during the ten years from 1980 to 1990, though over the past 100 years it averaged a 655 mm. Apart from rainfall, the park receives its sustenance in the form of water released into it through the Ghana canal, which originates from the Ajan bund, a seasonal reservoir of water to the south of the park. The seasonal floods in the northern rivers upstream, cause the annual inundation of the park. The change from a dry and moisture-less region to a water-filled wetland almost overnight, triggers a period of rapid growth in the vegetation and breeding period in the faunal species present in the park. However, by mid-summer most of the water evaporates, leaving pools of stagnant water teeming with fish and vegetation. One notices the soils of the wetland cracking due to lack of moisture. This cycle of water in the wetland contributes to the increase of niche in the spatial as well as the temporal scale. Different species occupy the wetland at different times of the year, while on the spatial scale, different depths of water are occupied by different vegetational communities and different faunal species.

Who are the stakeholders in this park? The unique character of Keoladeo National Park arises from the fact that the park was created by humans. The construction of the succession of tanks and the intricate system of water movement used the natural topography and hydrology of the area to provide for the requirements of the numerous species naturally found in the flood plains. For a long time, the area was treated as an important duck-shooting area by the then Maharaja of Bharatpur. During that period, local people living in the villages nearby were permitted to graze their cattle inside the park, except from December to March. They also collected fuelwood, and a variety of grasses having economic value. Before it was declared as a 'National Park', the notion of 'use' had been an integral part of its 'existence'.

The area was taken over by the State government of Rajasthan in 1956. A significant change in management came in 1982, when the park was declared a National Park and officials of the forest department were required, by law, to end all human interference within its boundaries. There followed a period of conflict, at times marked by violence between the villagers and the management of the park. However, a report of the Bombay Natural History Society (BNHS) in

1985 concluded that grazing per se did not damage the ecology of the park. On the contrary, the excess growth of *Paspalum*, an important grass species (which was earlier grazed on and controlled by cattle) caused difficulties for bulb, tuber and root-feeding avifauna such as the Siberian crane. As a consequence, permits for grass removal were given on a regular basis to people living in the villages around the park since 1986. Use by local people, albeit limited, is therefore a part of the management strategy of this park. They have an important stake in the park and its sustainable use.

While the management of KNP has seen phases of significant change, it is important to note that the government has been subsidizing the park. Table 3.1 gives an indication of the magnitude of this subsidy, viewed as the excess of expenditure over revenue.

TABLE 3.1
Revenue and Expenditures of KNP

Year	Revenue (Rs)	Expenditure (Rs)
1990–1	10,97,836	17,48,162
1991–2	17,37,712	14,79,042
1992–3	18,63,630	2,30,339
1993–4	20,27,825	19,79,443
1994–5	19,76,480	22,91,024
1995–6	24,52,000	37,07,400

Source: KNP

An important issue from the point of view of management and also from a macro economic viewpoint relates to the reduction of these subsidies. The single largest item of expenditure for the park authorities was the creation of open water bodies. Such open water spaces are the required habitats for several bird species, including the Siberian crane. However, in recent years, the aquatic area of the park has been shrinking due to the uncontrolled growth of weeds like the water hyacinth and *Paspalum Distichum*. Though several methods like bulldozing, cutting and burning have been tried to control the growth of these weeds, they have met with only limited success. Some observers like Vijayan (1988) have recommended that grazing by a limited number of buffaloes be reintroduced into the system. Though there are several people who empathize with the view that the local communities should have a stake in the management process, how far people's participation will be permitted in KNP is still an open question.

THE ECOLOGY OF KEOLADEO NATIONAL PARK

What do the Experts Say?

The biological diversity of Keoladeo National Park has been studied since the early 1950s. Most of these early studies revolved around the amazing diversity of waterfowl and the long-distance migration they carried out. Salim Ali's work concerning the migration patterns of long-distance migratory species of birds were some of the first kind of studies in the country (Ali, 1959). He also documented the problems the park went through immediately after independence when its very survival was endangered by an uprising of the local population who wanted to convert the area to agriculture (Ali, 1953).

Numerous studies on various species and their ecological interactions have since followed. A study by Schaller and Spillet (1965) notes the dangers of human interference and human predation (the Maharaja's shooting rights and local poaching). An account of the drought of 1979–80 is available in Breeden and Breeden (1982). They give a description of the changes which took place in the park's hydrology and species distribution. It also comments on the resilience of the park and its quick recovery after the drought.

The most comprehensive body of work on the biology and ecology of Keoladeo National Park is the result of a ten-year project by the Bombay Natural History Society (Vijayan 1987, 1988, 1991), which is summarily presented in Box 3.1.

Box 3.1
Summary of Findings from BNHS Study

1. Studies on the chemistry, hydrology, vegetation and fauna of the park are carried out. Effects on the park's ecosystem components by external influences have also been covered in terms of chemical and compound inputs into the system.

2. A water budget for the park is worked out, concluding that the dependence of the park's ecosystem on its water input is of paramount importance, both in terms of the amount and the timing. An

average of 15 MCM (million cubic metres) of water is estimated as required every year during the monsoons.

3. Other aspects include studies on biomass and production of macrophytes, interaction and linkages between cattle and vegetation, terrestrial vegetational distribution and mapping, associated distributions of avian species and listings of flora and fauna. The ecological interrelationships and life cycles of individual species, mostly avian are also studied.

4. It also comments on different techniques used to control the spreading of weeds and their consequences.

5. The importance of fish in this particular system is paramount. Their composition, population dynamics and community links are analysed. It has been shown that the community of fish have been changing over time from gill breathing species to air breathing, which can survive in weed infested, eutrophic habitat. The importance of fish as the major food for many of the bird species has also been elaborated.

6. Data on the habitat preference of fish species also show that the continued increase in weedy macrophytes like *Paspalum distichum* and *Ipomoea* would lead to inhibition in the free movement of fish, reduction of their planktonic food and depletion of dissolved oxygen.

7. The study maintains that of the 43 species present in the park, only six species breed in the park.

8. Numerous studies within the project outline the feeding and breeding requirements, breeding biology, nesting successes, population dynamics and habitat utilization of various bird species. Most studies aim at the effects on bird populations—egg-shell thinning and a drop in nesting success, is one of the direct results in raptures due to bio-accumulation (Muralidharan, 1993). These chemicals are the run-off of agricultural and industrial inputs which find their way into the park. Fertilizers and pesticides, in particular, appear to be causing the major damage.

9. As a conclusion, the project report submits that the hydrology of Keoladeo National Park is unique and requires careful monitoring to continue to host the numerous species found there. It also mentions the lack of a major secondary producer (previously the grazing mammals) and recommends removal of grasses from the park.

The diversity of mammalian species in the area is relatively low as compared to the number of bird species present in the park (28 species, including six species of larger herbivores). Consequently, their effect on the evolution of ecosystem dynamics is marginal. However, it had been thought, and in particular by villagers (WWF, 1996), that many species of birds depend upon the presence of the domestic buffalo that previously grazed the park. Though the linkage has not been proved, it is agreed in general that the presence of these mammals cleared up areas of weed-infested wetland by trampling and grazing and that their dung added nutrients to the wetland.

How to Assess KNP Biodiversity?

Different techniques of biodiversity assessment are available. One of the methods available is a combination of the 'species-based' and the 'ecosystem-based' approach. Such a combination can be used when relatively detailed accounts of the species found on the site and some knowledge pertaining to the hydrological regime and various other ecosystem processes are available.

The species approach implies an examination of the number of, and different kinds of species present in the park. Species identified as keystone, endemic, rare, vulnerable etc., should be accounted for. An ecosystem-approach is possible because the park is divided into different habitat types, each with its own associated assemblages and communities. The number of different ecosystems in the park is a measure of its diversity.[3]

Table 3.2 states aspects of KNP on which studies were conducted by BNHS.[4] Over time, focus seems to be on meteorology, hydrology, primary productivity of plankton, aquatic flora and aquatic microphyte productivity.

[3] To apply this combined approach some assumptions are necessary. The notable ones are: Species are distinct genetic groupings, that in the given case, can be assumed to best represent taxonomic distinctiveness. Species are optimal indicators of biodiversity as they comprise of genetic diversity and form the building blocks of ecosystems. Species richness, therefore, is relatively indicative of other biodiversity values; that is, areas of concentrated species, richness are likely to also represent considerable ecological heterogeneity or diversity. Ecological heterogeneity signifies species richness. Some species, e.g., endangered, keystone, rare, endemic, are more important than others.

[4] For this section, we have not included all the types of data collected from the park by the Bombay Natural History Society, but only those which would constitute the bare minimum required, to develop a picture of the park's biological diversity.

TABLE 3.2
Aspects of the Park Studied by BNHS: 1981–90

Topic	1981	1982	1983	1984	1985	1986	1987	1988	1989	1990
Meteorology	–	I	I	I	I	I	I	I	I	–
Hydrology	–	–	I	I	I	I	I	I	I	–
Water budget	–	–	–	–	I	I	I	I	–	–
Plankton primary productivity	–	–	I	I	I	I	I	I	–	–
Aquatic flora	I	I	I	I	I	I	I	I	–	–
Aquatic microphyte productivity	–	I	I	I	I	I	I	I	I	–
Aquatic macroinvertebrates	–	I	I	I	I	I	I	I	I	–
Fish fauna	–	I	I	I	I	I	I	I	–	–
Aquatic birds	–	I	I	I	I	I	I	I	–	–
Terrestrial flora	I	I	I	I	I	I	I	I	I	–
Grassland productivity	–	–	–	–	I	–	I	–	–	–
Abundance terrestrial insects	–	–	–	I	I	I	–	I	–	–
Land birds	–	–	–	I	I	I	I	I	–	–
Land mammals	–	–	I	I	–	I	I	–	–	–

Note: I in the table indicates that the aspect has been studied in that year

Source: BNHS

The major determinants of the park's biodiversity are discussed on the basis of inputs available from our study, supported, of course, by supplementary information. A number of distinctive habitats with varying communities are found in this small area. The variety of habitats present have been characterized by different plant associations and communities, and each such community further hosts its own specific fauna species (Perennou, 1987). Wetland, grass savannah, grassland with different kinds of shrubs and trees, and forest lands of different types are found within this small area.

The most important information for a biodiversity estimate is the 'species richness' or total number of species present in the park. Although a number of smaller organism groups are not represented in the study, as in most assessments, the larger plants and animals have been included in detail. In fact, even the major groups of the plankton and insect species have been evaluated. Number of species found on the park by the available data are 856. This count does not include the species of plankton and invertebrates.

TABLE 3.3

Changes in Species Composition in the Park: 1980–90

Stable or Increasing Populations	Decreasing Populations
Macrophytes, weeds or pests	Phyto-plankton of some genera
Prosopis juliflora	Floating and submerged aquatic plants
Air-breathing Fish	Siberian cranes
Grass preferring waterfowl	Gill-breathing fish
	Sarus crane
	Pheasant-tailed jacana
	Bronze-winged jacana

Source: BNHS

Table 3.3 lists species found to record a change in populations over the period of study. It is found that they correspond to the changes in the habitat consequent on human interference either by way of management or changed use patterns.

Dominating the list of increasing populations/biomasses are species which fall under the category of weeds or pests, these being predominantly emergent macrophytes. Also increasing in biomass and cover is *Prosopis juliflora*, a tree which spreads rapidly over most kinds of terrain. The waterfowl species preferring grassy habitat show an increase, possibly due to the removal of the primary consumer, the domestic buffalo, and the consequent increase in grassy wetland area and less disturbance.

The most publicized species in the group whose populations have shown a decline is the Siberian crane, whose population has dropped from about 200 in the 1960s to three in 1997. During the period of our study, the population dropped from 33 to ten. This decrease may have many reasons including change in the habitat, which the cranes frequent, brought about by an imbalance in the ecosystem processes, disturbance at its frequented habitats or along its route.

The park is home to four endangered species of birds and three endangered reptile species. In addition, there exist vulnerable species of mammals, birds and other amphibians. This in itself is reason enough to make an effort to maintain its character as suitable for these species.

Changes in the Species Composition of the Park

Seven species of fish which were recorded from the park earlier were noticed to have disappeared. Thirteen species are new additions to the park. Of the 43 species now found, only six species breed in the wetland, the rest come in with the seasonal canal water influx as is typical of a floodplain situation. This has to be viewed in the light of the instability in the quantum of water received by the park which has not been stable after 1983; till then a relatively steady supply of 14 m cu m of water was received.

The increase in weed species of macrophytes, and a consequent drop in open water, primary productivity points to eutrophication of the waters. The partial conversion of the park's wetland from open water to predominantly grass-dominated wetland is also changing the fish populations from gill breathing to air breathing survivors. This change in the wetland's vegetation is also effecting the species composition of avifauna. The trend is from open-water-loving species to grass-habitat-preferring species. This would point to a continuing change in wetland character which may have to be arrested if the original gill breathing fish and open-water avifauna species are to be protected. To some degree, the park management is attempting to fight the change, removing weedy macrophytes and controlling the hydrology.

A considerable amount of resources are spent by the management in conserving the unique habitat which KNP represents in ways more than one. At the same time, a number of different kinds of stakeholders have an interest in it. What is the economic value that they attach to it? How can this economic value be channelled into a source of funds which, if utilized in an appropriate manner, result in giving a fillip to its ecology and conserving it to ensure it is used wisely in the not-so-near future? These are some of the issues that shall be addressed herewith.

STAKEHOLDERS IN THE PARK

When it comes to valuation of this biodiversity rich wetland, the question is, who are the stakeholders who value it (and perhaps differently). Tourists probably constitute the most important stakeholders from the management point of view. Tourist numbers increased from 95,000 to 1,25,000 in the years from 1995 to 1998, indicating a large and growing tourism industry around Bharatpur town. The urban economy of the region benefits from this growth and has a stake in the efficient management of the tourist traffic into the park. Indirectly, they also have an interest in the ecological health of

TABLE 3.4
Stakeholders in KNP and Values they Derive

The stakeholders in the park can be identified as given below:

— the local rural population which derives a use value from the park, mainly through the collection of grass, fuelwood and fish.

— the local urban population which benefits from the income generated by the hotel and tourism industries.

— the tourists who derive the services of recreation, education and tourism.

— the management which is responsible for the maintenance of the ecological health of the park in a way such that the economic benefits continue to accrue;

— the community of scientists and ecologists who put a premium on existence value of the wetland ecosystem.

— non-users in the rest of India and elsewhere who value the existence of national parks and protected areas such as these.

Source: Author's estimates

the park, that ensures the continued accrual of this income. 'Use value', accruing from the tourism industry is, to some extent, complementary with the maintenance of the park as a healthy wetland system.

Ecologists on the other hand, view KNP as a man-made wetland with high ecological value. 'Existence value' is probably high in their scheme of thinking. For instance, the park is being used extensively for research and analysis, which is a kind of use value to the community of scientists.

From the foregoing discussion, it is clear that each category of stakeholders benefit from the unique ecology of the park. This is a situation in which total economic benefit is associated positively with preservation of the ecology. Its distribution between users and the extent to which users are able to reap the benefits depends on (i) the pressures created on the ecology by continuous use and the resultant changes in ecology and (ii) the manner in which the management allocates rights to the benefits accruing from the park.

Techniques for Valuing Biodiversity

A large number of techniques have been developed to assess the value of living resources and habitats rich in such resources. These can be classified into the following categories:

1. *Revealed preference based approaches:* These are based on market prices or surrogate market prices. The latter include techniques such as hedonic pricing, travel cost, production-function-based or alternative-technology-based approaches. Loss of earnings approaches and adjusted market price approaches are also variations on this theme.

2. *Stated preference based approaches to valuation*: Contingent valuation and its variations fall in this category.

3. *Ordinal ranking approaches to valuation:* These do not aim at giving one cardinal number to value but rank it as perceived by different stakeholders. This approach can also be referred to as the stakeholders' valuation approach.

Revealed preference approaches are used in contexts where a surrogate market for the environmental good is assumed to exist. Such a situation is found in Keoladeo National Park where tourism is the direct consequence of the rich diversity of flora and avifauna. It is safe to assume that the tourists' willingness to spend is directly related to the value that they place upon the visible biodiversity. In such a situation, a market for biodiversity exists and the need for using contingent valuation approaches, which simulate markets does not arise. A Travel Cost Method (TCM) can be used in this case.

However, tourists' valuation of biodiversity is not a complete valuation of different components of value accruing from it. It is due to this that we complement the tourism-related valuation with valuation by other stakeholders using a Multi-Criterion Approach (MCA). The latter gives an ordinal ranking of the different aspects of value that stakeholders see in Keoladeo National Park. Together, the two approaches capture significant aspects of biodiversity value and are expected to be useful in decision making for policy.

THE TRAVEL COST METHOD (TCM) FOR VALUING TOURISM SERVICES

Methods for valuation by stakeholders can be based on revealed or stated preferences. When preferences are expressed in terms of prices consumers are willing to pay, it is easy to estimate the demand for a good or a service. However, for subsidized public goods such as national parks, the price of admission cannot be used as an indicator of the value of the site. Instead, the travel costs incurred by individuals to reach the site can be taken as a surrogate for the value of site. Demand functions for tourism are set up making the probability of visiting KNP depend upon the amount spent on travel, either by way of total costs or by way of local costs, opportunity cost of time spent (reflecting the loss of income during that period), educational levels and reasons for visiting the park.

Such demand functions represent revealed preferences of an important segment of stakeholders, the tourists. Further, they capture the extent to which value of biodiversity conservation in a geographical area is reflected in the market for tourism. This is important in devising management and financing mechanisms that encompass all stakeholders. Since the travel costs will vary across individuals living at different distances from the site, such data from the tourists can be used to derive a demand curve for the site services. In this approach, the demand curve for the services of tourism are a proxy for the demand for conserving biodiversity in the park.[5]

[5] A complete write up on the method is given in the Section 'Methodology and Computational Details'.

Estimation of such a demand function is explained now. To begin with, tourists are classified representing different social groups, i, and distance zones, j. The dependent variable in the demand function is the visitation rate, $V(i, j)$ defined as tourist number in group i/ number of tourists visiting from zone j to which the group belongs. This is regressed on price as approximated by total and local cost variants in the two specifications[6] and other independent variables depicting the socio-economic characteristics of the respondent tourist, as:

$$V(i, j) = F(TTCP/LTCP, EVM, OPPTIME, H IPF) \quad (3.1)$$

where $V(i, j)$ = tourist number in group i/ number of tourists from zone j to which group i belongs; TTCP/LTCP = total travel cost/ local travel cost in two different specifications; EVM = reason for visiting park (education, recreation, religious etc); OPPTIME= opportunity cost of time spent; HIPF = household income.

Using survey data collected regarding tourists' travel and stay expenses[7], duration of stay and various socio-economic characteristics, a semi-log demand function (both in its total and local cost specifications) indicates that travel cost is a valid proxy variable for price in determining demand for tourism services.[8] Visitation is impacted significantly by travel cost in the semi-log demand function. Reason for visitation does not influence visitation significantly and household income seems to affect visitation negatively though the coefficient is very small. The equation explains 33 per cent of variation in visitation rate (which is acceptable with cross-section data).

The equation that gave the best fit is as follows:

$$\text{Log } V(i, j) = -2.975 -3.229 \text{ LTCP} -0.0511 \text{EVM} -1.402\text{e}-0.7\text{HIPF} \quad (3.2)$$

$$(-13.174) \quad (-2.181) \quad (-0.391) \quad (-7.645)$$

Adjusted R^2 = 0.335, Calculated F value = 19.47177; D.F: (3,107)

[6] Total travel cost is defined to include travel from place of residence, cost of travel within park, cost of boarding and lodging during stay and any other miscellaneous expenditure. Local travel cost excludes the first component on the assumption of the joint product nature of the visit to the park located as it is in a tourism region.

[7] The final set of usable responses consisted of 111 respondents, of when 68 were Indians and 43 were foreigners. Each respondent gave information on the number of members in his group/family. Hence, the total number of tourists covered in this manner were 305 consisting of 235 Indians and 70 foreign nationals.

[8] A specification using a semi-log function was found to be the best fit in this case.

The above exercise helps us to determine the value that one set of stakeholders in the park, the tourists, place on it. The average local cost incurred is Rs 303 per visitor. With about 1,25,000 visitors, the total amount that the tourists spend on it is Rs 370 lakh annually. Further, estimates of consumer's surplus and demand elasticities can help in the formulation of policy with respect to the management of these areas.

Table 3.5 gives the consumer's surplus as estimated from the semi-log form of the function relating visitation rate to travel cost, (its local variant). This gives an estimate of the 'willingness to pay' for preservation. At the level of average travel cost, the area under the demand curve and above the line of average cost represents the consumer's surplus enjoyed by the tourist. This is a measure of 'willingness to pay' for the services provided.

TABLE 3.5
Area under the Demand Curve and Consumer Surplus

Model specification: Using local cost variable	Total area	Consumer surplus per visit (Rs)
semi-log model (log of dep.)	505.44	202

Source: Author's calculations

In view of the joint product nature of the services provided by the park, it is considered more appropriate to estimate consumer's surplus in terms of local cost estimates. This amounts to about Rs 202 per visit if average local travel cost is taken as the reference point. If, however, entry fee alone is taken as cost as the forest department officials would do, the surplus is Rs 427.04 per visit by Indians and Rs 432 per visit by foreigners.

The demand functions were also used to estimate price elasticities of demand at the mean value of the variables. Table 3.6 gives these estimates for the five zones. The demand for the services of KNP turns out to be inelastic. The elasticity ranges from –0.24 to –0.01 for tourists coming from the five zones obtained from the functions based on the local cost variant of price. The inelasticity of demand for recreation with respect to its price has been observed in other studies as well (Navrud and Mungatana, 1994 for Kenya). Walsh (1986) gave an overview of the price elasticities of demand for various activities. The elasticity for 23 cases of outdoor recreation activities varied from –0.12 to –0.32. Low elasticities can be attributed to the following: (i) the expenditure on the good is a small part of total income and (ii) the service in question provides a specialized kind of recreational experience.

TABLE 3.6
Elasticity of Demand for Tourism Services: Zone-wise

Model	zone 1	zone 2	zone 3	zone 4	zone 5
Functions based on total local cost per tourist					
semi-log	–0. 05	–0.0727	–0.2366	–0.0778	–0.1130

Source: Author's calculations

All indications seem to suggest that the Indians visiting the park belong to the better educated group with higher levels of household income. Expenditure incurred on the visit is probably a small part of their household income. In this scenario, an increase in the entrance fee could probably be recommended as a part of park management.

The travel cost model estimates biodiversity value as reflected in the tourism service pricing at Rs 300 lakh annually. The inelastic nature of the demand signifies that increased entrance fee could be one device by which expenditure incurred on maintaining the park could be met.

VALUE ACCRUING TO STAKEHOLDERS OTHER THAN
THE TOURISTS: MULTI-CRITERIA ANALYSIS

Perceptions of Relative Value of Different Stakeholders

How to account for the perceptions of all the stakeholders in the park area? This is done through the ranking of different concepts of value using the technique of multi-criteria analysis. The categories of stakeholders concerned with the park are: scientists, villagers, non-users (residents of Delhi) and tourists (Indian and foreign tourists). Under the methodology of multi-criteria analysis, alternative methods can be used for arriving at the aggregated rank or score for different aspects of biodiversity value.[9]

A method of weighted expected valuation is used for here.

[9] The software called DEFINITE has been used for this exercise. See Janssen (1994) for details of the technique used.

TABLE 3.7

Aspects of Value, Their Nature and Stakeholders Interested

S. No	Aspects of value	Nature of value	Stakeholders interested in corresponding use
1.	Ecological functions	Regulation of water, nutrient cycle, flood control	Scientists, village residents, non-users
2.	Consumption	Timber, wood, irrigation water, water for domestic use, fodder, medicines	Villagers, scientists, non-users
3.	Livelihood	Providing livelihoods through tourism, fishing, fodder collection	Villagers, scientists and tourists
4.	Rarity value	Presence of unique or rare species	Scientists and tourists
5.	Services	Tourism value, education value, cattle grazing	Tourists, villagers and scientists
6.	Aesthetic	Scenic (real or perceived) or recreation value	Scientists, tourists and non-users
7.	Future/Option value	Possibility of new uses for conserved species in future	Scientists and non-users
8.	Ritual/Cultural value	Value related to religious beliefs and practices	Scientists and non-users
9.	Existence Value	Value linked to the right to live, regardless of use	Scientists and non-users

Source: Author's estimates

Table 3.7 gives the aspects of value considered in the ranking, their nature and the class of stakeholders approached. All stakeholders are not expected to be interested in every aspect of value. It may be pointed out that the manner in which questions relating to each of these was canvassed in different schedules varied in accordance with the ability of the respondent to answer in a meaningful manner. Further, the uses of the park and the values of the park as perceived by different stakeholders were expected to differ. The questions were designed in accordance with uses of the park perceived to be important for different sections of the stakeholders. For each stakeholder, the aspects of the park are taken as 'Alternatives' and individual respondents as 'Rankers', with equal weightage to all the individuals.

Value Ranking by Village Residents

Perceptions of village residents are based on a participatory rural appraisal study conducted by the WWF in six villages located around the park. The villages are Aghapur, Darapur, Ramnagar, Ghasola, Mallah and Baraso. In all the cases, the villagers were requested to rank their requirements from the park. It is to be noted that the ranking in the WWF survey was done on the basis of options that the respondents could relate to. Later, a correspondence was found between the categories selected by villagers and the categories defined above. These ranks were put together and the results are shown in Table 3.8.

TABLE 3.8
Value Rankings by Village Residents

Perceptions of village residents ranks	Option	Score	Corresponding category of use
1	Open grazing	0.86	Services/livelihood
2	Longer-duration permits	0.64	Livelihood/Services
3	Employment	0.71	Livelihood
4	Construction of gates For access	0.64	Others
5	Provision of water	0.50	Ecological function
6	Collection of dead wood	0.36	Consumption
7	Sharing Revenue	0.29	Others
8	Increasing wall height	0.00	Others

Source: Author's estimates

Value Ranking by Scientists

Table 3.9 shows the scores for alternative kinds of value as expressed by the scientists' group, some of whom have carried out certain studies on the park. The set included people who had specialized in different disciplines including biology, ecology and hydrology, all of which have some bearing on KNP. Further, some of them have conducted research studies in the KNP. Their value perception therefore reflects the impact of a particular kind of use to which such national parks can be put, to, namely that of research and study.

TABLE 3.9

Scientists' Perception of Value

Rank	Options	Score
1	Rarity value	1.00
1	Ecological	1.00
3	Existence	0.83
4	Future	0.67
5	Consumption	0.50
6	Livelihood	0.33
8	Services	0.17
7	Ritual/Cultural	0.25
9	Aesthetic	0.00

Source: Author's estimates

The scores[10] obtained indicate that alternative sources of value can be divided into three categories: (i) rarity, ecological function and existence values with scores of 0.80 and more are on top: (ii) consumption, livelihood and future use with scores between 0.5 and 0.8 come next and (iii) value generated by provision of services such as tourism, ritual and aesthetic value come at the bottom in the value indicators.

Value Ranking by Tourists

The tourists surveyed included both Indian and foreign nationals.[11] Table 3.10 gives the value rankings based on the perceptions of the complete sample, the Indians and the foreigners, respectively.

It is found that tourists as a group value the aesthetic, curiosity and existence aspects of the park, with existence getting a score less than the other two. The services and rarity-related values figure low in their way of viewing the park. There does not seem to be much difference between the value perceptions of Indian and non-Indian tourists. This is expected as the two groups do not differ much in terms of their education and awareness levels.

Non-User's Value Perception

Non-user perception was identified on the basis of a pilot survey of Delhi residents drawn from residential areas with differing kinds of

[10] Based on MCA technique.

[11] About 400 individuals were represented by the sample of 111 respondents who were interviewed.

TABLE 3.10
Value Scores from Tourists' Perception

Rank	Options	Score
1	Curiosity	1.00
2	Aesthetic	0.80
3	Existence	0.60
4	Services	0.40
5	Rarity	0.20
6	Others	0.00

Source: Author's estimates

environmental situations and differing population densities. The perception of these people regarding the main reason for the park's conservation and preservation reveals that from their point of view, the park should be preserved for maintaining the ecosystem stability. Ecological functions and consumption value featured prominently in their ranking of sources of value of KNP, as illustrated from the scores tabulated in Table 3.11. Interestingly, preservation for future generations, existence value and livelihood generation capability came next. Ritual, cultural and aesthetic values were at the bottom of the scale.

TABLE 3.11
Non-users' Perception of Value

Rank	Option	Score
1	Ecological	1.00
2	Consumption	0.87
3	Future	0.75
4	Existence	0.62
5	Livelihood	0.50
6	Future Use	0.38
7	Aesthetic	0.25
8	Ritual/Cultural	0.00

Source: Author's calculations

Values Across Stakeholder Categories and an Interpretation

Table 3.12 classifies value rankings of stakeholders into three categories: scores of 0.8 and above are ranked as 'high': those between 0.5 and 0.8 as 'medium' and less than 0.5 as 'low'.

TABLE 3.12

Classification of Perceptions of Value

Category	Scientists	Tourists	Village residents	Non-users
I. High	Rarity, ecological function, existence	Aesthetic curiosity	Livelihood and related services, employment	Ecological function, consumption
II. Medium	Consumption, livelihood, future	Existence	Ecological function	Existence, future, livelihood
III Low	Services, ritual cultural, aesthetic	Services, others	Others including ritual and cultural	Ritual, cultural, aesthetic

Source: Author's estimates

A fair degree of conflict is found to exist in the above rankings made by different categories of stakeholders. However, it is important to note the areas of agreement. Significantly, two non-village-based groups of stakeholders, the scientists and the non-users seem to realize the significance of livelihoods generated by KNP. This provides some common ground for policy making. Ecological functions of the wetland in preserving the water and nutrient flows seem to be given a high value by scientists, villagers and non-users outside the park. Such perceived congruence in value perception is an important point of take-off for policy.

Ritual, cultural and so-called aesthetic values seem to figure pretty low in the preference function of three of the four categories of stakeholders—namely the non-users, the village residents and the scientists. This is probably due to the fact that they have found a reflection in other ways such as in the ecological function and existence value concepts. Alternatively, it may mean that they reflect the value system of the stakeholders itself.

METHODOLOGY AND COMPUTATIONAL DETAILS

Conducting a Travel Cost Study

The Travel Cost Method (TCM) is typically used to capture the recreational value of sites, such as national parks and sanctuaries.

Sometimes, though less often, it has also been applied to problems like finding the value of collected forest products (not routed through the markets) for villagers, by examining the travel and time costs involved in collecting them. As these examples illustrate, the TCM can only capture the direct use value of an environmental good—other components of the Total Economic Value (TEV) (referred in the Chapter 'Environmental Economics through Case Studies') such as option value or non-use value cannot be quantified by this method.

Two Variables of the Travel Cost Method

The travel cost method focuses on estimating the following demand function:

$V = f (TC;X)$; where V = number of visits to the park, TC = travel cost to reach the park, X = vector of the relevant socio-economic variables.

Two approaches can be used—the Zonal Travel Cost Method (ZTCM) and the Individual Travel Cost Method (ITCM). Let us examine the difference between the two approaches. In the ZTCM the unit of analysis is zone. Under this method visitors are divided into different zones of origin. For instance, suppose we had to find the recreation value of an Indian sanctuary for Indian tourists. If our sample was large enough, we could divide the tourists into different zones, based on the states that they come from. A visitation rate is then calculated for each zone. This is defined as follows:

Visitation rate = (Number of visits to the park per year from the zone)/ (Total population of the zone). The visitation rate, therefore, tells us the average number of visits made by each resident of the zone to the site during a year. In this way, the effect of population on visitation is accounted for.

In the ITCM, on the other hand, the concept of zoning is absent. Here, the dependent variable is simply the number of visits made by the respondent to the site during a year. Hence, we can see that the number of observations in the case of the ITCM will be equal to the number of respondents, while in the case of ZTCM, it will be equal to the number of zones. The fundamental point of difference between the two approaches, therefore, is in the definition of the dependent variable. A comparison of the two approaches is also given in Table 3.13.

The choice of which of the two methods to use will depend upon the situation at hand. If the site is one that offers a unique recreation

TABLE 3.13

Comparison of the Zonal and Individual Travel Cost Methods

S. No.	Point of comparison	ZTCM	ITCM
1.	Unit of observation	The zone	The individual visitor
2.	The dependent variable	The visitation rate	The number of visits made by each visitor per period
3.	The nature of the independent variables	Only those characteristics which can be described at the zonal level are included	Individual-specific characteristics can be included
4.	Sample size requirements	The sample size should be large, so that several zones can be constructed	Sample size can be relatively smaller

Source: Author's estimates

experience, then, typically, visitors will come from even far-away regions to visit it. However, visitors who come from longer distances are generally not able or willing to visit the site more than once or twice in a year. In such a situation, if we were to use the ITCM approach, then the dependent variable (the number of visits made by each respondent) would not exhibit sufficient variation to make regression analysis possible. In that case, it is advisable to use the ZTCM. Note that a fairly large sample size is needed to make zoning feasible.

The ITCM, on the other hand, can be used successfully in those cases where the visitors are mainly locals. Thus, Durojaiye and Ikpi (1988) have used it to value urban recreation centres such as zoos and amusement parks in Nigeria—sites which are likely to be visited frequently by local residents, but which would not attract tourists from longer distances.

Steps Involved in the TCM

Preparation of Questionnaire

This is a very crucial step, as the quality of the data will depend upon the way that the questionnaire is drafted. The questionnaire that is prepared must keep in mind the following data needs:

1) Travel cost and travel time related data: We must know the place of residence of the visitor (this will give us the distance travelled in order to reach the site); the mode of transport; cost of travel; time spent on travel and on the site; and frequency of visits to the site.

2) Data on socio-economic status: We should know the household income level of the respondent. Often, people are reluctant to answer questions about their income level. In that case, it is advisable to construct some broad income bands and question them about which band they belong to. Besides, the questionnaire must also elicit information on other socio-economic characteristics such as education, age, gender, etc.

3) Data on perceptions and interest: Information on the perceptions of the respondents regarding environmental issues, and their interest in eco-tourism, wildlife etc., is often helpful when doing the analysis. Hence, questions, which probe the respondents' tastes and attitudes must also be included.

While it is obviously important to get as much information as possible, it is also important to remember that the respondents are tourists who will have come to enjoy a recreational experience. Very lengthy and time-consuming questionnaires may lead to non-response. Therefore, the questionnaire should be fairly concise; the time of interview should be kept to not more than about 20 minutes.

Pre-testing of Questionnaire

A pre-testing of the questionnaire is essential before the actual survey is carried out. This will help to point out flaws in the questionnaire, which can be corrected before the next stage. Additionally, it will also familiarize interviewers with the process of eliciting responses.

Selection of the Sample and Choice of Sampling Technique

The size and composition of the sample must be decided before the survey is carried out. For instance, we may decide to leave out the foreign visitors from the exercise in order to keep the analysis tractable.

It is also important to fix the sampling technique beforehand. In the KNP case, a stratified random sampling technique was used. Tourism data from the park authorities was used to determine the proportions in which Indian and foreign visitors should be included in the sample. Then, within the two strata, sampling was random.

Data Collection

The survey should be carried out in the peak tourist season, and preferably over a long period of time. All these are precautions to help ensure that the sample is indeed a random one. Interviewers must take care to maintain a neutral stance throughout the interview, and not influence the respondents' replies in any way.

Operationalizing the Method

1) Zoning

This is the first step in operationalizing the ZTCM (as already stated, zoning is not required in the case of the ITCM). Once the data has been collected, divide the entire area from where the visitors originate into zones of the park. Typically, zones have been constructed on one of the following bases:

i) In terms of political boundaries: For example, Tobias and Mendelsohn (1991) have treated the 81 cantons of Costa Rica as the zones of their study.

ii) In terms of increasing travel cost: This can be done by treating the park as the centre, drawing concentric circles around it, and treating these circles as the zones.

There are advantages to both these approaches. When the zones are defined in terms of political boundaries (such as states in the Indian context), data on socio-economic characteristics becomes easily available, e.g., we can easily find the figures for population, literacy rate, etc., at the state level. On the other hand, setting new zones based on increasing distance from the site may be a more logical approach to follow within the travel cost model.

2) Specifying the dependent variable:

Once the zones of origin have been defined, find the total population of each zone. Let us suppose that there are n zones in all. The dependent variable, which is the visitation rate, is then defined as:

V_j = (Number of visits to the park from zone j per year)/(Total population of zone j);

j = 1 to n.

Thus, the visitation rate tells us the average number of visits made by each resident of zone j during a year. In this way, the effect of population on visitation is accounted for.

In the case of the ITCM, of course, the above procedure does not have to be followed. There, the dependent variable will simply be the number of visits that the respondent makes to the site in a year.

3) Estimating the travel cost

Typically, the round-trip travel cost at the zonal level is found by either of the following two methods:

a) Using standard rules of conversion: Under this procedure, we can calculate the distance from the zone to the park, and then use a suitable average cost per kilometre. estimate to convert the distance variable into a cost variable. For example, Bojo (see Johansson 1987) has used a cost estimate of US$ 0.1 per mile for those travelling by car, and the economy class fare for those travelling by train.

b) Using the sample data: Using the actual information given by the respondents in the sample, an average travel cost can be derived for each zone.

One problem in the estimation of the travel cost has to do with the opportunity cost of time. It has been argued that the cost of time taken to reach the site and back should be included in the travel cost, because this represents loss of income-earning opportunities. At the same time, institutional constraints such as maximum working hours, paid holidays, etc., should also be taken into account. Because of these factors, the shadow price of the travel time may be substantially less than the wage rate. Accordingly, many researchers have used a shadow price of time equal to a quarter to one-half of the wage rate.

Durojaiye and Ikpi (1988) point out that the demand for recreation centres and the benefits derived from the trips is effected by the time spent on site and in travel. It is appropriate to include travel time as an additional cost if it confers a disutility on the recreationist. However, it may be the case that some people get a positive utility from the travel experience itself. In that case, including the cost of travel time will lead to an over-estimation of the total cost. The best way of determining whether it should or should not be included is, therefore, to question the respondents directly about their enjoyment of the travel time.

Some studies have also taken into account the value of the on-site time. This should certainly be taken into account if we expect the on-site time to vary systematically with the zone of origin. However, if this is not the case, then we can exclude it without affecting the shape of the demand curve.

4) Determining the other independent variables

The next step is to find out which other variables should be included in the regressions. If the ZTCM is to be followed, we will need zonal averages for each of these variables. This circumscribes the set of possibilities. For instance, while average income and education level can be used, it is meaningless to construct a zonal average for age or interest in the environment. The fact that individual-specific variables can be used, therefore, represents an advantage of the ITCM.

An important factor in this respect that should be included in the analysis but is often difficult to handle in practice is that of the availability of substitute sites. Just as the availability of substitutes will affect the individual's demand for a commodity, the availability of substitute sites to visit may affect the demand for a recreation site. Therefore, it has been suggested that the costs of travelling to alternative sites should be taken as independent variables in the regression equation. The problem, of course, remains as to which sites should be selected. In some cases, this is done by the researcher himself, based on his own perceptions of the market. Alternatively, it may be done by the direct questioning of the respondents as to which sites they consider are adequate substitutes to the site in question.

5) Estimating the demand function

Now estimate a statistical relationship of the following type

Visitation rate = f (Travel Cost, Income, Education, ...)

Different functional forms must be tried to estimate this relationship, e.g., linear, quadratic, log-linear, and double log—a priori, we cannot predict which form will perform the best. The form that yields the best results should be chosen. The travel cost coefficient should, of course, be negative and significant.

At present, there is no consensus on which functional form performs the best in the TCM. However, it has been noted that using different functional forms does often lead to significant differences in the consumer surplus estimates. Therefore, it may be a good idea to incorporate the results of a sensitivity analysis, based on use of different functional forms.

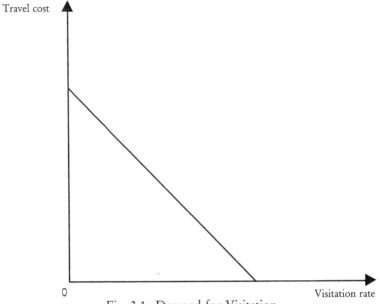

Fig. 3.1: Demand for Visitation

6) Generating the policy implications

Using the estimated demand function to predict values for the visitation rate at the different travel cost levels, a Marshallian demand curve of the type as shown in Figure 3.1 can be constructed.

The vertical intercept represents that level of travel cost at which the visitation rate to the site becomes zero—this may be called the 'choke price'. Having obtained this demand curve, the consumer surplus per person per visit for each zone can easily be found, by integrating the demand curve between the average travel cost for that zone and the choke price (all the other independent variables can be taken at their average values). Multiplying by the total number of visits from the zone will give us the total consumer surplus for the zone. Thus, if we add all the zonal consumer surpluses, we can get the total annual consumer surplus accruing to the visitors to the park.

Simultaneously, the ranges within which demand elasticities vary can also be predicted. This, as well as the consumer surplus estimates are significant for devising policy implications with respect to the fixing of different levels of the entry fee. The revenue derived from there has implications for park management and maintenance, which in turn enables the ecosystem integrity to be maintained.

There are a number of problems with the TCM, both theoretical as well as empirical, that a researcher should be aware of. Some of them are listed below:

(a) The assumption of identical preferences

What is done in the TCM is to construct a single demand curve for a large number of individuals (whether taken zone-wise or individually). This implies that we are making the assumption of identical preferences for all of them.

(b) Truncation bias

As mentioned above, data is collected in the TCM through an on-site survey. As a result, the data set that we get consists only of users; non-users (i.e. people whose visitation is zero as a result of higher travel costs) are by necessity excluded from the analysis. The bias that this exclusion introduces is called the truncation bias (visitation truncated at one), which may result in faulty consumer surplus estimates.

It has been suggested that the maximum likelihood method of estimation should be used rather than the OLS in order to avoid the problem of truncation bias. However, no consensus has yet been reached on the question of whether ML estimation performs significantly better than the OLS.

(c) The treatment of time

This has already been touched upon in the previous sections. The question of what rate to use when valuing travel and on-site time is a difficult one, and one that has not been conclusively answered. Hence, Bateman (1993) recommends that 'in such situations a sensitivity analysis can be carried out using a range of time value estimates based on wage rates. As a working approximation, we suggest that values of 0.25, 0.5, 0.75 and full wage rate be used.'

Problems Frequently Encountered

The following are some of the problems that may need to be resolved before the researcher can proceed with his/her analysis.

1. Tourists on package tours

Often the tourists to the site may be on a package tour. In that case, the questionnaire must be able to obtain complete information about the total number of sites that the tour covers, so that the correct portion of the total cost of the tour can be allocated to a particular site. Often a package tour will cover the cost of travel to a particular city, but the costs of going to and from the site and of moving around within the site have to be borne by the individuals themselves. In that case, those costs must also be elicited by the questionnaire. A proper division of the total costs between the different sites is also to be done for those tourists who are not on a package tour but are nevertheless visiting more than one place.

2. The joint product problem

It may be the case sometimes that the site in question is only one of a number of attractions in the vicinity. For example, the Keoladeo National Park in Bharatpur, Rajasthan attracts many of the tourists who come to visit the Taj Mahal and the city of Jaipur, as it is close to both these famed tourist spots. In this case, the following problem poses itself—if the site were to be by itself, would it still attract the same number of tourists? If that is not so, then the use of the TCM without correction for the effect of the other sites will lead to overestimation of the consumer surplus.

3. Foreign tourists

Foreign tourists are a particularly difficult manifestation of the multiple-site problem, as they typically come to visit the country as a whole. Some studies simply exclude them from the analysis in order to keep the problem tractable. See Navrud and Mungatana (1994) for their treatment of foreign visitors.

CONCLUSIONS AND POLICY RECOMMENDATIONS

Biodiversity valuation has important implications for decision making with respect to alternative uses of land, water and biological resources. Since all value does not get reflected in markets, its valuation also raises methodological problems regarding the kinds of value that are being captured by the particular technique being used. Simultaneously, in the context of a developing country, it is important to evolve methods of management that enable self-financing mechanisms of conservation. This implies that biodiversity value for which a market exists must be taken note of, while simultaneously making sure that the natural capital inherent in biodiversity rich areas is preserved and values which are crucial for some stakeholders but cannot be expressed in the market are reflected in societal decision making.

A focus on both the above aspects is necessary. It is important to take note of the nature of market demand for aspects of biodiversity that stakeholders, such as tourists, express a revealed preference for by way of paying a price for it. Simultaneously, it is important to examine the extent to which a convergence or divergence exists between value perceptions of this and other categories of stakeholders. It is in this spirit that two alternative methodologies are used here to arrive at an economic valuation of biodiversity in Keoladeo National Park. The travel-cost methodology captures the market-linked values of tourism and recreation. It throws up the following policy implications:

1. Keeping in mind the location of the park and the consequent joint product nature of its services, cost incurred locally is a better index of the price paid by tourists. It is found that demand for tourism services is fairly insensitive to price. A redistribution of the benefits and costs of the park through an increase in entry fee would not affect the demand for its services.

2. Cross-substitution between different categories of stakeholders can improve the financial management of the wetland. A part of the proceeds can go to the local management. Also, high-income tourists, scientists and even non-users with a stake in preservation can pay for or compensate low-income stakeholders for possible loss in welfare due to limits on extraction and use.

3. However, the limit to such a policy is determined by the number of visitors and their possible impact on the health of the wetland. Such a constraint did not appear to be operational in the context of the present park.

Identification and ranking of values of different aspects of biodiversity resources as perceived and expressed by different categories of stakeholders namely scientists, tourists, local villagers and non-users is an important object in the process of valuation. In the KNP study, a fair degree of congruence with respect to ecological function value and livelihood value is discovered to exist in the perceptions of diverse groups. Stakeholders as diverse as scientists, tourists, local villagers and non-users give high rankings to these uses.

The perceived congruence of value rankings suggests that it may be useful to bring together different stakeholders in an institution such as 'committee of stakeholders' at the local level in the management of wetlands. Plans for wetland conservation may need to be drawn up by this committee in collaboration with regional development planners. Such a policy approach shall bring wetland conservation in the mainstream in the context of development plans for the region. It shall also serve as a method of integrating local-level planning of wetlands with more macro level development plans. The appropriate institutional framework within which conservation of wetlands can be developed shall emerge from such a macro view of the alternatives to be considered. Witness in this context the changing approach to forest management in India in the last decade. Starting from small beginnings, joint forest management resolutions are now a part of forest policy in a large number of states. The present study on Keoladeo National Park indicates that a careful balancing of ecological constraints with economic benefits by the stakeholders can result in similar directions being given to wetland management.

REFERENCES

Ali, S. (1953): 'The Keoladeo Ghana Sanctuary of Bharatpur, Rajasthan', *Journal of Bombay Natural History Society*, 51: 531–6.

—— (1959): 'Local movements of resident water birds', *Journal of Bombay Natural History Society*, 56(2): 346–7.

Bateman, I.J. and R.K. Turner (1993): 'Valuation of the environment: Methods and techniques', in Turner, R.K. (ed.), *Sustainable Environmental Economics and Management: Principles and Practices*, Bellhaven Press, London.

Breeden, S. and B. Breden (1982): 'The drought of 1979–80 at the Keoladeo Ghana Santuary, Bharatpur, Rajasthan', *Journal of the Bombay Natural History Society*, 79(1): 1–37.

Brown, G.M and J.H. Goldstein (1984): 'A model for valuing endangered species', 11: 303–9

Chopra, Kanchan, Malavika Chauhan, Suresh Sharma, and N. Sangeeta (1997): *Economic Valuation of Biodiversity, Part I and Part II*, Report of Capacity 21 Project on Natural Resource Accounting, Monograph, Institute of Economic Growth, New Delhi.

Durojaiye, B.O. and A.E. Ipks (1988): 'The monetary value of recreational facilities in a developing economy: Acase study of three centers in Nigeria', *Natural Resources Journal*, 28(2): 315–28.

Eiswerth, M.E. and J.C. Haney (1992): 'Allocating conservation expenditures: Accounting for inter-species genetic distinctiveness', *Ecological Economics*, 5: 235–45.

Fisher, A.C., J.V. Krutilla and C.J. Cicchetti (1972), 'The economics of environmental preservation: A theoretical and empirical analysis', *American Economic Review*; 62: 605–19.

Hanley, N. and S. Craig (1991): 'Wilderness development decisions and the Krutilla- Fisher Model: The case of Scotland's flow country', *Ecological Economics*, 4(2): 145–62.

IIPA (1993): Wildlife Management In India, Mimeo, IIPA, NewDelhi, June.

Janssen, Ron. (1994): *Multiobjective Decision Support for Environmental management, Environment and Management*, 2 and 3. Kulwer Academic Publishers, Dordrecht, Netherlands.

Janssen, Ron and Marjan Van. Herwijnen (1994): *DEFINITE: A System To Support Decisions on a FINITE Set of Alternatives: User Manual*, Kluwer Academic Publishers, Dordrecht, Netherlands.

Kosz, Michael (1996): 'Valuing riverside wetlands: The case of the "Donau-Auen" national park', *Ecological Economics*, 16(2): 109–27.

Kothari, A., P. Pande, S. Singh, and D. Variava (1989): 'Management of sanctuaries and national parks in India', A Status Report, Indian Institute of Public Administration, New Delhi.

Krutilla, J.V.and Fisher, A.C. (1974): 'Valuing long-run ecological consequences and irreversibilities', *Journal of Environmental Economics and Management*, 1(2): 96–108.

Lockwood, M. (1997): 'Integrated value theory for natural areas', *Ecological Economics*, 20: 83–93.

Montgomery, A. Claire, Brown, M. Gardner Jr., and Darius. M. Adams (1994): 'The marginal cost of species preservation: The northern spotted owl', *Journal of Environmental Economics and Management*, 26: 111–128.

Munda, G. (1996): 'Cost-benefit analysis in integrated environmental assessment: Some methodological Issues', *Ecological Economics*, 19: 157–68.

Muralidharan, S. (1993): 'Aldrin poisoning of Sarus crane and a few other granivorous birds in Keoladeo national park, Bharatpur, India', *Ecotoxicology*, 2: 196–202.

Murty, M. N. and Susan M. Menkhaus (1994): *Economic Aspects of Wildlife Protection in the Developing Countries: A Case Study of Keoladeo National Park, Bharatpur, India*, Paper presented at REU workshop on methodological and other issues in Natural Resource Economics, Society for Promotion of Wasteland Development (SPWD), New Delhi.

Navrud, S. and E.D. Mungatana (1994): 'Environmental valuation in developing countries: The recreational value of wildlife viewing', *Ecological Economics*, 11: 135–51.

Perrenon, C. (1987): Vegetation Map of Keoladeo National Park, Bharatpur, Rajasthan, French Institute, Pondicherry, and Bombay Natural History Society, Bombay.

Perrings, C. and D.W. Pearce (1994): 'Threshold effects and incentives for the conservation of biodiversity', *Environmental and Resource Economics*, 4(1): 13–28.

Polasky, Stephen and Andrew. R. Solow (1995): 'On the value of a collection of species', *Journal of Environmental Economics and Management*, 29: 298–303.

Reid Walter, V., Sarah, R. Gomez, A. Sittenfield, D. Janzen, M. Collin, and C. Juma (1993): 'A New Lease on Life', in Walter V. Reid et al. (eds.), *Biodiversity Prospecting: Using Genetic Resources for Sustainable Development*, World Resource Institute, Washington.

Shogren, Jason. F. (1998b): 'A political economy in an ecological web', *Environmental and Resource Economics*, 11(3–4): 557–70.

Simpson, R.D., R. Sedjo, and J.W. Reid (1993): 'Valuing biodiversity for use in pharmaceutical research', *Journal of Political Economy*, 104(1), pp. 163–85.

—— (1996): *Marginal Values and Conservation Incentives in the Commercialisation of Indigenous Genetic Resources*. Working paper. Resource for the Future, Washington DC.

Soderbaum, P. (1992): 'Neoclassical and institutional approaches to development and the environment', *Ecological Economics*, 5(2): 127–44.

Solow, A., S. Polasky, and J. Broadus (1993): 'On the management of biological diversity', *Journal of Environmental Economics and Management*, 24: 60–8.

Schaller, G.B. and Spillett J. Juan (1965): 'The status of the big game species in the Keoladeo Ghana Sanctuary, Rajasthan, Cheetal', *Journal of the Wildlife Preservation Society of India*, 8(2): 12–6.

Tokias, D. and R. Mendelsohn (1991): 'Valuing ecotourism in a tropical rainforest reserve', Amkio, 20(2): 91.

Vijayan, V.S. (1987): Keoladeo National Park Ecology Study, Report January to June 1987, Bombay Natural History Society.

—— (1988): Ecology of Keoladeo National Park, Annual Report 1988, Bombay Natural History Society

—— (1991): Keoladeo National Park Ecology Study, 1980–90, Final Report, Bombay Natural History Society.

Walsh, R. G. (1986): *Recreation Economic Decisions: Comparing Benefits and Costs*, Venture Publishing, State College, PA, USA.

WWF-India (1996): Participatory Management Planning for Keoladeo National Park, Bharatpur, India, WWF India, New Delhi.

The Health Benefits of Improving the Household Environment
A Case Study of Andhra Pradesh

Gordon Hughes, Meghan Dunleavy, and Kseniya Lvovsky

WHY STUDY HOUSEHOLD ENVIRONMENT AND HEALTH?

Improvements in the household environment, notably better access to water, sanitation and clean cooking fuels, can have a remarkable impact on reduction in child mortality and other ill-health effects, possibly increasing an average life expectancy as witnessed in Andhra Pradesh. However, the nature of the relationships is complex, and the impact of various interventions differs significantly across locations and urban and rural areas. Generally, most cost-effective interventions have been found in rural areas, which have a lower level of services and higher child mortality. The largest portion of the health benefits from improving access to water in rural areas and sanitation in both rural and urban areas comes as a public benefit via a reduction in health risk for all members in the local community.

The status of health, particularly child mortality, and quality of household environment are immensely linked. The burden of disease at the household level is linked to contribution of environmental factors. Interventions outside the purview of the health sector, which are cost-effective in reducing the toll of premature mortality and morbidity are also to be identified. Because of the multidimensional nature of poverty, the health benefits of the provision of basic infrastructure services and reduction in health risks associated with the living conditions of the rural and urban poor are also to be focused.

Andhra Pradesh (AP) is the fifth most populous state in the country with approximately 76 million in 2000, almost 8 per cent of India's total population. The infant mortality rate (IMR) in 1996 averaged 65 deaths per 1000 live births, down from 73 in 1991 and lower than the national average of 72 (SRS, 1996). The State has remarkably improved water supply coverage in the past two decades. For instance, less than 3 per cent of people use surface water and less than 35 per cent people have access to water more than 15 minutes away. However, development of sanitation coverage has not shown the same progress: 73 per cent of people of the state still have no sanitation facilities (NHFS, 2000). Likewise, reliance on wood and dung cakes for cooking fuel continues for the majority of the population (89 per cent rural, 29 per cent urban; NFHS, 2000). The Gross State Domestic Product (GSDP) per capita of about US $ 320 per annum lies considerably below India's average of US $ 430 per capita per annum (1999). Disparities between rural and urban development indicators in AP also deserve notice, given that the rural population comprises 73 per cent of the state's total, and is relatively poorer than the urban population. The rural-urban gap is significant across multiple parameters, from IMR (73 in rural areas versus 38 in urban areas) (SRS, 1996) to maternal literacy (19 per cent and 46 per cent, respectively) (NFHS, 1995). Tremendous disparities in service coverage and mortality statistics among AP's 23 districts are also present.

Nearly one-fifth of the total burden of ill-health in AP can be attributed to environmental causes. Despite an increasing health burden related to exposure to urban, industrial and agrochemical pollution, traditional environmental risks like those from poor access to water and sanitation, and the use of biomass fuels by households continue to account for the larger role. In AP and India at large, modern forms of exposure to urban, industrial and agrochemical pollution add to the burden of ill-health from traditional household risks, but it is unlikely that they account for more than 2–3 per cent of the total burden of disease. In industrial countries with higher income level, the health damage caused by urban and industrial pollution may represent up to 4–6 per cent of the total burden of disease (see Figure 4.1).[1] This reflects (i) better health of their populations as measured by

---

[1] While the distribution of the disease burden due to modern environmental risks across countries/regions with different income levels resembles the Kuznet's curve, the

Box 4.1.

DALYs as a Measure of the Burden of Disease: A Methodology

Disability-adjusted life years (DALYs) are a standard measure of the burden of disease. The concept of DALY combines life years lost due to premature death and fractions of years of healthy life lost as a result of illness or disability. A weighting function that incorporates discounting is used for years of life lost at each age to reflect the different social weights that are usually given to illness and premature mortality at different ages. The combination of discounting and age weights produces the pattern of DALY lost by death at each age. For example, the death of a baby girl represents a loss of 32.5 DALYs, while a female death at age 60 represents 12 lost DALYs (values are slightly lower for males because of their lower life expectancy).

The use of DALYs as a measure of the burden of disease has provided a consistent basis for systematic comparisons of the cost-effectiveness of alternative interventions designed to improve health. When combined with the results of large-scale epidemiological studies, it enables public-health specialists to identify priorities and focus attention on development programmes that have the potential to generate large improvements in the health status of poor households in the developing world.

Source: Murray and Lopez (1996)

the total DALYs lost per million people and (ii) larger number of people who may be exposed to urban air pollution which is usually the largest component of the health damage caused by modern forms of exposure and a smaller role of other health risk factors prevailing in poor living conditions. In AP, urban air pollution is a growing problem, especially in central areas of Hyderabad, but the associated damage to health is still quite small relative to the damage caused by indoor air pollution in rural areas or poor quality of water and sanitation.

In 1990, 18 per cent of the total burden of disease in India was the result of diarrhoeal diseases, hepatitis, tropical cluster diseases, intestinal nematode infections and respiratory infections of infants and young children under the age of five years—(Murray and Lopez,

---

burden of traditional environmental risks declines as income grows, similarly to the total disease burden but at a much faster pace at higher income levels.

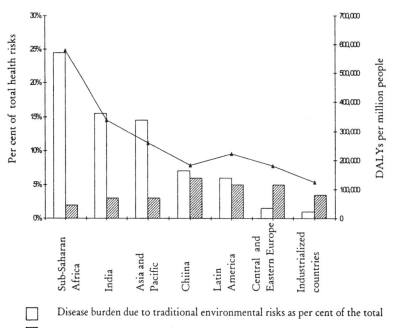

Disease burden due to traditional environmental risks as per cent of the total

Disease burden due to modern environmental risks as per cent of the total

—▲— Total disease burden, DALYs per million people

Source: World Bank, (2000a)

Fig. 4.1: Environmental Risks and the Disease Burden in
Different Regions and Countries

(1996, Annex Table 4.1). A large part of this burden was the result of
the death of infants under the age of one year, while the second largest
component consisted of the death of young children between one and
four years of age. For AP, the equivalent figure was 16 per cent of the
total burden of disease in the state. The incidence of this group of
diseases is strongly associated with the quality of the household and
community environment in which children are born, and live.

The burden of diseases related to water supply and sanitation in AP
can be further shown using case-load data reported to the Department
of Health in Andhra Pradesh in 1994–6 (see Table A.4.1). These data
demonstrate the consistently high proportion of communicable disease cases that are related to water and sanitation (42–59 per cent), and

the high contribution these cases make to the overall mortality from such diseases in AP (27–42 per cent).

TABLE 4.1

Incidence of Diseases Linked to Poor Water and Sanitation, 1994–6

Indicator	Reported number of cases	As per cent of communicable diseases	As per cent of all diseases
Cases	4,023,510	48.3	8.2
Mortality	1,909	31.9	5.2

Source: Director of Health—Monthly reports on communicable diseases

Diarrhoeal disease is the most frequently used indicator in studies examining the association of water supply and sanitation with health. Diarrhoeal diseases account for the largest component of the impact of poor quality of water and sanitation on health in terms of both mortality and morbidity, especially among children. The results of the study of the burden of disease for AP suggest that about 49,000 children aged less than five years die from diarrhoeal diseases each year. This represents about 19 per cent of all deaths of children in the age group of 0–4 years.

Respiratory diseases account for a greater proportion of mortality and morbidity in AP, India, and developing countries across the world, than do diarrhoeal diseases. However, the causal link between respiratory diseases and air pollution is less characterized than the link between diarrhoea and water-borne pathogens. Growing evidence from studies of the health effects of air pollution indicates that particles of small diameter can lead directly to respiratory infections and indirectly to exacerbated asthma attacks, allergies and cardiac dysfunction. Further, studies on women and children in indoor settings link exposure to cooking smoke from traditional biomass fuels to an increased incidence of respiratory diseases and a variety of other adverse health outcomes. The level and nature of exposure to indoor air pollution depends upon a combination of factors including type of fuel used, stove construction and house design. Overall, recent research suggests that the toll of premature deaths resulting from this exposure may be as high as 0.5 million each year in India or even higher. Most of these deaths are of children under the age of five years and are due to acute respiratory infections provoked or exacerbated by high levels of smoke resulting from the use of dirty cooking fuels.

BROAD FINDINGS FROM NFH SURVEY IN AP

The findings presented herewith are based on an analysis of the determinants of infant and child mortality in India utilizing the National Family Health Survey of 1992–3. The survey sample size was almost 90,000 households, including about 59,000 children born in the five years preceding the survey. Estimates of the contribution of the household environment to the burden of disease in AP are based on the specific results of this India-wide analysis[2]. The results of this study, at an aggregate level and in terms of the specific role of particular variables, seem to be broadly consistent with estimates derived from studies which rely upon different methods of analysis and sources of data (e.g., Vanderslice and Briscoe 1993, 1995; Esrey et al., 1991; Smith, 1998).

The key results from the epidemiological analysis with respect to the role of household environmental factors in infant and child mortality in India as a whole are shown in Figure 4.2.[3] In addition to environmental factors at the household and community levels, the model takes into account household wealth, mother's education, urban/rural household, a variety of household assets and a number of other principal household and behavioural characteristics. The child mortality reductions attributed to each risk factor in this analysis should not be understood as occurring in addition to the reductions in child mortality that take place over time due to general developmental advancement. For the time period of 1987 to 1992, the IMR in India changed from 81 per 1000 births to 66 (SRS Bulletin, 1996), for an average of 4.3 per cent change per year though there is some concern that this rate of change is decreasing and even plateauing in some states (Claeson, Bos and I. Pathmanathan, 1999).

---

[2] A similar analysis on the AP data was not possible, because a smaller sample size did not allow to establish statistically significant relationships with the variables of interest.

[3] A complete description of the statistical model including the list and qualifications of all variables used in the child survival analysis, as well as a discussion of various details of the statistical investigation can be found in Hughes and Dunleavy, (2000), and World Bank, (2000b).

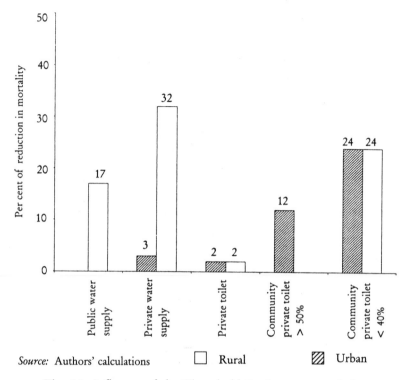

Fig. 4.2: Influence of the Household Environment on Infant
and Child Mortality: All India

The following findings for water and sanitation variables emerge
from the analysis:

1. Household access to a private water supply reduces child mortality by about 32 per cent in urban areas but by only 3 per cent in
   rural areas.[4] Thus, the direct health benefits of providing private
   water connections in urban areas to the households concerned are
   much larger than those in rural areas. This conforms with the
   familiar observation that water-borne diseases spread most rapidly
   in densely-settled urban communities with no or poor access to
   water.

2. There appears to be no significant difference between various
   types of private water supply—i.e., piped water, a hand pump or a

[4] A household with a private water supply is one with a piped water connection,
hand pump, or well, located in its yard or inside its dwelling.

private well—in terms of the health benefits provided in either urban or rural areas. This reinforces the inference that it is the quantity of water available that is the critical aspect of water supply from the point of view of health benefits.

3. There is no significant difference between urban and rural areas in the reduction in mortality resulting from access to private sanitation facilities. For both groups, household access to private sanitation reduces mortality by 3 per cent.

4. Similarly, there is no significant difference between the health benefits provided by latrines and flush toilets in the rural and urban areas.

5. The benefits from improving access to water in rural areas and to sanitation in both urban and rural areas are largely a function of the level of coverage of water or sanitation for the whole community. Investment in extending access, produces a small private benefit in the form of a reduced risk of child mortality for members of the household and a much larger public benefit via a reduction in the risk of mortality for all children in the local community—either the village in rural areas or the ward in urban areas.

6. Careful investigations suggest that these community benefits involve a threshold under which the whole community benefits as the proportion of households in the community with access to a private-water connection or with toilet increases up to a level of 50-60 per cent. Above this threshold, additional investments make little or no additional contribution to reducing the risk of child mortality in the community as a whole, though private benefits are not affected.[5]

7. Despite extensive and detailed investigations it was not possible to find any significant protective effect provided by household access to a public-water supply in rural areas or to public sanitation facilities in both urban and rural areas relative to the household having no access to supply of water or sanitation facilities.[6]

[5] Identifying such thresholds is difficult given the nature of the data available, so that a cautious interpretation of the results would rely upon the finding that increasing coverage of private water supply and private toilets, clearly reduces the risk of child mortality.

[6] Access to a public water supply includes access to a public standpipe, hand pump or well, which is shared with a group of other households or with the whole

The lack of any significant association between child mortality and access to a public-water supply in rural areas deserves particular attention. Almost all investments in extending rural water infrastructure have focused on providing access to public water supplies. Various community studies have suggested that these interventions have had beneficial health effects, especially when the schemes are well maintained and accompanied by an effective health education and hygiene programme. Unfortunately, the reality appears to be that the vast majority of public schemes in rural areas that were operating before 1993 did not meet these criteria and led to few or no observable health benefits.

The difference in the health impacts of private versus public supplies, highlighted by this analysis, is compatible with other studies which suggest that water quantity is the most important dimension of water supply with respect to its impact on health (Vanderslice and Briscoe 1993; Esrey et al., 1991). Households which rely upon public-water supplies must transport water over some distance to their dwelling, so that they may choose to rely upon other, often polluted, sources for many purposes. In particular, it is likely that they will not use as much water for washing and hygiene as households with a private water supply.

There are, of course, other benefits from investments in providing access to public supplies. The most important of these are the saving in time and increased productivity as well as possible health benefits for women and children other than reductions in child mortality that result from better access to water. Such benefits may be sufficient to justify the investments.

It is not surprising that there seem to be no health benefits from providing access to public sanitation facilities. These tend to be dirty and poorly maintained; they may even be regarded as unsafe, especially for women. Thus, people are often reluctant or unwilling to use them, so that they continue to rely upon fields or other places for defecation, in which case there is little reason to expect that access to public or shared toilets will have a significant impact on health.

Now consider the use of cooking energy in the rural and urban

---

Households without access to a water supply include those who rely upon surface water such as tanks, streams, canals or upon rainwater.

settings. Clean cooking fuel[7] rather than a dirty cooking fuel has a large effect on child mortality. Switching to a cleaner fuel reduces the risk of child mortality from all causes by about 45 per cent in rural areas, where 90 per cent or more of all households rely upon dirty fuels and by 18 per cent in urban areas (Mishra and Rutherford, 1997). Their investigation showed that switching from dirty to clean fuels would reduce the incidence of acute respiratory infections by 23 per cent. Statistical association between the type of a household fuel and child mortality is very strong, and is consistent with the growing body of literature on the health impacts of exposure to indoor air pollution due to the use of traditional biomass fuels. The use of these coefficients yields an estimated 610,000 deaths of infants and children under five years for all India which falls well into the range of 500,000–2,000,000 premature deaths from indoor air pollution provided by other studies (see Smith and Mehta, 2000; Bloom and Rozenfield, 2000).

What are the limitations of such studies? While interpreting the findings of this analysis, it is important to keep in mind that the use of cross-sectional data may result in biases of the estimates of programme effects because of possible non-random special allocation of public programmes, such as water supply or sanitation. For example, if the provision of shared water supply or sanitation facilities favours poorer areas with higher infant/child mortality, the results of the statistical investigation based on cross-sectional data may not be able to fully capture the benefits of these programmes.

HEALTH BENEFITS OF IMPROVING ACCESS TO WATER AND SANITATION IN ANDHRA PRADESH

A model (briefly titled as Hazard model)[8] with state and district level data for AP is used to derive estimates of the number of lives that

---

[7] In this analysis, clean fuels include electricity, LPG, bio-gas, kerosene and charcoal.

[8] The hazard model is a reduced form equation which means that it allows for changes in behaviour and other responses to a better or worse household environment—for example, in the period of breast-feeding, the probability of a baby having a low birth weight, nutrition and other aspects of the care given to babies and young children. The empirical analysis which determines the estimation procedures is complex and subject to differing interpretations. Given the nature of the factors which influence child mortality there is no single 'right' way of collecting and analysing data to address the issue. Thus, all estimates are subject to a significant margin of uncertainty.

might be saved by improving the household environment. The results are based on a number of important assumptions.

1. The estimates reflect the long-run impact of improvements in the household environment on infant and child mortality. For instance a part of the influence of lower exposure to indoor air pollution is mediated through such factors, the associated reduction in mortality will not be immediate but will only be observable after a period of three–five years.

2. The estimates are based on population and other data from the early 1990s—primarily, the 1991 Census and the 1992–3 National Family Health Survey. Rising incomes, better access to water and sanitation, and better health services tend to lower the toll of mortality per million people but in aggregate, this has been partially or fully offset by population growth.

3. There are concerns that the large reduction in the risk of mortality in rural areas associated with the use of a clean cooking fuel does not just reflect the influence of indoor air pollution but arises because the variable is acting as a proxy for some unobserved factor(s) which are correlated with a low mortality risk.

4. The results from the analysis of all of India are applied to AP at the district level, using a combination of analytical tools that (a) take into account unobservable differences between states that indirectly impact on child mortality and (b) incorporate the values of key parameters for individual districts.

5. The analysis is based on cross-sectional data that imposes limitations on the assessment of impacts of future interventions (e.g., predictions) to improve the household environment. Findings from this study are limited to statements on the magnitude and attributable risks associated with various factors as presented or recalled at the time of data collection. The extent to which these findings are applicable to future interventions need to be validated with longitudinal data and other studies.

This is another reason for using the lower 90th percentile confidence limits in this analysis. Even with this precaution, the estimates should be regarded as indicative and should be treated with appropriate caution in deriving policy conclusions from them. In this study, we focus on results and implications which appear to be robust in the context of such uncertainty.

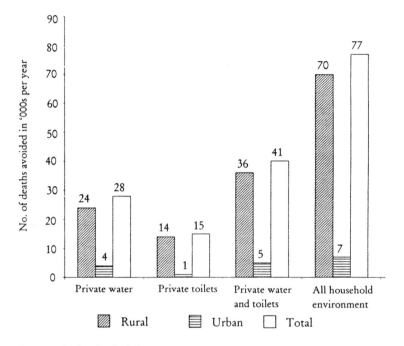

Source: Authors' calculations

Note: All household environment includes water supply, sanitation and clean fuels

Fig. 4.3: Reduction in Infant/Child Deaths due to Improvement
in the Household Environment, AP

Figure 4.3 shows the estimates of the total number of deaths of children under five years that could be avoided each year by improving the quality of the household environment. This is, of course, an unattainable target, but the reductions would be approximately pro rata for smaller increments.[9] Combining all of the improvements in the household environment would together reduce the number of infant and child deaths by at least 77,000 per year. On the assumption of no change in the use of clean cooking fuels, ensuring full access to private water and toilets would save at least 40,000 lives per year, again almost all in rural areas. Most of the reduction in mortality from

[9] Note that the sums of the estimates for the separate improvements are greater than the estimates for their combined effect because the proportional hazards model is multiplicative not linear.

expanding coverage of private water and toilets is the result of the increase in the proportion of households in the community with access to either or both private water and toilets.

While deaths of infants and young children represent the largest component of the burden of ill-health resulting from the poor quality of the household environment, it is useful to take account of the impact of these variables on mortality among older children and adults (primarily those aged over 60 years) as well as on morbidity. For this purpose, the ratio of the total number of DALYs lost to water-borne diseases to the number of deaths of young children from the same diseases was used to compute a multiplier representing the total number of DALYs lost as a result of water-borne diseases per death of a young child. A similar calculation for dirty cooking fuels was based on the total number of DALYs lost to respiratory infections and chronic respiratory conditions such as asthma and chronic obstructive pulmonary disease.[10]

Applying these multipliers yields the estimates of the overall burden of disease associated with the household environment. These estimates mean that the combined impact of all improvements in the rural household environment would be equivalent to an increase in life expectancy of about three years (for the whole population of the state, assuming an average life expectancy at birth of approximately 62 years).

Figure 4.5 shows that the combined effect of all improvements in the household environment could reduce the burden of disease by

[10] These multipliers of 45.5 and 41.8 DALYs per death, respectively, are likely to yield an underestimate of the total health damage associated with lack of water and sanitation and dirty fuels when these have the effect of worsening the severity or mortality rate of other diseases. For example, air pollution studies suggest that some of the worst effects of exposure to cooking smoke for women will take the form of disability and premature mortality resulting from cardiovascular conditions that are exacerbated by indoor air pollution. To avoid overestimates of the burden of disease associated with indoor air pollution, the DALY multiplier used was derived by considering only the total number of DALYs lost as a result of respiratory infections and chronic respiratory diseases by children under the age of 15 plus 25 per cent of the DALYs lost due to the same diseases by women aged 15 or greater.

Women are much more exposed to indoor air pollution than men and they are much less likely to be smokers. Hence, restricting the estimated multiplier as described provides a reasonable lower bound for the total number of DALYs lost as a result of diseases associated with indoor air pollution.

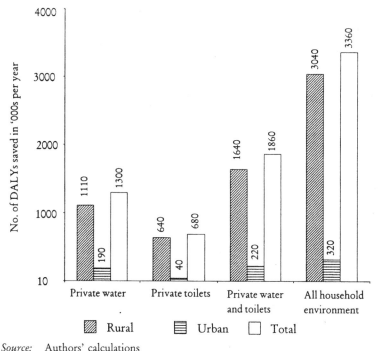

Source: Authors' calculations

Note: All household environment includes water supply, sanitation and clean fuels

Fig. 4.4: Total Health Benefits of Improvements
in the Household Environment

about 22 per cent for rural households 9 per cent for urban households, and 19 per cent for all households. The estimated benefit of the environmental improvements for all households corresponds closely to the estimate of the aggregate burden of disease associated with specific diseases linked to water and sanitation and to indoor air pollution.

However, this equivalence should not be interpreted as implying that universal access to private water and sanitation will effectively eliminate all incidence of diarrheal and other water-related diseases. Certainly, there will be a great fall in such incidence, but it is unlikely the reduction will be more than 70–80 per cent. The remainder of the improvement in health will come about via a lower incidence and severity of other diseases because the overall health status of the population is better.

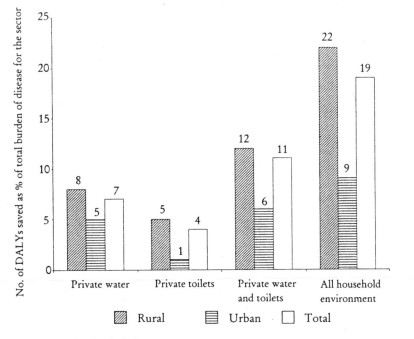

Source: Authors' calculations
Note: All household environment includes water supply, sanitation and clean fuels

Fig. 4.5: Health Benefits of Improvements in the Household
Environment, AP, as a Percentage of the Total Burden of Disease

One can also analyse the extent of disparities across the districts. There are large differences across districts in the health benefits generated by improvements in the household environment, which encompasses water, sanitation and indoor air pollution. For instance, the two districts with the highest rural burden of disease associated with the household environment are Kurnool and Mahbubnagar which rank among the poorest and least-developed districts in the state. The two districts with the lowest rural burden of disease are Chittoor and Guntur. Rural poverty in Chittoor is slightly lower than the average for the state, whereas Guntur is one of the poorest districts but it has a relatively low infant mortality rate and a high level of female literacy. Thus, the differences between districts are substantial and reflect indicators of human development other than income levels alone.

It is hardly surprising that Hyderabad has by far the lowest burden of disease due to household environment factors—its average is seven DALYs per 1000 people which is less than 30 per cent of the median value for the urban population of the state. The two districts with the highest burdens of disease for urban households are Srikakulam and Adilabad, both of which have relatively high levels of urban and rural poverty. The two districts—apart from Hyderabad—with the lowest burden of disease are Krisha and Rangareddi. The latter is part of the greater Hyderabad region but has a relatively high rural burden of disease. Overall, the burden of disease associated with the household environment for urban households is about 30 per cent of that for rural households. The major part of this difference is due to the contribution of indoor airpollution.

TARGETING INTERVENTIONS

Achieving such improvements will require a long period of time and large costs. The costs have been computed by estimating the annualized costs for rural and urban households of providing a private water supply, a private toilet and a clean fuel (see Annex A.4.1). According to the estimates, the total cost of providing universal access to a private water supply will amount to Rs 700 crore per year, while universal access to private toilets will cost Rs 1600 crore per year. If an interim target of achieving at least 60 per cent coverage of private toilets in all communities were adopted, then the cost would be much less at Rs 700 crore per year, almost the same as for private water supply. The total cost of switching all households to use of a clean cooking fuel would be Rs 2200 crore per year.

These costs may be compared with the associated benefits by calculating the average gross cost per DALY saved as a consequence of improvements in the household environment.[11] These estimates are shown in Figure 4.6. For rural households the average gross cost per DALY saved is Rs 12,000 with a range from Rs 4000 for private water supply to Rs 18,000 for private toilets. The averages for urban

[11] In this context 'gross cost' refers to the total cost of the intervention without making any allowance for any non-health benefits or 'willingness to pay' for the service(s) which may be associated with the intervention. The 'net cost' is the total cost minus the value of non-health benefits or the amount that households are willing to pay for the service.

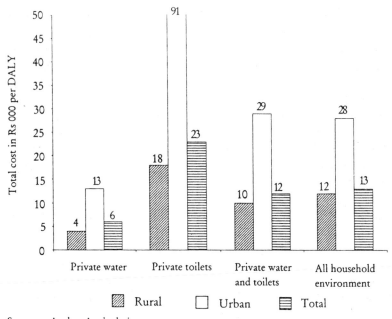

Fig. 4.6: Average Gross Cost per DALY Saved by Improving
the Household Environment

households are much higher, though the ranking of the three separate improvements is similar. For all improvements in the household environment the average gross cost per DALY saved is Rs 28,000, which is pulled up by the very high average of over Rs 90,000 per DALY saved for providing universal access toprivatetoilets.

As discussed above, the range of benefits generated by investments in water and sanitation is very large, so that the average gross cost per DALY saved also differs greatly across districts. Figures 4.7 and 4.8 show the 90th and 10th percentiles and the median of the average values by district for rural and urban households by district. For rural households the range of average gross costs per DALY saved by all improvements in the household environment is from Rs 10,000 to Rs 13,000 for the three best and worst districts for rural and urban households. Expressed as a percentage of the median value the ranges for specific improvements all lie between 25 per cent and

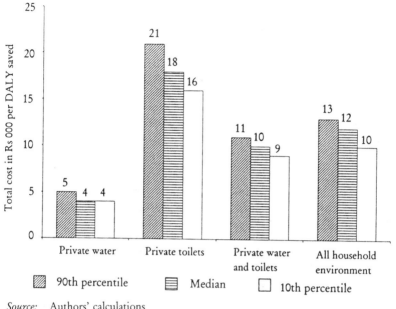

Source: Authors' calculations

Note: All household environment includes water supply, sanitation and clean fuels

Fig. 4.7: Range of Costs per DALY Saved by Improving the Rural
Household Environment

33 per cent. However, for urban households the ranges are much larger both in absolute and relative terms. For example, the average gross cost per DALY saved by improving urban sanitation has a 10th percentile of Rs 47,000 and a 90th percentile of Rs 155,000 with a median value of Rs 69,000. The costs are high in all districts, but the differences between districts are very important in such cases.

The gross cost per DALY saved provides a starting point to consider how to allocate the limited resources available for making improvements in the household environment. For example, the median for improvements in urban water supply is over three times the median for improvements in rural water supply. The median gross cost per DALY saved for addressing indoor air pollution in urban areas is about 50 per cent higher than the median for rural areas. However, three districts have a rural average gross cost per DALY saved for addressing indoor air pollution that is higher than the urban average gross cost per DALY saved for two districts.

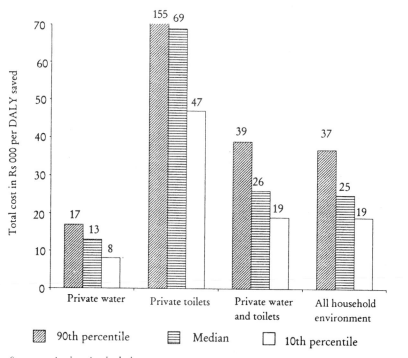

Note: All household environment includes water supply, sanitation and clean fuels

Fig. 4.8: Range of Costs per DALY Saved by Improving
the Urban Household Environment

So far, the analysis has assumed that there are no benefits from improving the household environment other than the reduction in the burden of disease discussed above. However, studies have repeatedly shown that even poor households are willing to pay significant amounts of money for a clean and convenient cooking fuel as well as for reasonable water supply, and something, though less, for sanitation which eliminates excreta from their immediate neighbourhood. Data in Annexure A.4.1 show how incorporating 'willingness-to-pay' estimates affects the cost-effectiveness of interventions and relative priorities.

The resulting estimates of the net cost per DALY saved may be compared with estimates for health sector interventions. Such comparisons must be used with care because of the uncertainty about the coverage and efficacy of public health programmes. Further, comparing preventive measures with curative measures is complicated by the difficulty of assessing tne benefits of avoiding episodes of ill-health rather than curing those who actually fall ill. Investments in infrastructure clearly fall into the category of preventive measures but tend to be more expensive than many public-health programmes because they offer higher levels of prevention with more certainty and over a longer term than alternative approaches to reducing the incidence of the diseases affected.

Subject to these qualifications, the net cost per DALY saved by investments in private access to water for rural households is about US $ 35, which is comparable with the most cost-effective health sector interventions in India that have a similarly significant impact on reducing the burden of disease (ASCI, 1996; World Bank 1997). The net cost per DALY saved for other improvements in the household environment vary from US $ 140 to US $ 350 with the exception of urban sanitation. To summarize, the analysis identified a number of interventions in improving the quality of the household environment, especially in rural areas, that are clearly justified by the health benefits and also revealed substantial differences in the measures of cost–effectiveness across interventions, districts and rural and urban populations.

POLICY CONCLUSIONS

The nature of the programmes required to achieve cost-effective environmental health improvements will differ. Within the limits of finance and 'willingness to pay' for services, it is important to focus future investments in rural drinking water programmes on providing household connections rather than public taps. Where schemes that provide public taps or other forms of shared access are implemented, it is crucial to ensure that (i) the facilities are properly maintained, (ii) they reflect the community's needs and priorities, and (iii) they are accompanied by effective programmes to promote hygiene and health education.

Programmes which provide household water connections in rural areas and sanitation in both rural and urban areas will generate substantial public benefits. It is, therefore, important to establish an appropriate balance between public funds and private contributions in financing the capital costs of such schemes, especially in the poor communities. However, in all cases there is a strong reason for covering their operating costs by user charges to ensure appropriate incentives for the use and maintenance of the systems (which is likely to affect the health outcomes of access to these services).

More attention should be paid to the potential benefits of ensuring the availability and promoting the use of modern fuels in rural areas. This would imply shifting away from across-the-board subsidies on kerosene and LPG which effectively limit their use by the rural poor, through rationing of supply, reducing incentives and potential market for the private sector, and illegal diversion of these products to non-domestic sector (e.g., transport). If necessary, alternative subsidy schemes should be carefully assessed and designed to target households in the greatest need while creating an open and competitive market, which will benefit all consumers.

REFERENCES

Andhra Pradesh (2000): *Report of Rural Poverty Reduction Task Force*, Hyderabad, May.

Administrative Staff College of India (1996): *Andhra Pradesh Burden of Disease and Cost-effectiveness of Health Interventions*, 2 volumes, Centre for Social Sciences, Administrative Staff College of India, Hyderabad.

Bloom, D. and A. Rozenfield (2000): *The Quality of Life in Rural Asia*, Oxford University Press, Hong Kong.

Claeson M., E. Bos, and I. Pathmanathan (1999): 'Reducing child mortality in India: Keeping the Pace', The World Bank, Washington D.C. (HD Technical Paper).

ESMAP (1997): *Household Energy Strategies for Urban India: The Case of Hyderabad*, Industry and Energy Department, The World Bank, Washington, D.C.

Esrey, S.A., J.B. Potash, L. Roberts and C. Shiff (1991): 'Effects of improved water supply and sanitation on ascariasis, diarrhoea, dracunculiasis, hookworm infection, schistosomiasis, and trachoma', *Bulletin of the World Health Organization*, 69 (5), 609–21.

Gomes, J. et al. (1998): 'Morbidity among farm workers in a desert country in relation to long-term exposure to pesticides', *Scand J. Work Environ and Health*, 24: 213–19.

Government of India (1996), Sampling Registration System, Registrar General of India, New Delhi.

Hernandez A.F., T. Parron and E. Villanueva (1996): 'Increased risk of suicide with exposure to pesticides in an intensive agricultural area: a 12 year retrospective study', *Forensic Sci. In.* 79: 53–63.

Hughes G.A. and M. Dunleavy (2000): 'Why do babies and young children die in India? The role of the household environment', manuscript, South Asia Environment Unit, The World Bank, Washington, D.C.

International Institute for Population Sciences (1995), National Family Health Survey–India, 1992–3, Mumbai.

—— (2000), National Family Health Survey-India, 1998–9, Mumbai.

Kenmore, P.E. (1991): 'Indonesia's Integrated Pest management: Policy, Production, and Environment', Paper presented at USAID-ARPE Environment and Agriculture Officers Conference, 11 September, Colombo, Sri Lanka,

Lessenger J.E., MD Estock, and T. Younglove (1995): 'An analysis of 190 cases of suspected pesticide illness', *Journal of American Board on Farm Practice*, 8: 278–82.

Meulenbelt de Vries I. J. (1997): 'Acute work-related poisoning by pesticides in The Netherlands; a one year follow-up study,' *Przegl Lek* 54(10): 665–70.

Mishra, V. and R.D. Rutherford (1997): 'Cooking smoke increases the risk of acute respiratory infection in children', *NFHS Bulletin*, No. 8 , IIPS Mumbai and East-West Centre, Honolulu.

Murray, C.J.L. and A.D. Lopez (eds.) (1996): *The Global Burden of Disease*, Harvard University Press, Cambridge, Mass.

—— (1994). 'Quantifying disability: data methods and results,' *Bull of WHO* 72(3): 481–94.

Murray, D.L. (1994): *Cultivating Crisis: The Human Cost of Pesticides in Latin America*, University of Texas Press, Austin.

Pitt, M.M., M.R. Rosenzweig and D.M. Gibbons: The Determinants and Consequences of the Placement of Government Programs in Indonesia. *The World Bank Economic Review*, 3: 319–48.

Rola, A.C. and P.L. Pingali (1993): *Pesticides, Rice Productivity and Farmer's Health: An Economic Assessment*, International Rice Research Institute, Los Banos, Phillipines and The World resources Institute, Washington D.C.

Ruijtenm M.W. et al. (1994): 'Effect of chronic mixed pesticide exposure on peripheral and autonomic nerve function', *Arch Environ Health*, 49: 188–95.

Sebastian, I., K. Lvovsky and H. de Koning (1999): Decision Support System for Integrated Pollution Control: A Software for Education and Analysis in Pollution Management, User Guide, The World Bank.

Sivayorathan C., et al. (1995): 'Protective measures use and symptoms among agro-pesticides applicators in Sri Lanka', *Social Science Medicine*, 40: 431–6.

Smith, K.R. (1993): 'Fuel combustion, air pollution exposure, and health: the situation in developing countries', *Annual Review of Energy and Environment*, 529–66.

—— (1998): *Indoor Air Pollution in India: National Health Impacts and the Cost-Effectiveness of Intervention*, Indira Gandhi Institute for Development Research, Mumbai.

Smith K.R. and S. Mehta (2000): The Burden of Disease from Indoor Air Pollution in Developing Countries: Comparison of Estimates, Presented at the WHO/USAID Global Technical Consultation on the Health Impacts of Indoor Air Pollution in Developing Counties, Washington, D.C. (3–4 May).

Vanderslice, J. and J. Briscoe (1993): 'All coliforms are not created equal: a comparison of the effects of water source and in-house water contamination on infantile diarrhoeal disease', *Water Resources Research*, (7): 1983–95.

—— (1995): 'Environmental interventions in developing countries: interactions and their implications', *American Journal of Epidemiology*, 141(2): 135–44.

World Bank (1993): *World Development Report 1993: Investing in Health*, Oxford University Press, New York.

—— (1997): 'New directions in health sector development at State level: An operational perspective', South Asia Health Unit, The World Bank, Washington D.C.

—— (1998): *Pollution Prevention and Abatement Handbook*, The World Bank Washington D.C.

—— (2000a): Health and Environment, Background paper for the World Bank Environment Strategy The World Bank.

—— (2000b): Andhra Pradesh, India—Water, Household Environment and Health, South Asia environment Unit, The World Bank Washington D.C.

ANNEXURE A.4.1

COSTS ESTIMATES FOR IMPROVEMENTS IN THE HOUSEHOLD ENVIRONMENT

The costs have been computed by estimating the annualized costs for rural and urban households of providing a private water supply and a private toilet. The annualized cost is equal to the sum of

(i) operating and maintenance costs (O&M), plus (b) an annuity on the capital investment over the lifetime of the installation using an interest rate of 12 per cent. In the case of shifting to a clean cooking fuel it is assumed that the alternative fuel is kerosene and that the cost is based on an average consumption of 20 litres per household per month using the import parity price for kerosene rather than the subsidized price at which kerosene is sold in ration stores. This reflects the full cost to the Indian economy of shifting from the use of dung or fuel wood to kerosene. We have not attempted to allow for the value of time saved by such a switch, since this is captured by the willingness-to-pay estimates.

The average annualized costs (in rupees per person per year at 1997–8 prices) used for these calculations were:

	Rural	Urban
Clean cooking fuel	419	402
Private water supply A	210	350
Private water supply B	100	250
Private toilet	250	400

The two estimates for private water supply refer to the average costs of providing a service to households with no access to a protected water supply (A) and to those that currently rely upon a public well or piped water supply in their community (B). In the case of sanitation, the costs are for providing private toilets, since the number of households with access to public toilet facilities is very small. The costs of a private water supply assume a single external connection for rural households or a single internal connection. In all cases, it is assumed that the average urban household size is 5.2 while the average rural household size is 5.4. For private toilets, the costs are based on a twin pit, pour-flush latrine for rural households and for 50 per cent of urban households, with the remaining 50 per cent of urban households served by a sewer connection, which is much more expensive, in order to avoid contamination to ground water caused by seepage from pit latrines in densely populated urban areas. The interest rate of 12 per cent used in computing the annualized costs is much higher than the interest rates typically used in India for such calculations but it reflects a realistic estimate of the opportunity cost of capital for the country.

On this basis the total cost of providing universal access to a private water supply will amount to Rs 700 crore per year, while universal access to private toilets will cost Rs 1600 crore per year. If an interim target of achieving at least 60 per cent coverage of private toilets in all communities were adopted, then the cost would be much less at Rs 700 crore per year, almost the same as for private water supply. The total cost of switching all households to use of a clean cooking fuel would be Rs 2200 crore per year.

NET COSTS OF IMPROVEMENTS IN THE HOUSEHOLD ENVIRONMENT

'Willingness to pay' estimates or WSS services were obtained from a review of seven available studies in India[12] and 'benchmarking'

[12] Undertaken by Smita Misra, World Bank. WTP studies for water and sanitation reviewed: AIMS (1996); Study on Willingness to Pay for Improved Water Supply, Sanitary Latrines and Sewage System for Rural Households (Punjab). A Report prepared by the Asian Information Marketing and Social Research (P) Ltd., for the Punjab health Engineering Department, Patiala and the World Bank. K. Choe, R.C.G. Varley and H.U. Bijlani (1996); Coping with Intermittent Water Supply: Problems and Prospects. Dehradun, Uttar Pradesh, India. Activity Report No. 26, Environmental Health Project, USAID, Washington, D.C. SRI (1997); Socio-Economic Profile and Willingness to Pay—Contingent Valuation study for the Gomti River Pollution Control Project at Lucknow—Phase I. A Report prepared by the Social and Rural Research Institute, New Delhi and Management Services Group, for the Water and Sanitation Office, DFID, 1997. Radhika Ramasubban, Bhanwar Singh, Ramesh Bhatia, John Briscoe, C.C. Griffin, C. Kim (1991); Willingness to Pay for Water in Kerala, India. Chetan Vaidya (1995); A Study on Willingness to Pay for Water and Sanitation Services—Case Study of Baroda. A Report prepared for the Human Settlement Management Institute, Housing and Urban Development Corporation. Marie-Helene Zerah (1997); Some Issues in Urban Water Management: Household Response to Water Supply Unreliability in Delhi. Working Paper, Centre de Sciences Humaines (CSH), Delhi. Smita Misra (1997); Measuring Benefits from Industrial Water Pollution Abatement: Use of Contingent Valuation Method in Nandesari Industrial Area of Gujarat, India. Working paper No. E/185/97, Institute of Economic Growth, University Enclave, Delhi, India. National Sample Survey Reports consulted: SSO, Sarvekshana Vol. XV No. 1, Issue No. 48, July–September, 1991 and NSS 43rd Round (July 1987–June 1988). SSO, Sarvekshana Vol. XIX No. 3, Issue No. 66, January–March, 1996 and NSS 50th Round (July 1993-June 1994). NSSO, Household Consumer Expenditure and Employment Situation in India, July 1994– June 1995, NSS 51st Round. NSSO, Household Consumer Expenditure and Employment Situation in India, July 1995–June 1996, NSS 52nd Round. NSSO, Household Consumer Expenditure and Employment Situation in India, January–December 1997, NSS 53rd Round. NSSO, Household

estimates from selected studies elsewhere. The need for bringing 'benchmarking' estimates was based on the following considerations. First, it was not possible to link the WTP with the quality of services in the Indian studies. Expectations about WSS service quality are often quite low in India that affects consumers' WTP. On the other hand, the types of private water supplies and private toilets envisaged here are certainly good enough for quite a few households to be willing to pay towards the cost of installing them and operating the services. Second, the baseline across seven studies, on which the WTP estimates were based, was difficult to clearly define and it most likely reflected some level of existing access to services. Based on these considerations and a range of 'willingness to pay' studies outside India, it was assumed that households are willing to pay an average of 3 per cent of their household expenditure for a private water supply and 2 per cent of their income for a private toilet relative to the baseline in which they have no access to protected water or sanitation.

Surveys have shown that, on an average, urban and rural households spend 5–10 per cent of their monthly household expenditures on purchases of one or more cooking fuels where these are available (ESMAP, 1997). The alternative is usually to allocate substantial amounts of time to collecting, transporting and using biomass fuels of various kinds. The question, then, is how much extra households are willing to pay to use a clean fuel, assuming that supplies and market access are liberalized. Based on analyses for the Philippines, where the prices of household fuels are not subsidized and markets are not subject to heavy regulation, the analysis has adopted the rather conservative assumption that willingness to pay is equivalent to 2 per cent of average household expenditure.[13]

Based on average household expenditures of Rs 20,000 per year for rural and Rs 32,000 per year for urban—taken from the NSS for 1997, adjusted to 1998 prices — the resulting estimates of 'willingness to pay' (in rupees per person per year) are presented in Table A.4.1

These figures are conservative so as to minimize the risk of understating the effective cost of reducing damage to health by measures which focus on improving the quality of the household environment.

Consumer Expenditure and Employment Situation in India, January–June 1998, NSS 54th Round.

[13] This is very much on the low side for urban households, but partially offset by the fact that the 38 per cent of urban households who do not use a clean cooking fuel fall disproportionately into the lowest two wealth quintiles.

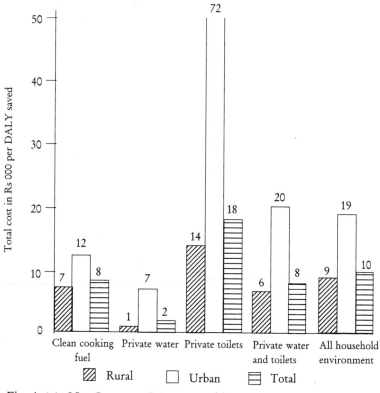

Fig. A.4.1: Net Costs per DALY Saved by Improving the Household
Environment

TABLE A.4.1
*Incidence of Diseases Linked to Poor Water and Sanitation
(Rural and Urban)*

	Rural	Urban
Clean cooking fuel	74	123
Private water supply given current situation of :		
No access	110	185
Public supply	74	123
Private toilet given current situation of :		
No sanitation	55	92
Public toilets	37	62

Source: Director of Health—Monthly reports on communicable diseases

COMPARING THE COST AND BENEFITS OF IMPROVEMENTS
IN THE HOUSEHOLD ENVIRONMENT

These estimates of the net cost per DALY saved may be compared
with estimates of the value that is attached to reducing the burden of
disease by one DALY—see figure A.4.1. Various methods may be used
to assess this value. One approach is to examine how much are people
willing to pay in order to reduce the risks associated, for example,
with occupational or road accidents in relation to the number of
DALYs lost as a results of such accidents. Typically, this yields values
for 'willingness to pay' per DALY in the range three to six times GDP
per capita. On the other hand, an alternative approach focusing on the
loss of potential income and output as a result of sickness or premature mortality tend to yield much lower values which depend heavily
on the age of the person at risk as well as the discount rate that is used.
For this analysis, we have used a figure of Rs 12,000 per DALY—
approximately equal to the estimated value of state GDP per person
for the year 1998—on the basis that this is likely to be the minimum
value that might reasonably be placed on a DALY in valuing the
benefits of environmental improvements.

On this basis, the value of the DALYs saved by the investments
required to provide universal access to private water supplies exceeds
the net cost per DALY saved by a large margin. The same is true for
measures to promote the use of clean cooking fuels, especially for
rural households. However, the net cost per DALY saved by investments in sanitation exceed the value of the health benefits, especially
for urban households.

IMPROVEMENTS IN THE HOUSEHOLD ENVIRONMENT
VIS-À-VIS HEALTH INTERVENTIONS

An alternative perspective is to consider where these measures would
rank relative to other possible health interventions in terms of net cost
per DALY saved. There are considerable difficulties in making such
comparisons because there may be substantial uncertainty about
the coverage and efficacy of public health programmes. Further,
comparing preventive measures with curative measures is complicated by the difficulty of assessing the benefits of avoiding episodes
of ill-health rather than curing those who actually fall ill. Investments in infrastructure clearly fall into the category of preventive

measures but tend to more expensive than many public health programmes because they offer higher levels of prevention with more certainty and over a longer term than alternative approaches to reducing the incidence of the diseases affected.

Subject to these qualifications, the net cost per DALY saved by investments in private access to water for rural households is about US $ 35. The net cost per DALY saved for other improvements in the household environment vary from US160 to US $ 350 with the exception of urban sanitation. These figures may be compared with estimates of the cost-effectiveness of a wide range of health interventions for Andhra Pradesh—see World Bank (1997) which is based on a study by the Administrative Staff College of India (1996).[14] The following list provides a summary of the results focusing on interventions that might be expected to save at least 100,000 DALYs per year.[15]

Measures costing < US $ 25 per DALY saved :

Hospitalization and treatment for meningitis (100,00)

Referral care for high risk pregnancies (300,000)

Secondary prophylaxis for rheumatic heart disease (140,000)

Outpatient treatment for epilepsy (110,000)

Rehabilitation for stroke victims (440,000)

University immunization programme (370,000)

Cataract surgery with spectacles (110,000)

Active screening and treatment for tuberculosis (1,100,000)

Treatment for acute respiratory infections in rural areas (410,000)

Measures with costs in the range US $ 25—50 per DALY saved

Hospitalization and treatment for measles (350,000)

Measures to prevent or treat strokes (470,000)

Treatment for acute respiratory infections in urban areas (120,000)

Aspirin treatment to prevent heart attacks (200,000)

---

[14] The ASCI report is not clear about the price baseline used in preparing their estimates of the net cost per DALY saved, so we have used an exchange rate of Rs 32 per US $ reflecting the exchange rate in early 1995.

[15] The number in brackets is the estimated number of DALYs saved each year by the intervention, rounded to the nearest 10,000.

Measures with costs in the range US $ 50—100 per DALY saved

Oral rehydration therapy (790,000)

Neonatal care for perinatal conditions (1,070,000)

Hospitalization and treatment for heart attacks (320,000)

Coronary bypass surgery for ischemic heart disease (480,000)

Hospitalization and treatment for diarrhoea (up to 4 yrs old) (560,000)

Measures with costs in the range US $ 100—200 per DALY saved

Inhaler therapy for asthma (100,000)

Intensive care for heart attacks (320,000)

Measures with costs in the range US $ 200—400 per DALY saved

Hospitalization and treatment for diarrhoea (> 4 yrs old) (220,000)

Various programmes to prevent or treat protein energy malnutrition (220,000)

Within this ranking, expenditures on extending access to rural water supply turn out to be one of the most cost-effective options among those with the potential to save large numbers of DALYs—at least 350,000 per year equivalent to 2 per cent of the total burden of disease in the state. A universal immunization programme is the only preventive intervention that is clearly more cost-effective. Among the treatment options examined, measures to identify and treat tuberculosis, to treat acute respiratory infections in rural areas and to rehabilitate victims of strokes are also more cost-effective. On the other hand, oral rehydration therapy, hospitalization and treatment for diarrhoea, and neonatal care for perinatal conditions are all significantly less cost-effective measures.

Expenditures on urban water supply and clean fuels in rural areas have net costs of US $ 160–180 per DALY saved, similar to the cost per DALY for providing intensive care to victims of heart attacks. It is clear that such expenditures would benefit a much larger proportion of the population, especially among those in poverty or with below average levels of household income.

In summary, measures that improve the quality of the household environment, especially in rural areas, by extending access to private water supply and by promoting the use of clean fuels are clearly cost-effective. This conclusion is justified both by comparison with alternative options for reducing the burden of disease in Andhra Pradesh and on any cost-benefit criterion which attaches even modest values to the benefits of lowering child mortality and preventing other adverse health outcomes.

Environmental Impact Assessment Process in India and Air Quality Management

P. Ram Babu

ENVIRONMENTAL IMPACT ASSESSMENT PROCESS IN INDIA

The Environmental Impact Assessment (EIA) process and associated practices are dealt with in this chapter. While explaining the EIA process cycle—Screening, Scoping, Baseline determination, Impact prediction, Assessment of alternatives and delineation of mitigation measures, Environmental Impact statement, Public consultation, Post project monitoring and auditing-practices prevalent in India, the examples of gaseous emissions and air quality are widely discussed. Also, there are comments on desirable trends that are a part of the present EIA practice in India and the areas within EIA to which the environmental economics toolbox can significantly contribute are offered.

The very first question any environmental manager would ask is, 'What is Environmental Impact Assessment'. It is an iterative process of assessing the various environmental dimensions, incorporating improvements and mitigation measures in the development of a project, commencing at its very outset. In this way, EIA can often prevent future liabilities or costly alterations in project design.

The logic for such an assessment is to say that environment and development are not separate challenges; they are inexorably linked. The challenge lies in achieving a situation that will enable environment and development to complement one another, and exist in harmony with one another. EIA offers a decision aid to planners to delineate the environmental consequences of a proposed development.

The objective of EIA is to foresee the potential problems that would arise out of a proposed development and address them in the project planning and design stage.

The EIA process should then allow for the communication of this information to (i) the project proponent (ii) the regulatory agency and (iii) the local stakeholders and interest groups.

What are the Indian Policies Regarding EIA?

The government of India passed the Environment Protection Act on 23 May 1986. The act provides India with a legislative framework accommodating for (i) protection and improvement of the environment and (ii) implementation of India's commitment relating to the protection and improvement of the environment, the prevention of hazards to human beings, other living creatures and property.

To achieve the above objectives, a notification on EIA was issued on 27 January 1994 and further amended in May 1994 and April 1997. Under the notification, an EIA is required where (i) any new project (of 29 sectors delineated in schedule 1 of EIA notification) is proposed (ii) pollution loads are increased through the expansion or modernization of any existing project.

Here, an EIA methodology is presented to demonstrate the management of air pollution. All the steps involved in this process are briefly described and illustrated with relevant examples from air quality monitoring.

EIA CYCLE AND AIR QUALITY MANAGEMENT

The concept of EIA cycle that it is a kind of feedback process in which the experience from project monitoring and auditing regarding environmental matters are used to further improvements in the project system. The EIA cycle consists of the following phases:

1. Screening.
2. Scoping.
3. Baseline determination.
4. Impact prediction.
5. Assessment of an alternative and delineation of mitigation measures.
6. Environmental impact statement and review.
7. Public consultation.

8. Post-project monitoring and auditing.

Screening—Which Projects Require EIA?

Screening is a method of eliminating projects that do not require detailed EIA from the review process. Screening criteria is based upon (i) scale of investment, (ii) type of development and (iii) location of development.

Screening methodologies are based upon (i) positive and negative lists, (ii) matrices and (iii) initial environmental examination.

Project screening determines whether to continue to the next phase of the EIA process, i.e., scoping. The project sectors, investment thresholds and locational details, that determine screening, are delineated in the EIA and Coastal Regulated Zones notifications of Government of India. Then, there are several external donor or lending agency regulations as well—a prominent one is the Asian Development Bank's process of screening. Each proposed programme or project is scrutinized as to its type; location—the sensitivity, scale nature and magnitude of its potential environmental impacts; and availability of cost-effective mitigation measures. Projects thus screened for their expected environmental impact are assigned to one of the following three categories:

1. Category A: Projects expected to have significant adverse environmental impacts. An EIA is required to address significant impacts.
2. Category B: Projects judged to have some adverse environmental impacts, but of lesser degree and or significance than those of category A projects. An initial environmental examination (IEE) is required to determine whether or not significant impacts warranting an EIA are likely. If an EIA is not needed, the IEE is regarded as the final environmental assessment report.
3. Category C: Projects unlikely to have adverse environmental impacts. No EIA or IEE is required, although environmental implications are still reviewed.

Scoping-Which Environmental Aspects are Significant?

Time, manpower, financial resources and data generally constrict EIA's. Scoping allows the EIA to focus on the most significant environmental issues inherent within the projects and its alternatives. Significance of an action must be analysed within the context of society as a whole, the affected region, the affected interest, and the locality, as appropriate. Both short-term and long-term effects are relevant. The following issues may be considered for determination of significance:

1. The degree to which the proposed action affects public health and safety.
2. Proximity to historical or cultural resources, parklands, wild and scenic places or ecologically-critical areas.
3. The degree to which the effects are likely to be highly controversial.
4. The degree to which the possible effects are highly uncertain or involve unique or unknown risks.
5. The degree to which the action might establish a precedent or affect future considerations.
6. The implications for cumulatively-significant impacts.
7. The degree to which the action might adversely affect districts, structures, or objects listed in, or eligible for, listing in the National Register of Historic Places.
8. The degree to which the action might cause loss or destruction of significant, cultural or historical resources.
9. The degree to which the action might adversely affect an endangered or threatened species or its habitat that has been determined as critical under the Endangered Species Act.
10. The degree to which the action threatens a violation of federal, state, or local law, or requirements imposed for the protection of the environment.

Indicative guidelines published by the Ministry of Environment and Forests (MoEF) are publicly available. They outline the significant issues to be considered in an EIA, based upon the project sector. For quantifiable impacts, the magnitude, prevalence, frequency and duration commonly determine the significance. For non-quantifiable impacts such as aesthetic or recreational value, significance is commonly determined through the use of socio-economic criteria or through the elicitation of stakeholder expectations. Once those impacts, which are potentially significant for a project have been identified, EIA must then attend to predict their effects.

There is always a common question regarding which projects and in which regions a detailed study of air environment is required? A broad classification of regions with regard to the available environmental space based on measurement of distance from the desired conditions would aid the scoping of projects. For instance, a project having large gaseous emissions in a moderate or poor air shed would require detailed air quality impact investigations.

Consider an example. A project with eight stacks of 30 metres height from the ground with a gas flow rate of 20,250 Nm^3/hr emits about 15g/s of gaseous pollutant. In coastal meteorological conditions, this could effect about 7 micrograms/m^3 ambient air quality increase. This increase can vary in the 300 sq km area from 2-15 micrograms/m^3. This is a large impact for the particular gaseous pollutant. The baseline of that pollutant has to be determined and the resultant ambient quality needs to be predicted with adequate accuracy. The stringency of emission controls would, of course, depend on the existing ambient quality status with regard to that particular pollutant.

The concept of airshed as delineated below can be an effective method of classifying the regions and could be a good tool for scoping an EIA. World Bank guidelines have introduced the concept of air shed of (i) good, (ii) moderate and (iii) poor quality based on the concentration level of PM_{10} (particulate <10 μm in size). Total Suspended Particulate (TSP) and sulfur dioxide (SO_2) would be the major guiding factors for selecting sites for power plants.

WB proposed classification of airshed are described in Box 5.1:

Box 5.1
Descriptions of Airsheds

Good
- PM_{10} and or SO_2: annual mean value <50 μg/m3 or 98 percentile of 24 h values over a period of a year $<$ 150 μg/m^3
- TSP: annual mean value $<$ 80 μg/m^3 or 98 percentile of 24 h mean value over a period of a year $<$ 230 μg/m^3

Moderate
- PM_{10} and or SO_2: annual mean value $>$ 50 μg/m^3 or 98 percentile of 24 h values over a period of a year $>$ 150 μg/m^3
- TSP: annual mean value >80 μg/m^3 or 98 percentile of 24 h mean value over a period of a year $>$ 230 μg/m^3

Poor
PM_{10} and or SO_2: annual mean value $>$ twice the trigger value with moderate air quality or 95 percentile of 24 h mean value over a period of a year $>$ trigger value for peak exposure levels in an airshed with moderate air quality.

What are the Impacts During Construction Phase?

The project construction phase (though generally short term in comparison to the operation phase) can lead to significant environmental impacts. Significant impacts can result through short-term, high-intensity pressures on the physico-chemical environment in relation to air, ground water, surface water, soils and land. Risks to fragile biological and ecological systems are of particular importance while assessing the construction stage impacts, in addition to hazards and risks posed to construction-stage workers.

The stress on infrastructure, socio-cultural incompatibility due to immigration of construction workers and living conditions and consequent public hygiene are also important issues to be considered while assessing impacts during the construction stage.

The impacts at the stage of decommissioning of the project, though significant, are not being considered in the present EIA practice in India, except in the mining sector. Submission of a mine rehabilitation plan is mandatory in the EIA process in India.

Pressure Due to Project and Baseline Determination

The pressure due to the project in the construction and operation stages, on the environment and baseline status of the relevant environmental components is determined in an EIA. The baseline status is to be determined for the area likely to be impacted. The relevant environmental components and parameters as also the impacted area for each of the environmental component is the output of the scoping step.

What are the Data Needs in an EIA?

Baseline setting also involves determination of all other relevant parameters of the environment that would be useful in impact prediction. For example, for a proposed liquefied natural gas (LNG) storage tank, the following parameters for water and air environment may be adequate as description of pressure due to project and baseline setting. In the water environment various parameters to be looked into are:

• Water usage
• Discharge quantity and characteristics (not very significant)
• Water bodies in the neighbourhood (not very significant)
• Surface water quality (if a coastal project, coastal water quality)

- Ground water quality (only in contiguous regions of potential spill)
- Ground water levels (only if project requires large ground water abstraction)
- Availability of water for use in the project and competing uses

Similarly, in an air environment, various gaseous emissions, meteorological details and ambient air quality are to be noted. The emissions during construction and operation phases have to be stated separately. Also emissions that are diffused, at ground level, and from stacks have to be separately mentioned. Spatial distribution and height of emissions is important as this determines subsequent dispersion as also the exposure of spatially-dispersed receptors with varying sensitivity. Boxes 5.2, 5.3 and 5.4 list some of them. The ambient air quality also be recorded by measuring stations' distance from the location of polluting project site.

Box 5.2
Emission Details from an LNG Storage Facility

Emission Parameter	Unit
Number of operating stacks	–
Height of stack from ground	M
Stack top diameter	M
Gas flow rate (each stack)	Nm^3 /hr.
Exit velocity (each stack)	m/s
NOx (total from 8 stacks)	g/s
CO (total from 8 stacks)	g/s
HC (total from 8 stacks)	g/s

Box 5.3
Micro-meteorological Parameters

Date	Wind velocity			Temperature			Relative humidity			Cloud cover		
	Km/hr			° C			%			Oktas		
	Max	Min	Avg	Max	Min	Avg	Max	Min	Avg	Max	Min	Avg

Box 5.4
Ambient Air Quality at Different Monitoring Locations

Ground Level Concentration
(24-hour average unless otherwise specified)

	SPM (mg/m^3)	RPM (mg/m^3)	SO_2 (mg/m^3)	NO_x (mg/m^3)	CO (8 Hrs) (mg/m^3)	HC (ppm)
Maximum						
Minimum						
Average						
Applicable Standard						

Impact Prediction

Impact prediction is a way of 'mapping' the environmental consequences of the significant aspects of a project and its alternatives. It should be noted that a certain element of uncertainty is always present when making predictions, particularly with respect to the environment. For this reason uncertainty within the EIA should always be taken care of in the prediction and presentation of impacts.

Within the EIA, impacts should be determined for
- Ambient air quality
- Surfaces and ground water quality
- Hydrology and sediment transport
- Climate, soils, materials and human health
- Land quality
- Land use
- Existing terrestrial plants and animals
- Community
- Effects on economic status
- Effects on health

How to define the impacted area? The impact prediction for each environmental component should cover the spatial region that would have significant impact. It is important to bear in mind that the impacted area is not simply determined by formulae like the distance at which the environmental change is less than x per cent. Such distances are not appropriate due to non-linearity in the pollutant's transportation phenomenon and location of various sensitive receptors. It is important to determine the sensitive receptors and the threshold values of quality of that environmental component and then determine the area for which the impact prediction exercise is to be undertaken. The practice in India has been to take a 10 km radius (25 km if the proposed facility has a stack-like thermal power) of the facility location. Ministry of Environment and Forests or Central Pollution Control Board (CPCB) has never explicitly recommended this practice.

In order to understand the impacted area, it is necessary to get a clear definition of 'no project scenario'. The impact prediction needs to be carried out for all the proposed alternatives of the project— including the 'no project scenario'. It is important to note here that the 'no project scenario' is not the same as 'no change' in the environmental quality. In case of LNG storage and distribution project, the fact that the fuel substitution can effect environmental improvement and 'no project' situation can lead to further degradation of environment should be brought out in the EIA. Of course, such estimates would involve a number of assumptions/projections regarding the regional economic growth. Such assessments can provide guidance to the public consultation process and decisions at the government as at this level the discussion would inextricably get linked to regional development.

How to get the predictions right or with some degree of certainty? The impact prediction usually involves the use of certain quantitative and qualitative models. Statement of applicability of such models in the specific situation should be made. There will be limitations of such models, which need to be stated clearly in the report. Statement of uncertainties in the impact prediction has to be determined and stated along with the attendant assumptions. For instance, the prediction of ambient air quality would have measurement errors, e.g., ambient air quality and meteorological parameters, modelling errors, e.g., applicability of assumptions, calibration etc.

The uncertainties would have to be stated in a form that aids decision-making when uncertainties related to a project cannot be used to provide a benefit of doubt in favour of the project. In contrast, it is the opposite—application of the precautionary principle, in such contexts, indicates that the benefit of doubt is to be used in favour of the environment, ecology and the stakeholders.

Measurements of Impacts

How to measure the impacts of environmentally-degrading pollutants? In the case of the prediction of impact on air environment, normally, impact on ambient air quality is what is considered. The prediction is undertaken for the ambient air quality parameters that are determined as significant in the scoping exercise. The choice of the prediction model would depend on specific meteorological and landscape characteristics. The models are different for hilly terrain, coastal regions and valley situations—of course, landscape characteristics determine the meteorological characteristics, too.

Ideally, impact prediction should go beyond the change in environmental status to predict the benefits and negative benefits to public health, resources and ecosystems. However, due to lack of information and knowledge regarding degradation of environmental status and its link to damages to human health, resources and ecosystems, one takes recourse to national standards or targets. This is justified, as such standards or targets are set based on appropriate studies though at a macro scale.

Taking recourse to national standards or targets in some situations can be grossly irrelevant. In such a situation, the burden of proof is with the project proponent. Table 5.1 gives the ambient air quality standards in India.

Although the zones, are largely defined, the zonation in the town/country planning documents are taken to provide the guidance in defining a zone in the specific context of a project. The forests, dominantly horticulture areas, wetlands and major water bodies and places of scenic value, outstanding beauty and cultural importance—though not covered by town and country planning zonation—are taken to constitute the sensitive zones.

Is there Consensus on How to Qualify Environmental Impact?

In the past, adequacy of adherence to these practices has been questioned, by the judiciary as also by the regulators and public. For example, a major power project proposal, near Mangalore has been objected to in a public interest litigation (PIL) in the Supreme Court of India, for its contribution to marginal increment in SO_2 ambient levels, though the resultant after the project is projected to be below the relevant National Ambient Air Quality Standards. The argument in support of such an objection was that the wet and dry deposition of

TABLE 5.1
National Ambient Air Quality Standards

Pollutant	Time weighted average	Concentration in ambient air (mg/m³) unless specified			Measurement method
		Industrial Aarea	Residential, rural and other areas	Sensitive area	
Suspended Particulate Matter (SPM)	Annual Average	360	140	70	High Volume sampler, (average flow rate not less than 1.1 m³/min)
	24 hours	500	200	100	
Respirable Particulate Matter (RPM)	Annual Average	120	60	50	Respirable particulate matter sampler
	24 hours	150	100	75	
Sulfur Dioxide (SO₂)	Annual Average	80	60	15	1. Improved West and Gaeke method
	24 hours	120	80	30	2. Ultraviolet fluorescence
Oxide of Nitrogen as NO₂	Annual Average	80	60	15	1. Jacob and Hochheiser modified (Na-Arsenite method)
	24 hours	120	80	30	2. Gas phase chemiluminescence
Lead (Pb)	Annual Average	1.0	0.75	0.50	AAS Method after sampling using EPM 2000Y equivalent filter paper
	24 hours	1.5	1.00	0.75	
Carbon Monoxide (CO)	8 hours	5.0 mg/m³	2.0 mg/m³	1.0 mg/m³	Non-dispersive infrared technique
	1 hours	10.0 mg/m³	4.0 mg/m³	2.0 mg/m³	

Source: CPCB, New Delhi, India

163

SO_2 would contribute to the acidity of the soils, which is already high in the forest of the western ghats, in the contiguous area of the project and the Forest Division is already incurring substantial expenditure neutralizing the soils.

Similarly another power project, north of Mumbai on the west coast of India, has been objected to, even though the resultant ambient quality is within the limits of national standards set for sensitive regions. The argument, here too, is very region specific—the specific horticulture practice, prevalent in this region, would not tolerate the levels of SO_2, permitted in the national standards for sensitive regions.

The above two instances bring out the fact that EIA is not documentation and demonstration of compliance with applicable regulations. It is the objective of EIA to prove and convince all the stakeholders that the proposed project does not inflict significant dis-benefits to the contiguous region and the livelihood of the people, and the mitigation plan put in place is adequate to mitigate the dis-benefits and cover any unanticipated risks.

What is Integrated Assessment?

The integrated impact assessment that includes the identification of the impacts resulting from the accumulation of impacts to the project region is a desirable part of an EIA for large projects. These impacts are often termed cumulative and can result through cross-media transfers and 'blending' of pollutants.

Adequate account of potential cumulative impacts should therefore identify: (i) Dispersal of pollutants, (ii) Cross-media transfer of pollutants and (iii) Accumulation of pollutants.

Environmental regulations in India do not specifically require the proponent to undertake such assessments. However, the EIA reviewer does examine the potential for cumulative impacts where (i) environmental problems are acute (eutrophication of water bodies, heavy metal contamination and entry into the food chain etc.); (ii) environmental media status is bad; and (iii) ecosystems are fragile, e.g., Doon valley etc.

Assessment of Alternatives and Delineation of Mitigation Measures

For any given project, various alternatives are compared from an environmental perspective. Alternatives should also consider the zero option. Options should then be ranked and selected based upon the best environmental option in relation to the level of accrual of economic benefits. Alternatives should address both the project location and its processes. Once alternatives have been reviewed, a mitigation plan is drawn for the selected option. The Environmental Management Plan (EMP) will form a crucial input in the stages of post-project monitoring.

The evaluation of options considering the environmental and economic benefits and dis-benefits has been a contentious issue of debate in the public consultation process and in the media. This is because, in the present-day practice of EIA, not much quantified information is available on the economic and environmental benefits and dis-benefits that can be compared and contrasted for arriving at a better decision. Social and environmental cost-benefit assessments with stakeholder focus can play a vital role in aiding to resolve a number of conflicts surrounding the developmental projects.

WHAT ARE THE ALTERNATIVES?

An insignificant process alteration or similar locational option is not in sync with the spirit of this step, in the EIA process. The alternatives should significantly differ in their environmental impact and there has to be a genuine search for economic and environmental trade-off. While a fuel choice of imported coal with larger sulfur content could be suitable for locations where acidification is not an environmental problem, such is not the case if the facility is to be located near the forests of western ghats, for example.

A set of criteria has to be developed to evaluate the alternatives. As impact prediction and assessment for all the alternatives could need deployment of disproportionate resources, screening based on expert opinion and qualitative assessments can be used for screening many options. However, the process has to be carried out diligently, in a demonstrable manner. Adoption of such a process would help resolution of a number of issues that would be raised in the public-hearing process or otherwise. The screening process based on the environmental criteria, could also be a part of pre-feasibility report of the project.

What is Impact Mitigation Plan?

The mitigation plans for control of adverse impacts arising out of developmental activity address the following:

- Pollution prevention
- End-of-the-pipe treatment technology
- Attenuation in the source-receptor pathway
- Protection of the sensitive receptors
- Risk mitigation measures (on-site and off-site)

The mitigation plan should also include compensation measures. The compensation measures need to be adopted only if an impact cannot be prevented or mitigated through rehabilitation and resettlement or the magnitude/extent of impact is not too large requiring resettlement and rehabilitation. The compensation has to be based on 'polluter pays' principle and the amount of compensation is to be estimated using damage costs.

The EIA should contain a 'commitment list' summarizing all mitigation proposals with explicit mention of organizations responsible for implementation and regulation. The list should provide details on what mitigation is intended to achieve, why it is assessed to succeed and the consequences of failure.

What is Environmental Management Plan?

Environment Management Plan should include:

1. Delineation of mitigation and compensation measures for all the identified significant impacts.
2. Delineation of unmitigated impacts .
3. Physical planning including work programme, time schedule and locations for putting mitigation and compensation systems in place.
4. Delineation of financial plan for implementing the mitigation and compensation measures in the form of budgetary estimates and demonstration of its inclusion in the project budget estimates.
5. Delineation of the Human Resource Plan in terms of the requirement of training in pollution prevention, staff for operation and maintenance of pollution control and monitoring systems, training for emergency preparedness and rescue operation and institutional strengthening for ensuring impact mitigation on the pathway and at the receptor site.

ENVIRONMENTAL IMPACT STATEMENT

The output from an EIA is called an environment impacts statement (EIS). This document assists the decision-making agency to assess the suitability of a proposed project. An EIS should provide clear information to the decision-maker on the environmental condition without the project and with the project and with project alternatives. In doing so, the EIS should also clearly outline any uncertainties of measurement, prediction and aggregation that may form an input to the decision-making process.

The EIS has to delineate all the impacts and shortlist the significant ones. The significant impacts have to be quantified or qualified for all the alternatives considered. As pointed out earlier, no project situation is one alternative. In addition, the project with and without the EMP should also be taken as an alternative. The EMP delineates measures to minimize and mitigate the significant impacts. The residual impacts have to be stated clearly for all the alternatives, which provides the basis for decision by the permitting authorities.

Comparing Apples and Oranges!

The decision, comparing the project alternatives based on their residual impacts, would involve comparing apples and oranges. For example, in the case of fuel choices as project alternatives, it may involve comparison of x, y, z increments in SPM, NOX and SO_2. It has been a practice in India, though never articulated, that the regulators ensure that the post-project situation is in conformity with the national standards and targets. Such an approach has been questioned widely in the past, and tools for such inter-comparisons are desirable.

In the past there have been instances, wherein the Batelle Environmental Evaluation System (BEES) has been used to compare benefits and dis-benefits associated with alternative projects and their varied impacts on different environmental components. The BEES impact scores are aggregated and normalized for each project, i.e., with the project, without the project, with project mitigation measures. Environmental issues of importance to be considered in this step are the same as the ones identified in project scoping, and any additional issues brought forward through consultation with the public.

Decision-making tools to aid project permitting, based on comparison of residual impacts of alternative project options, have been a subject of discussion in India. But the solutions that have emerged are highly prescriptive. It is proposed that investigations of environmental status, assimilative characteristics of environmental media, resource endowment in the region can be used to evolve a development project portfolio, for the region. Regulators can use such a desired portfolio as guidance for permitting decisions. Guideline documents, delineating desired process technology options for many industrial sectors and the zoning atlas brought out by CPCB in India has also been widely used in permitting decisions.

An alternative to the prescriptive approach is the social cost-benefit assessment of residual impacts for all project alternatives and marginal effectivity of investments in environmental management systems. These approaches involve adequate application of environmental economics' tools in the EIA process.

DECISION MAKING

The final step of decision making is based on the EIS and can involve varying levels of the activity. For non-complex projects, i.e., where impacts are minor, and assessed clearly and with low levels of uncertainty, the decision can be arrived at by Impact Assessment Agency. For projects involving significant impacts, uncertainties in prediction, complex trade-offs and conflicts, the decision is normally arrived at through a group decision involving a number of steps including evaluation of EIA and EMP by an expert panel.

The Impact Assessment Agency in the MoEF uses the services of expert committees in arriving at the permitting decision. The constitution of this committee reflects the likely stakeholder interests in such a decision, as also the expertise requirements. The expert panel, if necessary, may visit the site and call for additional investigations. It normally calls for a presentation by the proponent.

Recently, many proponents of large developmental projects are entering into discussion with the permitting authorities for setting the scope of EIA investigations. A similar trend is also seen in a proponent entering into dialogue with the neighbourhood, much ahead of the single point public consultation (or hearing). This is a healthy sign augering well for the EIA process.

PUBLIC CONSULTATION

In India, the public must be informed and consulted on a proposed development, after the completion of the EIA report. Any member of the public affected by the proposed development should have access to the executive summary of the EIA. This will include bonafide residents, local associates, environment groups and any other person located at the project site of the displacement.

The public should be involved in making oral/written suggestions to the State Pollution Control Board (SPCB) with jurisdiction of the region in which the project is located. Both the SPCB and the proponent should affect a public consultation programme. The objective of the public consultation programme is to identify the social and environmental risks of the different strategic project design components under consideration (capacity, process, site (s) etc). Risks can include: (i) involuntary resettlement; (ii) potential likelihood of influx of squatters; (iii) potential for media hostility; (iv) loss of the natural resource-base of the local population; (v) downstream impacts from polluting local water bodies; and, (vi) potential degradation of highly fragile natural habitats.

Consultation should identify and involve local representatives of potential project-affected groups and local government and non-governmental organizations (NGOs). India's statutory requirements oblige the SPCB to provide a summary of the outcome of the public consultation programme to the Impact Assessment Agency (IAA), together with the proponent's original EIA. At this stage, the proponent is also obliged to submit a modified EIA or respond to issues raised in public consultation process to MoEF which takes into account the issues raised within the consultation.

Table 5.2 provides a guideline for successful conduct of the public consultation process, as a part of EIA.

POST PROJECT MONITORING AND AUDITING

Monitoring should be carried out during the construction and it must be observed that operation of a project. During project operation, it must be observed that the prediction and agreements made in the EIS are complied with. If this is not the case and impacts exceed those predicted, corrective action should be taken. Monitoring and auditing will also allow the regulating agency to review the capacity and implementation of the EMP.

The EIA should contain a 'commitments list' delineating all mitigation proposals (after public consultation and review), implementation plan, monitoring plan for evaluating the success of mitigation and

TABLE 5.2

Guideline for the Successful Conduct of the Public Consultation Process

Objective	Issues to verify
Stakeholders identification	Is the sponsor aware of all those groups and individuals who will be directly affected by the social or environmental impacts of the project, and all those individuals and organizations who can contribute to, or hinder, the success of the project?
Impact identification	Have all social and environmental impacts of significance to the local population and other stakeholders been assessed in the EIA (including the indirect social impacts)?
Mitigation options	Have a wide range of compensation and mitigation options been presented to, and solicited from, the affected population?
Economic livelihoods	Are economic livelihood potential and social wellbeing of the project-affected groups comparable or better to the existing before the project?
Draft EIA	The draft EIA report and EMP have been released to the public and have been consulted upon?
Design changes	Those affected by the project are kept informed of changes in the project design, construction activities and operations as they arise?
Monitoring	Project-affected groups are proposed to be involved in monitoring the effectiveness of social and environmental impact mitigation and is a plan for the same presented?
Community development	Is the proponent working to promote local development within the wider community?

Source: CPCB

contingency/corrective mechanism under circumstances of failure/ineffectivity of mitigation measures. After reviewing the 'commitments list' which is not explicit in the present EIA practice, the Impact Assessment Authority draws a list of 'consent conditions' which include mitigation and compensation measures as also monitoring requirements by the proponent.

The important constituents of Monitoring System are: (i) what to monitor? (ii) who should monitor? (iii) evaluation system for monitored results, and (iv) feedback system for setting in motion corrective/contingency mechanisms.

The Monitoring System is generally complex and expensive and hence has to supplement the existing environmental monitoring systems in the region. The system has to be purposeful, analytic and not encyclopedic.

WHAT SHOULD BE MONITORED?

The parameters for assessing the following should be included in the monitoring plan:

1. The significance of impacts that were not included in the list of significant impacts despite objections in public consultation.
2. The uncertainties/non-specificities in the assumptions made while designing mitigation measures .
3. The affectivity of mitigation measures.
4. The early warnings for failure of mitigation and disaster-management systems.
5. The environmental parameters which will reach 10 per cent below the ambient quality standards/targets/thresholds at some sensitive receptors after the project implementation.

Who should Monitor?

The Post Project Monitoring Plan has to spell out responsibilities that are specific and clear. The monitoring responsibilities have to be shared amongst the IAA, PCBs, project proponent and the community. These commitments are incorporated into the consent conditions or post-project agreements. The EIA notification and subsequent modifications do not have guidelines requiring the sharing of responsibilities for post-project monitoring. As per the EIA identification, the responsibility of compliance (to consent/conditions) monitoring is with IAA who may specify the on-site data to be provided by the project proponent. The project proponent is required to file with the IAA, once in six months, a report delineating the demonstration of compliance.

However, it is desired that the project proponent should take the responsibility of demonstrating the compliance with the following:

- Pollution prevention/emission reduction commitments
- Emission standards and other related regulations
- End-of-pipe treatment commitments
- Human resource allocation and institutional-strengthening commitments

COMMENTS AND CONCLUSION

The following are the salient conclusions that follow from the discussion above:

1. The EIA process in India seeks active participation of three groups of stakeholders—project proponent, regulators and government, and the public at large including the neighbourhood.

2. The process mandated by the EIA notification of Government of India, delineates the prescriptive screening process.

3. In practice, scoping too has been highly prescriptive, but for the recent trends, wherein the proponent is entering into discussions separately with the regulators and the public to determine the scope of investigations to be included in the investigations.

4. Determination of project alternatives and their ranking based on the environmental viability has to be a part of the project's prefeasibility report.

5. The baseline environmental status determination, which requires the large deployment of resources, has to be designed prudently.

6. The impact predictions and associated EISs have to be made with qualifying statements of uncertainty. However, the uncertainty cannot be used to grant the benefit of doubt to the project proponent.

7. Reading of EISs and their interpretation for arriving at a decision of permitting, involves comparison of apples and oranges. Besides, the very characterization of impact as change effected by the project in the environmental quality doesn't appear to be sound. This has to be, to the extent possible, translated into damages to human health, materials, resources and ecosystems. Of course, such a characterization of impacts, also does away with the problem of comparing oranges with apples. It is precisely here that methods and tools of environmental economics can contribute and sharpen the EIA process.

8. It is important to grant explicit recognition to the fact that the EIA involves stakeholder dialogue and negotiation to arrive at internalization of environmental costs into the project planning. The process involves elicitation and understanding of stakeholder interests and arriving at a satisfying solution. The social cost-benefit assessment with stakeholder desegregation, can be an important tool in the EIA process to facilitate the negotiation process and resolve conflicts.

Social Forestry
A Case Study from Karnataka

K.N. Ninan and S. Jyothis

INTRODUCTION

Social forestry projects have been initiated in India since the early 1980s to meet the needs of local rural communities for fuelwood, fodder, food and small timber as well as regenerate and improve the tree cover on degraded forest and common lands. Thereby, it seeks to reduce pressure on natural forests. In view of their economic and social significance, social forestry projects have been accorded importance in the development plans of the country and the aid portfolio of donor agencies. In this chapter, we review the development of social forestry programmes in India, and the state Karnataka and then make an economic evaluation of a social forestry project in Karnataka. Using rigorous tests and sensitivity analysis, the analysis notes that at full benefits, net of all costs including the opportunity cost of grazing benefits foregone, the project reports high profits with the internal rate of return (IRR) exceeding 16 per cent. If benefits were to fall short by 50 per cent, and netted of all costs including the opportunity cost, the project still reports profits with the IRR exceeding 12.5 per cent. The study illustrates that social forestry projects are economically viable and socially desirable.

Indirectly, social forestry projects are aimed at reducing pressure on surviving natural forests, that are depleting fast due to economic and demographic factors as well as improving the natural resource base of the ecologically fragile regions. It also seeks to regenerate and make productive use of the country's degraded and extensive wastelands estimated at over 129.5 million hectares. Farm forestry programme is a component of social forestry programme. It was intended to induce farmers, especially in the ecologically-fragile and economically-disadvantaged regions such as the arid, semi-arid and hill regions of the country, to take up to tree-growing activities so as to make better and optimum use of their lands, as well as earn income by meeting the needs of rural and urban markets for fuel wood, bamboo, pulpwood, small timber, etc. Although the term social forestry and farm forestry have been ambiguously used, the two are, strictly speaking, not the same. While farm forestry has been promoted largely on commercial considerations and with profit motive in view, the same is not the case with social forestry which has broader social objectives in view, such as improving the tree cover on degraded forestlands and village commons, making productive use of the country's wastelands, promoting soil and water conservation, improving the landscape, etc. Notwithstanding its economic or social significance, investments in social forestry projects or any project for that matter will be undertaken only if they are viable and yield returns at least to cover the investment or expenditure made.

An economic evaluation of a social forestry project in Karnataka, which has been in the forefront in implementing social forestry projects in the country is presented here. In attempting this exercise the various steps to be taken for undertaking such an economic evaluation, as well as the use of standard economic tools and methods to assess the economic viability of a social forestry project are illustrated. In a way, the cost-benefit analysis as relevant for forestry studies has also been introduced here. Also presented are several exercises so that practising economists can get acquainted with the techniques of cost-benefit analysis as can be applied to analysis of land, water, soil and forest development projects.

SOCIAL FORESTRY PROGRAMME IN INDIA

Before analysing the case study, a brief review of the social forestry programme in India and Karnataka state is presented. The National Commission for Agriculture (in 1976) noted the widening gap between the demand and supply of fuel wood, fodder and industrial wood in the country. The Commission recommended taking up of the social forestry programme so as to bridge this gap as well as on environmental considerations. The programme envisaged raising plantations on all available private and community wastelands outside the forests, viz., along farm bunds, wastelands, strips along roads, rails and canals, compounds of industrial, educational and social institutions, etc. Specifically, the programme was to be implemented through different plantation models like farm forestry, community forestry, strip plantations, rehabilitation of degraded forests and development of recreation forests. The states were already implementing production forestry as a part of the state-plan schemes. To supplement the efforts of the state governments, the Government of India launched a Centrally-sponsored Scheme of Social Forestry including Rural Fuelwood Plantation (RFWP) programme during the Sixth Plan (1980–5) in 101 selected districts reporting acute shortage of fuel wood (Planning Commission, 1987). The programme was extended in 1982–three to fifty-six more districts, thus covering a total of 157 districts from various states and union territories. The Sixth Five Year Plan targetted raising fuel-wood plantations over 2.6 lakh ha, and supplying 580 million seedlings to farmers and children under the 'A Tree for Every Child Programme'. The outlay under the programme was Rs 97.21 crore out of which the central grant was Rs 50 crore. The achievements under the programme during the Sixth Plan were 3 lakh ha of plantation and distribution of 740 million seedlings. The Social Forestry Programme gained added impetus especially from 1982–3 onwards, when afforestation was included in the New 20-Point Programme. The programme received a fillip when the World Bank and other foreign donor agencies such as United States Agency for International Development (USAID), Danish International Development Agency (DANIDA), Swedish International Development Agency (SIDA), Overseas Development Agency (ODA), etc., came forward to support the programme. The Externally-aided Social Forestry Programme was commissioned under the State Sector Programme in eleven states initially and a few other states later. These foreign-aided projects were launched with a view to raising community forestry over 9.4 lakh ha and strip plantations over 6075 kms.

Information on the area afforested in India and Karnataka state during the plan periods from 1951–6 to 1993–4/1995–6 is furnished in Table 6.1. As evident, the area afforested in the country rose from 0.52 lakh ha during the First Plan to over 12.21 lakh ha during the Fifth Five Year Plan. Thereafter, during the Sixth and Seventh Plan periods

TABLE 6.1

Information on Area Afforested in India and Karnataka
State during the Plan Periods—1951-6 to 1995-6

Five Year Plan period/years	All India		Karnataka	
	Area afforested (lakh ha)	Cumulative	Area afforested (lakh ha)	Cumulative
First (1951-6)	0.52	0.52	0.002	0.002
Second (1956-61)	3.11	3.63	0.48	0.48
Third (1961-6)	5.83	9.46	0.64	1.12
1966-9	4.53	13.99	0.62	1.74
Fourth (1969-74)	7.14	21.13	0.61	2.35
Fifth (1974-9)	12.21	33.34	1.67	4.02
1979-80	2.22	35.56	0.08	4.1
Sixth (1980-5)	46.50	82.06	4.15	8.25
Seventh (1985-90)	88.86	170.92	6.67	14.92
1990-1	7.52	178.44	0.30	15.22
1991-2	10.16	188.60	0.34	15.56
1992-3	10.62	192.22	0.36	15.92
1993-4	9.64	208.86	0.46	16.38
1994-5	9.84	218.70		
1995-6	8.02	226.72		

Source: Forestry Statistics of India, 1995; The Citizen's Fifth Report, Centre for Science and Environment, New Delhi, 1999, p. 115

from 1980 to 1990 recorded a sharp rise in the area afforested in the country. Beginning from the First Five Year Plan period to 1995-6 over 22.6 million ha area was afforested in the country. Of this, over 19 million ha alone was afforested after 1980 when social forestry, including farm forestry, was taken up on a massive scale in the country. In Karnataka, the total area of afforestation rose from a negligible 0.002 lakh ha during the First Five Year Plan to about 1.67 lakh ha during the Fifth Plan. In Karnataka too, the area of afforestation registered a sharp rise between 1980 to 1990. By the end of 1993-4, over 1.6 million ha was afforested in Karnataka, of which over 1.2

TABLE 6.2

State-wise Distribution of Area Covered under Externally-Aided
Social Forestry Projects in India during 1981–2 to 1992–3

States	Total area covered under social forestry projects	
	('000 ha)	(per cent)
1. Gujarat	313.4	15.2
2. Tamil Nadu	302.9	14.7
3. Orissa	217.9	10.5
4. Bihar	168.2	8.1
5. Uttar Pradesh	161.9	7.8
6. Andhra Pradesh	150.7	7.3
7. Karnataka	149.5	7.2
8. Rajasthan	120.8	5.8
9. Himachal Pradesh	112.8	5.5
10. West Bengal	93.0	4.6
11. Kerala	85.3	4.1
12. Maharashtra	81.0	3.9
13. Haryana	67.0	3.2
14. Jammu and Kashmir	44.0	2.1
TOTAL	2068.4	100

Source: Forestry Statistics of India, 1995; Indian Council for Forestry Research and
Education, Dehradun

million ha alone was afforested between 1980 to 1993–4. The 1990s
has, however, witnessed a sharp reduction in the afforestation efforts
both at the all-India level and for the state of Karnataka.

Table 6.2 indicates the state-wise distribution of area covered under
externally-aided social forestry projects in India during the period
1981–2 to 1992–3. The area covered under social forestry in the 14
states under these externally-funded projects was over 2 million ha by
the end of 1992–3. Of these eight states, viz., Gujarat, Tamil Nadu,
Orissa, Bihar, Uttar Pradesh, Andhra Pradesh, Karnataka and Rajasthan
alone accounted for over three-fourths of the area covered under these

TABLE 6.3

Information on Externally-Aided Social Forestry Projects in India during 1981–2 to 1992–3

State	Donor agency	Project period	Project Cost (Rs lakh)	Farm forestry	Village woodlots	Strip plantations	Reforestation/ Rehabilitation of Degraded Forestlands
					Area Covered ('000 hectares)		
Gujarat	WB and USAID	5 years	12,965	230.5	35.0	17.5	30.4
Tamil Nadu	SIDA	1981–2 to 1992–3	14,454	103.2	187.7	7.9	4.0
Orissa	SIDA	1983–4 to 1992–3	10,651	88.5	74.2	0.6	54.6
Bihar	SIDA	1985–6 to 1990–1	5386	71.7	30.7	1.2	64.6
Uttar Pradesh	WB and USAID	5 years	16,116	147.2	14.0	0.7	–
Andhra Pradesh	SIDA	1983–4 to 1989–90	3838	108.1	25.0	3.8	13.8
Karnataka	WB and ODA	1983–4 to 1987–8	5523	120.5	25.0	4.0	–
Rajasthan	WB and USAID	5 years	3919	91.5	5.0	4.4	20.0
Himachal Pradesh	WB and USAID	5 years	5729	66.8	41.0	–	5.0

(cont.)

178

Table 6.3 (cont.)

State	Donor agency	Project period	Project Cost (Rs lakh)	Area Covered ('000 hectares)			
				Farm forestry	Village woodlots	Strip plantations	Reforestation/ Rehabilitation of Degraded Forestlands
West Bengal	WB	1981–2 to 1989–90	3486	52.0	6.0	20.0	15.0
Kerala	WB	1984–5 to 1989–90	5991	69.2	14.1	2.0	–
Maharashtra	USAID	1982–3 to 1989–90	5640	44.0	34.0	3.0	–
Haryana	WB and DANIDA	1982–3 to 1989–90	3332	30.0	12.0	9.5	15.5
Jammu and Kashmir	WB and DANIDA	1982–3 to 1989–90	2374	19.0	5.0	3.0	17.0
TOTAL			99,404	1242.2 (60.1)	508.7 (24.6)	77.6 (3.7)	239.9 (11.6)

Note: Figures in parenthesis give per cent share to total area covered under externally-aided social forestry projects
Source: Forestry Statistics of India, 1995; Indian Council for Forestry Research and Education, Dehradun

projects. Over 8 lakh ha was brought under social forestry in Gujarat, Tamil Nadu and Orissa between 1981–2 to 1992–3 under these projects. Table 6.3 presents more detailed information of these externally-aided Social Forestry Projects implemented in various states of the country during the 1980s and early 1990s. These projects envisaged an investment of over Rs 994 crore. As stated earlier, the World Bank and other donor agencies such as USAID, SIDA, DANIDA, ODA funded these projects. Out of the total area covered under social forestry in these projects over 60 per cent was accounted by farm forestry alone (over 1.24 million ha), 24.6 per cent by village wood-lots (over 0.5 million ha) and the remaining over 15 per cent (i.e., over 0.3 million ha) by strip plantations and reforestation or rehabilitation of degraded forestlands.

The above pertains to area covered under externally-funded social forestry projects. Information pertaining to the area brought under social forestry, including farm forestry, implemented under other schemes are not readily available. An Evaluation Report on Social Forestry Programme by the Planning Commission in 1987 noted that between 1980–1 to 1983–4 close to 4.81 lakh ha was covered under social forestry programme in the country. Of this, over 2.69 lakh ha was accounted by externally-funded social forestry projects and over 2.11 lakh ha by Rural Fuelwood Plantations (Planning Commission, 1987). Between 1990–1 to 1995–6, over 5.57 lakh ha of public lands were afforested, including forest lands. According to N.C. Saxena, some 18,000 million trees were planted in the country between 1980 and 1988, of which 10,000 million trees equivalent to an area of 5 million ha were planted on farm lands (cited in Citizen's Fifth Report, CSE, 1999). As per the above cited report, out of the 10,000 million trees planted on farm-lands; 7000 million trees was accounted by eucalyptus alone, of which 5000 milion trees are estimated to have survived. Because of its fast-growing characteristics, eucalyptus was the pre-dominant species distributed and grown. Other species such as Subabul (*Leucaenea Leucociphd*), Shisham (*Delbergia Sisso*), Kikar (*Accacia Nilotica*), Casuarina, Neem (*Azadirchi Indica*) and fruit trees were also distributed. The survival rates of plants in community plantations during 1980–1 to 1983–4 in selected ranges as per the Planning Commission Evaluation ranged from 74.6 per cent in Uttar Pradesh to over 99 per cent in Karnataka. However, a survey of 907 beneficiary households across 16 states revealed the survival rates of plants to be much lower. For instance, for seedlings planted in 1981–2, the number of the sample beneficiaries who reported survival rates of between 76 to 100 per cent at the end of planting season 1981–2 declined from 176 to 157 and then to 148 at the end of 1982–3 and 1983–4 planting seasons, respectively (Planning Commission, 1987). An evaluation by the Indian Institute of Public Opinion in 1987 covering 2000 beneficiaries each in five states, viz., Gujarat, Karnataka, Tamil Nadu, Uttar Pradesh and West Bengal, reported average survival rates of trees of all species in farm forestry during 1983–8 to vary from 43.7 per cent in Gujarat to over 70.4 per cent in Uttar Pradesh (Srivastava, 1992). An evaluation of social forestry projects in selected states by the NCAER in 1988 observed that in the 14 districts studied spread over six states survival rates ranged between 18.6 to 50 per cent. It exceeded 50 per cent in only two districts between 1980–3; in the remaining 12 districts these rates varied from 18.6 per cent in Ganjam district of Orissa to over 47 per cent in Ajmer district of Rajasthan. For the period 1983–8 these survival rates in these 14 districts ranged from 18.8 to 67 per cent (Srivastava, 1992). Insufficient rainfall, grazing, diseases and pests, inappropriate choice of areas taken up for plantations, improper preparation of treatment and work schedules and excessive targets, were among the several factors that contributed to the high tree-mortality rates (Srivastava, 1992). Among the species, the Indian Institute of Public Opinion (IIPO) study noted that the eucalyptus had the highest survival rate in almost all the states.

Generating additional employment through forestry activities was another objective of the social forestry programme. It was envisaged that during the Sixth Plan primary and secondary sector forestry activities would generate about 240 million man-days of employment every day. Keeping this in view the main thrust in the programme was promotion of a people's forestry programme. Data on employment generated in social forestry programmes are not readily available. The Planning Commission Evaluation Report of 1987 referred to earlier has furnished some estimates for various states in the country during 1983–4, which pertains to the initial years of the programme. Table 6.4 presents information on person days of employment on own work and on farm forestry reported by the beneficiary households across different states of India during 1983–4. As evident, taking all the states together the average person days of employment on farm forestry was about 52. This constituted about 10.6 per cent of the average person

TABLE 6.4

Person Days of Employment on Own Work and on Farm Forestry during 1983–4

State	Average Person Days Employed			
	Number reported	Own work including farm forestry	On farm forestry	Per cent of Col. 4 to Col. 3
(1)	(2)	(3)	(4)	
Andhra Pradesh	19	368	12	3.2
Assam	–	–	–	–
Bihar	57	404	18	4.4
Gujarat	48	418	83	19.8
Haryana	35	422	29	6.9
Himachal Pradesh	32	530	37	7.0
Jammu and Kashmir	–	–	–	–
Karnataka	62	433	56	12.9
Kerala	25	81	1	1.2
Madhya Pradesh	75	752	71	9.4
Maharashtra	57	340	42	12.4
Orissa	25	399	1	0.2
Rajasthan	70	795	122	15.3
Tamil Nadu	38	272	28	10.3
Uttar Pradesh	57	527	21	4.0
West Bengal	34	566	108	19.1
ALL STATES	634	492	52	10.6

Source: Government of India, Planning Commission 1987

days employed on own work including farm forestry reported by the beneficiary households. Across the states, one comes across wide variations in the average person days of employment in farm forestry ranging from one person day in Kerala and Orissa, to 108 person days in West Bengal and 122 person days in Rajasthan. The proportion of the average person days employed on farm forestry to total person days of employment (own work and farm forestry) ranged from 0.2 per cent in Orissa to over 19 per cent in Gujarat and West Bengal. The Planning Commission evaluation noted the average employment of wage labour on social forestry programme to be about 123 person days during 1983-4 for 37 reporting beneficiaries across states in India. This average varied from 15 person days in Madhya Pradesh to as high as 387 person days in Andhra Pradesh. The average income from wage employment on the social forestry programme for these beneficiary households was about Rs 1113 (Planning Commission, 1987).

There are several studies on social forestry programme and farm forestry programme in particular (Saxena, 1994; Saxena and Ballabh, 1995). These studies suggest that experience with the farm forestry programme has varied from region to region. Farmers in North Western states, who took to farm forestry in a big way in the initial years found to their consternation that when their eucalyptus crop was ready to be harvested, there was a steep fall in prices, resulting in their incurring losses, and subsequently losing interest in farm forestry (Saxena, 1994). Whether the sudden drop in prices was due to a glut in the market or due to buyers using their monopsony position to push down prices is a debatable point. In states like Gujarat, Karnataka and West Bengal the programme was reported to be successful with farm forestry spreading fast. Small farmers also benefitted from the programme by earning additional income. Studies that have tried to evaluate social forestry projects using project appraisal techniques are rare. A notable exception is a study by Nadkarni et al. (1994), that attempted to evaluate the economic and financial viability of 13 selected social forestry projects in Karnataka, from different agro-ecological zones. This study found that the internal rate of returns (IRRs) taking full benefits, net of all costs, including the opportunity cost of grazing benefits foregone to vary from 28 to 39 per cent across the different projects. At reduced benefits (by 50 per cent) and netted of all costs, including the opportunity cost, the IRRs ranged between 21.3 to over 34 per cent. The financial viability analysis showed the IRRs to range between 10.5 to over 46 per cent. This study, thus, found these selected social forestry projects to be viable, both economically and financially.

Social forestry programme has been criticized on a number of grounds. One is that eucalyptus which was widely distributed and grown mainly catered to the needs of the paper industry, rather than meeting rural needs as intended by the programme. Also it was reported that spread of farm forestry affected local food security in some regions by displacing food crops like *ragi* in Kolar district. Environmentalists criticized eucalyptus, which was the most popular species raised under the programme, on grounds that it led to depletion of ground water table, loss of crop productivity in neighbouring lands and also affected on-farm and off-farm biodiversity. With this review of social forestry programme in India, we now take up the case study.

MITTEMARI WATERSHED AREA IN KARNATAKA: LOCATION OF A SOCIAL FORESTRY PROJECT

As a case study, the social forestry plantation implemented in Mittemari Watershed development project, Karnataka will be evaluated. This Watershed Development Project, which is a sub-watershed of the Chitravathi district watershed is located in the semi-arid Kolar district of Karnataka State, India. This project was taken up for implementation in 1983–4 and is one of the oldest watersheds developed in the state. It received a national award for Best Productivity for Dryland Crop Production in 1987–8, apparently attributable to the watershed development. All components of watershed development activities have been implemented in this project. The area of the watershed is about 1245 ha of which 643 ha is cultivated land, 167 ha forestland, and the rest barren rocky wastes. About 750 ha in the project were identified for treatment under Watershed Development Programme (WDP). This includes 583 ha of drylands and 167 ha of forestlands. About 710 households with a population size of 2325 resided in the watershed, in the benchmark year 1983–4. Over 78 per cent of the households are mostly dependent on agriculture. The area receives an annual rainfall of 679 mm. The predominant crops sown in the watershed are groundnut and finger millet (UAS, 1990; Lakshmikanthamma, 1997).

Degraded forest lands and village commons were taken up for raising a social forestry plantation under the watershed development project. A mix of fuel, fodder and forest species were raised in the social forestry plantation. However, information pertaining only to 60 ha of this social forestry plantation wherein *Acacia Nilotica* was planted under this project was available. For this case study, only the social forestry plantation component of the watershed development is taken for an in-depth economic evaluation.

EVALUATION OF SOCIAL FORESTRY:
METHODOLOGICAL ISSUES, DATA AND APPROACH

What are Cash Flows and How Do We Make
the Time Series Data Comparable?

A project incurs costs over the years, so also the flow of benefits. These are often termed as time-series data on costs and benefits. In evaluating a project a number of conceptual and methodological issues merit clarification. First, the cash flows of costs and benefits arising from a project belong to different time periods, and have to be made into a comparable series by converting them into real prices or adjusting for inflation. However, if one expects a rise in real prices itself over time then the series of data has to be adjusted through use of an appropriate adjustment factor. While project appraisals take note of this factor, often they do not spell out whether the data series used for the appraisal are in real terms or at current prices (Nadkarni et al., 1994). Second, even if a series is inflation-adjusted, there is another element to be taken note of, viz., the time value or time preference of money. One hundred rupees received today will be preferred over Rs 100 (even if at real prices) received a year later due to time preference.

What is 'Discounting' and What Discount Rate to Use?

Additivity of cost and benefit flows over time is meaningful only after adjusting for such time preference values. Invariably, all such flows are to be converted into present values. To undertake the viability analysis, the present values of the cash flows of costs and benefits have to be computed through discounting. Then, there is the third question. What is the appropriate discount rate for undertaking this exercise? One view is that this rate should reflect the opportunity cost of capital. But given the institutional and market rigidities characteristic of developing countries, arriving at the correct opportunity cost of capital is not an easy task. It is, however, assumed to vary between 8 to 15 per cent in real terms in developing countries (Gittinger, 1982). A second proposition is to consider the borrowing cost of capital. Many governments tap the domestic and international markets to finance projects. But then project selection may be biased in favour of those with the best financial terms at the cost of economic efficiency. The third proposition is that it should reflect the social time preference rate, i.e., the rate at which the society weighs future consumption vis-a-vis present consumption. The World Bank, Indian Planning Commission and many researchers often use a discount rate of 12 per cent for project appraisals in developing countries. With a pure time preference rate of about 6 per cent, an elasticity of social marginal utility of about –1.75 and an economic per capita growth rate of GDP at 3.5 per cent, the estimate of social discount rate is 12.1 per cent. The 12 per cent rate then reflects the pure time preference, elasticity of social marginal utility of consumption and the per capita growth rate of consumption benefit. Use of such a high discount rate is not justified if the cash flows are in real terms. It also discriminates against investments with a long gestation period and implies that smaller time preference weights are attached to the stream of benefits and costs of future years. But, as noted earlier, society keeps the long-term horizon in view. Social discount rates are, therefore, generally lower than private discount rates (Dixon et al., 1994). But there is no magic formula to adjust the discount rate downwards (Pearce, 1992). Some have even suggested using zero discount rates for environment-oriented projects, but this has been criticized due to difficulties in demarcating environment-oriented projects from other projects; it may even lead to serious mis-allocation of scarce resources (Dixon and Meister, 1986; Pearce et al., 1990; Nadkarni et al., 1994; Dixon, et al., 1994). What then is the appropriate social discount rate? A number of studies have used discount rates ranging between 3 to 6 per cent in real terms to evaluate afforestation and conservation projects (Bojo, 1990; Pearce, 1992; Nadkarni et al., 1994). These rates could vary across countries depending on the circumstances of individual countries (Dixon and Meister, 1986). In UK, one study notes that a 5 per cent social discount rate was used to evaluate projects (Hanley and Spash, 1993). The UK Forestry Commission used even a lower discount rate, i.e., 3 per cent. Further, the Nixon administration in the US used social discount rates ranging from 3 to 12 per cent; for water resource projects like new dams, irrigation projects, etc., even lower discount rates were used than for other Federal projects (Hanley and Spash, 1993). In this analysis a discount rate of 3 per cent is used, and alternatively at 5 and 8 per cents, respectively, by way of sensitivity analysis. As noted earlier, the cash flows in our analysis are expressed in real terms and hence there is no justification to use high discount rates. However, since agencies like the World Bank use discount rates of 10 to 12 per cent to evaluate projects, we have also done a sensitivity analysis at 10 per cent discount rate.

What Time Horizon Should We Assume for the Analysis?

The length of the period to be considered for undertaking the appraisal is another issue of concern. This, it is suggested, should be coterminous with the economic life of the project or the technical life of a major investment incurred in the project. *Acacia nilotica* which has been raised in this social forestry plantation has a lifespan of about 25 years. Although the life span of *Acacia nilotica* can go up to 50 years or even more, social forestry projects, apart from environmental considerations have been raised in India primarily to meet the current needs of rural communities for fuel wood, fodder, small timber and supplementary food, and hence 25 years seems to be a reasonable upper limit for conducting our evaluation. Moreover, for most agricultural and related projects in developing countries, a project life span of 25 years is considered to be reasonable (Gittinger, 1982). Although the environmental benefits of social forestry projects may take a longer time to realize, it is difficult to quantify or value all of them.

The data for this study was collected in 1990 by S. Lakshmikanthamma for her doctoral work wherein the impact of WDP primarily from the farmer viewpoint was studied (Lakshmikanthamma, 1997). The reference year for the study was 1989–90. The analysis covers only 60 ha where *Acacia nilotica* were planted; information on the remaining lands where multi-purpose trees were raised are not available. Hence, the benefits and investments made in these lands are excluded from our analysis. Public investments in this watershed project have been incurred in the initial three or four years for soil and water conservation works, disseminating improved dry-farm technologies and afforestation. The cash flows of costs and benefits for the project are expressed at 1989–90 prices. The public investments were incurred in the initial few years and have been inflated to 1989–90 prices using the Consumer Price Index for Agricultural Labourers for Karnataka, the only available rural-specific price index.

COST-BENEFIT ANALYSIS OF THE PROJECT

What are the Costs and Benefits of the Project and How Do We Estimate Them?

The direct benefits (both marketed and non-marketed) from the project includes timber and non-timber benefits like pods, fuel wood, etc., from the community wood-lots raised on degraded forest lands and village commons used earlier by villagers for free grazing of their cattle. Being a public investment project, the opportunity cost of grazing benefits foregone by the villagers due to the establishment of community wood-lots on degraded forest lands and village commons used earlier by the villagers for free grazing of their cattle have been considered. For estimating the opportunity cost of grazing benefits foregone by the villagers, an earlier study wherein the animal pressure in standardized units per hectare of grazing lands available, animal grazing habits, the marginal value product of fodder grazed by ruminant livestock on Common Property Resources (Rs 271 per tonne) were used (Nadkarni et al., 1994). The opportunity cost is assumed to arise during the entire length of the project.

The capital investments incurred by the government or project implementing agency includes capital investments for raising community wood-lots on degraded forest lands and village commons. The indirect benefits are mostly environmental in nature such as an improvement in moisture availability. In addition to the initial capital investment for establishing community wood-lots, there are recurring costs for watch and ward (e.g., Rs 720 per month) and harvesting charges. *Acacia Nilotica* yields on an average 15 kg of pods per tree (from year 12 onwards) valued at Rs 0.15 per kg at 1989-90 prices; fuel wood of 0.5 tonne per tree when felled valued at Rs 350 per tonne, and timber yield of 0.424 cubic metre per tree valued at Rs 5313 per cubic metre (Nadkarni et al., 1994). The average density of the community wood-lot is about 200 trees per ha. As part of a sensitivity analysis there is the possibility that expected full benefits may not be realized. Hence, an across-the-board 50 per cent reduction in the expected benefits from the social forestry project is considered as one extreme possibility. This will test the rigorousness of our estimates under alternative scenarios. The cash flow of costs and benefits from the social forestry plantation over the 25-year period are presented in Table 6.5.

TABLE 6.5
Cash Flows of Costs and Benefits from Social Forestry Plantation in Mittemari Watershed Development Project, Karnataka

(Units: Rs)

Year	Establishment	Recurring Watch and Ward	Recurring Harvesting	Total Cost	Opportunity costs of grazing benefits foregone	Total Costs inclusive opportunity costs	Pods	Fuel wood	Timber	Total benefits
1.	4,19,874	720	–	4,20,594	52,166	4,72,760	–	–	–	–
2.	–	720	–	720	52,166	52,886	–	–	–	–
3.	–	720	–	720	52,166	52,886	–	–	–	–
4.	–	720	–	720	52,166	52,886	–	–	–	–
5.	–	720	–	720	52,166	52,886	–	–	–	–
6.	–	720	–	720	52,166	52,886	–	–	–	–
7.	–	720	–	720	52,166	52,886	–	–	–	–
8.	–	720	–	720	52,166	52,886	–	–	–	–
9.	–	720	–	720	52,166	52,886	–	–	–	–
10.	–	720	–	720	52,166	52,886	–	–	–	–
11.	–	720	–	720	52,166	52,886	–	–	–	–
12.	–	720	–	720	52,166	52,886	27,000	–	–	27,000

(cont.)

189

Table 6.5 (cont.)

		Cost				Benefits			
Year	Establish-ment	Recurring Watch and Ward	Har-vesting	Total Cost	Opportunity costs of grazing benefits foregone	Total Costs inclusive opportunity costs	Pods	Fuel wood	Timber	Total benefits
13.	–	720	–	720	52,166	52,886	27,000	–	–	27,000
14.	–	720	–	720	52,166	52,886	27,000	–	–	27,000
15.	–	720	–	720	52,166	52,886	27,000	–	–	27,000
16.	–	720	–	720	52,166	52,886	27,000	–	–	27,000
17.	–	720	–	720	52,166	52,886	27,000	–	–	27,000
18.	–	720	–	720	52,166	52,886	27,000	–	–	27,000
19.	–	720	–	720	52,166	52,886	27,000	–	–	27,000
20.	–	720	–	720	52,166	52,886	27,000	–	–	27,000
21.	–	720	–	720	52,166	52,886	27,000	–	–	27,000
22.	–	720	–	720	52,166	52,886	27,000	–	–	27,000
23.	–	720	–	720	52,166	52,886	27,000	–	–	27,000
24.	–	720	–	720	52,166	52,886	27,000	–	–	27,000
25.	–	720	154,440	155,160	52,166	207,326	27,000	2,100,000	27,032,544	29,159,544

Source: Authors' calculations

What are the Criteria Used for the Analysis?

For the analysis, three viability measures are computed, viz., the Net Present Value (NPV) i.e., the present value of benefits minus the present value of costs at 1989–90 prices where cash flows are summed up for 25 years; Benefit-Cost Ratio (B/C Ratio), i.e., the present value of benefits expressed as a ratio to the present value of costs, and the Internal Rate of Return (IRR) i.e., that rate which equates the NPV to zero.

The NPV, BCR and IRR are derived as follows:-

$$NPV = \sum_{t=1}^{t=n} \frac{B_t - C_t}{(1 + i)^t} \qquad (6.1)$$

where:

B_t = benefit in each year t

C_t = cost in each year t

t = 1, 2, ... n

n = number of years

i = discount (interest) rate

$$BCR = \frac{\sum_{t=1}^{t=n} \frac{B_t}{(1 + i)^t}}{\sum_{t=1}^{t=n} \frac{C_t}{(1 + i)^t}} \qquad (6.2)$$

IRR is that rate of discount which equates NPV to zero, i.e., when

$$\sum_{t=1}^{t=n} \frac{B_t - C_t}{(1 + i)^t} = 0 \qquad (6.3)$$

Another measure, though not favoured by economists is the 'Pay Back Period'. Essentially it refers to the period over which one can recoup the initial investment (Pearce and Nash, 1981). Thus, if one can recover the investment in a period of say 't' years, where 't' is some artificially established maxim, then one can undertake the project. This measure is used by some industries and agencies, but rarely by economists. Moreover, in the case of forestry investment the 'pay back period' is not a suitable measure to use since most often the forestry investment are recovered only in the final year when the tree or trees are felled. As our case study shows the NPV after deducting all costs including the opportunity cost of grazing benefits foregone (see Table 6.8, Column 9) turns positive only in the 25th year, i.e., after the trees are felled and when the timber value is added.

Analysis of the Results

The results of the analysis are presented in Tables 6.6 to 6.9. Table 6.6 which presents the NPVs for the social forestry plantation in Mittemari Watershed development project in million rupees at 1989–90 prices for cash flows summed up over 25 years indicates that at full benefits, net of costs, excluding opportunity costs, the NPVs under various scenarios range from Rs 23.6 lakh to Rs 136.40 lakh. If the opportunity cost of grazing benefits foregone by the villagers due to the establishment of the social forestry plantation on degraded forest lands and village commons used by them earlier for free grazing of their cattle are also included the NPVs under different assumptions and scenarios range from Rs 18.80 lakh to Rs 127.30 lakh. At reduced benefits (by 50 per cent) excluding opportunity cost, the NPVs range from Rs 9.8 lakh to Rs 65.70 lakh. If, however, the opportunity cost of

TABLE 6.6
Net Present Values for Social Forestry Plantation in Mittemari Watershed Development Project, Karnataka, in Rs lakh at 1989–90 prices   (cash flows summed up for 25 years)

Items	Discount rates			
	3%	5%	8%	10%
Full benefits, net of costs, excluding the opportunity cost of grazing benefits foregone	136.4	83.0	39.3	23.6
Full benefits, net of costs, including the opportunity cost of grazing benefits foregone	127.3	75.7	33.7	18.8
Benefits reduced by 50 per cent, net of costs, excluding the opportunity cost of grazing benefits foregone	65.7	39.2	17.6	9.8
Benefits reduced by 50 per cent, net of costs, including the opportunity cost of grazing benefits foregone	56.6	31.9	12.0	5.0

Note: Net Present Value: Present value of benefits minus present value of costs
Source: Authors' calculations

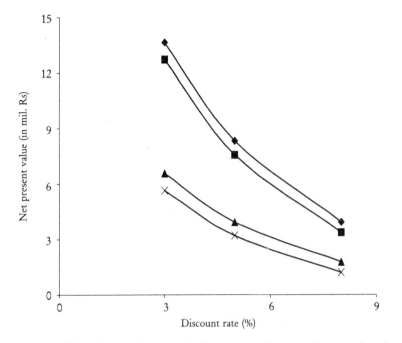

—■— Full benefits net of costs, excluding opportunity cost of grazing benefits forgone

—◆— Full benefits net of costs, including opportunity cost of grazing benefits forgone

—▲— Benefits reduced by 50 per cent net of costs, excluding opportunity cost of grazing benefits forgone

—✕— Benefits reduced by 50 per cent net of costs, excluding opportunity cost of grazing benefits forgone

Fig. 6.1: Relationship between Discount Rate and NPV

grazing benefits foregone are also added, the NPVs under various scenarios range from Rs 5 lakh to Rs 56.6 lakh. The relationship between discount rate and NPV is depicted in Figure 6.1. As evident, the relationship between discount rate and NPV is inverse.

Table 6.7 presents the BC ratios for the social forestry plantation in Mittemari Watershed development project. At full benefits, net of costs, but excluding opportunity costs, the BC ratios under various assumptions and scenarios are very high ranging from 6.85 to 28.61. When the opportunity cost of grazing benefits foregone are also

TABLE 6.7

*Benefit-Cost Ratios of Social Forestry Plantation
in Mittemari Watershed Development Project, Karnataka*

Items	Discount rates			
	3%	5%	8%	10%
Full benefits, net of costs, excluding the opportunity cost of grazing benefits foregone	28.61	19.22	10.38	6.85
Full benefits, net of costs, including the opportunity cost of grazing benefits foregone	10.08	7.36	4.46	3.15
Benefits reduced by 50 per cent, net of costs, excluding the opportunity cost of grazing benefits foregone	14.31	9.61	5.19	3.43
Benefits reduced by 50 per cent, net of costs, including the opportunity cost of grazing benefits foregone	5.04	3.68	2.23	1.57

Note: BC ratio: Present value of benefits expressed as a ratio over the present value of costs at 1989–90 prices for cash flows summed up over 25 years
Source: Authors' estimates

added, the BC ratios range from 3.15 to over 10. At reduced benefits, net of costs, excluding opportunity costs, the BC ratios range between 3.43 to over 14.3. If the opportunity cost of grazing benefits foregone are also added to total costs, the BC ratios under different scenarios range from 1.57 to over 5. It is significant that even when a high discount rate of 10 per cent (as used by agencies like the World Bank) is used, the social forestry project yields high returns.

The computational details are presented in Table 6.8. Detailed information on the cash flow of costs and (full) benefits, both undiscounted and discounted values at 3 per cent discount rate, over the 25-year period are presented for each of the 25 years. The table shows that at full benefits, net of costs, excluding the opportunity cost of grazing benefits foregone, the NPV is over Rs 136.40 lakh, and over Rs 127.30 lakh when opportunity costs are also added to total costs. The BC ratios are correspondingly 28.61 and 10.08.

Table 6.9 presents the IRR for the social forestry plantation in Mittemari Watershed development project. As seen from the table at

TABLE 6.8
Cash Flows of Costs and Benefits (Undiscounted and Discounted Values at 3 per cent Discount Rate) in Rupees from Social Forestry Plantation in Mittemari Watershed Development Project, Karnataka

Year	Total benefits	Total costs	Total costs inclusive opportunity costs	Discounted benefits $(5) = \dfrac{(2)}{(1+r)^t}$	Discounted costs $(6) = \dfrac{(3)}{(1+r)^t}$	Discounted costs inclusive opportunity costs	Discounted net benefits (a)	Discounted net benefits (b)
(1)	(2)	(3)	(4)	(5)	(6)	(7)	(8) = (5) − (6)	(9) = (5) − (7)
1.	–	420,594	472,760	0	408,343.69	458,990.29	−408,343.69	−458,990.29
2.	–	720	52,886	0	678.69	49,850.13	−678.67	−49,850.13
3.	–	720	52,886	0	658.90	48398.18	−658.90	−48,398.18
4.	–	720	52,886	0	639.71	46,988.53	−639.71	−46,988.53
5.	–	720	52,886	0	621.08	45,619.93	−621.07	−45,619.93
6.	–	720	52,886	0	602.99	44,291.19	−602.99	−44,291.19
7.	–	720	52,886	0	585.43	43,001.16	−585.43	−43,001.16
8.	–	720	52,886	0	568.37	41,748.70	−568.37	−41,748.70
9.	–	720	52,886	0	551.82	40,532.71	−551.82	−40,532.72
10.	–	720	52,886	0	535.75	39,352.15	−535.75	−39,352.15
11.	–	720	52,886	0	520.14	38,205.97	−520.14	−38,205.97
12.	27,000	720	52,886	18,937.26	504.99	37,093.18	18,432.26	−18,155.92
13.	27,000	720	52,886	18,385.69	490.28	36,012.79	17,895.40	−17,627.11

(cont.)

Table 6.8 (cont.)

Year (1)	Total benefits (2)	Total costs (3)	Total costs inclusive opportunity costs (4)	Discounted benefits $(5) = \frac{(2)}{(1+r)^t}$	Discounted costs $(6) = \frac{(3)}{(1+r)^t}$	Discounted costs inclusive opportunity costs (7)	Discounted net benefits (a) $(8) = (5) - (6)$	Discounted net benefits (b) $(9) = (5) - (7)$
14.	27,000	720	52,886	17,850.18	476.00	34,963.88	17,374.18	−17,113.70
15.	27,000	720	52,886	17,330.27	462.14	33,945.51	16,868.13	−16,615.24
16.	27,000	720	52,886	16,825.51	448.68	32,956.81	16,376.83	−16,131.30
17.	27,000	720	52,886	16,335.44	435.61	31996.9	15,899.83	−15,661.46
18.	27,000	720	52,886	15,859.65	422.92	31,064.95	15,436.73	−15,205.30
19.	27,000	720	52,886	15,397.72	410.61	30,160.15	14,987.12	−14,762.42
20.	27,000	720	52,886	14,949.24	398.65	29,281.70	14,550.60	−14,332.45
21.	27,000	720	52,886	14,513.83	387.04	28,428.83	14,126.79	−13,915.00
22.	27,000	720	52,886	14,091.10	375.76	27,600.81	13,715.33	−13,509.71
23.	27,000	720	52,886	13,680.68	364.82	26,796.9	13,315.86	−13,116.22
24.	27,000	720	52,886	13,282.21	354.19	26,016.41	12,928.02	−12,734.20
25.	29,159,544	155,160	207,326	13,926,761	74,105.28	99,020.52	13,852,655.33	13,827,740.56
Net Present Values				14,134,199	493,943.53	140,2317.8	13,640,255.87	12,731,881.6
BC Ratio							28.61	10.08

Note : (a) Discount Net Benefits here refer to full benefits, net of costs, excluding the opportunity cost of grazing benefits foregone.
(b) Discount Net Benefits here refers to full benefits net of costs including the opportunity cost of grazing benefits foregone.
Source: Forestry Statistics of India, 1995; Indian Council for Forestry Research and Education, Dehradun

full benefits, net of costs, excluding the opportunity cost of grazing benefits foregone, the IRR is 19.5 per cent. When the opportunity costs are also added, the IRR is over 16.4 per cent. At reduced benefits, net of costs but excluding opportunity costs, the IRR is over 16 per cent. When the opportunity cost of grazing benefits foregone are also included the IRR is around 12.5 per cent. Thus, looking at the three tables, the overall picture that emerges is that the social forestry project implemented as part of watershed development activities in Mittemari watershed development area is economically viable and yields high returns.

TABLE 6.9

Internal Rates of Return (per cent) for Social Forestry Plantation in Mittemari Watershed Development Project, Karnataka

Items	%
Full benefits, net of costs, excluding the opportunity cost of grazing benefits foregone	19.50
Full benefits, net of costs, including the opportunity cost of grazing benefits foregone	16.41
Benefits reduced by 50 per cent, net of costs, excluding the opportunity cost of grazing benefits foregone	16.01
Benefits reduced by 50 per cent, net of costs, including the opportunity cost of grazing benefits foregone	12.56

Note: Internal Rate of Return: It is the rate of return which equates the NPV to zero
Source: Forestry Statistics of India, 1995; Indian Council for Forestry Research and Education, Dehradun

Which Criterion Should We Use When There are More than One Project to Choose From?

In the foregoing we have illustrated the use of three alternate viability measures, i.e., NPV, BC ratio and IRR to assess the viability of the social forestry project. When there is only one project involved, one may employ any one or all of the above viability measures to decide whether to accept or reject the project in question. If however, the choice is between projects, the general rule is to select the project offering the highest NPV (Pearce and Nash, 1981). In making such a choice between projects one has to assess how far the projects to be appraised are comparable or exclusive. There are three contexts within which the NPV criterion may be used, viz., (i) Accept or Reject: wherein the agency or evaluator must decide whether the project in question is to be accepted or rejected. Faced with a single project, the NPV rule dictates that it should be accepted if the NPV exceeds zero, and rejected if it is less than zero; (ii) Ranking: given a series of investments with positive NPVs and a budget or capital constraint, one needs to rank them in order of preference and work down the list until a given budget is exhausted. This ranking need not necessarily be in terms of the NPV but could be in terms of the BC ratio and (iii) Mutual Exclusivity: here the agency or evaluator has to decide between the projects simply because undertaking one means that the other project cannot be undertaken (Pearce and Nash, 1981).

CONCLUSIONS

Investing in social forestry projects in India seems to be an economically-viable proposition. Using alternate viability measures, i.e., NPVs, BC ratios and IRRs, and under rigorous tests and sensitivity analysis, our analysis shows that if the expected full benefits are realized, the benefits from the social forestry project are quite high, with the IRRs ranging from 12.5 to over 19 per cent under various scenarios. Even if the expected benefits fall short by 50 per cent, netted of all costs, including the opportunity cost of grazing benefits foregone by the villagers due to establishment of community wood-lots on degraded forest lands and village commons used by them earlier for free grazing of their cattle, the social forestry project reports profits. If the direct benefits from some community wood-lots which we could not include in our analysis due to data gaps, and other indirect benefits, mostly environmental ones are also included, these profits may be still higher. Social forestry projects initiated in India to improve the tree cover on degraded forestlands and common lands, as well as meet the needs of local rural communities for fuelwood, fodder, small timber and supplementary food are thus economically viable and socially desirable.

REFERENCES

Bojo, Jan (1990): 'Benefit-cost analysis of the farm improvement with soil conservation project in Maphutseng, Mohale's Hoek district, Lesothio', in Dixon, John, David E. James, and Paul B. Sherman (eds.), *Dryland Management: Economic Case Studies*, Earthscan Publications Ltd., London.

Centre For Science and Environment (1999): *The Citizen's Fifth Report*, New Delhi.

Dixon, John, A. and Anton D. Meister (1986): 'Time horizons, discounting and computational aids,' in Dixon, J.A. and M.M. Hufschmidt (eds.), *Economic Valuation Techniques for the Environment—A Case Study Workbook*, The John Hopkins University Press, Baltimore.

Dixon, John, A., L.F. Scura, R.A. Carpenter and P.B. Sherman (1994): *Economic Analysis of Environmental Impacts*, ADB and The World Bank, Earthscan Publications Ltd., London, 2nd Edition.

Gittinger, J. Price. (1982): *Economic Analysis of Agricultural Projects*, EDI Series in Economic Development, The John Hopkins University Press, Baltimore, 2nd Revised Edition.

Hanley, Nick and Clive L. Spash (1993): *Cost-Benefit Analysis and the Environment*, Edward Elgar, Hants, U.K.

India, Planning Commission (1987): 'Evaluation Report on Social Forestry Programme', Programme Evaluation Organization, New Delhi, August.

Lakshmikanthamma, S. (1997): *Sustainability of Dryland Agriculture in India—A Case Study of Watershed Development Approach*, M.D. Publications, New Delhi.

Nadkarni, M.V., K.N. Ninan and S.A. Pasha (1994): '*The Economic and Financial Viability of Social Forestry Projects in Karnataka*', Joint Forest Management Working Paper No.16, Society for Promotion of Wastelands Development, and the Ford Foundation, New Delhi.

Ninan, K. N. (1998): *An Assessment of European—Aided Watershed Development Projects in India from the Perspective of Poverty Reduction and the Poor*, CDR Working Paper No. 98.3, Centre for Development Research, Copenhagan, Denmark, January.

Ninan, K.N. and H. Chandrashekar (1992a): 'The Green Revolution, Dryland Agriculture and Sustainability-Insights from India', in Peters, G.H. and B.F. Stanton (eds.), *Sustainable Agricultural Development—Role of International Cooperation*, IAAE, University of Oxford, Dartmouth, U.K.

—— (1992b): *Impact of Watershed Development Programmes on Dryland*

Development in India, Paper presented at the Second Meeting of the International Society For Ecological Economics, Stockholm, Sweden, 3–6 August.

Ninan, K.N. and S. Lakshmikanthamma (1994): 'Sustainable development—the case of watershed development in India', *International Journal of Sustainable Development and World Ecology*, Vol. 1, December.

Pearce, David (1992): *Assessing the Social Rate of Return from Investment in Temperate Zone Forestry*, GEC 92–07, Centre for Social and Economic Research on the Global Environment, University College, London.

Pearce, David and C.A. Nash (1981): *The Social Appraisal of Projects: A Text in Cost-Benefit Analysis*, Macmillan, London.

Pearce, David, Edward Barbier and Anil Markandya (1990): *Sustainable Development: Economics and Environment in the Third World*, Edward Elgar, Hants, England and Gower Publishing Co., Vermont, U.S.A.

Saxena, N.C., (1994): *India's Eucalyptus Craze: The God That Failed*, Sage, New Delhi.

Saxena, N.C. and Viswa Ballabh (1995): *Farm Forestry in South Asia*, Sage, New Delhi.

Srivastava, Manoj (1992): 'Survival rates in the social forestry programme', in Anil Agarwal (ed.) *The Price of Forests*, Centre for Science and Environment, New Delhi, pp. 190–204.

University of Agricultural Sciences (1990): 'Operational Research Project For Resource Management on Watershed Basis—Status Report of the Model Watershed Mittemari', Dryland Agricultural Project, Bangalore, March.

EXERCISES

Example 1

Numerical example of the calculation of net present value and benefit-cost ratio

Year	Cost	Benefit	discount factor $1/(1+.03)^t$	Discounted cost	Discounted benefit	Discounted cash flow
1	10000	0	0.9708738	9708.738	0	−9708.74
2	500	0	0.9425959	471.298	0	−471.298
3	500	0	0.9151417	457.5708	0	−457.571
4	500	12000	0.888487	444.2435	10661.84	10217.6
5	500	12000	0.8626088	431.3044	10351.31	9920.001
6	500	12000	0.8374843	418.7421	10049.81	9631.069

Year	Cost	Benefit	discount factor $1/(1+.03)^t$	Discounted cost	Discounted benefit	Discounted cash flow
7	500	12000	0.8130915	406.5458	9757.098	9350.552
8	500	12000	0.7894092	394.7046	9472.911	9078.206
9	500	12000	0.7664167	383.2084	9197.001	8813.792
10	1000	15000	0.7440939	744.0939	11161.41	10417.31
				13860.45 B/C Ratio	70651.38 0.196181	NPV = 56790.93

Discount Rate = 3 per cent
Column three presents discount factor at 3 per cent discount rate
Discount factor = $1/(1+r)^t$
where r = discount rate; and
t = time point
Column 5 presents the flow of discounted cost
The flow of discounted cost is arrived at by multiplying the cost flow (column 2) with the discount factor (column 4)
Sum of discounted cost = 13860.45
Column 6 presents the flow of discounted benefit
The flow of discounted benefit is arrived at by multiplying the benefit flow (column 3) with the discount factor (column 4)
Sum of discounted benefit = 70651.38
Net Present Value = Sum of discounted benefit – Sum of discounted cost
Therefore, NPV = 70651.38 – 13860.45 = 56790.93
B/C Ratio = The ratio of the sum of discounted benefit to the sum of the discounted cost
Therefore, B/C ratio = 70651.38/13860.45 = 0.196181

Example 2

Numerical example of the calculation of net present value and benefit-cost ratio

Year	Cost	Benefit	discount factor $1/(1+.05)^t$	Discounted cost	Discounted benefit	Discounted cash flow
1	10000	0	0.952381	9523.81	0	–9523.81
2	500	0	0.9070295	453.5147	0	–453.515
3	500	0	0.8638376	431.9188	0	–431.919
						(cont.)

Example 2 (cont.)

Year	Cost	Benefit	discount factor $1/(1+.05)^t$	Discounted cost	Discounted benefit	Discounted cash flow
4	500	12000	0.8227025	411.3512	9872.43	9461.078
5	500	12000	0.7835262	391.7631	9402.314	9010.551
6	500	12000	0.7462154	373.1077	8954.585	8581.477
7	500	12000	0.7106813	355.3407	8528.176	8172.835
8	500	12000	0.6768394	338.4197	8122.072	7783.653
9	500	12000	0.6446089	322.3045	7735.307	7413.003
10	1000	15000	0.6139133	613.9133	9208.699	8594.786
			13215.44	61823.58		NPV =
			B/C Ratio	0.21		48608.14

Discount Rate = 5 per cent
Column 3 presents discount factor at 5 per cent discount rate
Column 5 presents the flow of discounted cost
Sum of discounted cost = 13215.44
Column 6 presents the flow of discounted benefit
Sum of discounted benefit = 61823.58
Net Present Value = 13215.44 – 61823.58 = 48608.14
B/C Ratio = 61823.58 / 13215.44 = 0.21

Example 3

Discount Rate = 8 per cent

Numerical example of the calculation of net present value and benefit-cost ratio

Year	Cost	Benefit	discount factor $1/(1+.08)^t$	Discounted cost	Discounted benefit	Discounted cash flow
1	10000	0	0.9259259			-9259.26
2	500	0	0.8573388			-428.669
3	500	0	0.7938322			-396.916
4	500	12000	0.7350299			8452.843
5	500	12000	0.6805832			7826.707
6	500	12000	0.6301696			7246.951

Year	Cost	Benefit	discount factor $1/(1+.08)^t$	Discounted cost	Discounted benefit	Discounted cash flow
7	500	12000	0.5834904			6710.14
8	500	12000	0.5402689			6213.092
9	500	12000	0.500249			5752.863
10	1000	15000	0.4631935			6484.709
					NPV =	38602.46
				B/C Ratio	0.24	

Find out the discounted cost and benefit flow, NPV and B/C ratio and check your answer.

Example 4

Discount Rate = 12 per cent

Numerical example of the calculation of net present value and benefit-cost ratio

Year	Cost	Benefit	discount factor $1/(1+.12)^t$	Discounted cost	Discounted benefit	Discounted cash flow
1	10000	0	0.8928571	8928.571	0	
2	500	0	0.7971939	398.5969	0	
3	500	0	0.7117802	355.8901	0	
4	500	12000	0.6355181	317.759	7626.217	
5	500	12000	0.5674269	283.7134	6809.122	
6	500	12000	0.5066311	253.3156	6079.573	
7	500	12000	0.4523492	226.1746	5428.191	
8	500	12000	0.4038832	201.9416	4846.599	
9	500	12000	0.36061	180.305	4327.32	
10	1000	15000	0.3219732	321.9732	4829.599	
				11468.24	39946.62	NPV = 28478.38
				B/C Ratio	0.29	

Find out the discounted cash flow NPV and B/C ratio and check your answer.

Stakeholder Analysis in Joint Forest Management in India
A Case Study of Haryana Shivaliks

T.P. Singh and Ravi Hegde

Introduction

Conventional economic tools are often inadequate to examine the practicality and impacts of participatory natural resource management programmes that are marked by the presence of externalities, multiple and conflicting interests, and absence of clear property rights. Under such situations, a social analytical tool such as stakeholder analysis would be more useful for programme evaluation. Stakeholder analysis considers the key stakeholders, their private costs and benefits and the likely responses in a given situation or a system. It is useful in various contexts such as policy analysis, planning and project analysis. In this chapter, we seek to demonstrate the use of this technique through analysis of Joint Forest Management in the Shivalik Hills of Haryana, and observe that while there is a convergence of interests of stakeholders, the linkage between the resource managers and the markets is weak. Also it suggests that strengthening this linkage would be helpful for minimizing the conflicts as well as maximizing the benefits of forest management.

Forests provide a multitude of goods and services to mankind and contribute to the socio-economic and environmental welfare of a country. Their role has a far greater relevance for a developing country like India where farming is the mainstay of the national economy, which in turn is dependent on forest-based goods and services for sustained agricultural production. In addition, a range of forest produce (direct derivatives) provide livelihood security to millions of rural people and products (derived after value addition) as source of food, fodder, fuel, small timber and a variety of traded products.

India's forests and other natural resources are under enormous stress from rising human and livestock populations, rapid industrialization, urbanization and overall economic development. The past few decades have witnessed an unprecedented increase in demand for forest products, and the problem is likely to intensify further. India's population has risen from 361 million to over one billion from 1951 to 2000 with a corresponding decline in per capita forest area from 0.2 ha to 0.07 ha in the period 1951–95. The livestock population has increased from 292 million to 450 million during the same period. India supports about 18 per cent of the world population and 15 per cent of world's livestock, with only 2 per cent of world's geographical area, 1 per cent of world's forest area and 0.5 per cent of world's pasture land (Singh and Varalakshmi, 1998).

The magnitude of pressure on India's forests can also be understood by the fact that the total fuel-wood requirement is around 235 million m^3 per year as against the sustainably extractable amount of 40 million m^3. The estimated dry fodder requirement for livestock is about 780 million tonnes and that of green fodder around 932 million tonnes, while sustainable supply levels are about 56 per cent and 26 per cent, respectively. Further, industrial wood requirement, which has multiplied 24 times since independence, is 2.3 times greater than the sustainable supply level. Since independence, diversion of forest lands for non-forest users continued for quite some time with serious long-term implications. Between 1951 and 1980, about 4.3 million hectares (mha) of forest land was diverted for non-forest uses (GOI, 1987).

The impacts of permanent loss of forest cover due to forest diversion to non-forestry uses and degradation of growing stock due to excessive withdrawals are so massive that as much as 50 per cent of the land is degraded in India (Alcorn et al., 1990). Only 11.17 per cent of the land is under dense forest cover (FSI, 1997); 36.73 mha of land has good forest cover with more than 40 per cent crown density, and as much as 26.13 mha has got forest growth with 10 per cent to 40 per cent crown density, and about 5.7 mha has only scrub vegetation with crown density below 10 per cent. The ecological and regeneration status of forests is also being damaged by frequent forest fires. The Forest Survey of India estimated that nearly 53 per cent of the forest area is being affected by forest fire, 78 per cent of forests are subject to grazing, and 74 per cent forest area does not have adequate regeneration (FSI, 1996). The above situation has resulted in a serious resource imbalance. Attempts to deny or restrict access to forests with a view to conserving the remaining forests have escalated resource conflicts (Kothari, 1997).

The question of managing forest resources with due recognition of values and rights of various stakeholders is addressed. In that sense, this methodology of forest management cannot be put in any straight-jacket cost-benefit analysis. The stakeholder analysis is an alternative to such a pure economic method, but having the strength of accounting for the preferences and voices of people (i.e., stakeholders) at all the stages of designing, implementing and monitoring forest-related projects.

Need for Alternative Approach to Forest Management

A large body of research has probed the state of India's forests focusing on historical analysis of forest management, current forest utilization and policies (Damodaran, 1998). The earlier works have highlighted the radical shifts in resource management from the community-oriented approach in the pre-British era to the state-centrist approach during the British rule and in the post-independence era. They have also emphasized on the inadequacy of conservation strategies of the 1970s and 1980s based on 'untouched wilderness'. The history of the linkages between local communities and forest resources has led to the revival of the concept of community based conservation in the last two decades.

The Forest Department (FD), which is the present custodian of forests in India, is poorly equipped to save and augment forests from the mounting population pressure. As noted by Poffenburger (1990), a mere one lakh Forest Officers cannot possibly monitor the activities of the estimated 300 million rural population who are dependent on forests along with immense population of livestock. The realization that 'policing' by the Forest Department is not the solution to the problem of forest degradation has led to exploration of alternative approaches to forest management (Poffenburger et al., 1996), such as Joint Forest Management (JFM). JFM is a concept of developing partnerships between forest fringe user groups and FD on the basis of mutual trust and jointly-defined roles and responsibilities for the management of forests in the vicinity of the communities. The primary objective of JFM is to give users a stake in forest benefits and a role in planning and management for the improvement of forest conditions and productivity, while others include supporting sustainable forest management and equitable distribution of forest benefits (TERI, 1999). Based on the experiences of the ongoing joint protection efforts in some states like West Bengal, Haryana, Orissa, Bihar, etc., the Government of India issued the Guidelines on JFM on 1 June 1990, which envisaged involvement of local user-communities in protection and management of forests as partners with the FD. The resource users would organize themselves in the form of a formal institution, jointly manage the resources with the FD and share the benefits.

JFM is slowly emerging into a form of sustainable forest management tool, by seeking to balance the ecological, social and economic dimensions of forestry. Presently, 22 of the 28 states are at various stages of implementing JFM. There are 41,249 Village Forest Committees (VFC) in 17 states, and a total of 11.24 million ha of forest land is under Joint Forest Management in 14 states (TERI, 1999).

COMPLEXITY OF DESIGN AND ASSESSMENT OF JFM PROGRAMMES

Success of all programmes and projects depends on the basic framework, which they are founded on. Hence, they need careful designing before their implementation, and monitoring and evaluation during and after implementation with a view to measuring their progress and their impacts against the stated objectives. These operations are relatively simple and straight in scientific and technical projects where the output is tangible and measurable. On the other hand, designing of an approach like JFM and its assessment, which encompasses socioeconomic and environmental fabrics of society, is highly complicated due to following factors:

1. Issues or problems related to environment and natural resource base (such as air, water, forests, etc.) cut across social, economic and political boundaries, and issues related to their origin, use and impacts are wide-ranging. For example, deforestation can have negative implications not just at local levels, but at regional and global levels, and can have an impact on not only the present, but also future generations.

2. JFM related environmental resources are common property resources. For example, benefits of JFM like air, water and land including forests are for public consumption.

3. Forest resources have multiple and often competitive and conflicting uses. For example, forests and tree resources may have both productive and environmental benefits which are used by different sets of people; the timber of certain species may be required by a logging company, non-timber products by the local people, the land on which the forest comes up may be coveted by settlers and so on.

Under such complicated circumstances, designing a programme requires a holistic view of the issues. Further, the conventional economic methods (Pearce et al., 1989) are often inadequate to evaluate an approach such as JFM, as also to capture their implementability and distributional impacts (Chopra et al., 1989). By focusing on the measurement of costs and benefits of a project (or policy or programme) to the society as a whole, these techniques often do not adequately consider the distribution of costs and benefits among different stakeholders, or the winners and losers. More importantly, they overlook the fact that different stakeholders are unlikely to perceive the same environmental problems and seek the same solutions, and hence they use the same criteria for assessing the desirability or worth of a given intervention. As a result, these methods ignore the fact that several projects often fail due to opposition (or non-cooperation) of certain stakeholders who perceive that their interests have not been served.

Need for Social Analysis

Under such circumstances, social analysis, which is built beyond the conventional economic approaches, can provide a fillip, to account for the different interests of various stakeholders. Such analyses are based on the premise that every project is a social process, not merely a commercial investment, and brings into play an array of social actors (Cernea and Kudat, 1997). However, for long, projects were treated as technical or financial interventions. And hence, social dimensions of the projects aiming at bringing about a desired social change were ignored. The fact that economic processes do not occur in vacuum, but are always embedded in a social tapestry that affects their direction, face, shape and outcomes, underscores the criticality of social analysis.

Integration of economic, social, technical and environmental analyses could provide a consolidated knowledge that is distinctly more powerful in guiding project planning and execution than any of its separate parts being used in isolation. The social and behavioural mechanisms are intrinsic to development, and hence an intervention requires that the social fabric and the social context are explained and understood before-hand. Social analysis also helps to design the social goals and institutional framework within which the project operates. Another imperative for social assessment is to understand the social costs and risks associated and mitigation to be pursued, with a view to including them in the project design. Hence, social assessment is a necessary part of the set of analyses (economic, financial and technical) required for a project. Social assessments can enhance the quality at entry, increase economic returns and lay the groundwork for projects that have wider impacts and sustainability (Cernea and Kudat, 1997).

Evidently, in an approach like JFM in which multiple stakeholders are involved with a view to building an institution of communities to achieve the goals of natural resource conservation and economic development, social assessment is of paramount importance (World Bank, 2000).

WHAT IS STAKEHOLDER ANALYSIS?

One of the methods in social assessment is referred to as Stakeholder Analysis (SA). SA is an approach and procedure to gain an understanding of a system, process or a project. It involves identification of key stakeholders, an assessment of their interests and the ways in which these interests affect project riskiness and viability. It is linked to both institutional appraisal and social analysis: drawing on the information derived from these approaches and contributing to the combining of such data in a single framework. SA contributes to project design through the logical framework, and helps to identify appropriate forms of stakeholder participation (ODA, 1995).

By stakeholders is meant all those who affect, and/or are affected by the policies, decisions and actions of a system; they can be individuals, communities, social groups or institutions of any size, aggregation or level in society (Grimble and Chan, 1995). The term, thus, includes policy makers, planners and administrators in government and other organizations, as well as commercial and subsistence groups. Primary stakeholders are those ultimately affected, either positively (beneficiaries) or negatively (e.g., involuntary resettlement). Secondary stakeholders are the intermediaries in the aid-delivery process. This definition of stakeholder includes both winners and losers, and those involved or excluded from decision-making processes. Key stakeholders are those who can significantly influence, or are important to the success of the project (ODA, 1995). Geographically, stakeholders may be located in the project site (on-site) or elsewhere (off-site).

SA helps administrators and implementers to assess a project environment and to understand each others' perspectives in project negotiations. According to ODA (1995) it can help:

1. Elicit the interests of stakeholders in relation to the problems that the project is seeking to address (at the identification stage) or the purpose of the project (once it is started).
2. Identify conflicts of interests between stakeholders, that will influence assessment of project riskiness before committing funds (for proposed project activities).
3. Help to identify relations between stakeholders, and may enable 'coalitions' of project sponsorship, ownership and cooperation.
4. Help to assess the appropriate type of participation by different stakeholders, at successive stages of the project cycle.

SA aims to improve projects and policies in two ways:

1. To improve the effectiveness of programmes and policies on the ground, by explicitly considering stakeholders' interests, and identifying and dealing with conflicts (before they arise) over resources within and between stakeholder groups, and giving early consideration to ways of building on commonalities and complementarities of interest, and possibilities for cooperation and compromise.
2. To address the distributional and social impact of policies and projects in a better manner.

How did SA originate?

Stakeholder approaches and supporting methodologies in the field of management science have been established by the beginning of 1980s (Grimble and Chan, 1995). However, studies based on the concept of stakeholders and SA have taken hold in participatory programmes and natural resource management (NRM) around the 1990s (Grimble and Chan, 1995; Michener, 1998).

In the last few years, the use of the term stakeholders and the recognition of the need for some kind of SA has been emerging in various development and NRM circles (Michener, 1998; Grimble and Chan, 1995; Cernea and Kudat, 1997). However, there is still a need and scope for refinement of methodologies for systematically considering and incorporating stakeholder interests in analysis and policy making, and for linking these methods with both participatory as well as conventional micro and macro-economic approaches.

SA is related to participatory methods in several ways beginning from sharing important goals such as articulating and addressing the interests of the disadvantaged and less powerful groups. Although stakeholder approach is applied to a wide variety of areas in the development sector, there are several distinctive characteristics of NRM that make SA particularly relevant to the analysis. The rationale for using SA to address issues relating to NRM is that it can serve as a means of complementing and strengthening the policy and project assessment procedures, especially in dealing with stakeholder interests, where there are deficiencies in the conventional methods.

When is SA Required?

Consideration of the interests of different stakeholders would be useful in almost all policy-making and project-design contexts. Following are the key conditions where SA is likely to be particularly crucial (Grimble and Chan, 1995).

1. (a) Externalities: SA would be applicable where the externalities exist and (b) Unclear property rights (usufructs or ownership rights) over the resource: SA is more applicable to situations where resources (e.g., forests) are managed as common property rather than privately-owned; more particularly where traditional institutions regulating communal use and management are breaking down; and, where resources are officially owned by the state but function in practices as *de facto* open access resources.

2. Different levels of stakeholders with distinct interests and agenda: They include macro and micro interests ranging from government departments, environmental pressure groups and commercial and subsistence interests of the local farmers. In such contexts, not only the interests in natural resources but also the cognitive frameworks (knowledge base, decision-making criteria, etc.) and economic circumstances will vary considerably between stakeholders. SA would be

particularly valuable in these conditions, as opposed to situations where competition may exist over use of a resource but the main stakeholders share similar interests and are fairly homogenous (e.g., many small local farmers competing for the use of local forest produce on communal land).

3. Trade-offs to be made at the policy level over the use and management of resources: In a situation where national policy objectives encourage conservation, but local people are primarily interested in consumption or alternative uses, SA would be convenient.

What are the Contexts for SA?

Following are the broad contexts for the use of SA (Grimble and Chan, 1995).

1. Different institutional levels: The emphasis of SA, as said above, is to provide an analytical tool directly useful to policy makers and planners. However, policy is made and administered at different levels. Ranging from international enviornmental conventions, through national and regional natural resource management policy, right down to the level of designing and managing village-level community forestry and range-land projects, water-sharing schemes and the like. SA is applicable in capturing the views of all people at all levels.

2. National policy analysis: When a government wishes to establish an environmental policy and legislation to be applied across sectors, SA could be used to bring out the different sectoral interests in relation to natural resources and the environment. This would provide a basis on which a policy could be devised that is both feasible, and acceptable across government sectors.

3. Regional and local planning: SA would be particularly useful to analyze and help provide management/policy options in situations where the objectives and methods of national and regional governments interact and appear to be conflicting with the interests of the primary stakeholders.

4. Project analysis: SA would be applicable in designing and appraisal of projects where the activities of the project are likely to affect several local stakeholder groups with diverse interests (in relation to the project). These groups may be, for example, different villages, ethnic communities, farming groups and possibly men and women. Even within a village, it would be useful to examine how different subgroups behave and respond in a given situation.

SA can be used for the following purposes: (i) *ex ante* appraisal of projects and policies; (ii) *ex post* evaluation of projects and policies; (iii) research on natural resource management and change, designated to increase the understanding of general issues related to conservation and degradation; and (iv) analytical support to an on-going process of conflict resolution and cooperative management of a resource, e.g., village common pool resource.

How is SA Conducted?

SA is conducted in the following steps.

Step 1: Identifying Key Stakeholders and their Interests

The purpose of this step is to identify and list all the stakeholders and their interests and expectations. Many of the interests may be more obvious, while some others may be difficult to define, especially if they are hidden, multiple or in contradiction with the stated objectives. The thumb rule is to relate each stakeholder with either the problems that the project is trying to address its stated objectives.

This is achieved by preparing a table of stakeholders with their level of functioning (such as primary and secondary) to answer the following questions:

- Who are the potential beneficiaries
- Who might be adversely impacted
- Who are the vulnerable groups
- Who would be the supporters and opponents
- What are the relationships among the stakeholders
- What are the stakeholders' expectations of the project
- What benefits are likely to accrue
- What stakeholder interests conflict with the project goals
- What resources would the stakeholders be able to and willing to provide

Step 2: Determining Stakeholder Influence and Importance

The influence and importance that a stakeholder can have on the project is reflected in terms of the overall effect it can have on the project, such as in deciding which decisions are to be made or in facilitating or hindering its implementation (World Bank, 2000). 'Influence', refers to how powerful a stakeholder is. 'Importance' refers to those stakeholders whose problems, needs and interests are the priority of the project. If these 'important' people are excluded and are not assisted, then the project cannot be deemed a 'success'. The following questions would be helpful for the analysis:

- What are the relationships between various stakeholders
- Who has power over whom
- How are the stakeholders organized, and how can that organization be influenced or built upon
- Who controls the resources
- Who has control over information

Step 3: Drawing Out Assumptions and Risks Affecting Project Design and Participation

Based on the interests and expectations of stakeholders along with the influence and power they can wield on the system, one needs to anticipate their responses in order to construct the framework for the project. This can be achieved by making certain assumptions about the behaviour of stakeholders. Eventually, the success of a project depends, partly, on the validity of the assumptions made about its stakeholders, and the risks facing the project. Some risks are associated with the project, while some arise during implementation due to the conflicting interests among stakeholders.

Step 4: Formulating a Stakeholder Participation Strategy

It is important to define who should participate, in what ways and at which stage of the project depending upon the interests, influence and importance of stakeholders.

How to Use the Findings and Limitations of a Stakeholder Analysis?

The results of a stakeholder analysis will help to prepare the project concept note and design, and the same could serve as a basis for revision later in the project, should the situation warrant. The findings can also be used in periodic monitoring and evaluation.

It is important to recognize that there are some limitations with SA (Grimble and Chan, 1995).

1. It tends to treat different stakeholder groups as distinct entities. In reality, however, social groupings are generally not distinct and there are overlaps between groups.

2. Stakeholder groups are defined here based on each group having a distinct set of interests that distinguishes it from the others. This, however, is one of the many ways of defining groups, and may not be desirable in community initiatives that are based on cooperation amongst the participating communities. For instance, in an approach like JFM, extent of group identity, intergroup cooperation and the history of community institutions are possibly more important than the existence of shared interests in determining the success of community efforts.

3. There is an inherent methodological limitation in SA since it is aimed at specifically dealing with, analysing and managing sets of divergent interests of stakeholders. There could be some situations having conflicting interests that are based on fundamentally different conceptions and there may be no conceptual grounds on which they can be compared. Then, development of methodological tools for comparison and management becomes difficult.

4. Methods being used in SA need to be refined for application in different contexts, and procedures further developed for specific stages of analysis, in particular for conflict resolution and management. It has been shown that SA is an eclectic approach drawing concepts and methods from management science, Rapid Rural Appraisal (RRA), Participatory Rural Appraisal (PRA), common property resource theory, farming systems economics, environmental economics and political economy. The adoption of the approach to suit different purposes will similarly require inputs from a diverse range of disciplines and experience, including those not traditionally involved, such as business management and political science.

Who are the Stakeholders in JFM?

In a typical JFM programme varieties of stakeholders having varied interests would be operating at different levels of functioning as shown in Table 7.1. They are briefly discussed here.

Resource User Groups

Resource users are particularly interested in availability of the resources at present as well as over time. In the Indian context, a sizeable population is dependent forests. These include the relatively poor inhabitants of agricultural villages and tribal hamlets, whose quality of

TABLE 7.1
Stakeholders in a Typical JFM Programme

Level of stake	Stakeholders	Interests (in the order of priority)	Impact of interests on forest resources
Primary (local on-site)	Specific resource users	Availability of specific products Sustainability of such products	– or no impacts +
	Women	Fuelwood, fodder, water availability Sustainability	– or no impacts +
	Head-loaders and wood smugglers	Fuelwood and fodder Wood products	– –
	Neighbouring communities	Forest products	–
	User industries	Availability of forest product	?
	JFM committee	Forest protection	+/–
Primary (local off-site)	FD	Forest protection and augmentation	+
Secondary (local off-site)	Panchayat	Local resource management Control over funds Over-all economic development	+/–
Local/ regional	NGOs	Development of the weaker sections Natural resource conservation Institutional learning	+/– +/–
Local / regional	Political parties	Community organization	+/–
State / National level	Governments	Economic development Legal control on resources Natural resource conservation	+/– +
National / International	Donor agencies	Resource conservation and economic development (regional/ global level)	+

Note: Positive and negative impacts are designated by + and – signs, respectively
Source: Authors' estimates

life is intimately linked to the productivity and diversity of living organisms in their own restricted catchments. In a country where the subsistence of over 70 per cent of the population is dependent on land and land-based resources through agriculture and forests (Romm, 1981), community-based management systems have been crucial in sustaining the resource base and preventing them from becoming open access resources.

It is estimated that in India there are about 100 million forest dwellers in the country living in and around forest lands, and another 275 million who depend on forests for their basic livelihood security (Singh and Varalakshmi, 1998). Besides fuel wood, fodder and wood products, forests also provide a variety of non-wood products such as fruits, seeds, honey, medicinal herbs and so on. Collection of non-wood forest products (NWFP) and sale is a major activity in states such as Bihar, Andhra Pradesh, Maharashtra, Madhya Pradesh and Orissa, that have large tracts inhabited by tribals. Non-wood forest produce such as grasses, bamboo, canes, *bhabbar*, etc., used for artisan activities play an important role in the livelihood strategies of the rural poor.

Considering the high dependence on forests for these products, deforestation and decline in forest conditions can have very serious implications for rural populations and for public policy. In this context, the need for inclusion of the needs and interests of user communities and their empowerment in the conservation agenda was emphasized (Gadgil, 1993).

Women and JFM

Status of women in rural India is often not commensurate with their role in house management. As the 'hearth managers', they have to arrange for cooking fuel and water, and also for supply of fodder for livestock, besides their critical role in farming and other activities. Therefore, it is the women who suffer the most from the scarcity of fuel, fodder and water as a consequence of deforestation and forest degradation, and that is why they have a higher stake in forest management. Interventions and practices geared towards forest protection under JFM might impact women both positively as well as negatively (TERI, 1999). While women's involvement in JFM is encouraged in several states through the passage of resolutions that specifically address their enrolment to the committees, the criticism is that women's involvement is often more symbolic than active (Saxena et al., 1997; TERI, 1999). Even in areas where women's groups have been formed, the women are often ignorant and, thus, are dependent on their men or the FD to manage the affairs of the groups.

De Facto Users Under Open Access Regime

Under open access conditions, a variety of de facto users exist, such as head loaders, illicit collectors and neighbouring communities. Such practices that do not have provision *de jure* are discouraged under JFM since they provide legal backing to protection and policing by the participating community. Therefore, such interests are likely to be adversely impacted by JFM.

User Industries

User industries such as rural and cottage industries and industries using forest produce as raw material form a crucial link in the production-consumption chain of forest products by way of utilizing the raw-produce and converting them into products. Impact of JFM on such users is still not well-documented. In one case in the state of Haryana, it is reported that the local paper and pulp industry had to revise its raw-material mix due to escalation of costs in the post-JFM period leading to conflicts (Mahapatra, 1998).

Forest Department and JFM

Forest Departments (FD) are the legal custodians of forests. The story of state control over forests, started during the British rule, continued even after independence, leading to gradual erosion and loss of rights enjoyed by the communities. The forest department in the post-colonial period continued to concentrate on revenue benefits of forests. The colonial powers pursued the policy of supplying cheap raw materials to feed the industries. The 1952 Policy of Independent India maintained the status quo by perpetuating the monopoly rights of its predecessors. This ensured that monopoly rights in respect of forest resource continued to be vested with the state, which was justified on grounds of national interests in terms of criticality of such sectors as defence, communication, industries, etc., which make use of timber products.

In spite of the Social Forestry programme in the 1980s, pressure on natural forests continued to grow, and hence the situation called for evolving a new programme for management and conservation of the remaining forests. This led to the recognition that forest policies cannot be framed in isolation from the people, but must be complemented by an environment promoting sustainable use of the resource in close cooperation from the resource user groups. It was also realized that for a community-based resource management to be effective, some of the authority that the communities lost over time must be restored with adequate economic incentives.

Panchayat

Panchayats, the self-governance institutions at the village level, are the basic developmental administrative unit of the government, and their role has recently been significantly expanded with the 73rd amendment to the Indian Constitution (1992). The role of Panchayats in JFM is still unclear at the moment and the level of influence that the Panchayati Raj system should wield on the functioning of JFM institutions is a subject of debate in India (TERI, 1999).

The enhanced role of Panchayats is important for two reasons:

1. In view of the emphasis on overall village development under JFM and the Panchayat's control over funding for local development activities, its involvement can be beneficial since it can provide developmental assistance to often cash-strapped JFM institutions. Decentralisation has provided them powers for implementation of schemes for economic development and social justice, and made them a key institution in village self-governance which is important for JFM as well.

2. Matters falling within the ambit of Panchayat comprise NWFP, fuel and fodder, including social forestry and farm forestry. These are the forest usufructs provided to people under JFM agreement. This amendment, hence, empowers Panchayats, subject to state legislation, to implement NWFP, fodder and fuel development programmes that lie at the heart of JFM (TERI, 1999).

NGOs

The need for the involvement of NGOs in forest management activities is recognized by the government, as is reflected in the guidelines issued by the Government of India (1990). As provided by the guidelines, committed voluntary agencies/NGOs with proven track records, are well-suited to motivate and organize village communities and also to act as an interface between the FDs and local village communities for revival, restoration and development of degraded forests. NGOs have the required level of motivation and commitment, rapport with the local communities and identification with participatory ideals and objectives, that are often lacking in the FD.

Donor Agencies

One of the concerns of the international donor agencies is the continuing deforestation and the consequent impacts in terms of loss of biological diversity and climate change. The JFM programmes in India were started mostly with financial assistance from international donor agencies. Their interest in JFM is based on their commitment to conservation of the natural resources and the environment and, overall human welfare, globally. As far as JFM is concerned, this interest not only ensured flow of financial assistance but also provided the legitimacy for the JFM. They have been able to provide a common platform for interaction between FDs, NGOs, researchers and the villagers from the areas where JFM is being implemented. These fora have facilitated different agencies to interact, exchange and share ideas, experiences, methodologies etc., within India and in the international level. An important outcome of such as interaction has been the recognition of the need to adopt a process approach, rather than a project approach to implement JFM (Singh and Varalakshmi, 1998a).

Various Departments in State and Central Governments

While the FD is primarily responsible for the protection and augmentation of forests, various departments such as agriculture, horticulture, animal husbandry, rural development and so on are concerned with the core issues of poverty eradication and all-round development of people. If these objectives are to be fulfilled, programmes and policies of various departments, and state and central governments should be compatible with each other. Therefore, initiating interdepartmental linkages to bring about holistic rural development is very crucial in JFM. Getting other departments to involve themselves in the JFM programme is not solely to ensure fund-flow. There is a need for other departments to become active in JFM areas in their own sphere of expertise. In several states, provisions exist to include representatives from related departments.

The Case of JFM in Shivalik Hills, Haryana

The Shivalik Hills form a belt of low-lying rugged hills along the foot of the Himalayas, extending from the Brahmaputra valley on the east to the Potwar plateau and the Bannu plains (in Pakistan) on the west. The belt covers about 3 million ha in the four north-western states of Haryana, Punjab, Himachal Pradesh and Jammu and Kashmir; and extends over about 400 km in these states, falling between 75 ° 35' to 77 ° 30' E and 30 ° 10' and 30 ° 30' N. These hills are characterized by extremely rugged and broken steep slopes, serrated outlines, and sheer precipices 70 m or higher, standing out sharply at places. The elevation varies from between 280 to 1500 m above mean sea level.

The past systems of forest management in the Shivaliks have recognized the degradation that has become endemic to the forest due to increasing pressures. The ecological history of the area shows that it had a rich forest cover earlier (Chopra et al., 1989; Singh and Varalakshimi,1998).

The seriousness of the problem of land degradation in the Shivaliks came into sharp focus in the mid-70s when deforestation in the catchments of Sukhna lake reached alarming levels, causing serious problems of soil erosion and siltation. Various engineering and vegetative measures became ineffective due to the lack of cooperation from the villagers in maintaining these measures. This led to the evolution of the participatory approach of forest management by enlisting people's participation in the protection and management of forests, jointly with the Haryana Forest Department (HFD) under the JFM programme (Chopra et al., 1989).

The strategy adopted for obtaining people's cooperation was based on the construction of water-harvesting structures to provide irrigation water to rainfed agriculture and that resulted in increased crop-yields by two to three times. This proved to be very effective in eliciting the participation of local communities. Water stored in earthen dams was distributed equally among all the households irrespective of land ownership, helping communities to gain confidence in the participatory approach. With effective conservation, distribution, and management of stored water, Water Users' Association (WUA) came into existence. This captured the attention of farmers and gave a new direction to the concept of watershed rehabilitation. In addition to the protection provided to forests, the catchment was treated by constructing silt detention structures and plantation of trees and grasses. The *bhabbar* grass that has predominant use among the people, was available for harvesting within a year of planting. The grass productivity increased from 40 kg to 2000 kg per ha by 1986, besides an increased tree cover. For sustaining the interests of villagers it was considered necessary to share the increased productivity of forest produce between the HFD and community. For this purpose, the WUAs were reorganized into Hill Resource Management Societies (HRMSs) registered under the Societies Registration Act of 1860.

Subsequent to a decade of experimentation in select villages such as Sukhomajri, Dhamala, Jatanmajri and Nada, the HFD developed a number of strategies to enlist the participation of communities from a number of villages in forest protection and management. These strategies effectively motivated the communities to establish social fencing and other protection and management systems.

Socio-economic Profile of Village Communities

The project covers 38 villages, with 2726 families with a total population of 18,184. The population density of the HRMS villages is 121 persons/km^2 as against the state average of 372 persons/km^2. The family size varies from 6.8 to 11.6. Children constitute about 48 per cent of the population. The average number of female members in the villages is about 824 per 1000 males. The literacy rate of women is 40.47 per cent as against the male literacy rate of 69.1 per cent.

Most of the villages are heterogeneous comprising of 5–10 castes. However, some of them are mono-caste villages. Castes in Haryana, quite akin to the Indian context, have come to serve as a reflection of the socio-economic status of people. Castes such as *Jats* and *Gujjars* have larger land and livestock holdings and are considered as dominant, while *Bhanjaras* and *Bhanjdas* are more or less resourceless and are involved in forest-based crafts such as rope making (from *bhabbar* grass) and basket making (from bamboo) respectively, while the rest are either into agriculture or wage-earning.

About 48 per cent of the families in Haryana JFM villages are engaged in farming; 23 per cent are wage earners, and 20 per cent are in service sectors. The size of land holding varies from 6 *bigha*s to 48 *bigha*s. Among the total livestock population, buffaloes are the maximum in number (44 per cent of total livestock and 2.44 animals per household) followed by cows (23 per cent); bullocks (12 per cent), goats (9.16 per cent) and camels (0.36 per cent). Green grass is the commonly used fodder. In all, 43 per cent of the families of the JFM area collect grass from the forests, 33 per cent from agricultural fields, and 24 per cent both from 'forest' as well as the fields.

All the villages have metallic roads and electricity connection. The pattern of energy consumption in the HRMS areas suggests that firewood is the primary source of fuel for 99.45 per cent of the area and dungcake accounts for 75.45 per cent households. In the case of commercial fuels, kerosene is used by 24.83 per cent of the households, while only 4.73 per cent of the households use Liquified Petroleum Gas (LPG).

Benefit Distribution Under JFM

The benefits under Haryana JFM consist of water, fodder, *bhabbar* grass, bamboo, etc. Benefits are shared on the basis of an equitable distribution. Different HRMSs have evolved different methods for meeting the needs of different sections considering the resource status of the households, needs for forest products, ability to pay and so on. The specific benefits are shared in the following way.

Fodder

A nominal fee is payable for cutting grass in their respective area, as decided by the HRMS. This amount depends on factors such as the lease amount payable to the FD and the households' ability to pay. In several instances, the fee varies depending on the size of livestock holding. Women-headed and resource-poor households are exempted or subsidized, widows with no earning members are provided grass free of cost. Since grazing in the forests is totally banned, households having goats are allowed to graze them on the village commons. In several cases, big landowners allow the poor to cut grass from their fields.

Bhabbar grass

Netting on the cots in the villages are made of *bhabbar* grass; the weaving is done by the family members. Each member in the HRMS is allowed one or two head-loads of *bhabbar* every year. The *Bhanjara* community which makes ropes from *bhabbar* is allowed to cut more grass than the above stipulated norm. The community members are employed for grass-cutting, wherein they get half of the harvest in lieu of their wages.

Bamboo

Bhanjadas are weave baskets from bamboo. They are provided with an annual permit for bamboo by the HFD on nominal fees. They are also responsible for proper harvesting of bamboos, clearing the forests of debris and preventing fires and thefts. Other members of the villages obtain fodder and fuel wood but not bamboo from the same bamboo forest.

Irrigation Water

One of the activities in JFM is the management of water-harvesting structures and the regulation of water use by charging a fee to the user, and the auctioning of the dam for pisciculture. There are both landed and landless people in a village. While the landed need the irrigation water, the landless do not. Nonetheless, all of them are involved in the management of water-harvesting structures. Both the groups have equal access to the water, although the landless have little use of it. In several cases, the landless sell their share of water to the landed at a mutually-agreeable price or that determined by the HRMS. In some cases, the landless give their water rights to the landed in exchange for cutting grass from the fields of the landed. In several other cases, the landless relinquish their rights on water, and in lieu of it are not charged any fee for grass.

STAKEHOLDER ANALYSIS IN SHIVALIK JFM

An attempt has been made to use SA in the JFM Programme in the Shivalik Hills of Haryana. The objective of this analysis is to acquaint the readers with the process of conducting SA step by step, and using its findings for decision making. Although the JFM in the Shivaliks is over a decade old, for the purpose of understanding, the present analysis is carried out as a case of an *ex ante* appraisal.

In the context of an analysis using SA, a combination of tools and techniques needs to be applied for gathering information on various aspects. However, the present analysis draws inputs from our work in the field of JFM in the Shivaliks (Singh and Varalakshmi, 1998; Varalakshmi, et al., 1999; TERI, 1999).

TABLE 7.2
Stakeholders in Shivalik JFM

Level of stake	Stakeholders	Interests (in the order of priority)
Primary (local on-site)	Farming groups (*Gujjars and Jats*)	Availability of water Fodder and fuelwood
	Forest dependants (rope-maker and basket weavers)	Availability of specific forest products Sustainability Fuelwood Fodder Water
	Wage-earners (non-farming groups working for wages in villages and towns)	Fuelwood Fodder Water
	Women (mainly at home)	Fuelwood, fodder, water availability Sustainability
	HRMS (association of user groups)	Forest protection Water management and distribution
	Wood Smugglers	Wood products
	Neighbouring communities	Forest products
Primary (local off-site)	HFD represented by Beat Guard / Forester / Range Officer/ DFO	Forest protection and augmentation
	Ballarpur Industries (BPM)	Availability of bubbar grass at cheap prices
Secondary (local off-site)	Panchayat	Local resource management Control over funds Overall economic development
Local/ regional	NGOs (TERI, etc.)	Natural resource conservation Institutional learning Over all development
Local/regional	Political parties	Community organization
State/National level	Governments	Economic development Natural resource conservation
National/ International	Donor agencies (Ford Foundation)	Resource conservation and economic development (regional/ global level)

Source: Authors' estimates

Stakeholders and Their Interest

Primary Stakeholders

1. Local on-site: Among the primary stakeholders on-site, the important ones are the people who are primarily dependent on forest resources for livelihood, such as the *bhanjaras* and *bhanjdas*. Besides *bhabbar* grass and bamboo, they require fuel wood and fodder for their own use. Farming groups are important in many respects. They are the dominant sections of the population in terms of sheer number, land and livestock resources they control, and their requirement of forest-based resources such as water for irrigation, fuel wood and fodder for household consumption. Wage-earning groups are also in significant numbers, and have varying requirement for forest-based resources such as fuel wood, grass and fodder. Women have a higher stake in forest-based resources and the JFM. Equal share in irrigation water for the participating households and its saleability in the emerging water-market in the locality has enhanced the economic stake of all the households in JFM.

HRMS is the formal institution of participating communities, and has multi-faceted stakes in JFM. It has to ensure forest protection, distribution of benefits among the participating households and also the development of the village.

When the common pool resource management turns out to open-access regime, a range of *de facto* users emerge (such as head-loaders, smugglers, adjoining communities and so on). However, in the context of Shivalik JFM, such activities are curbed.

2. Local off-site: FD has an enhanced stake in JFM since it is sharing the responsibility of forest protection and development with the interest groups. A responsible and mature community organization, capable of ensuring forest protection is their interest.

The Ballarpur Paper Mills (BPM) had, for long, monopoly access to *bhabbar* that is used as a raw-material for paper making. It used to buy 80 per cent of *bhabbar* from the area. An area of forest used to be leased out to it at a nominal price by the HFD. After the formation of HRMS, the mill had to buy the *bhabbar* from the society since the forest is now leased out to them. With the price of bhabbar increasing and the mill being unable to buy at the price, they switched to wood-based raw material in 1997. With the demand for *bhabbar* coming down, and HRMS not agreeing to reduce the price of *bhabbar*, many villages are unable to sell their *bhabbar*. This results in a stand-off between the mill and the HRMSs (Mahapatra, 1998).

Secondary Stakeholders

Panchayat, although a major stakeholder *de jure*, does not have much say in JFM. Tata Energy Research Institute (TERI), which is the NGO facilitating the implementation of JFM, is interested in ensuring the conservation of forest resources and the well-being of the communities. JFM is also offering an opportunity for institutional learning. Political parties do not have a major role in the Shivaliks since JFM is not very high on their agenda. State and national governments also have stakes in JFM through their commitment to the development of the communities and natural-resource conservation. The Ford Foundation, as a donor agency, is committed to global sustainable development and natural-resource conservation, and has its interests in JFM.

Various related departments and other institutions such as agriculture, animal husbandry, soil and water conservation, Rural Development etc., are not included due to their lesser involvement in JFM per se.

Stakeholder Influence and Importance

As shown in the methodology, the second step in conducting SA is to identify the relative power, influence and importance of the stakeholders summarized in Table 7.3.

The farming groups have a higher influence in the community, mainly deriving their power from being large in number, by their control over the local resources, and their socio-economic status. They are important to the project also, since they can contribute to the project's success, and, in turn, can potentially be benefited from the project. Forest dependants such as *Bhanjadas* and *Bhanjaras* are relatively weaker due to their social and economic marginalization in the society. However, they are important to the project since they have a direct economic stake in the forest resources. Further, they possess the key skills required for local value addition of the products, and can largely be benefited from the project. Similarly, wage earners too do not have much influence, but can be important to the project. Women are a special category of stakeholders and are important to the project since they have a large stake in the project. The HRMS has a high influence on JFM by providing local organization and leadership,

TABLE 7.3
Stakeholder Influence and Importance

Level of stake	Stakeholders	Degree of influence	Variables affecting the relative power and influence	Degree of importance
Primary (local on-site)	Farming groups	High	Socio-economic and political status Control over resources	High
	Forest dependants	Low	Skills	High
	Non-farming groups	Low	–	High
	Women	Low	–	High
	Wood smugglers	–	–	Low
	Neighbouring communities	Low	–	Low
	BPM	High	Control over market	High
	HRMS	High	Organization and leadership Control over strategic resources	High
Primary (local off-site)	FD represented by Beat Guard /Forester/ Range Officer/DFO	High	Authority of leadership Control over strategic resources	High
Secondary (local off-site)	Panchayat	–	Control over resources Legal backing	Medium
Local/ regional Political	NGO	High	Key knowledge Negotiating position	High (initially)
Local/ regional	Political parties	–	Political power	Low
State/ National level	Governments	High	Authority Legal power Control over budget	Low
Inter-national	Donor agencies	High	Monetary Political	High

Source: Authors' estimates

and can effectively regulate the behaviour of resource users towards forests and ensure effective protection.

FD is an important stakeholder in terms of authority and control over forests. It can provide the necessary legal and financial back-up for JFM, and also benefit from effective forest conservation likely to be brought about from the project. Panchayats do not seem to have much influence and may not be important for the project. TERI, as an NGO, is influential in terms of its credibility and the consequent influence over the policy-making bodies. It possesses key technical knowledge and can monitor the progress through research, and it can also benefit through institutional learning. It is important for the project since involvement of an NGO is a necessary condition for JFM.

Political parties may be locally influential. However, JFM per se may not be very important for them, and, hence, are not important from the project point of view. State and national governments wield influence over JFM through their authority in decision making and control over the budget.

A donor agency has considerable clout in the state and central governments and in policy making. It can provide the necessary financial resources and technical inputs for the programme.

Responses of Stakeholders

In the third step, assumptions regarding the roles and responses of the stakeholders are made. Before implementation of JFM, certain assumptions are to be made about the behaviour of the communities and their responses vis-à-vis JFM. It could be expected that JFM would work well if these assumptions remain valid. Table 7.4 captures the likely project impacts and the consequent responses of the stakeholders.

The striking features are that there is an apparent match of interest of most of the stakeholders (Table 7.2), and the likely impacts of the projects are consistent with their interests and expectations (Table 7.3). If JFM ensures protection to forests, FD's interests in terms of forest conservation are fulfilled. From the communities' perspective, their interests are best served if the programme offers a set of benefits such as irrigation water for agriculture, fodder for livestock, fuel wood and also specific products such as *bhabbar* grass, bamboo, and so on. Interests of the dominant farming groups are served since water is available for their farmlands and also fodder for their livestock. Forest-dependent communities could greatly benefit from JFM since forest produce of their interest is available at a lesser investment of their labour and money, and also the long-term sustainability of these

TABLE 7.4

Stakeholder Responses and Roles

Level of stake	Stakeholders	Impact of project	Likely response towards project	Resources which would be mobilised by the stakeholders
Primary (local on-site)	Farming groups	Water Fodder and fuelwood	+	Time and effort (individual)
	Forest dependants	Bamboo/*Bhabbar* Water Fodder and fuelwood	 +	Time and effort (individual)
	Wage earners	Water for sale Fodder and fuelwood Increased wage (indirectly)	+ +	Time and effort (individual)
	Women	Water Fodder and fuelwood	 +	Time and effort (individual)
	Wood smugglers	Non-availability	–	Nil
	Neighbouring communities	Non-availability	–	Nil
	BPM	Increased *bhabbar* availability Higher prices for *bhabbar*	+/–	Uncertain
	HRMS	Say in resource management Village development Institutional learning	 +	Time and effort at the community level Monetary (at a later stage)
Primary (local off-site)	FD	Effective forest conservation and development Job made simple	+ +	Legal backing Monetary

Level of stake	Stakeholders	Impact of project	Likely response towards project	Resources which would be mobilised by the stakeholders
Secondary (local off-site)	Panchayat	Natural resource conservation	+	Institutional
		Village development	+	Monetary
		Dilution of power and responsibilities	–	Uncertain
Local/ regional	NGOs	Natural resource conservation	+	Technical
		Village development		Legal
Local/ regional	Political parties	Community organization	+/–	Uncertain
State/ National level	Governments	Natural resource conservation Village development	+	Legal Monetary
International	Donor agencies	Natural resource conservation	+	Monetary
		Village development		Institutional

Note: Positive and negative responses are designated by + and – signs, respectively.
Source: Authors' estimates

resources is ensured to a large extent. For the non-farming groups, the major benefit, besides fodder and fuel, is water. They can benefit not only from sale of their share of water, but also from the enhanced opportunities for wage earning as a result of flourishing agriculture. Hence, all of them are likely to respond positively towards JFM.

The response of the illegal users can be expected to be negative since they are the losers. The response of the BPM is difficult to predict and its response could be positive or negative depending upon the way it perceives the JFM. It is important to highlight the fact that although it appears to be a loser initially, it can benefit from the programme in the long run because of enhanced land productivity and assured supply of *bhabbar*.

The FD can be expected to provide the necessary support not only through legal and institutional means, but also through initial financial assistance. On the other hand, the response of the Panchayat is not easy to predict. The state and central governments can be expected to be positive about the programme.

In all, in the Shivaliks, due to the potentially positive impact of the JFM programme at all levels, majority of the stakeholders can be expected to respond positively. It can also be assumed that interest groups are willing to invest their time and effort individually, and also collectively through HRMS.

Participation Strategy

The final stage in SA is to formulate a participation strategy for stakeholders as presented in Table 7.5.

The present participation patterns of stakeholders indicates that, although there is consultation amongst other stakeholders, the linkage with BPM (or with market in general) is not existing. If the BPM were to be an active partner in JFM, it would, probably, be possible to maximize the revenue brought about by the utilization of *bhabbar* grass by the BPM. This linkage is necessary not only for maximizing the profitability of the products generated under JFM, but also for a more evolved and successful model of JFM. In view of this, the participation strategy needs to be revised (Table 7.6).

It can be seen that the at the identification stage, the FD should take

TABLE 7.5

Existing Participation Matrix

Type of participation	Who	Consult whom	Partnership with	Control and responsibility
Identification	FD	Interest groups NGO	Interest groups NGO	FD and HRMS assisted by NGO
Formulation	FD and HRMS assisted by NGO	Interest groups Panchayat	Interest groups Donor agency	FD and HRMS assisted by NGO
Implementation	FD and HRMS facilitated by NGO	NGO Donor agency	Interest groups Donor agency	FD and HRMS Facilitated by NGO
Monitoring and evaluation	NGO	Interest groups HRMS Donor agency	FD and HRMS	NGO assisted by FD and HRMS

Source: Authors' estimates

TABLE 7.6
Recommended Participation Matrix

Type of participation	Who	Consult whom	Partnership with	Control and responsibility
Identification	FD	Interest groups NGO	Interest groups NGO Donor agency	FD and HRMS assisted by NGO
Formulation	FD and HRMS assisted by NGO	Interest groups Panchayat	Interest groups Donor agency[b]	FD and HRMS assisted by NGO
Implementation	FD and HRMS facilitated by NGO	NGO Donor agency	Interest groups Donor agency[b] BPM[a]	FD and HRMS Facilitated by NGO
Monitoring and evaluation	NGO	Interest groups HRMS BPM[a] Donor agency[b]	FD and HRMS	NGO assisted by FD and HRMS

Note: a, b are added on to make the participation more functional.
Source: Authors' estimates

the initiative and consult the interest groups and the NGO and forge a partnership with them and the donor agency. The FD, NGO and the community institution—HRMS—should begin the project formulation in consultation with interest groups, Panchayat, BPM (wherever *bhabbar* is the major produce, otherwise it is the network of traders) and the donor agency. The total responsibility should be shared by the FD and HRMS, to be assisted by an NGO. At the implementation stage, which would be in partnership with the interest groups, the donor agency and BPM, the NGO needs to assist the FD and HRMS in implementation. The responsibility of monitoring and internal evaluation would be that of the NGO in partnership with FD and HRMS which would consult interest groups, BPM and the donor agency.

The above findings could be used either to provide an understanding of the entire intervention in an *ex ante* appraisal, or be used as basic framework for monitoring and evaluation and a more improved form of JFM. The same approach can be used to other areas where JFM is still emerging.

Are Stakeholders' Interests Free of Conflicts?

In this context, SA has to provide answers to a number of questions such as:

- Which stakeholders' interests are going to receive priority?
- How the interests of all the important and influential stakeholders will be met in order to ensure their cooperation
- What is the common ground on which compromise between pertinent stakeholders can be based?
- How are the conflicts between stakeholders going to be resolved or controlled?

This process of managing stakeholder interests and conflicts is being institutionalized under the JFM. However, the actual process is still to develop.

There are several conflicts arising in JFM in the Shivaliks at various levels—within and between villages and societies. The causes of conflicts range from resource demarcation, benefit sharing, fund-utilization, financial transparency and so on. Some of them are major while some minor, but a large number of them have been resolved amicably.

As the JFM institution matures and becomes more widespread, the degrees of conflicts are likely to increase. As a more lucrative range of NWFPs mature, and the sharing of timber harvests becomes regularized, questions of equity and distribution of benefits is likely to create new management challenges and conflict-resolution skills (Saxena, et al., 1997; Singh and Varalakshmi, 1998; TERI, 1999). Therefore, conflicts are liable to increase over resources' use between adjoining villages, the landless, non-forest fringe villages migratory herders, etc. The typical conflict mechanisms in a JFM programme are depicted in Table 7.7.

There could be four general categories of conflicts based on the actors involved and the relative power they wield: micro-micro, micro-macro, macro-micro or macro-macro (Conroy et al, 1998 as cited in TERI, 1999). Micro-micro conflicts occur between subgroups of one protection committee (multiple hamlets, villages, power-groups within a village, etc.) or with other communities, but they are more or less on an equal footing.

Macro-micro conflicts arise between stakeholders on an equal footing, as when government agencies like the FD take decisions that adversely impact micro-level stakeholders such as FPCs. Such conflicts

TABLE 7.7

Conflict Matrix

	Directly related to protection	Indirect effect on protection
Conflicts within protection community	One sub-group refuses to abide by protection and harvesting rules	Conflicts between two sub-groups who refuse to co-operate any longer in various issues leading to violation of protection
Between protection communities and other stakeholders	Other interested parties (other villagers, timber merchants, etc.) do not recognize the community's protection rules	Conflicts not relating to issues other than protection (such as personal disputes, party-politics, etc.) indirectly affecting forest protection

Source: TERI, 1999

are very common and stem from policy decisions of the state (such as benefit sharing, access to NTFP, marketing, etc.). Saxena (1997) recounts a situation in Orissa where bamboo is made available at subsidized prices to paper industries, and often the communities resort to stealing. When one community protecting the bamboo found that all the bamboo in the final harvest of 1997 went to a private contractor holding a 10-year lease beginning 1989, it resulted in a micro-macro conflict.

Micro-macro conflicts arise when the micro-level stakeholders take decisions that go against agreements worked out with higher level stakeholders (say FD). The failure to ensure protection of a forest by the participating community would lead to such conflicts. Macro-macro conflicts represent a difference in objectives between departments, programmes, etc. of the government. For example, the transfer of ownership rights of NTFPs in scheduled areas to Panchayats might lead to conflicts between the JFM programme and Panchayat Raj programme of the government.

Conflicts have arisen due to the complexity and diversity of stakeholders and stakes, both within and between villages, and between/among HRMSs. The origin and nature of conflicts are influenced by the socio-economic profile of the community, functioning of HRMS and the level of community participation in the deliberations. In several cases, conflicts that have arisen over resource demarcation, benefit sharing or fund-utilization, indicate the improved understanding and increased involvement by the community members.

Arbitration for Conflict Resolution

Despite the best efforts at minimizing disputes, they are bound to surface when arbitration becomes necessary. Dispute arbitration is a pivot upon which the rest of the institution rests, and effective and quick resolution is necessary. In a study conducted in Bolangir district of Orissa, where originally 45 communities had been active in forest conservation, in 1998 the number reduced to 30, which was due to their inability to resolve conflicts (Conroy et al., 1998 as cited in TERI, 1999).

Broadly, there can be two types of approaches that can be applied to stakeholder interests and conflicts. Following (Grimble and Chan, 1995), such approaches lie along a continuum:

$$\leftarrow - - - - - - - \text{Continuum} - - - - - - - - \rightarrow$$

Round table negotiations	Top-down analysis
Conflict resolution reached through the initiative of primary stakeholders, where outsiders play a marginal and supportive role.	Participation of primary-local stakeholders is minimal.

Although the two approaches outlined above are generally applicable to different contexts, they are not mutually exclusive. On the other hand, using them in a combination would be more effective. For example, the top-down approach may be used to identify several feasible options, which are then selected and modified through discussion with various stakeholders.

Dispute arbitration is possible by a number of entities including formal arbitration by the FD, informal intervention by the FD, NGOs, Panchayat, the committee and village members themselves, as well as other interested parties such as the political leaders, religious leaders and so on (TERI, 1999).

CONCLUSION

We have tried to give an understanding of the SA, and take the reader through the various steps of conducting it so that it can potentially become a useful technique in social cost-benefit analysis.

As JFM is emerging as an important institution for sustainable forest management approach in India, the basic framework for the programme has to be robust with a holistic view of the issues. As a typical Natural Resources Management (NRM) programme, JFM has diverse stakeholders having a wide array of interests. Hence, it is important to analyze the stakeholders' interests beforehand and anticipate conflicts with a view to resolve them as and when they surface. SA could be specifically useful in this area.

It is clear from the SA of Shivalik JFM, that although there is a common interest of all the stakeholders, the direct linkage between JFM and the market in general, and with BPM in particular, is missing. Strengthening this linkage could not only minimize conflicts, but also help maximize the revenue to HRMS.

The SA emerged in response to the perceived deficiency of conventional approaches for assessing and designing projects and policies. While SA seeks to fill this gap, it is again emphasized that it complements approaches such as Benefit-Cost Analysis (BCA). Nevertheless, though SA has limited objectives and is not necessarily useful in all contexts, it is believed that it will be an important aid both to understand problems and to improve policy and project design in many developmental situations.

Evidently, in spite of the limitations, SA has potentially a wide range of applications. It is better developed as an analytical tool rather than as a method for conflict mitigation or resolution. It is a useful tool for policy makers and planners working in the area of natural resource management. Its specific advantage is that it provides procedures for getting to the heart of a problem and for understanding (and coming to grips with) the reasons underlying a potential or actual conflict of interest that might threaten the very success of a project.

REFERENCES

Alcorn, J. S., D. Berwick, D. Groenfeldt, M. Flickinger, and Hatziolos (1990): *Opportunities for Eco-development in buffer Zones: An Assessment of Two Case Studies in Western India*, Biodiversity Support Programme, WWF, Washington, USA.
Arnold, J. E. M. (1990): Social Forestry and Communal Management in India, Social Forestry Network, Paper 11b, Overseas Development Institute, London.
Bhatt, C. P. (1990): 'The *Chipko Andolan*: Forest conservation based on people's power'. *Enviornment and Urbanization*, 2: 7–8.

Cernea, M. M. and A. Kudat (eds.), (1997): *Social Assessments for Better Development: Case Studies in Russia and Central Asia*, The World Bank, Washington D.C.

Chopra, K., G. Kadekodi, and M. N. Murty (1989): *Participatory Development*, Sage Publication, New Delhi.

Damodaran, A. (1998): 'Stakeholder management policies for sustainable biodiversity services in India', *Decision* 25 (1–4): 63–78.

FSI (1996): *The State of Forest Report, 1995*, Forest Survey of India, Dehra Dun.

—— (1997): *The State of Forest Report, 1996*, Forest Survey of India, Dehra Dun.

Gadgil, M. (1993): 'Biodiversity and India's degraded lands', *Ambio*, 22 (2–3): 167–72.

Gadgil, M. and R. Guha (1992): *This Fissured Land: Ecological History of India*, Oxford University Press, New Delhi.

—— (1995): *Ecology and Equity: The Use and Abuse of Nature in Contemporary India*, Penguin Books, New Delhi, p. 213.

GOI (1987): *India's Forests*, Ministry of Enviornment and Forests, Government of India, New Delhi.

Grimble, M. and M. Chan (1995): 'Stakeholder analysis for natural resource management in developing countries: some practical guidelines for making management more participatory and effective' *Natural Resource Forum*, 19 (2): 113–24.

Kothari, A. (1997): 'India explores joint management of protected areas', *Ecodecision*, Winter, 49–52.

Mahapatra, R. (1998): 'Sukhomajri at the crossroads', *Down to Earth*, 15 December, pp. 29–36.

Michener, V. J. (1998): 'The participatory approach: Contradiction and co-option in Burkina Faso', *World Development*, 26 (12): 2105–18.

ODA (1995): *Guidance Note on How to Do Stakeholder Analysis of Aid Projects and Programmes*, Overseas Development Administration, London.

Pearce, D., A. Markandya and E. B. Barbier (1989): *Blueprint for a Green Economy*, Earthscan, London.

Poffenburger, M. (1994): 'The resurgence of community forest management in eastern India', in Western, D. and R. M. Right (eds.): *Natural Connections and Perspectives in Community Based Conservation*, Island Press, Washington D.C., pp. 53–7.

Poffenburger, M, P. Bhattacharya, A. Khare, A. Rai, A. Roy, S. B., N. Singh and K. Singh, (1996): *Grassroots Forest Protection: Eastern Indian Experience*. Research Network Report # 7. Asia Forest Network, Berkley, p. 84.

Poffenburger, (1990): Forest Management Partnerships: Regenerating India's

Forests, Executive Summary of the workshop on Sustainable Forestry, September 10–12, New Delhi.

Romm, J. (1981): 'Uncultivated half of India', *Indian Forester*, 107: 1–21.

Saxena, N. C. (1996): Joint Forest Management in India, Empowering the people or another development bandwagon, CIFOR, Bogor, Indonesia.

Saxena, N. C., M. Sarin, R. V. Singh and T. Shah (1997): Western Ghats Forestry Project: An independent study of implementation experience in Canara Circle, Karnataka Overseas Development Administration, New Delhi.

Singh, T.P. and Varalakshmi (1998): The Decade and Beyond—Evolving Community-State Partnership, TERI, New Delhi.

Sivaramakrishnan, K. (1995): 'Colonialism and Forestry in India, Imagining the past in present', *Comparative Studies in Society and History*, 37 (1): 3–40.

TERI (1999): National Study on Joint Forest Management, Report submitted to the Ministry of Environment and Forests, Government of India, New Delhi.

Varalakshmi, V., R. Hegde and T. P. Singh (1999): 'Trends in grassroots institutional evolution—a case from joint forest management programme in Haryana, India', *International Journal of Sustainable Development and World Ecology* (6): 1–11.

World Bank (2000): Social assessment http://wbln0018.worldbank.org/essd/kb.nsf/

Valuing the Health
Impacts of Air Pollution[1]

Jyoti Parikh

HEALTH IMPACTS OF AIR POLLUTION

Environmental degradation of air, water or soil, always affects different segments of society differently. First, it is often in a polluted environment where the poor often find a place to live. Second, the basic health, sanitary and dietary conditions of the poorer sections of the population make them more vulnerable to a degraded environment. Third, while discussing the economic costs of pollution, the burden of the cost of remedial measures (like medical expenses) puts a relatively higher strain on the poor man's resources as compared to other sections of the society.

The levels of air pollution are rising in practically all the cities and towns. The consequences of this pollution need to be estimated and valued so as to draw attention to the extent of social costs and the need for remedial measures. We start with a case study of air pollution in Mumbai to estimate the health costs using the cost of illness method, where data was available for 12 years to measure the cost of morbidity. The cost elements include costs of medicines, doctor's visits, travels, hospitalization and so on, depending on the fractions incurring these costs. The loss of productivity is measured in simple terms as loss of workdays. A discussion on cost of human mortality is also included. To illustrate, the cost of mortality is estimated using several approaches, viz., statistical value, human capital approach and workmen's

---

[1] Material for this chapter is taken from a project report on Economic valuation of air quality degradation in Chembur, Mumbai, India, by Indira Gandhi Institute for Development Research (IGIDR).

compensation act. Also projected here are the difficulties in measuring these costs in the face of slum population, poverty and inability to pay by the poor. The survey carried out also shows the illnesses and deaths among vulnerable groups viz., different age groups, poor people staying on certain sites and so on.

We aim at establishing the physical linkages, i.e., the impacts of air pollution on human health, and subsequently leading to increased morbidity. The human body possesses a particularly useful and ingenious faculty to deal with urban air pollution. But, with large quantities of pollutants the ability of lungs to supply oxygen to the brain and other organs gets affected. The body functions suffer and the chain reaction affects the general well-being of a system. The economics follow from such physical linkages.

In a developing country such as India, where the longevity and the general health status of the average citizen is increasing, it is difficult to determine the detrimental effects of air pollution. The numbers, if correlated without care, may suggest that even as pollution levels rise, status of health is improving. Clearly, such a conclusion misleads the policy makers. The fact is that without the muffling effects of air pollution, perhaps present-day health status of the average Mumbai resident would have been much better! Such calculations of improvement of health status on account of poor air quality are an integral part of economic valuation of environmental degradation.

There are costs associated with air pollution. However, the true costs are much higher, as the health expenditure could have had much better uses that could bring human welfare or earn reasonable rate of return elsewhere through other investment opportunities. Various components of the health expenditures interpreted economically are:

- Opportunity cost of money spent on curative medicine
- Opportunity cost of money spent on preventive medicine
- Opportunity cost of social infrastructure on health, e.g., money invested in hospitals, dispensaries and clinics for treatment of diseases caused by air pollution. For example, if done nothing for over ten years, an extra hospital may be needed to help the increased number of patients
- Opportunity cost of time of medical doctors/nurses
- Direct cost to the economy from lost output due to sickness/ decreased productivity of patients suffering from diseases caused by air pollution e.g., output lost, workdays lost

- Future costs and opportunity costs due to present exposure, e.g., costs that will be incurred in the future due to exposure to air pollution today

As the morbidity and mortality on account of air pollution increases, society must design ways to deal with the associated diseases, work-loss days and a population generally having a poor health status. One might argue that this is not a problem, given that the market will deal with the demand for greater health care by financing more dispensaries, hospitals and health-care facilities. However, given the high degree of government subsidy involved in hospitals, society faces a huge opportunity cost on the subsidy thus set aside. Also, hospitals that cost Rs 20 crore to build and equip in 1970s and 1980s will now cost perhaps ten times more. Health care will become much more expensive, the government will be less and less able to finance medical treatment for its citizenry and most definitely, society will pay a high opportunity cost on capital thus sunk into more hospitals.

The economic valuation of these impacts is performed using 'willingness to pay' type of estimates, average wages, average productivity losses, reduction in Intelligence Quotient (IQ) points among the surveyed population, duration of illness related to air pollution and its translation into productivity loss, materials damage, etc. Bart Ostro of the Californian Environment Protection Agency has made some significant contributions to the monetization of such damages. He used dose-response relationships developed in the US.

However, such a dose-response curve specific to India is lacking. Given below is a case study carried out in the Indian context.

Development of the Dose-Response Relationships

Using data from the Chembur area of Mumbai city, the study conducted by the Environmental Pollution Research Center (EPRC) at King Edward Memorial (KEM) Hospital has established the medical links between air pollutants and health in general. The first thing to do is to correlate respiratory disorders to ambient air quality and demonstrate that morbidity/mortality is a function of air pollution. For this, the work done since 1978, by KEM hospital, under the guidance of doctors Kamat and Mahashur, is used here (see Box 8.1 below). Many of the symptoms such as respiratory morbidity (e.g., coughs, colds, asthma), work-loss days and absenteeism are linked to air pollution.

Box 8.1
Air Pollution: Related Symptoms and Impacts

Syndrome	Details	Data Source
Cough	Per cent of population suffering using time series data	Kamat and KEM
	Probability of cough using cross sectional data [the logit model]	Mahashur and EPRC
Dyspnea	Per cent of population suffering using time series data	Kamat and KEM
	Probability of dyspnea using cross sectional data [the logit model]	Mahashur and EPRC
Work-day Loss	Time series data	Kamat
Hospitalization	Cross sectional Data: Hospital costs associated with treatment	Mahashur and BMC
Mortality	Cross sectional data	BMC

Additionally, we use characteristics of the subject (age, exposure years, type of housing, type of occupation, income levels, type of neighbourhood etc.) and an index of environmental pollution or air quality status. We are looking at the effects of Nitrogen dioxide (NO_2), Sulphur dioxide (SO_2) and suspended particulate matter (SPM) in ambient air on human health.[2] These pollutants may be used in isolation or in combination. However, intuitively, and certainly desirable, so far as the medical literature goes, an index of air quality is a better-suited determinant of one's health status.

The following steps are followed and indices created:

1. An index has been created by dividing ambient air pollutant level with that of the recommended standard. Having created such an index for each pollutant, they have been regressed on health variables using equal weight for each pollutant.

[2] We recognize that SO_2 and NO_2 levels in Chembur are well within the recommended industrial standards. The fact is that Chembur is a residential area as well, and ammonia and carbon-monoxide are the two bigger culprits. Ideally, we would like to monitor their effects on health; but data is lacking.

2. Each pollutant level is regressed to health effects individually.
3. Values of concentration in ambient air higher than that which the standard prescribes is calculated, and all such values are arithmetically added to get an index.

However we would like to point out that such methods leave much to be desired. Certain considerations are critical:

1. Simply adding pollution to get aggregates will be incorrect. These numbers say nothing about the composition of the ambient air and the intensity of the damage it can cause. Different pollutants have different impacts on humans, animals, soils and plants.
2. Ideally, we would like to assign weightage to each of the pollutants with respect to the damage they are doing to the respiratory system. Assigning equal weights implicitly assumes that pollutants are causing equal damage. This is a fallacy. For instance, standards recommend 60mg/m3 for each pollutant. Yet damage caused by 60mg/m3 of NO_2 and 60mg/m3 of SO_2 differ greatly. Hence, weightage ought to be assigned as per damage done.
3. The joint effect of pollutants must be recognized and accounted for. For example, the combined effect of SO_2 and SPM is far more damaging to the upper respiratory system than their effect taken individually.

How to Define an Appropriate Air Pollution Index?

Ideally, the air quality index has to be an aggregated one, based on the weights assigned to different pollutants. There is a need for revising these relative weights in Indian conditions which may have different effects due to differences in health and nutrition standard's diet and lifestyle indicators. However, we are unable to do this for want of data. Box 8.2 shows the methodology followed in arriving such an index.

METHODOLOGY OF DATA AND INFORMATION COLLECTION

Cross-Sectional Studies

From the available cross-sectional studies on population, we have information on different aspects of the health status of the population, which are coded as shown in Box 8.3:

Ultimately, the data was aggregated into two categories so that a

BOX 8.2
Computation of Aggregated Air Quality Index

Air Quality Index (AQI)

The concept of an air quality index is nothing new. The notion that air quality needs to be seen as an integrated whole of various pollutants rather than discrete compartments of individual pollutants is supported intuitively and logically.

The problem, however, is in designing this index. Ideally, a unit change in the pollution index should have a fixed change in the impacts it is reputed to affect. In other words, the AQI needs to be a weighted index incorporating the adverse impacts of various pollutants. Different pollutants cause different impacts on health and property and, hence, there cannot be a single component of an AQI which suits all occasions. AQI designed to capture health impacts will be different from the AQI designed to capture impacts on property values. Again, the AQI designed to capture respiratory diseases will be different from the AQI for cardiovascular diseases. The AQI, therefore, needs to be defined for the purpose for which it is computed.

For computing, the relative toxicity weightages of various pollutants can be used. For respiratory diseases, these have been calculated and are given below.

Pollutant	Relative Toxicity
NO_X	1.00
CO	0.02
HC	0.055
SO_X	4.15
SPM	2.81

$$AQI = NO_x*[1] + CO*[0.02] + HC*[0.055] + SO_x*[4.15] + SPM*[2.81]$$

Source: Sterling et al., (1967)

simple model could be applied. The aggregation was based upon whether the subject had any symptom or not, i.e., Dyspnea/cough = 1 if yes, = 0 if not.

Time Series Studies

For data on the exposure and incidence of morbidity, we have data from two sources: (i) household data, where subjects maintained

Box 8.3
Codes for Health Status

	Health status	Code
Cough	No cough	0
	Dry cough for one year	1
	Productive cough for one year	2
	Dry cough for two years	3
	Productive cough for two years	4
Dyspnea	No dyspnea	0
	Dyspnea (parox)	1
	Dyspnea (external)	2
	Dyspnea (both)	3

diaries over a certain time period, and (ii) data from hospitals recording the number of patients admitted on account of respiratory disorders.

The Data Set and Associated Problems

Quantitative data that has been collected for over 2000 household-level subjects over two to three years is difficult to analyse for several reasons: (i) not all these subjects were exposed to Chembur air throughout the day. Many leave Chembur to work in areas that had better or worse air quality; (ii) we lack data on a day-to-day basis to correlate the diary-data to air quality on that particular day; (iii) personal expenses per person are difficult to compile.

Similarly, several problems arise in using the data from hospitals. (i) People do not go to hospitals for the respiratory disorders unless the disorder is of an extremely severe nature. To that extent, the study underestimates the health effects of air pollution, and (ii) the study counts the physical incidence of morbidity rather than the economic burden of such morbidity. Two problems become obvious using hospital statistics.

1. It is difficult for a valuation team to capture the economics that underly this morbidity. The data does not comment on the type of medical cost incurred by the patient, the 'value' of discomfort suffered, the number of workdays lost in the process and the

number of work days lost for other members of the family on the same account.

2. The data does not comment on the amount of money spent on avertive/preventive medicine that is attributable to air pollution related morbidity.

Thus, having left much of the impact unaccounted, the true economic value of loss is bound to be underestimated. Due to the reasons mentioned above, the present valuation can be considered a gross underestimation of the damage suffered on account of air pollution. An appropriate questionnaire must be designed, by cooperative consultation between doctors, air-quality monitoring authorities and the valuation team, so that the numbers will feed directly into the valuation exercise.

Morbidity and Mortality

Morbidity related to air pollution embraces the following: respiratory symptoms (e.g., cough, cold, asthma, bronchitis), eye and skin irritation, a general feeling of listlessness, 'feeling down', work-day loss (WDL) due to illness and in extreme cases, death. A more subtle, yet real cost that air pollution imposes upon society is exacerbation of respiratory morbidity. They inflame the respiratory tract, intensify the irritation and discomfort and thwart an early recovery. These effects, however important and significant, are difficult to determine.

Illnesses (e.g., one's own and those of their friends, neighbours, relatives) impose costs on the individual and the society in many ways. One obvious cost is the bills a patient must pay for a doctor's consultation fee, the medicines, the earning lost because a work day is lost, cost of the trip to and from the doctor's, etc. Society too loses because its mandays in terms of productivity are lost, more people are ill or 'down', others must be found to substitute for the absentee and make-do in his/her absence. Often, the cost is not just the individual's discomfort, but family members as well, who have to accompany them to the hospital or share the extra burden at home.

When air pollution causes excess mortality, a problem is faced in calculating the statistical value of life. Statistical value of life (SVOL) measures are not person-specific. That is, we are not valuing the life of a specific person, which is always non-measurable especially from that person's viewpoint or his loved ones. However, a society finds certain deaths intolerable and takes measures involving costs to avoid certain number of deaths, be it to prevent accidents, fire, health hazards, and so on. Wage rates offered for risky jobs also gives an idea concerning SVOL.[3]

Insurance policies taken out by the people provide one indication of such valuation. Compensation provided by factories, railways, airlines and the like in case of accidents also provide some indication. Although these issues are not addressed here it is important to be aware of these issues in valuing deaths due to pollution.

MODELLING HEALTH EFFECTS OF AIR POLLUTION

Data and Statistics

It is clear that not all morbidity and mortality is caused by air pollution. The question is, 'How much of the human mortality and morbidity suffered is on account of air pollution?' Statistical and econometric analysis is needed to establish these relationships.

Here data from two sources are used: the first, collected by Kamat and his team, the second collected by Mahashur and his team under EPRC. The data from Kamat is in time series, and that from Mahashur is cross-sectional in nature.

Dose-response models are developed now. The following relationships are formulated: (i) Dyspnea and SPM, (ii) cough and SO_2, (iii) WDL and NO_2, (iv) Dyspnea and NO_2, and (v) mortality and SO_2. A number of logical functional forms were also attempted and the ones which gave better representation of the relationship are presented. The functional forms differ with the pollutants-health-impact relationship as is to be expected in any such econometric exercise.

Econometric Specification and Estimation

In the study being conducted by the EPRC at KEM hospital, cross-sectional data are collected for 300 households from the three housing colonies: Telecom factory, Tolaram and Collector's Colony. The variable to explain is the illness symptom, which is not a continuous

---

[3] Indian statistical-value-of-life figures yield low numbers. The reason is that in the Indian context, abundant supply of labour drives wages down and forces people to accept higher and higher levels of risk without giving them the bargaining power to demand higher wages to compensate for risk undertaken.

BOX 8.4
The Logit Model

The logit model estimates the probability of a certain event occurring, given a certain set of independent variables. The dependent variable (y^*) is a latent variable and is not observable. What we observe is a qualitative variable y_i, defined by

$$y_i = 1 \text{ if } y^* > 0$$
$$= 0 \text{ otherwise}$$

$$y_i = \beta_0 + \sum_{j}^{k} \beta_j x_{ij} + u_i \qquad (1)$$

1. Let P_i be the probability of $y_i = 1$ i.e. in our case, the subject is suffering from cough.
2. The error term is assumed to be logistic and we obtain

$$\log \frac{P_i}{1 - P_i} = \beta_0 + \sum_{j=1}^{k} \beta_j x_{ij} \qquad (2)$$

then

$$\frac{\partial P_i}{\partial x_i} = \beta_j^* P_i (1 - P_i) \qquad (3)$$

The left-hand side of the equation (2) is called a log-odds ratio. The log-odds ratio is a linear function of the explanatory variables. After estimating the parameter, we can predict the effect of changes of any of the explanatory variables on the probability of the observation belonging to either of the two groups. (e.g., equation (3)).
The detailed formulation of logit model can be obtained from any of the econometric textbooks [e.g., Pindyck and Rubinfeld (1981)].

but takes several discrete positions (as shown in Box 8.3). Therefore, ideally one should use a multi-nominal logit model. However, we aggregated the options into just two choices (having a symptom or not) to analyse the effect of change in air pollution levels on the population having dyspnea so that a simple logit formulation can be employed. The logic and steps involved in logit specifications are summarized in Box 8.4:

The estimated dose-response equation with standard error in parentheses is:

LOGIT (DYS) = 0.012 TE + 0.477 SEX + 0.901 SM – 5.682

$$(.0069) \quad\quad (.43) \quad\quad (.73) \quad\quad (1.9)\ n=300 \quad (8.1)$$

where

TE = Total Exposure in terms of SPM; SEX = Male, Female; SM = Smoking:1 = Yes and 0 = No; DYS = Dyspnea: 0 = no, 1 = yes

The estimated logit function is then interpreted as the probability function for suffering from dyspnea. Total exposure (TE), dummy for smoking (SM) (1 if yes, 0 if no) and sex are statistically-significant variables in deciding upon the probability of having dyspnea (DYS).

The change in probability that an observation will lie in either of the groups can be obtained by substituting the explanatory variables. As an approximation, we can assume that the initial probability for explanatory variables at their mean values of sample observations to be equal to the sample probability (33/300, 11 per cent). Then,

Change in Prob (DYS) per Unit Change in SPM = 0.012 * 0.11* 0.89
(from equation (3) in the Box 8.4)   = 0.00113

This, however, is the mean change in probability of having DYS per unit. The upper and lower bounds of changes can be obtained from using the coefficient and adding and subtracting the standard error in the above equation, respectively. Therefore,

Upper Change Prob (DYS) per unit change in SPM =

$$(0.0116+0.0069)\ *0.11*0.89 = 0.0018$$

and

Lower Change Prob (DYS) per unit change in SPM =

$$(0.0116-0.0069)*\ 0.11*0.89 = 0.00046$$

Similar studies elsewhere estimate the difference between the level of exposure and the standards promulgated. They use this differential to calculate excess morbidity by taking into consideration the coefficients they estimated from their dose-response curves.

One should note that taking the entire Mumbai as mixed to set standards is more of an administrative convenience than a medical edict. This standard, however, is not supported by any medical evidence (i.e., there is no reason to believe that people in Mumbai have a higher threshold of resistance as compared to people elsewhere or that morbidity is zero below the standard prescribed). Since we do not have an India-specific medical criteria for SPM, we shall be calculating the incremental change in dyspnea consequent to 100 unit change in SPM. Otherwise, we could use the residential standards that are considerably lower.

What if the original environmental concentration itself is below the standards? For this, incremental changes in mortality/morbidity corresponding to changes in air quality when the original concentrations are below standards can be worked out. When the ambient concentrations are below permissible standards, it is legally acceptable to let air quality degrade up to that level. However, standards being more of administrative conveniences than medical edicts, such a degradation of quality is anyway bound to have adverse health impacts. One could compute the cost of no-action (business as usual scenario) by finding out the incremental degradation permissible.

Finding out the number of excess dyspnea cases calls for the estimation of change in probability of individual subjects and estimation of the probability distribution. As a demonstrative step for valuation exercise, however, assume that 15 per cent of the population, originally suffering from dyspnea will move into no dyspnea category, if air quality could be brought down to the minimum possible levels. The various costs associated with this, as estimated by medical doctors, can be valued at the rates obtained from brief inquiry by us, as shown in Table 8.1.

The following categories of morbidity levels can be made to show the differentiated cost of treatment depending upon the differentiated level of morbidity.

1. 50 per cent of people suffering from dyspnea have either bronchitis or asthma.
2. Bronchitis/asthma patient needs medical attention in the following manner.

    (a)   Mild attacks, 100 per cent once a year
        (i)   No visits to the doctor
        (ii) One work day lost
    (b)   Moderate attacks 40 per cent, once in a year
        (i)   Two doctor visits per attacks
        (ii) Three work days lost

TABLE 8.1
Morbidity and its Economic Burden

Morbidity-related support sought	Cost in Rs Range	Cost in Rs Average
Medical consultation (out-patient)		
Doctor's fee (per consultation)	20–200	50
Cost of diagnostic tests (per case)	50–500	150
Medicines (per day)	20–100	50
Transport (per visit)	10–100	40
Hospitalization		
Doctors fee	300–2000	1000
Diagnostic tests	1000–3000	2000
Accommodation	2000–3000	300
Food (two persons, per day)	50–300	150
Transport (per stay)	200–1000	500
Medicine (per attack)	1000–3000	1500
Full-time assistant (rupees per day)		83
Work days lost (rupees per day)		83

Source: IGIDR Survey

(c) Severe attacks 5 per cent of total cases once in a year
   (i) 5 days in hospital
   (ii) 10 work days lost

From these statistics, one can now calculate the economic costs of air pollution with respect to it's effect on cases of dyspnea and it's aggravation.

The economic value of the private burden of dyspnea caused to people in Chembur alone due to poor air quality is in excess of Rs 35 lakh. When other 'free' services are included, costs rise by about Rs 20 lakh more! Note also, that these annual estimates do not include government subsidies, and are thus underestimates of the true economic burden of air pollution. The estimates are shown in Table 8.2.

Similarly we formulated a logit model for cough in the following manner:

$$\text{logit [COUGH]} = f\,[\text{SM, TE, TE}^2\,] \qquad (8.2)$$

where

TABLE 8.2
Total Economic Value Associated with Increased Dyspnea

Severity of attack	# of people	Loss suffered	Rupees	Rs (1000s)
Mild attack (A)	6585	One work day loss	546,580	546
Moderate attack (B)	2634	Consultation (50*2)	263,400	2028
		diagnosis (100)	264,300	
		Medicine (50* 5)	658,531	
B = 40% A		Transport (40*2)	210,730	
		Work days lost (3*83)	632,189	
Free C = 26% B	(684)	Consultation	68,400	307
		Diagnosis	68,400	
		Medicine	171,000	
Severe attacks (D)	329	5 days in hospital	329,000	1936
		Diagnosis tests	329,000	
		Consultation	329,000	
D = 5% A		Food	246,938	
		Transport	164,625	
		Work day loss(asst)	136,638	
		Work day loss	273,277	
		Medicine	493,875	
Severe, Free E = 39.6% D	Free (131)	Accommodation	139,000	625
		Diagnosis	139,000	
		Consultation	139,000	
		Medicine	208,500	
Total (Private)		(A+B+D-C-E)		3578
Total (Social)		(A+B+C+D+E)		5442

Source: Author's estimates

SM = smoking, TE = Total Exposure, TE^2 = square of TE

Using the example data, the estimated logit model is as follows:

Logit [COUGH] = -6.9242 + 1.4657 SM + 0.015 TE + 0.227 TE^2
    (1.9)   (.55)   (.007)   (.23) ; n = 300

TABLE 8.3

Expenditure per Individual Case of Asthama/Bronchitis Attack

Severity of sickness	Expenditure (Rs) per person	Per cent of Annual (average) Income
Mild attack	83	0.28
Moderate attack	769	2.5
Severe attack	5885	19.4

Source: Author's estimates

Standard errors are provided in parenthesis. The variables SM and TE are significant at the 5 per cent confidence level. The variable TE^2 included to capture the non-linear effects of pollutant concentration on human morbidity is not significant, but shows the correct sign.

Absenteeism and Workday Losses

Exposure to air pollution causes illness and could cause work loss and increase restricted activity days because of cough, colds, other respiratory diseases, asthama, breathlessness and a general feeling of 'being down'.

One might argue that it would be unfair to attribute all of such morbidity to air pollution. That would grossly overestimate the costs of air pollution. People fall sick for various other reasons. Not all loss incurred during illness can be attributed to air pollution. The question is, 'what is the percentage of these total cases of morbidity that can be attributed to air pollution per se and not other factors?' To complicate matters, there may be those who are ill, but may well have recovered sooner, had air pollution not aggravated their symptoms and slowed down their recovery. To capture all such incidence we estimate the following relationship:

$$\text{Absenteeism (per cent)} = f\,(NO_2) \qquad (8.3)$$

The left-hand-side includes absentees from school and work in Chembur during 1978–80 as a percentage of the population under survey. The data is part of the work done by Kamat of KEM hospital for the residents of Chembur. The independent variable is NO_2 levels as measured by BMC. The results are as follows:

$$\text{Absenteeism per cent} = 0.039 + 0.32085\,(NO_2)$$
$$(2.09) \qquad (0.145) \qquad ; n = 16, \quad R^2 = 25.69\%$$

The preliminary data suggests that 25 per cent of the variation in recorded absentees are explained by ambient air quality. Since estimation of the monetary value here, will overlap with that of dyspnea, it is not estimated.

Morbidity and SO_2 Levels

Likewise, the following equation is estimated to estimate the morbidity status due to exposure to SO_2:

$$\ln [\text{cough}] = f (\ln SO_2) \tag{8.4}$$

The independent variable values are taken from BMC. The dependent variable 'cough' is arrived at by Kamat from his health study. It records the percentage of the population suffering from acute or chronic cough for three months or more. Monthly averages are used. The results are as follows:

$$\ln [\text{cough}]= 2.1157 + 0.11643 * \ln (SO_2)$$
$$(0.289) \quad (0.0577) \quad\quad ; n = 43, \quad R^2 = 9\%$$

The independent variable takes the expected sign and is significant at the 5 per cent level. Since the equation is a log-log type, coefficients stand for the elasticities. A 1 per cent rise in pollutant concentration levels will lead to a 0.11643 per cent increase in the percentage of population coughing. The data shows that 13.644 per cent of the population is complaining of chronic and/or acute cough. Attributing that to the study area, a staggering 1,12,380 people in M-ward are complaining of cough!

$$\partial (\text{cough}) / \partial (SO_2) = a1 * \text{cough}/SO_2 \text{ (MEAN)}$$
$$= 0.11643 * (13.64\% \text{ of } 823297)/61.95$$
$$= 0.11643 * 112380/61.95$$
$$= 211.05$$

This can be monetized to give an economic value of incremental changes in SO_2. Here again, a double counting with dyspnea is possible, hence the monetization exercise is not undertaken.

Analysis of Mortality Rates

It is not only patients suffering from respiratory disorders but also others that are then affected by air pollution. The other bias arises from the fact that not all patients who die of air pollution and respiratory deaths are included in respiratory deaths, although it was air pollution that was the main factor. Therefore, taking only respiratory deaths would prove too narrow, and unembracing. We, therefore, broaden the concept of mortality caused by air pollution and use total death rates in the city.

To capture the above mentioned effects, we estimated the following equation:

$$TDR\%_{WARD} = f\ (log\ Population,\ PDEN_{WARD},\ SLUMS_{WARD},\ HOSP_{WARD},\ SO_2)\quad (8.5)$$

where:

$TDR\ per\ cent_{WARD}$ = total death rate per ward, log Population is per ward, $PDEN_{WARD}$ = population density per ward, $SLUMS_{WARD}$ = slums per ward adjusted for population size, $HOSP_{WARD}$ = hospitals, dispensaries and clinics per ward adjusted for population size; SO_2 = average SO_2 levels taken from monitors corresponding to the particular ward.

The independent variables are population of the ward, PDEN (population density), SLUMS (defined as population of the ward/no. of slums), HOSP (defined as population of the ward/no. of hospitals) and SO_2, concentration of Sulphur Dioxide in g/m^3.[4]

Variables of population size and density are used to bring out the effects of crowding and congestion, weighted heavily in both medical and environmental literature. The number of slums per ward is introduced to recognize the problems of sanitation and poor nutritional status associated with slums, and their possible effect on the death rate in the ward. SLUMS takes the value of population in ward per slum. The higher this number the better environmental quality in a certain ward, *ceteris paribus*. HOSP referring to hospitals, dispensaries, clinics and maternity homes is similarly computed. The more hospitals in the neighbourhood is assumed to reflect on opportunities for citizens to secure an improved health status.

The regression was conducted for the year 1989–90, the last year for which the report of the executive health office is available. A better set

---

[4] The estimates were conducted with the data readily available. The statistics on the actual population staying in the slums as well as the number of beds available in different hospitals were not readily available. We agree that the population in slums and beds per ward represent the congestion and health services better.

of independent variables could have been the percentage of slum population in each ward and the number of hospital beds per population head because the variables as it is taken now could pose problems. For example, a big slum is equated with a small slum and a 100 bedded hospital is equated with a dispensary as far as the regression goes. The results are as follows:

$$TDR \text{ per cent}_{WARD} = 4.1517 - 0.6723 \log P + 0.00000577 PDEN + 0.000169 SLUM$$
$$(0.171) \quad (0.245) \quad (0.0000018) \quad (0.00023)$$

$$+ 0.00168 \text{ HOSP} \quad + 0.0052 \text{ } SO_2$$
$$(0.00163) \quad (0.0038); \quad n = 20, \quad R^2 = 72\%$$

Standard errors are in parenthesis. As expected, the total death rate increases with rising SO_2 levels, slums per ward and population density. Variables of population and density are significant at the 5 per cent level. Coefficients of SO_2 and hospitals are significant at 10 per cent confidence level. Notice that the HOSP variable takes a positive (+) sign and is significant. Apparently, and supported by intuition, higher death rates and associated morbidity within a ward imply a greater need and demand for health services.

We recognize that the concentrations of SO_2 in Mumbai are below the permissible industrial air pollution stipulated standards, yet the sulphur dioxide levels correlate with death rates. Although this sounds counter-intuitive, it is not unique. Epidemiologic studies undertaken in several locations indicate that SO_2 acting alone or as a surrogate for other sulphur-related species, is associated with increased risk of mortality. The report of Lipfert (1991) cites many cases of correlation of SO_2 to total mortality even when the range of concentrations are below World Health Organization (WHO) stipulations. The possible explanation for such behaviour could be that the ambient air quality monitors are not able to capture the actual exposures for the pollutants (such a possibility is indicated in Mumbai where the ambient sulphate level was far exceeded by the personal exposure). Added to this could be the fact that SO_2 may be acting as a surrogate for all sulphur-related species like sulphates and sulphurous acid particulate. The synergestic action of sulphur-based pollutants with particulate could also be a reason for this behaviour. Possibility of a lower threshold for the population, where air pollution acts in synergy with other health issues (general insanitary condition, poor nutrition etc.) cannot be ruled out.

VALUATION OF HEALTH EFFECTS

Classically, valuation exercises are done for the changes in the pollutant concentration from its present level to the acceptable standards. However, as explained earlier, this cannot be attempted here. Till the time the actual causal relationships are established, it will be meaningless to argue for a reduction in existing pollution levels. We are, therefore, attempting only to demonstrate the valuation exercise by evaluating the economic value of a 10-unit change in SO_2 concentration.

Taking the partial differential of the equation estimated earlier with respect to sulphur dioxide, we get the excess death rate attributable to SO_2.

$$\partial TDR/\partial SO_2 = 0.0052$$

$$\Delta TDR \text{ (per cent) } = 0.0052 * \Delta SO_2 \qquad (8.6)$$

For a 10-unit change in sulphur dioxide, the number of excess deaths/deaths avoided can be calculated as follows:

Excess death rate	= 0.0052 *10
Normal death rate in Mumbai	= 0.76%
Population of Chembur	= 823297
Number of normal deaths	= 0.76 *823297/100 = 5971
Number of excess deaths	= 0.052*5971
	= 325

The valuation of mortality can be done using one of the several standard ways. For the purpose of this valuation, we use two approaches: the Human Capital Approach and the Wage-Risk Differential.

Statistical Value of Life	= Rs 2,87,230 per life
Human Capital Approach	= Rs 3,83,433 per life
Workmen's Compensation Act of India	= Rs 2,13,144 per life

Cost of Lives lost/saved in M ward as per the equation presented above:

a. Statistical Value of Life approach	= 325*287230 = Rs 93.35 million
b. Human Capital Approach	= 325*383433
	= Rs 125 Million

c. Workmen's Compensation Act   = 325 * 213144

                                            = Rs 69.27 Million

Discussion on Health Costs

We have tried to drive home the point that the costs of air pollution, just like air pollution itself, are all-pervasive. The costs imposed on society come in various shapes and forms. Often, given the existence of externalities, people do not perceive them as such a huge problem. But for society, as we have demonstrated here, these costs are real, and significant.

The techniques whereby relationships between pollutants and morbidity can be established have been demonstrated as also the techniques that can be used to conduct the economic valuation of the damage done. A comprehensive list of the various forms in which pollution exacts its toll on society has not been provided here. Only a few aspects of the costs (WDL, a few respiratory syndromes, hospitailization costs, and mortality) were considered. Nor are the costs mentioned earlier are a comprehensive list of factors that capture all the costs air pollution imposes on our society.

As mentioned previously, the costs imposed on society with respect to the discomfort related to morbidity, the suffering of unreported cases, costs of preventing morbidity, aversive expenditure, and numerous other factors are not given here. Many costs go without mention. What this study presents in terms of valuation, is only, at best, the tip of an iceberg, using central estimates, accounting for only dyspnea and death attributable to air quality degradation of $10mg/m^3$, where social loss exceeds Rs 10 crore per year. This cost is, clearly, very significant.

Social Opportunity Cost Pricing

In the case of air pollution in Chembur, the cost of air pollution is not just the cost of medicine bought by Chembur residents to combat the respiratory disorder/cough/cold.

In certain cases, the 'value' of morbidity and mortality may appear to be 'too small' for a single person or a group of individuals; not appearing to justify investment in one more hospital, or the financing of an expressway or the installation of an abatement plant. A more dynamic and informed perspective would be to understand that such morbidity and mortality is going to be faced, and at an increasing rate, over time. When the capacity of the government to provide subsidies on health is constrained, when building more hospitals is too expensive, when the productivity and, therefore, the earning capacity of people is low, society is caught in a vicious downward spiral. See Appendix A.8.1 for some details of social costs of morbidity and mortality.

Using 1992 figures, the Brihanmumbai Corporation (BMC) is spending Rs 405 crore on public health including medical relief, hospitals, medical education, air pollution control activities etc. The receipts from the public during the same period is just Rs 11.70 crore. Had it not been for air pollution causing mortality or compounding other morbidity, a percentage of these costs could have been saved, both by the private patient and the public in general.

The following must be considered to arrive at the true economic cost society is bearing on account of air pollution: (i) annualized cost of hospitals, clinics, dispensaries, (ii) social cost of hospitals, clinics and dispensaries, (iii) subsidies on treatment and medicine, (iv) the opportunity cost of the number of doctors treating air pollution caused/aggravated cases, (v) investment in research on the effects of damages caused by air pollution and (vi) the returns foregone on a perhaps more lucrative investment e.g., in preventive rather than curative medicine, education, etc.

Yet another aspect of investment in health care needs elaboration. The cost of health care is calculated on the assumption that we already have sufficient health care infrastructure to take care of excess demand so that incremental cost of treatment will remain constant. However, this is not true. The fact that we are underprovided in health care is obvious from the crowding in the hospitals. The percentage of ailing population who do not go to hospitals because of crowding is about 8 per cent (NSS, 42nd Round) for Urban Maharashtra. This clearly demonstrates the case for new hospitals, more doctors, more paramedical staff and the entire health-care paraphernalia. The cost of new hospitals and, consequently, unit cost of treatment will be much higher in new hospitals as compared to the existing ones. This, in turn, will drive the average medical costs up and also necessitate excessive government subsidy. We will have to capture all these cycle of events and quantify them.

All such avenues must be researched and the costs added up, considering all the heads discussed above. Without these costs to bear, society would save a phenomenal amount each year, and benefits would be recurring. This money could be harnessed to an alternative investment and spent on other issues that need immediate attention and financial help. Were doctors not busy treating respiratory diseases, they could be saving other lives! Research could be done in other areas of national importance. Money now being spent on curative medicine could be used to prevent the diseases from happening in the first place.

Considering all these aspects of opportunity and social-cost pricing, the costs of air pollution become all the more distressing, and the agenda for action, and action itself, becomes all the more imperative.

Distributional Aspects of Air Pollution

Slums are typically located close to either an industry, or the highway/railway lines or the solid waste dumping yards, all of which are environmentally-damaging areas. In a study conducted by the Tata Institute of Social Sciences for Mumbai on urban environmental management, indicates that most of the slum dwellers in M-Ward are

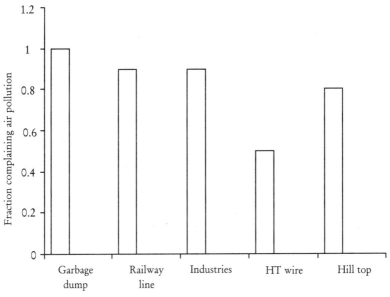

Source: Panwalkar et al., 1992

Fig. 8.1: Population Perceiving Air Pollution

troubled by the presence of air pollution (by perception) and also exhibited symptoms of diseases that could be related to air pollution (Figure 8.1).

The second aspect of the problem is that poorer sections of the population are exposed to the worst of all possible environmental hazards. For example, in the M-Ward, let us take the case of slum dwellers in marshy land near solid waste dumping sites. This has the added impact of odours and toxic gases. They are exposed to water pollution in the marshes; the land around them is chronically degraded due to their unavoidable action (using the surroundings for public toilets) they have to bear with the putrification of the solid waste in the adjacent garbage dumping site. They use the most polluting of all fuels (paper, wood, cow dung, coal) and use them in the most inefficient manner, both environmentally and economically. The limitation of space in their houses exposes practically every member of the family to the higher levels of pollution.

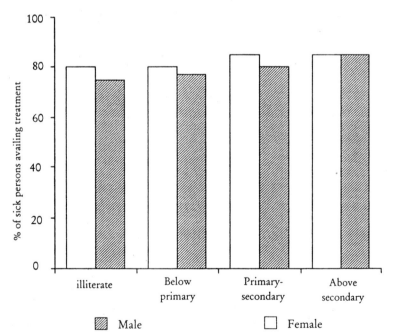

Source: NSS 42nd Round, Urban Maharashtra

Fig. 8.2: Sickness by Levels of Education

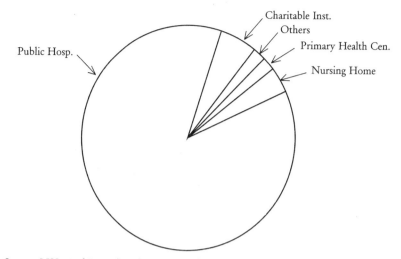

Source: NSS 42nd Round, Urban Maharashtra

Fig. 8.3: Type of Medical Service Availed (In-Patients)

Yet, it is not only the poor but all sections of society, whether illiterate or graduate, who suffer in the urban areas. Figure 8.2 shows that none can escape.

In continuation with the second point, it is true that in India, the government supports much of the health-care system and the poor people can freely avail of it. This argument is theoretically correct but a casual look at the data presented in Figure 8.3 would indicate that it is only 46 per cent of population that is treated in free wards. Of this only 44.21 are below 40 per cent fractile income group (NSS, 42nd Round for Urban Maharashtra).

This essentially means that more than half of the poor population pays for hospitalization charges, and consultation and medical expenditure out of their own pocket. In the case of hospitalization, the government supports only the consultation, medicine and food for the patient, and every other expense (transport, food for the assistant, opportunity cost of patient and assistant) has to be borne by the poor. Because of low income, further pressures are placed on the poor. It will be interesting to study what the social value of his income is. The significance of his WDL and associated opportunity cost will become clear when we realize that a meal that sustains life and employment itself, is dependent on each day's earning.

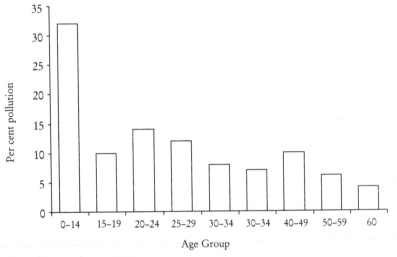

Source: Census figures, 1981

Fig. 8.4: Distribution of Pollution by Age Group

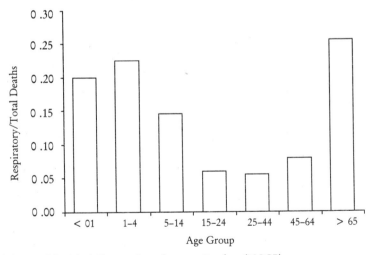

Source: Municipal Corporation of greater Bombay (MCGB)

Fig. 8.5: Fraction of Respiratory Deaths to Total Deaths

Age Distribution of Air Pollution Impacts

Air pollution does not distinguish between young and old as far as its entry into the lungs is concerned. Once inside, however, the impact could be drastically different. It has been observed that the young as well as the old, are particularly susceptible to air pollution.

An age distribution of Mumbai pollution given in Figures 8.4 and 8.5 presents the fraction of respiratory deaths to total deaths at different age groups. It can be clearly observed that the fractions show significant increase at either end of the spectrum.

A detailed analysis of the extent and burden of costs of degradation will be necessary especially on the young of today, who will be the ones to bear the costs of environmental degradation that we cause today.

REFERENCES

Kamat, S.R. (1992): 'Killing us Softly', in *The Hindu Survey of Environment*, Madras (now Chennai).

Kamat, S., et al., (1984): *Bombay Air Pollution—Health Study*, United Arts, Bombay.

Lipfert F.W. (1991): 'Mortality and Air Pollution', *The Handbook of Environmenetal Chemistry* Springer Verlac, Berlin, pp. 75–177.

Mahahur, A.A., Dalal Nepa (URBAIR) (1993): *Health Morbidity Relating with Air Pollution in Chembur in 1978 and 1990*.

Pindyck, R.S. and D.L. Rubinfeld (1981): *Econometric Models and Economic Forecasts*, Mc Graw Hill International Book Co. Singapore.

Sterling T.D., S.V. Pollack, J.J Pharz (1967):Urban Hospital Morbidity and Air pollution, A Second Report, Archives of Environmental Health, 15, September, pp. 362–4.

Appendix A.8.1
Social Opportunity Cost

Opportunity cost refers to the best alternative use to which particular resources could be put, if they were not being used for the purposes being costed. For example, the opportunity cost refers to the wages forgone in job B by a worker busy doing Job A rather than Job B. Further, if job A pays him Rs X/hr, the opportunity cost to the worker of a work hour lost is Rs X.

In the case of environmental pollution and the impact on human health, several such opportunity costs are incurred. Costs incurred on account of air pollution are both direct and indirect. Simply pricing the medicines used to cure bronchitis, for example, is not an adequate and comprehensive measure of cost imposed on humans by air pollution. Other costs are involved. The list includes loss in work days, opportunity cost of the money spent on curative medicine by both the patient in particular, and the public in general.

To get the comprehensive costs incurred by society, all types of costs must be accounted for. They are as follows: i) direct cost of pollution, ii) external cost of pollution and iii) costs arising from intertemporal considerations.

The direct cost of the activity is the fact that human labour, capital, enterprise, etc., was invested in the production of goods which is required for pollution control. Suppose these factors could be employed elsewhere, devoted to some other activity to the value of Rs X, then the opportunity cost of the activity presently engaged, in is Rs X.

Pertinent to the issue of health effects of air pollution, doctors, medical equipment and resources harnessed in the medical treatment of pollution-caused symptoms and associated research, have a high direct opportunity cost. If doctors were not busy curing patients of basic upper respiratory diseases, they could use their potential elsewhere, perhaps in valuable research. Perhaps they could be improving the quality and quantity of preventive rather than curative medicine. Scarce capital spent on building hospitals, for example, could be spared, and perhaps used for other purposes in the economy. Rather than spend money on expensive medicines, the poor could have invested in a house, better nutrition and their children's education.

The second component of opportunity cost is accrued in the future cost. Air pollution is causing upper respiratory diseases, a reduction in the efficiency of lung functioning and an increased incidence of coughs and colds. This translates into general weakness, increased casual leave of working people, a lower output for agricultural workers, a decreased productivity of urban workers to do work and so on. This lost output has an economic cost. Some of these costs may be incurred over time, with chronic effects of air pollution, say after five years of exposure to noxious fumes. An appropriate discount rate must then be used to calculate the present value of the future loss/cost incurred. This external cost must be accounted for and included in the estimation of the true opportunity cost of air pollution to society.

The final element in opportunity cost pricing arises from intertemporal considerations. Suppose urban air quality is deteriorating over the years. Then clean, fresh urban air may be a resource that will be hard to find in the future, a 'luxury' afforded only in 'the good old times'. This places a scarcity premium on the resource, its value depending upon the stock of the resource at present, the rate of deterioration, the social discount rate, and other parameters. Having considered all the aspects of this cost, it will be found that the free market, unaided, undervalues the 'price' of clean air because it does not account for the scarcity premium that the resource commands. Thus, the true opportunity cost [OP] of resource use is as follows:

OP = DC + EC + UC,

where DC is the direct cost, EC is the external cost, and UC is the user cost associated with the resource consumption/ degradation.

Economic Benefit-Cost Analysis of a Proposed Solid Waste Resource Recovery Plant

*Paul P. Appasamy**

INTRODUCTION

Solid Waste Management in Indian cities is becoming a problem due to rapid population growth and changes in lifestyles. Average per capita generation of wastes is about 0.5 kg per day in larger cities. The Municipal Corporation of Lucknow which has to dispose off 1500 tonnes per day is considering a proposal for a biomethanation plant to convert about 200 tonnes of organic wastes into biogas. The biogas would be used in a gas engine to recover about 5 MW of power, which would be sold to the state electricity grid. seventy-five tonnes per day of organic manure, a by-product would be sold to tea gardens or other buyers.

A cost-benefit analysis is used in evaluating this project in a 'with-without' framework. It is assumed that the solid waste would be landfilled if the project did not exist. Two alternatives are considered here, namely biomethanation, which would convert methane to carbon dioxide (CO_2) while the other alternative is landfill. Even with the gas collection, under this alternative, considerable quantities of

* Acknowledgements: Enkem Engineers and Infrastructure Development Finance Corporation supported the study, provided the data, and permitted publication of the results. P. Narahari Reddy carried out the field work in Lucknow with assistance for the Municpal Corporation. K.S. Kavi Kumar, Assistant Professor shared his knowledge of the Clean Development Mechanism and its relevance to this study. I am grateful to all these organizations and individuals for their assistance.

methane would be released. The environmental damage caused by releasing methane is averted in the first alternative and can be valued as a benefit of biomethanation.

Although the biomethanation option is comparatively very expensive, it also provides substantial benefits, while the landfill option is highly dependent on the price of land and generally has negative benefits. Also, the environmental benefits of biomethanation are quite large when compared to the landfill option. Sensitivity analysis shows several policy-oriented results.

With increasing urbanization and changes in lifestyles, solid waste management is becoming a major problem in cities and towns in India. According to the Census 2001, the urban population of India is about 285 million which is expected to reach about 400 million by 2011. Income and the standard of living has also gone up leading to the generation of wastes, such as plastics, paper, etc., in large quantities. Average per capita generation of wastes in large cities in India is about 0.5 kg per day, which means that a city of four million would generate about 2000 tonnes per day of domestic solid waste, not counting construction debris and other types of industrial/commercial waste. These wastes have to be collected, transported and disposed in an environmentally-sound manner.

The public is more concerned about the efficiency in removal of garbage from the streets, since accumulation on the streets is not only unsightly but a public-health hazard. The outbreak of 'plague' in Surat brought the environmental risks posed by uncollected waste to the consciousness of the public and the municipal authorities. Thus, there are social costs associated with uncollected garbage. On the other hand, a clean street is a benefit to the residents and to others using that locality. Therefore, primary collection at the household level must be viewed not only as a municipal service but also as an environmental benefit to the local population. Primary collection of solid waste is a local 'public good', which must be collected and disposed off at an optimal level by weighing these benefits against costs of collection. Alternative institutional options are being considered in many cities, such as neighbourhood organizations, (non-governmental organizations) NGOs, or private contractors in conjunction with the municipal authorities who are expected to provide this service. This is the first stage in urban solid waste management.

On other hand, secondary collection involves collection of wastes from a transfer station and transportation to the nearest landfill. This is largely a technical function and can be done either by the municipal authority or by a private operator. Optimal routing, vehicle and fuel requirements for this activity are to be estimated and managed. Municipal agencies generally perform this step reasonably well, since the number of transfer stations is generally small. Vehicles can ply from the transfer stations to the landfill. The public is generally not aware of transfer stations and landfills unless they happen to live in proximity to either of these.

The neglected area in solid waste management is disposal activity. Some NGOs are propagating decentralized disposal using vermiculture, etc., which can deal with part of the organic waste. But, it must be recognized that not all the urban solid waste can be disposed in this manner. However, such decentralized systems must be encouraged so that the burden on the municipal authorities is reduced. Similarly, recycling and reuse of the non-organic wastes will reduce the quantity to be collected and disposed.

In most cities and towns, the collected waste is dumped in low-lying areas, euphemistically called landfills, with the ostensible purpose of reclaiming land. This causes serious environmental problems at the local level—pollution of ground and surface water, gas generation that could cause explosions, rodents and other disease-bearing vectors that may proliferate at the site. Thus, there are major environmental costs associated with improper disposal, that are rarely recognized or discussed, since there is much more interest in primary collection because of its greater visibility. It is increasingly recognized that landfills are also major sources of greenhouse gas (GHG) emissions.

The concern on disposal of urban solid waste in India was first taken up by a High Power Committee set up by the Planning Commission in 1995 (Planning Commission, 1995). According to the report, apart from the mega cities, as many as 33 cities with population over one million will require solid waste disposal system established during the Ninth Five year Plan period. Several techno-economic studies have been carried out in India, exploring the alternatives available to the disposal and recycling of solid waste. The notable ones are by Reyer et al. (1999), which explores the alternative under a linear programming model for the city of Bangalore; Reddy and Galab (1999) which provides an assessment of solid waste in the city of Hyderabad.

A particular option of disposing solid waste from the city of Lucknow, using a cost benefit analysis, is analysed. In particular, the externality benefit of abating global climate change is evaluated and accounted.

WHAT ARE THE OPTIONS FOR THE PROPER DISPOSAL OF URBAN SOLID WASTE?

There are at least four possible disposal options: (i) Sanitary landfilling, to reclaim land for other uses; (ii) Composting, which will produce fertilize (iii) Incineration, where the solid waste is used as a fuel and (iv) Biomethanation, which produces fertilizer and generates gas which can be converted to power. Other technologies such as pyrolysis are used in other countries.

Each of these options has the associated costs and benefits. Sanitary landfilling and composting require large areas of land. Urban land values have been going up tremendously, and local governments have to decide if they will allot large tracts of land for this purpose, even if the reclaimed land can be ultimately used for a park. Moreover, it is not advisable to use reclaimed land (from dumping solid waste) for constructing houses or other buildings. It is often not recognized that the use of public land has an opportunity cost of not utilizing the land for some other purpose.

The other aspect of disposal that is of interest is the energy/resource value of the waste. Two possible useful outputs are fertilizer and power that can be produced from the waste. Composting has been recommended in India because of the high organic content of the waste. Unlike wastes in western countries, which have high calorific value and low moisture content, and can therefore be used as a fuel, power generation in India has to take a different route, such as biomethanation. This involves gas generation followed by power production in a gas turbine. While these technologies have been tried out on a small scale for relatively homogeneous wastes such as vegetable wastes, poultry wastes, etc., they are yet to be tested at the municipal level for urban solid waste.

This case study is an attempt to study the economics of one method of resource recovery, namely biomethanation in a benefit-cost framework. Sanitary landfilling is used as the 'baseline' option against which the comparison is made.

There are three major stages in the process of biomethanation for resource recovery:

1. The wastes must be segregated to remove the non-organic fraction and could be sold as recyclables after sorting.
2. The organic waste must be digested to produce biogas, which is a mixture of methane and CO_2. The solid residue after digestion can be collected as fertilizer and sold in bags.
3. The gas has to be passed through a gas engine to produce electricity and can be used or sold to the grid.

There are very substantial investment and operating costs at each stage. On the other hand, there are at least three products—Power, Fertilizer and Recyclables—that can be considered as the direct benefits of biomethanation. The reduction of methane, a GHG, is a global environmental benefit. There are also local environmental benefits such as avoiding water pollution, explosions due to gas, etc. Wetlands and water bodies can also be protected instead of filling them up.

THE CONTEXT OF BIOMETHANATION CASE STUDY

The city of Lucknow (Uttar Pradesh) is faced with the problem of disposing 1500 tonnes of solid waste in an environmentally-sound manner. The Supreme Court of India had given a directive in 1996 to all local bodies and State Governments to improve the solid waste management practices in Class I cities (i.e., with population of one lakh or more) expeditiously. Many of the urban local bodies in the country are examining various options for solid waste collection and disposal. As a matter of policy, the Government has also recommended state and local governments to consider privatizing urban services and infrastructure wherever possible.

Lucknow has a population of about 25 lakh and generates solid waste of approximately 0.6 kg. per capita per day. Of this, around 1300 tonnes are collected by the Municipal Corporation. Waste disposal rates are likely to increase in the future. The waste has a high percentage of volatile matter (>65 per cent) and a calorific value of more than 2500 cal/gm on a dry basis. Recyclables such as paper, plastic, cloth and metal account for about 10–12 per cent of the waste. Hence, if the recyclables and inert materials are separated, the organic waste can be used for the production of biogas. The current practice of open dumping at locations such as low-lying areas or wetlands end up causing environmental problems at those sites. After considering a number of options such as landfilling, incineration, pyrolysis, briquetting etc., the Municipal Corporation has chosen anaerobic digestion followed by power generation as a suitable option (NIDC, 1996).

The Municipal Corporation has requested a consortium of engineering companies to set up a plant that would handle about 300 tonnes of solid waste in a digestor to produce biogas and an organic manure. Pre-treatment and sorting of the waste would be done before it is fed to the digestor, where about 100 tonnes of inorganics would be removed. The remaining 200 tonnes of organics would be digested to produce biogas. The biogas would then be used in a gas engine to recover about 5 MW of power. All the methane would be converted to CO_2 and water. The high capital cost of the project has to be ultimately met by the sale of the power generated and the organic manure, for which contractual arrangements have been made. The Central Government has sanctioned a capital grant (a subsidy) of Rs 15 crore to help defray the capital costs. Since a financial institution was also interested in extending finance, it wished to take a decision after making an economic assessment of the benefits and costs to society, including the environmental aspects.

How Can Benefit-Cost Analysis be Applied to a Solid Waste Disposal Project?

The objective is to get a complete economic picture of the project, including the benefits and costs that accrue to society and to groups that are not part of the project. The methodology of 'Economic Benefit-Cost Analysis' (BCA) is well-established in the literature and is generally used for decision-making for large public projects and policies (UNIDO, 1972; Bojo, 1992; Murty et al., 1993). More recently, BCA has been increasingly used in the assessment of environmental projects and policies. Since economic BCA differs in many ways from financial analysis, these aspects are briefly explained below.

With-Without the Project

The biomethanation project option is considered to be an alternative to the baseline alternative of landfilling. Then such a project is to be considered to be 'incremental' over the baseline. The purpose of BCA is then to determine if the additional benefits on account of the project exceed the additional costs. This situation is called 'with the project'. In other words, the project must be considered in relation to a baseline, i.e., what would have happened in the absence of the project? A baseline scenario (without the project) must be assumed in order to carry out a 'without' analysis. This is not the same as a 'do nothing' or 'business-as-usual' scenario. In the present case, the Municipal Corporation like in all other Class I cities, is required to dispose of its solid waste in an environmentally-sound manner. In the absence of the biomethanation plant, the solid waste would have to be disposed of in a sanitary landfill or by composting or by incineration. Open dumping (the existing practice) is not legally acceptable. In this analysis, we assume that the alternative would be a sanitary landfill with little or no 'externalities' (social costs) other than GHG emissions. We would have to estimate the hypothetical costs—capital and operating—for the sanitary landfill. We would also have to estimate the environmental costs of landfilling.

The analysis can be summarized as shown in Box 9.1:

BOX 9.1
Enviromental Lists of Landfilling

	With Project	Without Project
Benefits	Benefits of Biomethanation (B_1)	Benefits of landfill (B_0)
Costs	Costs of Biomethanation (C_1)	Costs of landfill (C_0)
Net benefits	$N_1 = B_1 - C_1$	$N_0 = B_0 - C_0$

Costs include the environmental costs in both cases. All benefits and costs are expressed in terms of Net Present Value using an appropriate discount rate.

If $N_1 > N_0$, then $(N_1 - N_0)$ would be the gain to society by undertaking the project.

If $N_1 < N_0$, then the project is not viable in an economic sense.

Valuation of Benefits and Costs

In economic analysis, all the benefit (outputs) and costs (resources) as well as any environmental benefits and costs have to be valued at their true resource prices. For example, land, which is a major resource has to be valued at its resource cost. Similarly, the outputs of the project must be valued at their 'shadow prices', if the contractual arrangements differ from the market price. Conceptually, one may also have to value several other resources such as labour and foreign exchange at their shadow prices (UNIDO, 1972). But this is not done here, since these are assumed to be the same as the market price. Market price reflects true resource prices, when markets are not distorted by monopoly power, government intervention, etc.

Non-economic Costs and Benefits

There are many financial costs such as interest charges on capital, subsidies, royalty, duties, etc., that are to be included in financial analysis, but not in economic analysis. The rationale is that these are simply financial transfers that have no bearing on the economic value of the resources or outputs of the project.

Social Discount Rate

Projects involving streams of benefits and costs over a long period of time need to be evaluated after necessary discounting. This step is necessary as the benefits and costs accruing in different periods are not comparable in terms of their opportunity values and, hence, they are not even additive. Discounting the benefits and costs over time requires a value for the discount rate[1]. In this analysis, the opportunity cost of capital is used as the rate of discount, i.e., the return that the promoters would get if they were to invest their resources in some other project. Since the financial institutions currently treat 14—15 per cent as the appropriate rate of return for their projects, it was decided to use 15 per cent in this solid waste project. It must be noted that the discount rate is 'the pure rate of time preference' and is not a deflator to adjust for price changes. This is because, all costs and benefits are initially expressed in terms of prices with 2000 as the base year. We assume that the real value of all resources and outputs remain the same in the future years. But they need to be discounted to bring them to the present value, to account for the opportunity cost of capital[2].

[1] In 'Social Forestry: A Case Study from Karnataka', Ninan and Jyothis explain the rationale for this in some detail.

[2] In financial analysis, on the other hand, inflating the costs and benefits to the future change in prices is done, before any discounting is done.

Transport Costs

It is assumed that all inputs are available at the factory gate or at the landfill at the costs mentioned. Similarly, the value of the outputs (benefits) are at the point of generation and not at the point of use. Thus, transport costs are embedded in the case of inputs. In the case of outputs, the cost of the output to the final user would be greater on account of the transport cost.

Environmental Costs

While solid waste management takes care of the environmental problems of the city's wastes, the disposal options themselves can add to local or global pollution. The costs imposed on society by such a pollution must be accounted. If damage costs are not available, then the cost of abating pollution can be used in its place.[3]

Local Environmental Costs

In the case of biomethanation, there are air emissions of NO_x, particulates, SO_2, etc., from the final stack. NO_x is normally the pollutant of concern in gas engines. Since we were informed that the emissions are within emission limits, we have assumed that there are no social costs due to air pollution. Since most of the liquid effluents are to be recycled, there may not be water pollution to any significant extent. In this analysis, we ignore any social costs on account of local air and water pollution.

In the case of sanitary landfilling, leachate collection will result in effluents that would have to be treated, particularly for organics. Otherwise, there would be contamination of ground or surface water. Air emissions from the landfill other than carbon dioxide and methane (which are discussed later) are unlikely to exceed emission standards. Thus, in the case of the landfill also, we are ignoring the social cost of local pollution. We have ignored this cost in the computations. Both biomethanation and landfills would also have potential safety problems due to the generation of gas and the possibility of explosion.

[3] Ideally, one may like to develop the kind of model suggested by Murty in this book to arrive optimal price or pollution tax for abatement (at which marginal abatement cost and marginal damage costs are equal). Alternatively, the abatement costs are to be consistent with the pollution standards, as is done in this analysis.

Global Pollution

Of much greater importance are the GHG emissions from the disposal of solid waste. In India, landfills have been identified as the third largest source of methane emissions (Gupta et al., 1998). In the case of sanitary landfills, the landfill gas consists of methane (55 per cent) and CO_2 (45 per cent) and small quantities of other pollutants. If there is gas collection, then about 40 per cent of the methane generated can be recovered and converted to CO_2 with or without power generation. The remaining 60 per cent is released into the atmosphere. In the case of biomethanation, we are assuming that all the methane after digestion is converted to CO_2.

WHAT ARE THE ENVIRONMENTAL COSTS OF GREENHOUSE GAS EMISSIONS?

Greenhouse gases like CO_2 and methane are 'uniformly mixed pollutants' in the sense that they have the same effect on the atmosphere, regardless of their geographic point of origin. Hence, the impact of a tonne of CO_2 on the global environment is the same whether it is emitted in India or the US. In theory, emission taxes or fees should be set at that level where the marginal damage caused by one additional tonne of CO_2 equals the marginal cost of abatement. In practice, because of the difficulty in estimating damage costs, the marginal cost of abatement is used as a proxy.

A recent IPCC working group report (1999) indicates that at present, the lowest cost of CO_2 abatement is equivalent to US $ 35 per tonne of CO_2. However, since the marginal damage cost is likely to be less than the abatement cost, it may be prudent to assume a value much less than US $35 per tonne of CO_2. We have assumed the value used in California of US $9 per tonne (Carlin, 1995).

There is also considerable debate in the literature on the Global Warming Potential (GWP) of methane vis-à-vis CO_2. Michaelis (1992) uses a 'lifetime'OPPNB factor of 10. Although in terms of warming potential, methane would be 58 times higher than CO_2, it degrades more quickly than CO_2. White et al., (1995) cite an IPCC study that says that on a weight basis 1 kg of methane will cause an equivalent contribution to global warming of 35 kg of CO_2 taken over a 20-year time span. A study by W.S. Atkins (1996) cited another IPCC study, which indicates that the GWP of methane is 24.5 times that of CO_2 on a weight basis. In this study, we have used this figure since it is a fairly recent estimate of GWP of methane. Since the CO_2 damage cost is assumed to be US $9 per tonne, the methane damage cost is assumed to be 9×24.5 = US $220.50 per tonne of methane. The key point to be noted is that the capture and conversion of methane to carbon dioxide has significant environmental benefit, in the form of lowered environmental damage.

How are the Costs and Benefits of Biomethanation Calculated?

The detailed project report (DPR) prepared by the Consortium contains the technical and financial details on which the following analysis is based. As mentioned earlier, the financing arrangements, subsidies etc., are not relevant for economic analysis.

Project Costs

Land

1. The land provided for the project must be valued at its opportunity cost. The land requirements are 20,245 m². The land registration office in Lucknow has valued this particular area at Rs 608/ m² . (The market value may differ, but in this case may not be reliable for long-term analysis.) The resource value of the land = $20,245 \times 608$ = Rs 1.231 crore.
2. The non-recyclable inert materials have to be disposed off in a sanitary landfill. The rejects of 50 tonnes per day would require a landfill area of 76,042 m².[4] The land cost would be Rs 4.623 crore. Since the materials are inert, it is assumed that there would be no gas generation.

---

[4] Computation of Land Requirements for Landfill

$$\text{Land Requirement in m}^2 = \frac{\text{Annual Quantity of} \times \text{Number of years Solid waste (tonnes)}}{\text{Density (times / m}^3) \times \text{Depth (m)}}$$

Density = 0.9 tonnes / m³

Sanitary Landfill area requirement for inerts in Option 1 = $\dfrac{50 \times 365 \times 15}{0.9 \times 4}$ = 76042 m²

Sanitary Landfill area requirement for Option 2 = $\dfrac{270 \times 365 \times 15}{0.9 \times 4}$ = 410625 m²

Thus, the total land costs would amount to Rs 5.854 crore.

Capital Costs

The investment costs given in the DPR amount to Rs 65 crore. However, three items, namely (i) the import duty on the gas engines of Rs 2.85 crore, (ii) the loan processing fees of Rs 0.40 crore and (iii) the interest charge of Rs 1.50 crore cannot be included in an economic analysis. The remaining capital costs amount to Rs 60.25 crore.

Capital cost has been divided between 2000 and 2001 as Rs 30.125 crore in each year. It is assumed that the life of the plant is 30 years. The total discounted value would be Rs 56.33 crores.

Leasing Cost

The gas engines used for power generation will be leased over a ten-year period. The annual cost would be Rs 1.8 crore towards investment and Rs 2.9 crore towards operation and maintenance for a total annual cost of Rs 4.7 crore at current prices. It is assumed that there will be no additional costs for the remainder of the project. As shown in Table 9.1, the leasing cost is from 2002–11 only. The present value of the leasing costs discounted @ 15 per cent is Rs 17.837 crore for the above period.

Operation and Maintenance Costs

The annual operation and maintenance costs given in the DPR amount to Rs 2.45 crore. However, two items, namely land (Rs 0.002 crore) and royalty (Rs 0.13 crore) cannot be included for economic analysis. The discounted values of the operation and maintenance cost would be Rs 11.46 crore for the period up to 2030.

Project Benefits

Power

The net power available for sale is 1,15,558 kwh /day. The consortium has entered into an agreement with the State Electricity Board (SEB) to buy the power at Rs 3.16/kwh from 2002 onwards. The power tariff for 2002 was fixed using a base of Rs 2.25/kwh in 1995 prices, with an inflation rate of 5 per cent. Therefore, in 2000, prices the equivalent price would be Rs 2.87/kwh. Thus, the annual value of the power in 2000 prices = Rs 11.94 crore per year. The discounted value of the power up to 2030 at 15 per cent would be Rs 58.98 crore.

TABLE 9.1
Present Value of Costs of Biomethanation Plant

(in Rs crore)

Initial Costs (in crore)			
	Land for Plant	=	Rs 1.231
	Land for Landfill	=	Rs 4.623
	Capital Cost (2000)	=	Rs 30.125
	Capital Cost (2001)	=	Rs 26.205
	(discounted @ 15 per cent)		
	Total	=	Rs 62.184
Recurring Costs (in crore)			
Year	2002 ... 2011		Present value discounted @ 15%
1) Leasing Cost	Rs 4.7 ...	Rs 4.7	Rs 17.837
2) Operation and maintenance	Rs 2.32 ...	Rs 7.32	Rs 11.460
			Rs 29.297
Present Value of Project Costs	=		Rs 91.481

Sources: SEBs and author's calculations

Manure

The market value of organic manure is about Rs 2 per kg or Rs 2000 per tonne. Although the promoters have made a contractual arrangement to sell the manure for Rs 2900 per tonne with a buyer, it would be more appropriate for economic analysis to price any resource at its opportunity cost. The value of the manure would be Rs 2000 × 75 × 360 = Rs 5.40 crore per year. The discounted value of the manure up to 2030 at 15 per cent = Rs 26.68 crore.

Recyclables

The estimated value of the recyclables such as paper, plastics and cloth, of 40 tonnes / day at Rs 1.50 is around Rs 60,000 per day. The actual price that a buyer may offer may be less, depending on his transport cost. The value of the recyclables (at the factory gate) would be Rs 2.16 crore per year. (It is assumed that the plant operates for 360 days in a year.) The non-recyclable inerts of 50 tonnes which would be disposed off in a landfill, as mentioned earlier, would have no value. The discounted value of the recyclables would be Rs 10.67 crore for the period up to 2030 at discount rate of 15 per cent.

TABLE 9.2
Present Value of Benefits of Biomethanation Plant

(in Rs crore)

Recurring Benefits (in crore)			Present Value
	Year 2002	2030	Discounted @ 15%
Power	Rs 11.94 ...	Rs 11.94	Rs 58.98
Manure	Rs 5.40 ...	Rs 5.40	Rs 26.68
Recyclables	Rs 2.16 ...	Rs 2.16	Rs 10.67
Total			Rs 96.33

Sources: SEBs and author's calculations

Environmental Costs

Local Pollution

It is assumed that all the air emissions are within the standards and that the effluents are recycled. We are not including any local environmental costs.

Global Pollution

The biogas from the digestor is said to be a mixture of methane (23 tonnes) and CO_2 (35 tonnes) per day. If it is assumed that all the methane is converted to CO_2 in the gas engine, the CO_2 equivalent would be an added 63 tonnes per day.[5] Thus, the total emission of CO_2 would be 35 + 63 = 98 tonnes per day. The damage value of the CO_2 at US $ 9 per tonne would be: 98 × 360 × 9 × 45.65 = Rs 1.45 crore.

---

[5] Conversion of methane to CO_2

$$CH_4 + 2 O_2 \longrightarrow CO_2 + 2H_2 O$$

By weight = 16 g + 64 g $\longrightarrow$ 44 g + 36 g

Therefore, 23 tonnes of methane $\longrightarrow$ $\dfrac{23 \times 44}{16}$ = 63 tonnes of CO_2

(Assuming an exchange rate of US $ 1 = Rs 45.65) The discounted value of the GHG at 15 per cent up to 2030 would be Rs 7.16 crore.

Summary of Benefits and Costs

1. Benefits—Present value up to 2030 at 15 per cent

Power	Rs 58.98 crore
Manure	Rs 26.68 crore
Recyclables	Rs 10.67 crore
Total	Rs 96.33 crore

2. Costs—Present value up to 2030 at 15 per cent

Land	Rs 1.23 crore
Landfill for Inerts	Rs 4.62 crore
Capital	Rs 56.33 crore
Leasing Cost	Rs 17.84 crore
O & M Cost	Rs 11.46 crore
Total	Rs 91.48 crore

   Present value of net benefits (excluding environmental costs)
   = Rs 96.33 – Rs 91.48 = Rs 4.85 crore

   Present value of environmental costs = Rs 7.16 crore

   Present value of net benefits (including environmental costs)
   = – Rs 2.31 crore

WHAT ARE THE BENEFITS AND COSTS OF THE BASELINE OPTION—LANDFILLING?

The Municipal Corporation cannot continue the practice of open dumping. A wetland is not an appropriate disposal site. It is also likely that the ground water in the area is getting contaminated. There are also other environmental problems associated with open dumping. In the light of the Supreme Court decision, other options such as composting, sanitary landfilling, incineration etc., need to be considered. The status quo or 'business-as-usual' scenario cannot be used as the baseline. We have used sanitary landfilling as the baseline since it is the most widely used practice for disposal of solid wastes. We have assumed that it would be a lined landfill with provision for gas and leachate collection. The collected gas would be flared and the uncollected gas would be released to the atmosphere. Other options such as composting, power generation from landfill gas or pelletization could also have been compared. We could not do so due to the limited time available for gathering the necessary data.

Land Costs

The most expensive component is the land necessary for a landfill. In this analysis, we have assumed that about 10 per cent or 30 tonnes would be removed by ragpickers etc., before the landfilling actually takes place. Hence, 270 tonnes of organic and inorganic material would be deposited in the landfill. We have estimated the land requirement for depositing 270 tonnes of waste per day up to a depth of 4m over a period of 15 years. The market price of land in the outskirts of Lucknow was found to be Rs 608 / m² from the land registration office. We have assumed that after 15 years, the landfill would be covered and used later as a park or recreation area. The value of the recovered land is assumed to be equal to the cost of obtaining a second landfill site for the next 15 years. Therefore, there would only be the initial cost of land for the first landfill.

Required land area $= 410{,}625$ m² (For details see foot-notes 1 and 2)

$$\text{Cost of Land} = 410{,}625 \text{ m}^2 \times 608 \text{ Rs / m}^2$$
$$= \text{Rs } 24{,}96{,}60{,}000 = \text{Rs } 24.97 \text{ crore}$$

Recurring Costs

Annualized Capital Costs

For sanitary landfilling, costs relating to equipment, civil works, gas and leachate collection system etc., have to be incurred. A consulting firm ERM, UK estimated these to be US $ 3.30 per tonne for India using a discount rate of 5 per cent for a period of 15 years (ERM, 1996). The undiscounted cost would be US $ 4.77 per tonne. For disposal of 270 tonnes per year, the undiscounted annualized capital cost would be $4.77 \times 45.65 \times 270 = \text{Rs } 58{,}793$ per year.

Operation and Maintenance Cost

The other costs associated with operation and maintenance would be US $1.80 per tonne for India. The undiscounted cost would be US

$2.60 per tonne. For disposal of 270 tonnes per day the equivalent operation and maintenance (O&M)cost for a year would be 2.60 × 45.65 × 270 = Rs 32, 046 per year.

Thus the recurring cost would be = Rs 90,840 per year
                                    = Rs 0.01 crore (rounded off)

Benefits

Recovered Land

The value of the recovered land from the first landfill is used to finance the second landfill for the next 15 years. The value of the second landfill would be available only after 30 years of use and 10 years of post-closure. Since the discounted value would be small, this benefit has been omitted.

Gas Recovered from the Landfill

The quality of the gas generated from the landfill would be on average 150 m³ per tonne of solid waste.

150 m³ × 270 tonnes = 40,500 m³ of biogas is generated per day

Since the methane content is assumed to be 55 per cent and the collection efficiency of 40 per cent; effective quantity of methane collected = 40,500 × 0.55 × 0.40 = 8910 m³. The value of the methane collected is assumed to be the same as natural gas. The price of natural gas inclusive of royalty and cess was Rs 2235 per 1000 m³ in 1994–5 prices (Sankar, 1998). Due to inflation, the value is assumed to be Rs 2800 per 1000 m³ or Rs 2.80 per m³ at 2000 prices. Value of the gas collected per year = 8910 × 2.8 × 365 = Rs 91,06,020 = Rs 0.91 crore.

Environmental Costs

There are two sets of environmental externalities.

Greenhouse Gas Emissions

1. Methane Emissions:

Uncollected methane (60 per cent) emitted to the atmosphere per day = 150m³ × 392 860 × 10⁻⁹ × 270 × 0.60 = 9.55 tonnes per day (White, et al., 1995)

Methane is assumed to have a damage value of US $ 220.5 per tonne
Damage value of methane emitted

from the landfill   = 220.5 × 45.65 × 365 × 9.55
       = Rs 3.432 crore per year

2. Quantity of methane collected = 9.55 × 0.40/0.60 = 6.37 tonnes

The collected methane is assumed to be converted to CO_2 by flaring

$$\text{Quantity of } CO_2 = 6.37 \times 44/16 = 17.52 \text{ tonnes/day}$$

Damage value of CO_2 = 17.52 × 365 × 9 × 45.65
       = Rs 0.263 crore per year

3. Quantity of CO_2 emitted from the landfill

= 150 × 883930 × 10^{-9} × 270 = 35.80 tonnes/day (White et al., 1995)

Damage value of CO_2

= 35.80 × 9 × 45.65 × 365 = Rs 0.537 crore per year

Total annual GHG emission damage = 0.537 + 0.263 + 3.432 = Rs 4.232 per year

Discounted costs of GHG for 30 years at 15 per cent
       = 4.232 × 6.566 = Rs 27.79 crore

Local Pollution

1. Other air emissions will also occur from the landfill.
2. The leachate collected from the landfill would have to be treated.

These costs are excluded from the analysis.

Summary of Benefits and Costs

Benefits

Annual value of the benefits = Rs 0.91 crore

Present value of the benefits = Rs 5.98 crore

discounted at 15 per cent over 30 years

Costs

Cost of land = Rs 24.97 crore

Annual cost of landfill = Rs 0.01 crore

Present value of costs = 24.97 + 0.07 = Rs 25.04 crore

discounted at 15 per cent over 30 years

Net Present Value

1. Excluding environmental costs = Rs 5.98 – Rs 25.04
   = – Rs 19.06 crore
2. Of environmental costs alone = Rs 27.79 crore
3. Including environmental costs = – Rs 46.85 crore

WHAT ARE THE MAJOR CONCLUSIONS OF THE STUDY?

The economic BCA analysis for the biomethanation project inclusive of environmental costs is given in Table 9.3.

TABLE 9.3
Present Value of Benefits and Costs

Present Value @ 15 per cent over 30 years	Biomethanation project (Rs crores)	Sanitary landfill (Rs crores)
Benefits	96.33	5.98
Costs	91.48	25.04
Net benefits	4.85	–19.06
Environmental costs	7.16	27.79
Net social benefits	–2.31	–46.85

Gain to Society of biomethanation = Rs –2.31 – (–46.85) = Rs 44.54 crore.

Sources: SEBs and author's calculations

The major conclusions can be summarized as follows:

1. Biomethanation has high benefits and high costs compared to the sanitary landfill. The cost in the case of the sanitary landfill is extremely dependent on the price of land. The large negative benefit is due to the fact that the land cost was estimated to be Rs 25 crores.

2. Both biomethanation and sanitary landfill emit GHGs, but the major difference is that the sanitary landfill emits some methane (even after provision of gas collection) which is much more detrimental to the environment than carbon dioxide.
3. The gain to society of nearly Rs 45 crore consists not only of the net social benefit of biomethanation, but also the averted cost of the landfill option. Thus, the assessment of biomethanation (from a social standpoint) must also take into account the benefit of not having a landfill, except for disposing the inert materials.

HOW WOULD THE CONCLUSIONS CHANGE IF THE ASSUMPTIONS WERE ALTERED?

Biomethanation necessarily has high risks—technical and economic. The technical risks are beyond the scope of this analysis. However, if less power is generated than assumed or if the recyclables have no value, then the calculations would change as shown below:

1. No benefit from recyclables: If the benefit from the biomethanation plant is restricted to power and manure, and there is no value addition from recyclables,
   Net benefit excluding environmental costs = 58.98 + 26.68 – 91.48 = - Rs 5.82 crore
   Net benefit including environmental costs = –5.82 – 7.16 = - Rs 12.98 crore
   The social gain from biomethanation would be
   = - Rs 12.98 – (– Rs 46.85) crore = Rs 33.87 crore.
   Biomethanation would be preferred to sanitary landfilling even if there was no value addition from the recyclables.
2. Revenue from power generation is less than anticipated and there is no benefit from recyclables: Table 9.4 table provides three scenarios of 50 per cent, 75 per cent and 100 per cent power generation of the optimal level of power generation of 5 MW.

Even the worst case (Scenario I) has a net benefit which is preferable to the sanitary landfill. The indifference point between biomethanation and sanitary landfill would be when the power generated is 42.6 per cent of the optimal level (i.e., about 2.23 MW) and the economic value of the recyclables is zero. Below 2.23 MW, the sanitary landfill would be more attractive. On the other hand, if the price of power was

TABLE 9.4

Sensitivity Analysis—Power Generation

Present value of benefit/cost	SCENARIOS		
	I	II	III
(Rs crore)	50% Power (2.5 MW)	75% Power (3.75 MW)	100% Power (5 MW)
Power	29.49	44.24	58.98
Manure	26.68	26.68	26.68
Total benefits	56.17	70.92	85.66
Direct costs	91.48	91.48	91.48
Net benefits	-35.31	-20.56	-5.82
Environmental costs	7.16	7.16	7.16
Net social benefits	-42.47	-27.72	-12.98

Source: Author's calculations

higher than assumed or if recyclables had value, the indifference point would correspondingly change. Many such scenarios could be generated with sensitivity analysis.

WHAT ARE THE GLOBAL ENVIRONMENTAL BENEFITS OF
THE BIOMETHANATION PROJECT?

The global environmental benefits of a project like biomethanation would be a reduction in GHG emissions when compared to a baseline, that in this case could be sanitary landfilling. The GHG emissions are not actually very different, but the GWP is significantly different because biomethanation captures all the methane and converts it to CO_2. In the case of the sanitary landfill (even with gas collection), 60 per cent of the methane escapes into the atmosphere. We have assumed in the analysis that methane has a GWP of 24.5 times that of CO_2 (W.S. Atkins Consultants, 1996). In other words, emitting one tonne of methane is equivalent to emitting 24.5 tonnes of CO_2. We can calculate for the landfill and biomethanation option the GWP in CO_2 equivalents as shown in Table 9.5.

The annual reduction in GWP of emissions from biomethanation

TABLE 9.5

Global Environmental Benefits of Biomethanation
(emission in tonnes per day)

Option	CO_2 emissions	Methane emissions	GWP in CO_2 equivalents	GWP reduction in CO_2 equivalent
Landfill (with gas collection)	53.32 tpd	9.55 tpd	287.3 tpd	0
Biomethanation	98.3 tpd	0	98.3 tpd	189 tpd

Sources: Author's calculations

compared to landfilling would be 68,985 tonnes/year of CO_2 equivalent. If the landfill did *not* have gas collection, the GWP reduction would be even higher and the global environmental benefits of biomethanation would be greater. The choice of the baseline is, therefore, of key importance.

One of the ways that emission reduction credits can be obtained is through joint ventures by institutions in developing countries and partners from developed countries. If these reductions are certified to be genuine emission reductions, a developed country providing the investment for the project could claim these as credits under the Clean Development Mechanism (CDM) of the Kyoto protocol. However, it would be up to the host developing country to decide whether or not to participate in the CDM process. The certified emission reduction requires 'environmental additionality' which refers to GHG reductions that are additional to any that would occur in the absence of the project (Toman, 2001). In our case study, the additionality is due to the capture and conversion of methane in biomethanation, compared to sanitary landfilling which emits much of the methane to the atmosphere.

WHAT ARE THE POLICY IMPLICATIONS OF THE STUDY?

Cities will be generally reluctant to use technologies like biomethanation on account of the high capital costs. Landfills are the preferred option because public land is often available without having to pay the full resource cost and recurring costs are quite low in comparison. But, land has increasingly become a scarce resource in the major cities. Finding suitable land may become difficult in the future. Also, methane emissions from landfills is a serious negative externality that will have to be controlled. At the present time, local governments are unlikely to be aware or concerned about global environmental problems.

Private-sector firms would be hesitant to finance projects with such high investments without some public assistance or guarantee. Since there are significant societal benefits, financial institutions/government may wish to extend financial assistance in the form of subsidies, grants, low interest loans etc., demonstrate to the use of this technology. If the technology is found to be viable, then assistance could be extended on a wider basis to other large cities.

REFERENCES

Asia Bioenergy (India) Ltd. (2000): *Power Generation and Organic Fertiliser Production Plant from Municipal Solid Waste at Lucknow, Uttar Pradesh*, Detailed Project Report, Chennai.

Bhide, A.D. and B.B. Sundaresan (1983): *Solid Waste Management in Developing Countries*, Indian National Scientific Documentation Centre, New Delhi.

Bojo, Jan (1992): *Environment and Development: An Economic Approach*, Kluwer Academics, Dordrecht.

Boyd, R. and Anil Markandya (2000): *Cost-Benefit Analysis and Cost Effectiveness Analysis* (mimeo), University of Bath, U.K.

Carlin, J. (1995): 'Environmental Externalities in Electric Power Markets: Acid Rain, Urban Ozone, and Climate Change', *Monthly Energy Review*, U.S. Energy Information Administration, Washington D.C., November 1995.

Central Pollution Control Board (1996): *Comprehensive Industry Document and National Environmental Standards for Gas-based Thermal Power Plants*, New Delhi.

Environmental Resources Management (1996): *Municipal Solid Waste Management Study for Madras Metropolitan Area*, Chennai.

Expert Committee (1998): *Solid Waste Management in Class I Cities in India*, Interim Report of the Committee constituted by the Honourable Supreme Court of India, New Delhi, June.

Gupta, S., Krishna Mohan, R. Prasad, S. Gupta and A. Kansal (1998): 'Solid waste management in India: Options and opportunities', *Resources, Conservation and Recycling*, 24: 137–54.

IPCC Working Group (1999): *Technological and Economic Potential of Green House Gas Emissions Reduction*, Third Assessment Report.

Michaelis, P. (1992): 'Global warming: Efficient policies in the case of multiple pollutants', *Environmental and Resource Economics*, 2 : 61–78.

Murty, M.N., Gopal K. Kadekodi and N. Mongia (1993): *Environmental Impact of Projects-Planning and Policy Issues*, Institute of Economic Growth, Working Paper No. 158, New Delhi.

National Industrial Development Corporation (1996): *Prefeasibility Study on Municipal Solid Waste Management at Lucknow*, sponsored by Uttar Pradesh Non-Conventional Energy Development Agency, Lucknow.

Planning Commission, Government of India (1995): *Report of High Power Committee on Urban Solid Waste management in India*, New Delhi.

Reddy, Sudhakar and S. Galab (1999): *Management of Urban Organic Waste in India: A Case Study of Hyderabad City*, Monograph, Centre for Economic and Social Studies, Hyderabad.

Reyer, Gerlagh, Pieter van Beukering, Madhu Verma, PP Yadav and Preety Pandey (1999): *Integrated Modelling of Solid Waste in India*, CREED Working Paper No. 26, Amsterdam.

Sankar, U. (1998): 'The energy sector', in *Economic Instruments for Environmental Sustainability*, Sankar U. and O.P. Mathur (eds.), National Institute of Public Finance and Policy and Madras School of Economics, New Delhi and Chennai.

Toman, Michael A. (2001): 'Establishing and Operating the Clean Development Mechanism', in *Climate Change Economics and Policy*, Resources for the Future, Washington, D.C.

UNDP/World Bank (1993): *Community Based Solid Waste Management— Panaji Case Study*, New Delhi.

UNIDO (1972): *Guidelines For Project Evaluation*, Vienna.

W.S. Atkins Consultants (1996): *Centralised Anaerobic Digestion – Review of Environmental Effects*, sponsored by U.K. Ministry of Agriculture, Fisheries and Food, London.

White, P.R., M. Franke and P. Hindle (1995): *Integrated Solid Waste Management: A Lifecycle Inventory*, Blackie Academic and Professional, London.

Fiscal and Institutional Approaches to Pollution Abatement
A Case Study of Water Pollution

M.N. Murty

Dealing with Water Pollution

This chapter provides some insights into the approaches for water pollution abatement. A review of empirical works in India is attempted with a more detailed description of some selected case studies. Studies in India by and large have recommended a hybrid instrument of pollution tax-standards for controlling industrial water pollution. However, in the case of industrial estates containing small-scale enterprises, the approach of collective action is recommended. In some recent studies in India and abroad, empirical support is provided to a new model of pollution control in which the local community, market, and government play equal role.

Water resources are important environmental resources. The very process of economic development creates demand for several services offered by the water resources. Industries and households demand water for industrial processes, domestic uses and drinking. In addition, water acts as a public good service as in waste disposal. Agricultural activities create demand for irrigation, another example of private good service and to carry fertilizer and pesticide residues, a public good service, from the water resources. Water resources have natural regenerative or renewable capacity and they can accept certain amounts of pollution loads without affecting themselves. That means, this natural regenerative capacity of water imposes a constraint on the functioning of waste disposal services. If the water demand for waste disposal exceeds the supply constrained by its natural regenerative capacity, the degradation of water resources starts. Given the public good nature of waste disposal service, the demand may exceed the natural supply. The problem then, is to look for instruments and institutions to reduce water demand for waste disposal services to their natural levels of supply.

The fiscal and institutional approaches for water pollution abatement by industries, illustrated with some case studies, are dealt with here.

In 'Alternative Instruments and Institutions for Pollution Abatement', a brief account of the alternative instruments and institutions for water pollution abatement is presented. The section 'A Look at Environmental Regulation in India' provides a case study of using pollution taxes. 'Tax Standards Approach for Industrial Water Pollution Abatement in India' describes the institutional approach of collective action to control water pollution by the industries. 'Collective Action' deals with a new model explaining the industrial pollution abatement in the developing countries. Finally 'Conclusion' sums up the approaches to pollution abatement.

ALTERNATIVE INSTRUMENTS AND INSTITUTIONS FOR
POLLUTION ABATEMENT

Pollution is an economic externality (as explained in 'Enviromental Economics through Case Studies'). Alternative institutions for the control of environmental pollution are: (i) Government (e.g., pollution control boards), (ii) market, (where the sellers and buyers meet) and (iii) community or associations of people (who may like to avoid or control pollution). A practical policy may involve all these institutions. Normally one does not come across a market situation with producers of waste and processors of waste acting with the same price/ cost arrangements to abate such pollutants. Therefore, it is generally stated that market forces fail to control environmental pollution.[1] Government has been viewed as an alternative institution to deal or manage the environment. Community action or people's participation

---

[1] Waste disposal service of environmental resources is a public good with a property that the exclusion is not possible by charging a price for it.

is now gaining prominence as an alternative to governmental agencies for the management of environmental resources.[2]

What can the Government do?

Non-market policy instruments include command-and-controls (CACs). Market-based instruments consist of pollution taxes (Pigou, 1920) and marketable pollution permits (Dales, 1968). These are often referred to as economic instruments. The choice between these instruments depends both on their efficacy in achieving the target level of emissions as well as on the relative size of the welfare losses they produce (Baumol and Oates, 1988). Government can use non-market policy instruments, market-based or economic instruments or a combination of the two.

The CAC instruments are in the form of fines, penalties and threats of legal action for closure of the factories and imprisonment of the owners. They can be used either for facilitating the use of specific technologies for environment management or for the realization of specific environmental standards. Most often the cost of imposing and implementing compliance are generally higher when CAC instruments are used than with economic instruments. Furthermore, under CAC instruments, there can be no incentives for firms to innovate or invest in more efficient pollution control technologies or in cleaner process technologies.

What are Economic Instruments?

Economic instruments can be divided into three categories: (i) price-based instruments, (ii) quantity-based instruments and (iii) hybrid instruments. These instruments are often called market-based instruments.

The price-based instruments were first suggested by Pigou in 1931 in the form of taxes and subsidies to deal with detrimental and beneficial environmental externalities in production and consumption. Instances are pollution taxes on a polluting commodity either at the production stage (e.g., on paper, leather, electricity, etc.) or at the consumption stage (e.g., on cigarette, packed food, etc.) or on a

---

[2] This alternative is now becoming attractive because of high monitoring and enforcing costs to the Pollution Control Boards (PCBs) and other governmental agencies and the presence of non-benevolent governments especially in many developing countries.

polluting input (e.g., fuel inputs, chemicals, etc.). The pollution tax or Pigouvian tax is a corrective instrument to realize the socially optimal level of economic activity generating pollution. Also, there can be subsidies on commodities, the production of which generate environmental benefits (e.g., tree *patta* scheme, under which for every four trees one protect one gets a free tree).

Let us illustrate the Pigouvian Tax/subsidy framework diagrammatically. In Figure 10.1, MCA, MD respectively represent the marginal cost of abatement and marginal damages from pollution. Abatement costs are incurred by the producers or firms. Damage costs are incurred by the consumers or affected people. P^m, P^* stand respectively for pollution loads with and without tax instrument; 't' stands for the pollution tax. With the polluters using the pollution abatement technologies, the Pareto optimality requires that the pollution can be reduced up to the level at which MCA is equal to MD. If a tax equivalent to 't' on per unit of pollution is levied on the polluter-based on the 'polluter pay principle', the polluter has an incentive to reduce pollution up to the optimal level, P^*, in the free market. The

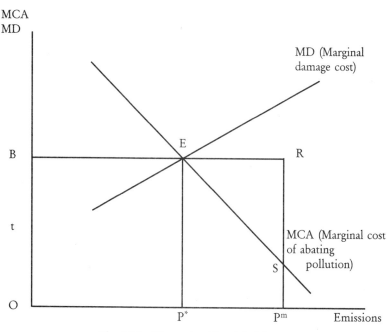

Fig. 10.1: Pigouvian Tax Model

polluter has two choices: (i) pay tax equivalent to P^*ERP^m or (ii) reduce pollution load from P^m to P^* incurring the cost equal to P^*ESP^m. If he reduces pollution, he will save cost equal to ERS. Therefore, given the tax rate equivalent to 't', he chooses to reduce pollution rather than paying the tax.

The damages from pollution are felt by a large number of people (more so with water pollution). Therefore, the damages from a unit of pollution at margin is the sum of marginal damages to all the affected people. To design a Pigouvian tax, we require information about abatement-cost functions of polluting firms and damage functions for all the affected people. The cost of collecting the information to estimate these functions can be prohibitively high. For example, lakhs of people are affected from the pollution of a major river like the Ganges or an urban airshed like Delhi. Therefore, it may not be economically feasible to design the Pigouvian tax.

What are quantity-based instruments? Dales (1968) has suggested an alternative to the pollution tax, a system of tradable pollution rights for the management of environment. This is known as a quantity-based instrument. He has proposed that the property rights be defined to the use and abuse of environment. One who pollutes less than the tolerant or set limit (or environment target) gets an entitlement to trade his rights. Such an entitlement can be offered for sale to a bidder. This system is like a tax to achieve the specified environment target at a minimum cost.

For example, in the case of air pollution, under this approach, first the optimal level pollution in a given geographical area is determined. The level of pollution to be tolerated is then divided into a number of permits among the various polluting units within the area (either by free distribution or by auctioning). Firms which are already comparatively more efficient in controlling their wastes or pollution (the ones that face lower unit cost for pollution control) may continue their original level of production and emissions. But they will have some extra pollution permits (or entitlements) to spare. They can sell such extra permits to firms that are less efficient in controlling their wastes (to those that face higher unit costs for pollution abatement). Provided monitoring is possible and effective, the net result is that total pollution is kept within the prescribed levels. The more efficient firms will sell their surplus permits to less efficient firms that require more permits in order to continue with original production plans. In this process, a market for pollution permits is created, in which trading in permits takes place up to the point at which the aggregate supply of permits is equal to the aggregate demand for permits and the equilibrium permit price is equal to the marginal cost of abatement to each firm.

Mixed Instruments: A Practical Approach

In practice, we can also have a mixture of both CACs and economic instruments. Economic instruments alone may not be feasible because their high imposition requires a lot of information on firm level emission, technology etc., which are not easy to come by. CAC measures alone are inefficient measures (they may result even in the use of costly pollution abatement technologies by the firms). Similarly, the estimation of damages to affected people in the case of pollution tax, and knowing a prioi the optimal level of pollution in the case of tradable permits, poses practical problems for the design of economic instruments. Fixation of pollution standards (Minimum National Standards (MINAS)) a priori by Pollution Control Boards (PCBs) and using either pollution tax or marketable permits instrument to induce the polluter industry to meet those standards is a hybrid method, using regulatory and economic instruments. However, in this case the criteria for fixation of environmental standards is a subject of debate, about whether they have to be decided on a scientific basis or on the basis of referendum or political process. For instance, scientifically, they are to be based on the evidence concerning the effects of air pollution on health or of polluted water on fish and human life. They can be alternatively decided through a political process by having a referendum on the choice among alternative sets of pollution standards. Still, there are issues such as: should standards be set at state levels or national, should the standards be compromised between the industry and people, and so on.

However, we need an estimate of pollution abatement cost as a starting point. It is feasible to obtain an estimate of this if (i) the polluters are much less in number than the affected people and (ii) tangible information can be obtained about technologies used by the polluters, pollution loads and levels of production. Using the firm-level data on pollution loads, costs of abatement and production levels, the pollution abatement cost functions can be estimated using econometric techniques (some of which are referred in 'Environmental

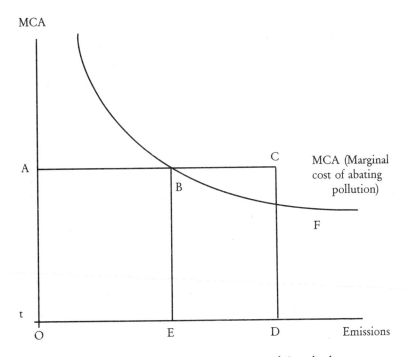

Fig. 10.2: Adhering to Environmental Standards

Economics through Case Studies). Given the environmental standards and the estimated marginal abatement cost function, a rate of tax can be fixed such that, the firms will automatically have an incentive to reduce pollution for meeting the standards. This is explained in Figure 10.2.

Let the emission standard be OE. Let the current rate of the firms emission be OD. If the firm has to reduce pollution load from D to E as per the environmental standard, the rate of tax equivalent to OA will make the firm to do so. The rate of tax 't' in this case is the marginal abatement cost corresponding to the level of pollution permitted by the given standard. The firm has an incentive to carry out pollution abatement rather than paying tax because the cost of abatement given by the area BFDE in the figure is lower than the tax liability given by the area BCDE. Similarly, marketable pollution permits can be used to obtain the reduction in pollution loads by firms, as required by environmental standards. It can be shown that the taxes standards or tradable permits and standards method results in the adoption of least cost technologies by the firms (Baumol and Oates, 1988).

Why do we still need some elements of CAC measures? There can be many situations in which CAC instruments are unavoidable. In several cases, the social cost of a particular activity depends on factors beyond the control of those directly involved. For example, the effects of discharge of effluents into a river depends upon the conditions of the river at that particular point of time. Similarly, stagnant air can trap air pollutants, perhaps even collecting them becomes hazardous. Therefore, exogenous meteorological conditions may contribute to occasional crisis requiring temporary emergency measures in the form of CAC. Pollution tax rates cannot be changed at short notice to deal with emergencies and even if the changes are effected, polluters response follow with a longer time lag. Marketable permits also result in long-run adjustments in environmental quality and are not suitable for emergencies. CAC measures on the other hand, can be quickly operated to deal with more than the normal amount of emissions arising out of emergencies, since they do not require extra monitoring.

But, in practice, pure CACs are not easy to impose as the policing cost is quite high. A mixed strategy is an alternative strategy with lower costs. It also helps to realize given environmental standards. This is often referred as 'tax standards approach'.

Community Action or People's Participation

The strategy other than governmental and economic instruments is the community action. With the failure of the legal system to control pollution and difficulty in introducing tax-subsidy-quota systems, it is important to look for institutions that are an alternative to the government for controlling environmental externalities (World Bank, 1999; Murty et al.,1999). The alternatives can be (i) collective action of all the agents relevant for managing the environment and (ii) a purely market option. At this stage, it is useful to introduce an important conceptual framework from environmental economics that can help in understanding the emergence of collective actions.

Coase (1960) has argued that many types of externalities can be optimally controlled by creating specific property rights among concerned agents. The concept of property rights has already been dealt in 'Environmental Economics through Case Studies'. An important statement by Coase, now known as the Coase theorem, is explained as follows: Consider a situation of an externality (say pollution). There are two agents involved here, namely, the one which generates pollution and the other affected by it. Let there be a bargain between them regarding the compensation to be paid by the generator to the affected party. For the moment, assume that the cost of bargaining is zero. According to the Coase theorem, given the initial property rights to any resource, either to the generator of the externality or to the affected party, the bargaining between the two parties results in the optimal control of externality. The final outcome of bargaining is invariant to the initial property rights. For example, in the case of air pollution, whether the right to clean air is vested in the affected people or whether the right to pollute is given to the polluter, the finally bargained amount of compensation would be the same. This result is illustrated through Figure 10.3. In this figure, pollution load is measured along the x-axis and the MCA and the MD are measured along the y-axis. The optimal pollution load is given as OE. For the pollution loads higher and lower than OE, there are incentives to bargain for gain between the polluter and the affected party. If the polluter has the right to pollute beyond OE, then the MD is higher than MCA for the pollution loads, the affected party has an incentive to pay the polluter any rate lower than MD for a unit reduction in pollution and the polluter has an incentive to accept that amount at any rate higher than the MCA. Therefore, bargaining between the two parties takes place until the pollution load is reduced to OE. Similarly, since MCA is higher than MD for pollution loads lower than OE, the polluter has an incentive to offer a payment to the affected party at any rate lower than MCA and the affected party has an incentive to accept the same at any rate higher than MD. Again, the bargaining between them leads to the optimal pollution load OE.

In practice, there are several practical problems for the Coasean bargaining to work in controlling the environmental externalities. First of all, in reality, the transaction costs or costs of bargaining are not zero but positive. It can be shown that with positive costs of bargaining, the resulting pollution load through bargaining can be higher or lower than the optimal pollution load 'OE' depending on the initial property rights.

There are practical difficulties in applying this model in handling pollution matters in actualities. Firstly, with the positive transaction

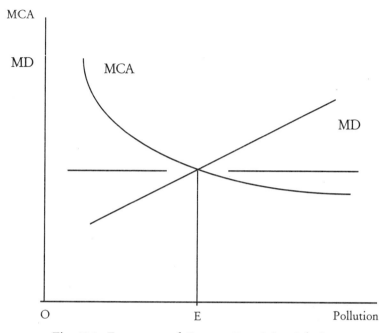

Fig. 10.3: Emergence of Coasean Bargaining Solution

costs, the final result will no longer be invariant to the initial property rights. Secondly, one of the key assumptions in the Coasean solution is that all the externalities are captured in the value of property rights and there are incentives for gainful bargaining. This can work well for the externalities on a smaller scale or local externalities of the type described by Coase (a building that blocks a windmill's air currents; a confectioner's machine that disturbs a doctor's quiet etc.). However, many environmental externalities occur on a grander scale with a large number of receivers and many times, a good number of generators. Take the case of pollution of a river, in which a large number of firms as generators, and individuals as affected people are involved. Here, defining individual property rights and facilitating bargaining is a bit difficult, as more than one individual is involved as generator and receiver. One way of dealing with this problem is to create a common property right to the river for all the affected people as one group and have an association of polluters of the river as the other group. The third problem for Coasean bargaining arises again in the context of defining the property rights for an environmental resource. The environmental resource is a stock affecting the welfare of both the present and future generations. Capitalization of future benefits from this resource is not possible because property rights to future generations of affected people cannot be defined. One approach in order to take care of the future, is to consider the government as its representative. The government can compete in the market for environmental property rights of the future generation and pay for it by issuing a debt which has to be serviced by future generations . Another approach is based on the assumption that the present generation has a bequest motive to the future and wants to bequeath to the future the preserved resources. However, both government intervention and bequest motive are outside the scope of Coase's property rights' approach.

In the Coasean bargaining solution, the government has a minimal role to play. Its role is only to create property rights and protect them, and then the free-market bargaining between the agents will optimally control the externality. Various institutional alternatives for the control of environmental externalities contain some elements of market mechanism with the government playing only a limited role. Given the doubtful quality of government and transaction costs of government instruments, it is imperative to look for new institutions to define and implement property rights for the environmental externalities. Under all such considerations, collective action can be a viable option.

A LOOK AT ENVIRONMENTAL REGULATION IN INDIA

India is having a comprehensive environmental legislation regarding pollution control measures. By and large, it is only using CAC measures.[3] India has not implemented the choice of a mix of instruments (mentioned in 'Alternative Instruments and Institutions for Pollution Abatement?' above) for the control of industrial pollution so far. There are several empirical studies in India, now, exploring the possibility of using economic instruments and the institutions facilitating people's participation in the management of environmental resources (Mehta, et al., 1996; Murty, et al., 1999; Pandey, 1998; Misra, 1999; World Bank, 1999). These studies demonstrate the possibilities of using economic instruments for the control of pollution by

---

[3] For a list of some major ones regarding water pollution see 'Pollution Control in Tanneries'.

industries, especially by the big factories, and the use of institutions facilitating collective action to control industrial pollution by the small-scale industries in an industrial estate, and the management of forest resources.

Environmental Legislation in India

There is a spate of environmental legislations in India starting from the early 1970s. Chronologically, they are the Wildlife Protection Act of 1974; the Water (Prevention and Control of Pollution) Act of 1974; the Water Cess Act in 1977; the Forest Conservation Act in 1980; the Air (Prevention and Control of Pollution) Act in 1981; the Environment (Protection) Act of 1986 and the Public Liability Insurance Act of 1991. In 1988, the Water Cess Act of 1977 was amended as the Water (Prevention and Control of Pollution) Cess Act, along with the Air Act of 1981.[4] 'Pollution Control in Tanneries' by Sankar also provides some more details regarding environmental regulations in India.

Of these, the acts that directly concern industrial production in India are the Water Act (1974), the Water Cess Act (1977 and 1988), the Air Act (1981 and 1988) and the Environment (Protection) Act or EPA (1986). While the first two have laid the foundation for legislations in the context of air and water pollution in the country, the EPA is designed to fill the gaps still remaining in the legal framework for the control of industrial pollution. The third is more of a revenue-generating legislation than a measure to restrict the consumption of water by industrial units in the interests of resource conservation.

Three issues of substance are dealt with by these three acts.

1. They detail the institutional foundations of environmental regulation of industrial pollution. The early acts provided for the setting up of PCBs at the central and the state levels, empowered to prevent, control and abate air and water pollution and to advise governments on matters pertaining to such pollution. The CPCB also coordinates the activities of the State Boards. The acts also specify that industrial units are to provide on demand all information regarding their effluents and treatment methods.

---

[4] The Water (Prevention and Control of Pollution) Act and the Air (Prevention and Control of Pollution) Act are hereafter referred to as the Water Act and the Air Act, respectively.

2. They set the national standards for air and water quality. The actual standards are laid down by the Central Pollution Control Board (CPCB, 1995), in consultation with institutions such as the National Environmental Engineering Research Institute (NEERI) in Nagpur. The standards, termed Minimum National Standards (MINAS) are defined for the country as a whole, although individual states have the option of making them more stringent. Standards are currently specified in concentration units. For example, in the case of waste water milligrams per litre of certain parameters like biological-oxygen demand (BOD), chemical-oxygen demand (COD), suspended solids (SS), total dissolved solids (TDS) and pH values are used. In the case of air pollution[5] suspended particulate matter (SPM), sulphur dioxide (SO_2) and nitrogen dioxide (NO_2), are measured. These standards are further specified, in the case of water pollution, according to the sink for the waste water and, thus, specific standards exist for discharge into surface water, streams, rivers and coastal areas.

3. They lay down regulatory procedures for ensuring that standards are met by individual units. Following the (yearly) application by an industrial unit to the State Pollution Control Board (SPCB), a consent order is issued once the board is satisfied that effluent treatment will ensure the realization of the relevant water or air quality standards. But in case of non-compliance with these standards, the boards are empowered to take action against such industrial units, with measures ranging from fines to imprisonment cutting off electricity and water connections.

4. In addition, the EPA of 1986 gives powers to the central government to pursue any means deemed necessary to protect and improve the quality of the environment, including coordinating the activities of the various state governments.

TAX STANDARDS APPROACH FOR INDUSTRIAL WATER POLLUTION ABATEMENT IN INDIA[6]

How to estimate the appropriate pollution tax or subsidy with a Tax Standards Approach? The design of tax for the water pollution

[5] There is a move to change over to a system of load-based standards (where load equals concentration times volume), but these have not yet been detailed.

[6] This section is mainly drawn from James and Murty(1996).

abatement in India requires information about the standards for different water pollution parameters and the estimates of abatement cost of water pollution at different rates of water pollution. They are used to estimate the marginal abatement cost function. Given the standards, the pollution tax required to make the factories to meet the standards can then be estimated. Econometric techniques are used to estimate all such parameters. Two different methods are demonstrated here, ultimately aimed at designing taxes for water pollution abatement. They are: the conventional 'cost-function' approach, and 'output distance' method. In both the methods, the total and marginal abatement costs and, hence the tax rates are estimated.

The Conventional Cost-function approach

It is now mandatory, as per the Air and Water Pollution Acts, to set up an effluent treatment plant for abatement of water pollution. Assuming that there are only two inputs required for an effluent treatment plant, namely labour and capital, a general form of the (total) abatement cost function be specified as:

$$C = [\, V, \frac{BODINF}{BODEFF}, \frac{CODINF}{CODEFF}, \frac{SSINF}{SSEFF}, \quad w_k, w_l\,] \quad (10.1)$$

where

C = the total annualized cost (in Rs) of the effluent treatment plant

V = the annual volume of wastewater (in kilolitres) treated by the plant

BODINF = concentration of BOD in the influent (milligrams per litre)

BODEFF = concentration of BOD in the effluent (milligrams per litre)

CODINF = concentration of COD in the influent (milligrams per litre)

CODEFF = concentration of COD in the effluent (milligrams per litre)

SSINF = concentration of SS in the influent (milligrams per litre)

SSEFF = concentration of SS in the effluent (milligrams per litre)

w_K = the price of the capital used in the effluent treatment plant

w_L = the price of the labour used in the effluent treatment plant.

The cost function is further specified as linear in logarithms as:

$$Ln\ C = \alpha + \alpha_v\ lnV + \alpha_b\ ln\ \frac{BODINF}{BODEFF} + \alpha_c\ ln\ \frac{CODINF}{CODEFF} \qquad (10.2)$$
$$+ \alpha_s\ ln\ \frac{SSINF}{SSEFF} + \alpha_k\ lnw_k + \alpha_l\ lnw_l$$

where

Ln and ln stand for logarithms (taken at the base .... e). The a's are coefficients with respect to the three parameters BOD, COD and SS, and the volume of waste water treated.

What is important for estimating abatement tax is the marginal abatement costs. There are three points to be noted about the marginal abatement cost function (say, with respect to COD in waste water).

1. The cost of abatement is incurred in the context of reducing the quantity of COD (or BOD or SS) in the effluent. Hence, the appropriate partial derivative of the total abatement cost function is that with respect to the product of CODEFF (or BODEFF or SSEFF) and the volume of waste water in which this concentration is found.

2. Since this marginal cost represents the cost of reducing the quantity of COD (or BOD or SS) in the influent waste water, and since the variable in question is the ratio of BODINF/BODEFF, it is clear that a reduction in the quantity of COD in the effluent represents an increase in the ratio.

3. Since these are marginal costs for the reduction in the COD (or BOD or SS) load (concentration times volume), and since the volume matters in the total costs of abatement, the marginal cost has to be divided by the (average) volume of waste water treated.

The marginal abatement cost functions, therefore, have a negative sign. The marginal cost function corresponding to a decrease in COD in wastewater, accordingly, is given by

$$MCA_c = \frac{\delta C}{\delta(CODEFF) \times V} = \frac{-\alpha_c.\ C}{CODEFF \times V} \qquad (10.3)$$

where

MCA stands for marginal abatement cost, δ stands for derivatives.

The value of the parameter α_c is obtainable from a regression technique. The MCA can be estimated by setting the level of all other variables except the one with respect to which the derivation is carried out (i.e., CODEFF) are taken to be at their mean values within the sample. However, these can be varied, and the actual estimates can use maximum, mean and median values of both CODINF and volume.

The marginal abatement cost function with respect to volume of waste water is the standard partial derivative of the total abatement cost function with respect to the volume of waste water treated (in kilolitres) per annum. Using the equation (10.2), this is deduced as :

$$\text{MCA}_v = \frac{\alpha_v \cdot C}{V} \qquad (10.4)$$

Again, although the estimated total cost function uses mean values of all variables except for volume V, simulations can be made with maximum and median values of CODINF as well.

The tax rate, now is calculated simply by substituting the actual (average) concentration of the effluent (e.g., CODEFF) in the waste water by the standard (i.e., by 250 milligrams per litre) in the expression for the corresponding MCA. Likewise, the procedure can be repeated to get the tax rate required to support the BOD standard or the standard for SS (see CPCB, 1995 for a detailed account of these standards). The methods used to collect the data necessary for the estimation of the tax rates and the results of the estimation, including the various tax rates, are detailed and analysed. This method is now demonstrated for waste water, based on an all India level data.

The Data

Normally, the data required to estimate the abatement cost function are not collected in full by the CPCB or the various SPCBs or any other government or private agency. Therefore, a questionnaire-based survey may be necessary, backed by selected factory visits, in order to compile the data on influent and effluent quality as well as on costs and input prices.[7] The questionnaire response from 82 large- and medium-sized firms falling under highly-polluting industries at the all-India level identified under the Water Cess Act of 1977 forms the basic data base for estimating the abatement cost relations.

---

[7] 'Influent' refers to the waste water proceeding out of the production plant, prior to treatment, while 'effluent' refers to wastewater after treatment, prior to discharge into the environment.

The categories of highly-polluting industries identified by the Water Cess Act of 1977 (Schedule I) are: (i) ferrous metallurgical, (ii) non-ferrous metallurgical; (iii) mining industries; (iv) ore-processing industries; (v) petroleum industries; (vi) petro-chemical industries; (vii) chemical industries; (viii) ceramic industries; (ix) cement industries; (x) textile industries; (xi) paper industries; (xii) fertilizer industries; (xiii) coal (including coke) industries; (xiv) power (thermal and diesel) generating industries; and (xv) processing of animal or vegetable products industries. The Central Pollution Control Board has further specified 17 categories of highly-polluting industries within these general categories.

The states identified are Tamil Nadu, Kerala, Andhra Pradesh, Karnataka, Maharashtra, Gujarat, Orissa, West Bengal, Delhi and Harayana.

Estimate of Total Abatement Cost Function

The aggregate (total) abatement cost function to be estimated is taken to be a function of the quality of effluents and influents and of the cost/prices of two primary inputs namely, capital and labour. Further, instead of taking influent and effluent quality as separate variables, the ratio of influent quality to effluent quality is taken in the cost function. This is a more intuitive approach, since costs are incurred in the process of *reducing* the amounts of BOD, COD and SS in the influent waste water.

Various steps involved in the estimation process are summarized now.

1. *Computation of capital cost of effluent treatment plant*: This is often termed as the price of capital measured by the rate of return on capital stock. This can be derived using a value-added approach. By definition, the value added by a production plant is the turnover minus the sum of material inputs used in production. Since there are only two primary inputs entering in the cost computations, this value-added comes from the two factors, namely labour and capital. Subtracting labour costs yields the value-added due to capital alone. For this estimation of this value-added by capital, secondary data from the Annual Survey of Industries is used.[8] Dividing this by the relevant estimate of invested capital (available from the data of the Annual Survey of Industries), yields

the rate of return on capital. Adding to this the rate of depreciation yields an estimate of the price of capital services. Since the (financial) capital used in the effluent treatment plant is assumed to be shifted out of main production to this alternative use, the same price applies to the capital invested in the effluent treatment plant.

Total Value-Added	=	Turnover − Material Cost
	=	Value-Added by Capital and Labour (i.e., the Primary Factors).
Value-Added by Capital	=	Total Value-Added − Value-Added by Labour (i.e., labour cost).
The Rate of Return on Capital	=	Value-Added by Capital / Invested Capital.
And, the Price of Capital	=	Rate of Return on Capital + Rate of Depreciation.

2. *Adjusting to economies of scale:* There is one additional practical aspect of estimating (as opposed to theoretically derived) marginal costs of abatement that is worth mentioning. Since the influent and effluents are given in concentration units (i.e., milligrams per litre) and the volume of waste water in kilolitres (i.e., 1000 litres), it is appropriate to convert the concentrations also into milligrams per kilolitres. This is done simply by multiplying the concentrations by 100. Further, since the cost is in terms of lakhs of rupees per annum and it is desirable to have the tax per unit of effluent in terms of rupees, the marginal cost is multiplied by a factor of one million. Since the tax on annual waste water quality is in terms of rupees per milligram, and the excess is likely to be in terms of even kilograms (given the high volumes treated per plant), it is sensible to have a tax in terms of rupees per 100 grams, by multiplying the marginal cost estimate by 100 × 1,000 since 1000 milligrams make a gram.

3. *Econometric functional forms and estimation problems:* Alternative functional forms of the cost function are: a full translog specification, a truncated translog specification, a full Cobb-Douglas

[8] At this stage, an assumption of 'capital and labour invested in the effluent treatment plant as perfectly substitutable with those employed in the main plant' is made.

specification, or a linear form etc. The appropriate one is to be selected on the basis of goodness of fit. There are possibilities of multi-collinearity between the effluent/influent ratios.[9] Since the R^2 value and the significance levels were the highest for the specification with the COD ratio and the input prices, this was chosen as the base estimation. In addition, the cost function was estimated with (i) the COD ratio without input prices; (ii) the BOD ratio and input prices, and (iii) an index which converted BOD ratios into COD ratios using fixed weights. Four alternative specifications of total abatement cost functions can be tried.

Estimation 1

$$\text{Ln C} = \alpha + \alpha_v \ln V + \alpha_c \ln \frac{\text{CODINF}}{\text{CODEFF}} + \alpha_k \ln w_k + \alpha_l \ln w_l \qquad (10.5)$$

Estimation 2

$$\text{Ln C} = \alpha + \alpha_v \ln V + \alpha_c \ln \frac{\text{CODINF}}{\text{CODEFF}} \qquad (10.6)$$

Estimation 3

$$\text{Ln C} = \alpha + \alpha_v \ln V + \alpha_c \ln \frac{\text{BODINF}}{\text{BODEFF}} \qquad (10.7)$$

Estimation 4

$$\text{Ln C} = \alpha + \alpha_v \ln V + \alpha_c \ln \frac{\text{CODINF}}{\text{CODEFF}} \qquad (10.8)$$

where

Ln and ln = natural lagaarithm

The corresponding estimated regression equations are presented in Table 10.1 where CODINF refers to the COD index of influent quality and CODEFF refers to the COD index of effluent quality.[10]

---

[9] Indeed this was confirmed by a high correlation between pairs of effluent ratios and by a rise in the R^2 (and adjusted R^2) and in the significance of the ratios when tried singly.

[10] These indices were constructed as follows: First the coefficient of the ratio of BODINF/BODEFF in the regression of the ratio of CODINF/CODEFF on the former ratio obtained (say, ß) was used to construct weights. While the COD ratio of any given firm was assigned a weight of $1/(1 + ß)$, the BOD ratio was assigned a ratio

TABLE 10.1

Parameter Estimates of Total Abatement Cost Functions: Four Alternative Models: Explained Variable = Log of Total Abatement Cost

	Estimation 1	Estimation 2	Estimation 3	Estimation 4
α	−1.06 (−0.98)	−5.05 (−8.67)	−4.87 (−9.01)	−5.03 (−8.84)
α_V	0.46 (10.10)	0.49 (13.51)	0.47 (13.63)	0.48 (13.73)
α_C	−0.12 (−1.65)	−0.20 (−2.54)	–	−0.21 (−2.59)
α_B	–	–	−0.18 (−2.35)	–
α_K	1.16 (6.56)	–	–	–
α_L	0.53 (2.87)	–	–	–
R^2	0.75	0.57	0.56	0.57
Adjusted R^2	0.74	0.56	0.56	0.56

Note: R^2 is square of multiple correlation coefficient. The figures in parentheses are heteroscedasticity-corrected t-statistics

Source Author's calculations

Estimated Pollutant-specific Marginal Costs of Abatement and Tax Rates

The total abatement cost functions thus estimated are now useful to derive the marginal abatement costs as well to arrive at pollution tax rates. Let equation 10.5 be retained to calculate these, because of the better statistical fit of this specification to the data (the higher R^2). From this estimated equation, it is now possible to estimate averaged total abatement cost for any given set of all the explanatory variables. It is useful from the policy point of view, to estimate the marginal abatement costs for variations in the volume of waste water and quality of influent treated. The first gives a measure of eco-nomies of scale in the treatment plant design. The maximum volume reported in the sample was used as one extreme. The median value was chosen as the low end of the scale for volume of waste water. As compared to the situation with maximum volume of waste water, the marginal abate-ment cost is substantially higher with median volume of waste water, confirming the presence of extensive economies of scale.

---

of ß/(1+ß). The resulting weighted index is the independent variable CODINF/CODEFF.

Then let us take the case with the influent quality of waste water. The maximum and the median levels were chosen once again, and marginal costs were observed to rise with a fall in influent quality. This was however done only in the case of the estimates from the regression with COD ratio, volume and the input prices as independent variables. The total abatement costs corresponding to those variations in volume of waste water and CODINF can be now used to deduce the marginal costs. These marginal average costs are treated as the relevant tax rates.

Since the variation is reflected in the tax rates computed in each case and since the tax rates are the variables of real interest, the results of various combinations of volumes of waste water and COD levels are shown in Table 10.2

TABLE 10.2

Tax Rates in Rupees for 100 Grams Reduction in COD per Annum

	Maximum volume	Average volume	Median volume
Maximum CODINF	0.10	0.41	8.08
Average CODINF	0.08	0.32	1.84
Median CODINF	0.06	0.24	4.82

Note: Derived from equation 10.5; Maximum annual volume (in kilolitres) is 47,320,000 while the average and median volumes are 3,676,400 and 12,570, respectively; Maximum CODINF (in milligrams per litre) is 106,000, the average is 12,570 and median is 1,340

Source: Author's calculations

Table 10.2 reveals that there is a sharp increase in tax rates as the volume of waste water decreases, indicating that there are significant economies of scale in pollution abatement technologies. Also, except for the case of median waste water volume, the marginal costs (and hence the tax rates) increase as the influent concentration of the pollutant (COD) decreases. The pattern of tax rates is the same, with the rate rising as the volume of waste water decreases.

Table 10.3 shows the computations of estimating tax liability corresponding to the extent of excess COD and the volume of waste water. These tax rates, by themselves, do not give any indication of the relative magnitudes of cost to the concerned firm. For the firms in the sample with excess COD concentration above the standards in their

TABLE 10.3
*Cost Implications of the Effluent Tax: Liability as a
Proportion of Turnover*

Firm	Excess COD concentration (milligrams per litre)	Annual volume of waste water (kilolitres)	Annual tax liability (Rupees)	Annual turnover (Rupees millions)	Tax liability as a percentage of turnover (%)
1	6	67,450	1,273.02	235.93	0.0005
2	30	30,175	2,847.55	152.01	0.0019
3	38	74,550	8,911.17	122.40	0.0073
4	65	106,500	21,775.40	223.93	0.0097
5	68	793,070	169,638.00	999.50	0.0017
6	72	29,465	6,673.33	26.78	0.0025
7	75	639,000	150,753.00	3,290.00	0.0046
8	84	6,390,000	1,688,430.00	1,400.00	0.1206
9	90	106,500	30,150.60	815.38	0.0037
10	150	42,600	20,100.40	150.00	0.0134
11	230	6,035	4,366.25	23.14	0.0188
12	240	2,564,880	1,936,340.00	180.35	1.0737
13	350	514,750	566,719.00	1,078.90	0.0525
14	500	2,662,500	4,187,580.00	407.75	1.0270
15	650	2,662,500	5,443,850.00	184.00	2.9586
16	825	9,052,500	23,492,300.00	7,279.50	0.3183
17	950	284,000	848,683.00	180.05	0.4714
18	1,085	7,100	24,232.10	60.00	0.0439
19	6,250	79,875	1,570,340.00	10.31	15.2313
20	26,924	104,370	8,839,320.00	39.30	22.4919
21	32,250	213,000	21,607,900.00	146.70	14.7293

Source: Murty and James in Murty, et al., (1999)

waste water, the tax liabilities calculated using the average tax rate of
Rs 0.32 per 100 grams of COD. There are two points that emerge from
this exercise.

Some comments can be made on these tax estimates:

1. Only 21 out of the 82 firms in the sample exceed the COD standard. That is, less than a third of the firms in the sample are defaulters. Of these, Table 10.3 shows that about ten firms have excess concentrations of COD equal to or less than 150 milligrams per litre. About eight firms have an excess COD concentration of between 150 and 1000 milligrams per litre, while three firms have substantial excesses over the standard (over 6,000 milligrams per litre). However, their tax liability is based on excess concentration times the volume of waste water, and hence a firm with only 84 milligrams per litre excess COD and 6.39 million kilolitres of wastewater volume per annum ends up with a tax liability of over Rs 16 lakh. Further, the maximum tax liability of Rs 2.35 crore falls on a firm with an excess COD concentration of 825 milligrams per litre but over 9 million kilolitres of waste water volume per annum, and a firm with an excess of nearly 27,000 milligrams per litre in its effluent is liable to pay only around Rs 88 lakh since its volume of waste water per year is just 0.1 million kilolitres.[11]

2. The ratio of annual tax to turnover becomes significant (e.g., above 4 per cent) for only four firms out of 21 (or about 14 per cent of the defaulters). While it is true that firm profits are a better indicator of the 'bite' of the tax; such a measure gives a rough relative picture of the effectiveness of the tax.

3. In terms of revenue to the government, it is illustrative that from this handful of firms, the revenue raised (the sum of the tax liabilities) is around Rs 6.8 crore. There is, thus, considerable potential in such a tax for abatement enforcement and revenue generation.

Output Distance Function Method

The conventional production function defines the maximum output that can be produced from an exogenously given input vector while the cost function defines the minimum cost to produce the exogenously given output. The output and input distance functions generalize these notions to a multi-output case. The output distance function (Murty and Kumar, 2001) describes 'how far' an output

---

[11] Note, however, that in the case of an economic instrument like the pollution tax, polluting firms informed of excess emission would prefer to spend on effluent control rather than on paying the tax. Given time, therefore, the total taxes paid could be far short of the assessed tax liability.

vector is from the boundary of the representative output set, given the fixed input vector. The input distance function shows how far, is the input vector from the input vector corresponding to the least cost for producing a given vector of outputs.

The assumptions about the disposability of outputs become very important in the context of a firm producing both good and bad outputs. The normal assumption of strong or free disposability about the technology implies that we can reduce some outputs given the other outputs or without reducing them. This assumption may exclude important production processes, such as undesirable outputs. For example, in the case of water pollution, BOD, COD and SS are regulated and the firm cannot freely dispose of them. The assumption of weak disposability is relevant to describe such production processes. The assumption of weak disposability implies that a firm can reduce the bad output only by decreasing simultaneously the output of desirable produce.

Suppose that a firm employs a vector of inputs $x \in \mathfrak{R}^N_+$ to produce a vector of outputs $y \in \mathfrak{R}^M_+$, $\mathfrak{R}^N_+$, $\mathfrak{R}^M_+$, are non-negative N- and M-dimensional Euclidean spaces, respectively. Let $P(x)$ be the feasible output set for the given input vector x and $L(y)$ the input requirement set for a given output vector y. Now the technology set is defined as:

$$T = \{(y,x) \in \mathfrak{R}^{M+N}_+, y \in P(x), x \in L(y)\}. \qquad (10.9)$$

The output distance function is defined as,

$$D_O(x,y) = \min\{\theta > 0 : (y/\theta) \in P(x)\} \; \text{œ} \; x \in \mathfrak{R}^N_+ \qquad (10.10)$$

The derivation of absolute shadow prices for bad outputs using the distance function requires an assumption that one observed output price is a shadow price. Let y_1 denote the good output and the remaining $m-1$ outputs are pollutants or bad outputs. Assume that the observed good output price (r_1^0) equals its absolute shadow price (r_1^s) (i.e., for $m = 1$, $r_1^0 = r_1^s$). Fare et al., (1993) have shown that the absolute shadow prices for each observation of undesirable output ($m = 2, \ldots, M$) can be derived as,

$$(r_m^s) = r_1^0 \; \frac{\partial D_0(x,y) / \partial y_m}{\partial D_0(x,y) / \partial y_1} \qquad (10.11)$$

The shadow prices reflect the trade off between desirable and undesirable outputs at the actual mix of outputs, which may or may not be consistent with the maximum allowable under regulation (Fare et al., 1993, p. 376).

Translog Output Distance Function and Data on Indian Water Polluting Industry

In order to estimate the shadow prices of pollutants (bad outputs) for the Indian industry using equation (10.16), the parameters of output distance function have to be estimated. The translog functional form (Pittman, 1981; Fare et al., 1990; Coggins and Swinton 1996) is chosen for estimating the output distance function for the Indian water and air polluting industries which is given as follows:

$$\ln D_o(x, y) = \alpha_0 + \Sigma\beta_n \ln x_n + \Sigma \alpha_m \ln y_m + 1/2\Sigma \Sigma \beta_{nn'} (\ln x_n)$$

$$(x_{n'}) + 1/2 \Sigma \Sigma \alpha_{mm'} (\ln y_m) (y_{m'}) + \Sigma\Sigma\gamma_{nm}(\ln x_n)(\ln y_m) + i_i D_i \qquad (10.12)$$

where x and y are respectively, Nx1 and Mx1 vectors of inputs and outputs, and D_i stands for the dummy variables used for time periods and industry specifications. The data used here is from two surveys of water and air-polluting industries in India.[12] The data from these surveys provide information about the characteristics of polluting firms for the years 1994–5, 1996–7, 1997–8, and 1999–2000. It consists of sales value, capital stock, wage bill, material input cost, waste water volume, influent and effluent quality for BOD, COD and SS, capital stock, wage bill, and fuel and material input cost for a sample of 60 firms for the year 1994–5 and for a sample of 120 firms for the three years during 1996–9. Thus, the data constitute an unbalanced panel. These firms in the sample belong to tanneries, chemicals, fertilizers, pharmaceuticals, drugs, iron and steel, thermal power, refining and others. For estimating the output distance function, the technology of each water-polluting plant is described by joint outputs: sales value (good output) and COD, BOD and SS (bad outputs) and inputs: capital, labour, fuel and materials. In the case of air-polluting industries, the bad outputs considered are SO_2, NO_x and SPM. However,

---

[12] A Survey of Water Polluting Industries in India, 1996 and A Survey of Water and Air polluting Industries in India, 2000, Institute of Economic Growth, Delhi.

most of the firms in the sample could not provide all the required information about air pollution.

The water-polluting firms in the Indian industry are supposed to meet the standards set for the pollutants (35mg/l for BOD, 250mg/l for COD and 100mg/l for SSP) by the CPCB. CAC regulatory instruments are used to make the firms realize the standards. Most of the firms in the sample have effluent treatment plants and in addition some firms are using process changes in production and input choices to achieve the effluent standards. However, there is a large variation in the degree of compliance among the firms measured in terms of ratio of standard to effluent quality. The laxity of formal environmental regulation by the government, use of CAC instruments, and the absence of informal regulation (see Murty et al., 1999; World Bank, 1999) by the communities in the neighbourhood of the firms can be regarded as factors responsible for large variations in the compliance to the pollution standards by the firms.

Estimates of Shadow Prices of BOD, COD and SS and Pollution Taxes for the Indian Industry

The translog cost function given earlier is estimated using the linear programming method with the data for the Indian water polluting industries (Murty and Kumar, 2001). Table 10.4 provides the descriptive statistics of estimated shadow prices of BOD, COD and SS for the Indian industry. The estimates of firm specific shadow prices of BOD, COD and SS could be interpreted as the marginal costs of pollution abatement. These marginal costs are found to be increasing with the

TABLE 10.4

Descriptive Statistics of Estimates of Shadow Prices of Water Pollutants for Indian Industries (Rs lakh per tonne)

Industry/ Pollutant	Mean	S.D.	Minimum	Maximum
Overall				
BOD	00.132901	00.060858	00.001130	00.36
COD	00.506225	00.266572	00.003972	01.74
SS	00.166764	00.086278	00.006226	00.68

Source: Murty and Kumar (2001)

degree of compliance of firms with respect to each pollutant. Taking the index of non-compliance by the firms as the ratio of effluent concentrations of BOD, COD and SS it is found that the higher the index, the lower the shadow price. That means there is an increasing marginal cost of abatement.

The standards given for BOD, COD and SS are, respectively, 35mg/l, 250mg/l and 100mg/l. Following the tax-standards approach (Baumol and Oates, 1988) if taxes are designed and levied such that the tax on each pollutant is equal to the marginal cost of abatement corresponding to the standard, the polluting firms will have incentives to comply with the standards. As explained in the previous section, using the estimates of marginal cost of abatement based on conventional cost functions, the earlier studies in India (Mehta et al., 1995; Murty et al., 1999) have also dealt with the problem of designing the pollution taxes using the tax-standards approach. The taxes on BOD, COD and SS are respectively estimated as Rs 20,157, Rs 48,826, and Rs 21,444 (all in 1996–7 prices).

COLLECTIVE ACTION: AN EXAMPLE OF INDUSTRIAL WATER POLLUTION ABATEMENT IN INDIA

Use of CAC instruments by the government in a situation of non-availability of economically-viable technological options for pollution abatement has been causing considerable hardship to small scale enterprises in India. The government has not made any sincere efforts to promote economically-viable pollution abatement technologies for the small scale enterprises via research and development (R&D) in the public sector. Secondly, the presence of scale economies in pollution abatement, especially in the water pollution abatement, has compounded problems for the industrial estates in India. In such a situation, it is not economical for the small scale enterprises to have their own individual effluent treatment plants.

Collective action involving all the relevant parties for water pollution abatement (factories, affected parties and government) is now seen as an institutional alternative to deal with the problem of water pollution abatement in industrial estates in India (Murty, et al., 1999). Collective action in industrial water pollution abatement is meant to bring about the necessary institutional changes that are compatible with the choice of cost-saving technologies. For example, a Common

Effluent Treatment Plant (CETP) can be adopted if necessary legislation is in place to define the property rights of the factories and the affected parties. A CETP for an industrial estate confers the benefits of saving in costs to the factories and the reduction in the damages to the affected parties. There are many incentives for polluters, affected parties and the government to promote collective action in industrial water pollution abatement.

Collective Action in Developing Countries: Is it Possible?

There may be several constraints for collective action in industrial pollution abatement. Some of these constraints can be in the form of:
- Inadequate and ambiguous environmental laws protecting the rights of affected parties to clean environment,
- Lack of public awareness about the magnitude of damages to the community from pollution and the presence of environmental laws protecting the rights of people,
- Lack of resources of local communities to organize themselves as politically-active groups for taking recourse to legal action against polluters,
- Inadequate resources at the disposal of small enterprises to organize themselves as a club for setting up a CETP,
- The problem of agreeing upon a cost-sharing arrangement for a CETP by a club of factories,
- The problem of designing methods of charging factories and households for treating effluents by a CETP organized by a club of affected parties/municipal committees, and
- Political uncertainty in the case of clubs of affected parties and the uncertainty of continuance of agreement for cost sharing by a club of factories.

Incentives for Collective Action

The government can play an enabling or catalytic role in the collective action by aiming to remove some or all of these constraints. In a democracy, the legislature can enact environmental laws and create legal institutions to protect the rights of citizens to clean environment. Public awareness about the magnitude of damages from pollution can be promoted by creating institutions for environmental education. The government or NGOs can even provide subsidized legal facilities to local communities. It can give small enterprises concessional financial loans and technical help for setting up CETPs. NGOs can provide expertise to a club of factories to work out mutually-agreeable methods of sharing the cost of CETP.[13]

There are many incentives for polluters, affected parties and the government to promote collective action in the industrial water pollution abatement, some of them are listed below:

Incentives to Polluters

1. CETP is less expensive in terms of capital and operation cost.
2. It is easy for a club to secure financial support from Government and NGOs.
3. With CETP, water can be treated economically to produce process-grade water which can be reused and recycled in the industry. It is an important incentive to form a club in the water-scarce regions.
4. The size of an industrial estate depends upon the water availability and the facility to dispose the waste water on a sustainable basis. The CETP may help achieve both these objectives.

Incentives to Affected Parties

1. Improved quality of drinking water.
2. Reduction in the damages from water borne diseases.
3. Recreational facilities from the preserved water body.
4. Reduction in the cost of legal action against polluters.
5. Increase in the access to legal institutions.

Incentives to Government

1. Reduction in the burden of various government agencies working for abating and controlling the water pollution.
2. Respectability for the catalytic role rather than the unpopularity for the coercive role.

Recent studies (Murty and Prasad, 1999; Murty et al., 1999) in India about the historical developments leading to the adoption of CETP technologies by some industrial estates in Andhra Pradesh, Haryana

---

[13] A method of sharing the cost of CETP is an important component of contract arising out of collective action of small-scale enterprises in an industrial estate. Therefore, the method of cost sharing should be such that it is mutually acceptable to all enterprises. Appendix A.10.1 presents some of such cost-sharing methods.

and Tamil Nadu states clearly provide evidence for the role of collective action involving affected people from pollution, the factories, NGOs and the government. There are three processes involved in the collective action for control of water pollution in an industrial estate. These are: (i) collective action of affected parties; (ii) collective action of factories and (iii) the bargaining between a coalition of affected people and a coalition of factories. The collective action of affected people is possible, if the damages from pollution are substantive enough to justify the transaction costs of coalition and bargaining. The factories in an industrial estate have to take recourse to pollution-abatement methods taking into account of possible collective action by the affected people in the form of cost sharing. The available pollution abatement technology may provide small factories a broad spectrum of technological choices out of which the CETP may be the least-cost technology. Therefore, the collective action by the factories can be technology-driven. Finally, the bargaining between a coalition of affected people and a coalition of factories produces the end result of collective action, that is, the realization of prescribed environmental standards.

Collective Action and Estimation of the Cost of Water Pollution Abatement for an Industrial Estate

A collective action programme is not costless. They constitute the costs to factories, government and affected parties. The factories incur the cost of abatement to meet the standards. The affected people incur the cost of public litigation cases and the cost of organizing themselves as a society. The government incurs the cost of financial incentives provided to the factories. A method of estimating the cost to the factories is given below with a case study.

Given a threat of closure or legal action by an association of affected people, small scale industries in an industrial estate are made to reduce pollution to meet the prescribed standards. The industries have a choice between the following technologies to meet the standards: (i) in-house treatment, (ii) CETP and (iii) a mixture of both. Given the scale economies in water pollution abatement, in-house treatment is not economical for small scale enterprises. A survey of pollution abatement practices of isolated industries (Murty et al., 1999) shows that the capital cost of effluent treatment plant to meet the water-pollution standards for small-scale enterprises is almost equal to the capital cost of the main plant. The industries may prefer therefore to go for a CETP, which is possible only if they are located as a cluster in an industrial estate. They can have a CETP only if there is a contract among the factories about (a) sharing capital and the operating costs, (b) the prices charged for treating the pollutants and (c) the quality of influent accepted by the CETP.

The industrial estates normally contain heterogeneous factories belonging to different industries with varying pollution loads and concentrations. With an agreement among the factories to supply waste water of standard quality or concentration to the CETP, some factories in the industrial estate may have to do 'in-house treatment' to bring the pollution concentration in the factory effluent to the standard acceptable to the CETP factory. Therefore, the cost of water-pollution abatement in an industrial estate will be: In-house treatment cost plus the cost of CETP.

Estimating in House Treatment Cost

In a recent interesting case study of water pollution abatement in Nandesari industrial estate in Gujarat, Misra (1999) has estimated the cost of alternative technologies for meeting the standards of water pollution.[14] The average volume of waste-water discharges by the factories in the industrial estate is 7.3 million litres per annum. Between different establishments it ranges from 0.1 million litres per annum to 69 million litres per annum. The initial level of COD concentration in the factory effluents ranges from 100 mg per litre to 10,000 mg per litre. In order to meet the effluent standard acceptable to CETP on an average, the initial level of COD concentration is 3450 mg per litre. The reduction of COD concentration during in-house treatment is on an average is 2615 mg per litre. The cost of in house treatment ranges from Rs 0.40 lakh to Rs 139 lakh per annum with an average of Rs 15 lakh. The total in-house treatment cost for the Nandesari industrial estate is estimated as Rs 1000 lakh (Misra, 1999).

[14] Based on time series primary data on various components of water pollution abatement cost (the labour costs, capital costs, material costs and energy (fuel and power) costs) and the volume and characteristics of influent waste water and effluent wastewater from the records maintained by the factories for a sample of 45 factories from Nandesari industrial estate (out of 250 small-scale factories) producing different kinds of organic and inorganic chemicals and pharmaceuticals during 1993-4 to 1995-6.

Estimating CETP Cost

The CETP accepts the effluent from the factories after the primary treatment and treats it further for meeting the effluent standard of 35mg/l, 250mg/l and 100 mg/l of BOD, COD and SS, respectively. The capital cost of CETP at Nandesari at 1996 prices is Rs 373 lakh. Taking the cost of capital services as 28 per cent (18 per cent of opportunity cost plus 10 per cent rate of depreciation), the annualised cost of capital of CETP is estimated as Rs 104 lakh. The operation and maintenance (O & M) cost of CETP is reported as Rs 10 lakh. The total annual cost of CETP is estimated as Rs 224 lakh. Adding to this the cost of in house treatment by the factories, the total cost of pollution abatement to meet the water-pollution standards by the Nadesari industrial estate is estimated as Rs 1224 lakh. This is the cost of pollution abatement for the industrial estate through the institutional arrangement of collective action described above. It is expected to be much lower than the total cost of achieving the standards through in-house treatment by the factories of Rs 3820 lakh.

LOCAL COMMUNITIES, MARKET, AND GOVERNMENT: AN EMERGING NEW MODEL OF POLLUTION ABATEMENT

There is now evidence of a number of industries in developing countries complying with the environmental standards even in the absence of any formal regulation by the government.

Two case studies will be cited as examples, one from Indonesia and another from India. Take the interesting success story of PT Indah Kiat Pulp and Paper (IKPP) in Indonesia, described in World Bank (1999). IKPP is the largest and the cleanest paper producing company in Indonesia. Clean up began in some of its mills in 1990s with pressures from local communities. Local villagers claimed damages from the mills with the help of local NGOs. Indonesia's national pollution control agency, BAPEDAL, has mediated an agreement in which IKPP acceded to the villagers' demands. The need to go the Western bond market to finance the expansion of IKPP to meet the growing export demand, has made the company to go for cleaner technologies. The good performance of the company in pollution management has resulted in the increase of its stock value in comparison to the Jakarta's composite stock index.

Murty et al. (1999) report the results of a survey of a number of industrial estates in Andhra Pradesh, Tamil Nadu and Gujarat states of India and an all-India survey of large scale water-polluting factories providing evidences of local community pressure resulting in the industries complying with the standards. A number of agencies such as local communities, elected representatives (members of Parliament, State Assemblies, Municipal Committees), industries, NGOs and government are found to be involved in the processes leading to the establishment of CETPs in the industrial estates. There are also several examples of physical threats and public litigation cases against the factories to claim damages from pollution by the local people, resulting in the big factories complying with the standards.

To drive the point home, take another example of the Pattancheru industrial estate in Andhra Pradesh. Local opposition to pollution started in 1986 when about 3000 villagers marched to the Chief Minister's office after suffering large scale crop losses and health damages due to contamination of ground water and the pollution of a nearby river. In 1989, about 5000 people held a demonstration before the state assembly, demanding an end to industrial pollution. In the same year, farmers blocked the highway running through Pattancheru for two days. Not withstanding these threats, the villagers had also filed court cases by jointly sharing the cost with a contribution of Rs 200 per household. The main demands involved in the petition are: (i) providing water supply to the villagers, (ii) providing medical facilities and free treatment to the pollution affected villagers and livestock, (iii) preventing pollution from further spreading and the immediate closure of hazardous industries, (iv) payment of compensation to all the victims of pollution by the factories, (v) to take action against the industries flouting environmental laws and (vi) to constitute a team of environmental experts and economists for an on-the-spot survey and study of water and air pollution and losses incurred on account of pollution, and furnish a report to the Supreme Court.

In response to this court case, the Supreme Court of India had ordered (Supreme Court Order on 11.12.1989 in W.P. No. C967/89) the constitution of an expert committee for undertaking a study of pollution problems in the affected areas. The expert committee submitted its recommendations with respect to the following issues in the writ petition: (i) providing water supply by tankers to the affected villages mentioned in the writ petition on a temporary basis till a permanent scheme is provided, (ii) addressing health aspects in the affected villages referred to in the writ petition, (iii) payment of compensation, (iv) environmental awareness and training, (v) Common Effluent Treatment Plants and (vi) monitoring.

This legal action through the collective efforts of people has ultimately forced the factories in the industrial estate to have a CETP in order to comply with the water pollution standards. Similar experiences are reported from many other industrial estates in India.

Communities as Informal Regulators

Informal regulation by local communities is resulting in the factories complying with standards as explained by the examples given above. The amount of influence the local communities exert on the factories to undertake pollution depends, among other factors, upon their affluence, the degree of political organization, education and environmental awareness. Pargal and Wheeler (1996) have found a negative relationship between BOD load in a factory effluent and per capita income and educational levels of local communities in a sample of 243 factories in Indonesia. Similarly, Murty and Prasad (1999) have found a negative relationship between BOD effluent-influent ratio and a relative index of development of local community, and the political activity of local community measured in terms of percentage of votes polled in the recent election to the Indian Parliament.

In developed countries, contesting environmental regulations by local communities and industries is now becoming an important component of enforcement of environmental laws. Some recent studies (Naysherki and Tietenberg, 1992; Miller,1998) have reported that US Environmental Protection Agency (USEPA) encourages private litigants to bring suits against polluters. Private litigation now constitutes a major component in the enforcement of US Clean Air Act. The European Commission, in its 1993 Green paper, has clearly signalled its intent to support the rights of individuals to pursue polluters for compensation due to environmental damages (Heyes, 1977). Baik and Shogren (1994) have reported that lawmakers in Canada are committed to empowering private agents in virtually every aspect of the pollution control process, from the drafting of regulations to undertaking enforcement.

Can Market bring Clean Technologies?

The market agents, consumers, producers and stockholders have incentives for pollution control. Consumers regulate the market for pollution-intensive commodities by expressing preference for green products or commodities produced using cleaner technologies. Investors have also incentives to invest in the industries using cleaner technologies. Higher levels of observed pollution in a firm is an indication to the investors, that the firm uses inefficient technology resulting in the loss of profits. The losses in profit may occur because of a reduced demand for its products by green consumers, increased cost due to higher penalties imposed by the government for non-compliance with the pollution standards and the settlement of compensation to the victims. In this case, there may be a downward revaluation of the firm's stocks in the capital market. On the other hand, a good environmental performance by the firm may result in upward evaluation of its stocks.

Some recent studies have shown that the stock markets in both developed and developing countries react to the environmental performance of the firms. Studies about stock markets in US and Canada show that the gains from good news or bad news about environmental performance are in the range of 1 to 2 per cent (World Bank, 1999). Also, studies about the firms, behaviour with respect to environment-performance-related changes in stock prices show that the firms react to such changes by reducing the pollution loads (Konar and Cohen, 1997). The recent World Bank sponsored studies about this phenomenon in some developing countries like Argentina, Chile, Mexico, and the Philippines, show that stock prices are extremely volatile to news about environmental performance of firms. The gains in stock prices due to good news about environmental performance averages to 20 per cent in these countries.

CONCLUSION

The economic instruments, pollution tax, and marketable pollution permits can control better the environmental externality of industrial pollution. However, there are limitations on their implementation. In practice, one has to use hybrid instruments like pollution-tax standards or pollution-permits' standards. Many recent studies about the use of hybrid instruments in India for water pollution abatement recommend the use of tax-standards approach.

The case study about designing a tax-standard method for water pollution abatement described in this chapter, clearly brings out the merit of using a tax-standards approach. This approach can benefit those affected by pollution, industry and the government, in contrast to CAC measures or regulations currently in practice in India. In the context of a selected number of firms from all over the country, the methodology of determining a set of tax rates to enforce the existing standards for water quality in the country is demonstrated here. Such an analysis can be easily extended, provided adequate data is available, to the case of pollutant-specific or even industry-specific tax rates.

There are limitations on conventional instruments like pollution taxes, marketable permits and CAC instruments for controlling industrial pollution, especially if there are non-convexities in pollution abatement and the government is non-benevolent. Collective action based on Coasean bargaining solution can control water pollution even with convex pollution abatement technologies and a non-benevolent government. The collective action is possible if there are institutional arrangements in which all the relevant agents: polluters, affected parties and the government come together. Such collective actions involving affected parties, industry, government and NGOs have emerged as institutional alternatives to deal with the problem of water pollution abatement in many industrial estates of India.

There can be constraints to collective action. The government and NGOs can play a catalytic role to remove some or all of these constraints. Also, there are incentives for collective action for all the agents involved in water pollution abatement, as demonstrated by a case study in this chapter. These incentives highlight the roles of different parties, especially the catalytic role of government.

The new model of pollution control as described in the recent studies (Murty, et al., 1999; World Bank, 1999) highlights the importance of informal regulation by the local communities when the formal regulation is weak or absent. Market also plays an unexpected role in this model. It is a set of institutions: local community, market and government that deals with the environmental pollution.

REFERENCES

Aigner, D.J. and S.F. Chu (1968): 'Estimating the industry production function', *American Economic Review*, 58: 826–39.

Baik, K. and J.F. Shogren (1994): 'Reimbursments for citizen suits', *Journal of Environmental Economics and Management*, 27(1): 1–21.

Baumol, W.J. (1972): 'On taxation and control of externalities', *American Economic Review*, 42(3): 307–22.

Baumal, W.J. and W. Oates (1988): *The Theory of Environmental Policy*, 2nd Edition, Cambridge University Press, Cambridge.

Barbara, A.J and V.D. McConnell (1990): 'The impact of environmental regulations on industry productivity: Direct and indirect effects', *Journal of Environmental Economics and Management*, 18: 50–65.

Christensen, P.P. (1989): 'Historical roots for ecological economics-biophysical versus allocative approaches', *Ecological Economics*, 1(1): 17–36.

Coggins, J.S. and J.R. Swinton (1996): 'The price of pollution: A dual approach to valuing SO_2 allowances,' *Journal of Environmental Economics and Management*, 30: 58–72.

Conrad, K. and C.J. Morrison (1989): 'The impact of pollution abatement investment on productivity change: An empirical comparison of the U.S., Germany and Canada', *Southern Economic Journal*, January, 55: 684–98.

Coase, R.H. (1960): 'The problem of social cost', *Journal of Law and Economics*, 3: 1–44.

O'Connor, D. (1992) 'The use of economic instruments in environmental management: the experience of East Asia', in *Economic Instruments for Environmental Management in Developing Countries*, Proceedings of a workshop held at OECD Headquarters in Paris on 8 October 1992, OECD, Paris.

Cropper, M.L. and W.E. Oates (1992): 'Environmental economics: A Survey', *Journal of Economic Literature*, 30(1): 675–740.

CPCB (1995): Standards for Pollutants, Central Pollution Control Board, New Delhi.

Dales, J.U. (1968): *Pollution, Property and Prices*, University of Toronto Press, Toronto.

Dasgupta, A.K. and M.N. Murty (1985): 'Economic evaluation of water pollution abatement: A case study of paper and pulp industry in India', *Indian Economic Review*, 20(2): 231–67.

Fare, R. (1988): *Fundamentals of Production Theory*, Springer-Verlag, Berlin.

Fare, R., S. Grosskopf, C.A.K. Lovell and C. Pasurka (1989): 'Multilateral Productivity Comparisons when Some Outputs are Undesirable: A Non-Parametric Approach,' *Review of Economics and Statistics*, 71: 90–8.

Fare, R., S. Grosskopf, C.A.K. Lovell and S. Yaisawarng (1993): 'Derivation of shadow prices for undesirable outputs: A distance function approach', *Review of Economics and Statistics* 75: 375–80.

Fare R,. S. Grosskopf and J. Nelson (1990): 'On Price Efficiency', *International Economic Review* 31: 709–20.

Fare R., S. Grosskopf, and C.A.K. Lovell (1994): *Production Frontiers*, Cambridge University Press, Cambridge.

Fare, R. and D. Primont (1995): *Multi-Output Production and Duality: Theory and Applications*, Kluwer Academic Publishers, Netherlands.

Gollop, F.M, and M.I. Roberts (1993): 'Environmental regulations and productivity growth: The case of fossil-fuelled electric generation', *Journal of Political Economy*, 101: 654–74.

Gray, W.B, and S.J. Shadbegian (1993): 'Environmental regulation and manufacturing productivity at the plant level', Working Paper No 4321, National Bureau of Economic Research, Washington

—— (1995): 'Pollution abatement cost regulation and plant level productivity, Working Paper No. 4964, National Bureau of Economic Research, Washington

Gupta, D.B., M.N. Murty and R. Pandey (1989): Water Conservation and Pollution Abatement in Indian Industry: A Study of Water Tariff; National Institute of Public Finance and Policy, New Delhi.

Hakuni, M. (1994): 'Efficiency in the Finnish sulphate paper industry in 1972–90', Finnish Forest Research Institute, Research Report No. 157.

Heyes, A.G. (1977): 'Environmental Regulation by Private Contest', *Journal of Public Economics*, 63: 407–28.

James, A.J. and M.N. Murty (1996): Water Pollution Abatement: A Taxes-Standards Approach for Indian Industry, Working Paper No. E/177/96, Institute of Economic Growth, Delhi-110007.

Jorgenson, D. and P.J. Wilcoxen (1990): 'Environmental regulation and US economic growth', *RAND Journal of Economics*, 21: 314–40.

Konar, S. and M. Cohen (1997): 'Information as Regulation: The effect of community right to know laws on toxic emissions', *Journal of Environmental Economics and Management*, 32: 109–24.

Kumar, Surender (1999): 'Economic Evaluation of Development Projects: A Case Analysis of Environmental and Health Implications of Thermal Power Projects in India', A Ph.D Thesis, Jawaharlal Nehru University, New Delhi.

Mehta, S., S. Mundle and U. Sankar (1995): *Controlling Water Pollution: Incentives and Regulation, SAGE*, New Delhi.

Miller, J. (1998): 'Private enforcement of federal polluton control laws', *Environmental Law Reporter*, Vol. 14.

Misra, S. (1999) 'Water Pollution Abatement in Small Scale Industries: An Exploration of Collective Action Possibilities in Nandesari Industrial

Area in Gujarat', A Ph.D thesis submitted to the University of Delhi, Delhi.

Murty, M.N. (1991): 'Management of common property resources: limits to voluntary collective action', *Journal of Environmental & Resource Economics*, 4: 581–94.

—— (1995): 'Environmental Regulation in the Developing World: The Case of India', *Review of European Community and International Environmental Law*, 4(4): 330–7.

Murty, M.N., A.J. James and Smita Misra (1999): *The Economics of Water Pollution: The Indian Experience*, Oxford University Press, New Delhi.

Murty, M.N. and U.R. Prasad (1999): Emission Reductions and Influence of Local Communities in India, in Murty, M.N., A. James and Smita Misra (1999): op cit.

Murty, M.N. and Surender Kumar (2000): 'Measuring Cost of Environmentally Sustainable Industrial Development in India: A Distance Function Approach', Forthcoming in *Environmental and Development Economics*, Cambridge University Press, New Delhi.

—— (2001): *Environmental and Economic Accounting for Indian Industry*, A Report of Research Project funded by the Capacity Building Project in Environmental Economics in India, World Bank. Forthcoming, Oxford University Press, New Delhi.

Myers, J.G., and L. Nakamura (1980): 'Energy and pollution effects on productivity: A putty-clay approach', in Kenderick D. (ed.), *New Developments in Productivity Measurement and Analysis*, University of Chicago Press, Chicago.

Nandy I., R.A. Daryapurkar and S.N. Kaul (1991): *Common Effluent Treatment Plant—An Overview*, National Environmental Engineering Research Institute (NEERI), Nagpur.

Naysherki, W. and T. Tietenberg (1992): 'Private enforcement of federal enviromental law', *Land Economics*, 68.

Pandey, Rita (1998): Pollution Taxes for Industrial Pollution Control, Mimeo, National Institute of Public Finance and Policy, New Delhi.

Pargal, S. and David Wheeler (1996): 'Informal regulation of industrial pollution in developing countries: Evidence from Indonesia', *Journal of Political Economy*, 104(6): 1814–27.

Pigue, A.C. (1970): *The Economics of Welfare*, London: McMillan.

Pittman, R.W. (1981): 'Issues in pollution interplant cost differences and economies of scale', *Land Economics* 57: 1–17.

—— (1983): 'Multilateral productivity comparisons with undesirable outputs', *Economic Journal:* 93: 883–91.

Porter, M.E., and C. van der Linde (1995): 'Towards a new conception of the environment competitiveness relationship', *Journal of Economic Perspectives*, 9: 97–118.

Shephard, R.W. (1953): *Cost and Production Functions*, Princeton University Press.

—— (1970): *Theory of Cost and Production Functions*, Princeton University Press, Princeton.

Yaisawarng, S, and Klein, D.J. (1994): 'The effects of sulphur dioxide controls on productivity change in the U.S. Electric Power Industry', *Review of Economics and Statistics*, 96: 447–60.

World Bank (1999): *Greening Industry: New Roles to Communities, Markets and Governments*, Oxford University Press, New York.

Approaches to Natural Resource Accounting in the Indian Context

Gopal K. Kadekodi

INTRODUCTION

Valuation of natural resources and their accounting as part of income accounting are two separate issues, but they are related. Unlike many other goods and services which society buys from the market, natural and environmental resources may or may not have a market. Yet, from time immemorial, societies have always recognized their value and price. Natural resources are, like human-made capital, to be designated as natural capital; they are part of the national wealth or stock. Their use or abuse is a flow towards the welfare of society. Since their use adds to the welfare and abuse reduces it, their accounting on the lines of capital formation is necessary to understand the state of welfare of a nation. In a sense, valuation and income accounting are to be integrated within the national income accounting.

At present, accepted income accounting methods do take note of contributions by production factors such as labour and capital (as flows), but do not take cognizance of changes in natural and environmental resources. Integration of contributions by all the natural resources with income accounting requires a unified methodology on the lines of defining income within the framework of national income accounting.

While the development of the methodology of integration is still at a crossroad, the case studies presented here can provide the progress made in this direction in India.

The starting point for a discussion on Natural Resource Accounting is the conventional income accounting in a national, state or even a regional framework. The System of National Accounts (SNA) was developed by the United Nations, after the Bretton Wood Convention. Most countries by now have systematized the computation of national and domestic products and income, regularly on an annual basis. In India, they are compiled and published by the Central Statistical Organization (an organ of the Ministry of Planning, Government of India), under the title National Income Accounts. The incomes are identified as contributions by various resources of the country, such as labour (e.g., salary and wages, self-employment income), returns to man-made capital (e.g., profits or interests), returns to land (e.g., rent) and so on. Now, it has been realized that one of the basic resource categories of a country, namely the natural resources, also contribute to wealth and income, but they are not properly accounted for in the conventional income accounting. When it comes to natural and environmental resources, it is the concept of sustainability that will be the guiding principle to determine the contribution of the resources. Hence, one starts with the concept of Sustainable Accounting.

Natural and environmental resources may or may not command a market price. That calls for both a theory of valuation and methods of estimation (Bateman, and Turner, 1993; Smith, 1996; O'Connor et al., 1998; Garrod and Smita1999). Among many reasons to value natural resources is to use and integrate these values with the flow of natural and environmental resources in measuring the welfare of a nation. The flow changes in natural resources bring about stock changes as well. Therefore, the values of both the flow and stocks of natural resources are to be integrated along with all other income and wealth accountings. This branch of enquiry is generally termed as Natural Resource Accounting. Two different aspects of such accounting are discussed namely a satellite accounting system and an integrated environmental and economic accounting system.

We also discuss the logic, methods and complexities of such resource accounting in the Indian context. To begin with in 'System of National Income Accounting', a brief account of the method of conventional System of National Accounting is described. This will be followed by 'National Resource Accounting' to highlight the logic, methodology and methods of integrating resource accounting with the conventional system of income accounting. In 'Case Studies in Natural Resource Accounting', several studies are presented to demonstrate and illustrate the methods of both satellite accounting and integrated environmental and economic accounting. This is followed by a brief comment on the Indian experience in Natural Resource Accounting in 'Some Lessons from Indian Income Accounting'.

SYSTEM OF NATIONAL INCOME ACCOUNTING

What is the System of National Accounting (SNA)?

After the second world war, the League of Nations Committee of Statistical Experts felt the need for economic accounting at nation/ state levels, as an aid to formulate development strategies. They first published, in 1947, a document called '*Measurement of National Income and the Construction of Social Accounts*'. Subsequently, the UN Statistical Office in 1953 formalized the methodology and published a document called '*A System of National Accounts and Supporting Tables*', often referred to as SNA. SNA is essentially a statistical compendium showing the expenditures and incomes of a nation on an annual basis. Some of the major components of this compendium are gross domestic and national products; gross and net national incomes; accounts of taxes and subsidies; accounts of external transactions; sectoral level private and government consumption expenditures; savings, investments and capital stocks at sectoral levels; and sectoral level income, expenditure and value added. SNA is an important macroeconomic tool for understanding the growth and development status of a nation.

As far as income accounting is concerned, Hicks (1940, 1946) provided the basic principle to define income as a welfare indicator. He advocated the inclusion of all current consumptions in the income measure that do not impoverish future consumptions. Obviously, expenditures on private and public consumptions and investment (for the benefit of future consumption etc.) are part of this welfare indicator. Such welfare benefits emerge out of the use of resources of the economy. Examples are labour, land, man-made capital, materials produced by various production processes and so on. But there is one problem in accounting regarding the contribution of man-made capital. Man-made capital, as a stock, is part of the national wealth. This wealth is used as input in the production of commodities and services whose consumption enhances welfare. However, its use may lead to its own depreciation. If this depreciation is not accounted as a cost in the current income accounts, the current state of the economy is made to look better. But it will mean a smaller stock of capital for the future and, hence, a lower level of production and less welfare in the future at the cost of an inflated welfare now. Such an income-generation process is not sustainable in the long run. The Hicksian solution is to account for all such depreciation as costs in current income accounting. That is how a concept of net domestic product (NDP) evolved. In most countries, national income accounts have evolved methods to adjust for the net contribution by man-made capital in this way. One can get a perfect natural resource accounting if the same is attempted for natural resources as well.

The conventional System of National Accounts (SNA) was first started in the United States of America in 1942. The 1953 UN document (1968) systematized the procedure. The starting point for such an accounting is an identity, all valued in market prices as shown in Box 11.1

BOX 11.1
Basis of National Income Accounting

Aggregate supply of   =   Aggregate demand
an economy

Domestic productions   =   Intermediate use in production
+Imports   processes + Private Consumption
                              expenditure + Public consumption
                              expenditure + Gross investment +
                              Exports

Using the Input-Output Transactions framework (perhaps familiar only to economists), the gross domestic product (GDP) is defined as shown in Box 11.2:

BOX 11.2
Definition of Gross Domestic Product

GDP = Domestic production – Intermediate use consumption
= Private consumption + Public consumption + Gross investment
+ Exports – Imports

Under each of the terms used in the Box 11.2, there may be several sectors such as crop agriculture, plantation, mining, fishery, forestry, processing industries (such as textiles, tobacco, leather, etc.), manufacturing industries, service sectors (such as education, health, banking and so on). The production of many of these goods and services do depend upon or require natural resources both as stocks and flows (e.g., water, forest, ponds, lakes, ocean, air, minerals, etc.). From the GDP, by deducting the depreciation of man-made capital, one gets at the true measure of income, namely NDP.

NDP = GDP – capital depreciation

For any accounting year, some further adjustments such as adjusting for changes in the stocks of goods (which have neither been consumed or invested, nor exported) may become necessary. The method of SNA is basically mathematical, tracing all flows of incomes or goods and services in the economy in an accounting year.

An added element to SNA is the statement on the man-made capital stocks in the economy. The accounting identity for this is:

Closing capital stock = Initial capital stock + Investments during the accounting period – Capital depreciation.

The same logic can also be used to develop accounting for natural capital.

NATURAL RESOURCE ACCOUNTING

What is Sustainable Accounting?

Natural resources such as soil, water, forests, minerals, wildlife etc., are capital stocks, to be termed as natural capital. They also contribute to the welfare of the economy. If such natural capitals are left out from the framework of income accounting, there can be either an underestimation or overestimation of the income of a country. If there is any regeneration of forests, it adds to the stock of natural capital. If deforestation takes place, this depletion reduces the same stock. If crude oil depletion takes place for the benefit or welfare of the present generation, less will be left to the future generation. Now, one would like to see an accounting of income to be developed accommodating all the resources, including the use and abuse of renewable and non-renewable resources. Thus is all about sustainable accounting; only with such an accounting system, the linkages between environment and development can be better understood.

It is sometimes difficult to understand 'natural and environmental resources' as natural capital. It is a stock in exactly the same sense that man-made capital is considered. It has the characteristics of repeated use, depreciation and possibility of replacement and can enjoy rent for its use or abuse. Its accounting however, both as stock and flows (i.e., use or non-use benefits from it) is not yet within the framework of income accounting.

The concept of resource accounting evolved almost three decades ago in the early 1970s, at the end of the development of methodologies for project evaluation. With growing concern about the gaps in the SNA, procedural steps are being developed to account for natural resources. SNA has one basic deficiency that it can take note of only such production and consumption processes where there is a market price. Classical examples of this lacuna are many.[1]

Talking of sustainable accounting, two additional lacunae or difficulty are to be noted. First, non-imputation of the values of environmental goods and services used in production processes and the second, absence of any allowance for depreciation, degradation or depletion of natural resources. Improvement in the methods of SNA were debated in the 1992 United Nations Conference on Environment and Development (UNCED), held at Rio de Janeiro, which recommended all nations, and the United nations in particular, to develop a system of Integrated Environmental and Economic Accounting (IEEA).

What is Integrated Environmental and Economic Accounting ?

The main objective of environmental and economic accounting is to expand the existing systems of national economic accounts in order to integrate environment and social dimensions in the accounting framework. Alternatively, at least satellite systems of accounts for natural resources be developed to arrive at what is currently being coined as 'Green GNP'.

What is the satellite system of resource accounting? It is essentially a modified income accounting system, showing environment-related sectoral activities separately along with their physical accounts of flow changes, valuations and possible links to the main SNA. United Nations Statistical Division (UNSTAT) in 1993 came up with a

---

[1] Some standard examples are: decline in national income if one married his house maid (thereby taking her off from paying any salary), barter exchange of salt and butter (or hides and skins by the tribals), home-grown food consumption (predominantly in rural India), or food distributed and consumed through charities and so on.

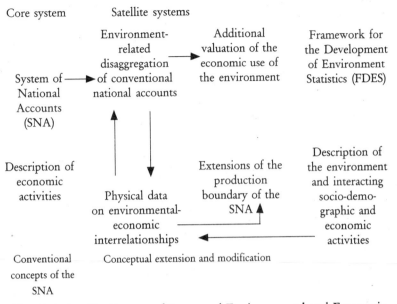

Fig. 11.1: Satellite System of Integrated Environmental and Economic Accounting (SEEA)

document describing the methodology of this System of Environmental and Economic Accounting, as a revised SNA. The main reason for such a satellite accounting system was the non-availability of market data for all the non-produced tangible and non-tangible resources and assets. Figure 11.1 demonstrates this.

Such satellite accounts have been attempted by UN agencies (UN, 1993), and also independently by countries such as Norway (Alfsen and Torstein, 1990), the Netherlands (NCBS, 1993) and several others. Under this method, as suggested by several scholars (Peskin, 1989), stock and flow changes in environmental resources are to be treated in a separate table, leaving the basic income accounting table unchanged.

The major components or steps for such an accounting system are:

1. Identification of environmentally-related sectors/economic activities.

2. Physical accounts of those sectors/activities: Stocks, flows or changes in stocks, factors affecting the changes in stocks (sectoral intermediate demands, consumption, depletion, degradation, regeneration, etc.).

3. Valuation of the changes in stocks and flows.
4. Aggregation of values.

Let us illustrate the satellite accounting system with one example of a natural resource. Consider forests as an example of natural capital. Can one develop a satellite accounting (or any integrated accounting) for it as easily as for man-made capital? The answer is 'yes' in theory, but 'difficult' in practice. First, the major difficulty arises from the distinction between depreciation and depletion. In the case of depreciation, it can remain as a notional value judgment. The same cannot be said about natural resources when they actually degrade and deplete. Second, accounting for additions to forest stock is not easy. It takes place both through natural regeneration and plantation. For each of these, one ought to have good data and information about the investment costs and survival rates. In other words, it is not as simple as accounting for capital formation in the usual national income accounting sense. Third, the flow from forest stocks is only partially recorded and accounted as legal extractions: much of it is not. Then there are several natural phenomena such as forest fires, landslides, earthquakes, floods etc., on account of which there are changes in this natural capital. In short, physical accounting of forest stock and flows is a complex task.

A satellite accounting for forest resources is demonstrated now. Based on detailed studies by Madhu Verma (2000) and Chopra and Kadekodi (1997), dimensions of forest-related stocks and flows and their physical accounts of forest resources for the state of Himachal Pradesh are shown in Table 11.1. It illustrates the various physical flow components of forest resources with their links to various economic sectors. There are two major components in this physical accounting table. They are: (i) the physical stock accounts on forest area and growing stocks and (ii) the details of flows from forests as a natural resource. One can easily notice the complexity in getting quantitative information on each of these components. While the growing stocks may be changing at an annual increment of 1.28 m³, the annual productivity or extraction is at the rate of 0.43 m³ per hectare. The flows consist of direct extractive activities such as salvage, timber for right holders (peculiar to the HP state), fuel wood collection, minor forest products and so on. Directly, forests also perform a consumptive function as providing tourism to wildlife sanctuaries. Indirectly, they provide a number of ecosystem services such as water-

TABLE 11.1
Physical Accounts of Forest Stock of Himachal Pradesh

Stocks and flows from forests	Physical value	Possible valuation methods	Value (Rs) per hectare of geographical area of forest	Area under tree and shrubs only
Forest Stock Accounts				
1. Total geographical forest area of HP	35,407 km²	NA		
2. Area under tree cover and scrub forest	12,521 km²	NA		
3. Total growing stock	10.25 crore m³	1. User Cost method	1.10 lakh	2.85 lakh
		2. Present Value method		
		3. Net Present Value method		
4. Area lost due to forest fire (1995–6)	571.43 km²	NA		
5. Forest area diverted (as on Dec. 1996)	33.88 km²	NA		
6. Area afforested (as on 31.12.96)	38.90 km²	NA		
7. Annual Increment	1.28 m³/ha [a]	NA		
8. Annual Productivity	0.43 m³/ha [a]	NA		
Forest Flow Accounts (annual flows)				
(A) Direct Consumptive Uses :				
9. Salvage	3.50 lakh m³	1. Direct market price technique	0.08 thousand	0.22 thousand
10. Timber for right holders	1.06 lakh m³		0.16 thousand	0.42 thousand
11. Fuel wood	27.60 lakh tonnes	2. Indirect estimates	0.75 thousand	1.92 thousand

(cont.)

Table 11.1 (cont.)

Stocks and flows from forests	Physical value	Possible valuation methods	Value (Rs) per hectare of	
			Geographical area of forest	Area under tree and shrubs only
12. Fodder 4.81 thousand	92 lakh tonnes			1.86 thousand
13. Minor forest produce	1,161.56 tonnes		0.067 thousand	0.17 thousand
Total Direct Consumptive Uses			3.0 thousand	7.0 thousand
(B) Direct Non-consumptive Uses				
14. Eco-tourism	66.56 lakh tourists	1. CVM 2. Travel-cost method	18.0 thousand	46.0 thousand
Total Direct Benefits			21.0 thousand	53.0 thousand
(C) Indirect Uses				
15. Watershed	6.77 crore m³ (growing stock in river basin forest circle) and 36,986 km² (entire forest area)	1. CVM 2. Change-in-productivity approach 3. Replacement cost approach	2.0 lakh	5.16 lakh
16. Micro-climatic functions	9,69,018 households	1. CVM 2. Indirect estimates	0. 39 thousand	1.0 thousand
17. Carbon sink	12,521 km² (area under tree cover and scrub forest)	1. CVM 2. Indirect estimates	48 thousand	1.23 lakh

(cont.)

Table 11.1 (cont.)

Stocks and flows from forests	Physical value	Possible valuation methods	Value (Rs) per hectare of	
			Geographical area of forest	Area under tree and shrubs only
18. Biodiversity/endangered species	8,966 (total no. of species in HP) and 125 (endangered species)	1. CVM 2. Option value 3. Bequest value	20 thousand	20 thousand
19. Employment generation	48.4 man days	1. Direct costing	0.06 thousand	1.7 thousand
Total Indirect Benefits			2.68 lakh	6.90 lakh
TOTAL ECONOMIC VALUE			2.89 lakh	7.43 lakh

Note: (a) There could be many more economic values associated with forests. Instances of 'Direct Use Values' are genetic material, human habitat, cultural and educational use; 'Indirect Use Values' are air and noise pollution reduction, micro-climatic regulation, nutrient recycling, flood control and soil conservation; 'Non-Use Values' are intrinsic worth.

(b) [a] relate to some selected districts of HP only

(c) CVM = Contingent Valuation Method

(d) NA = Not Applicable

(e) Indirect Estimates include opportunity costs, replacement costs, productivity change, etc.

Sources: Items 1 and 2: State of Forest Report 1997; 3 and 9–20: Madhu Verma (2000); 4 and 5: Forestry Statistics of India 1996; 7 and 8 : Chopra and Kadekodi (1997)

shed development, act as a carbon sink, and protect the biodiversity and micro-climatic environment.

There are a number of methods to value the use and non-use functions and services provided by natural and environmental resources. Some details of all such methods have already been briefly introduced in 'Environmental Economics Through Case Studies' and dealt within various chapters in this book. Table 11.1 also lists the use of different appropriate methods in deriving the values of various ecosystem services.

Another illustration of satellite accounting is from a study by Brandon and Hommann (1995). They estimated the cost of environmental degradation, depletion and associated costs (what they call costs of inaction) at the national level, for a large number of natural resources. These costs and values were not integrated into the national income accounts. Table 11.2 shows their estimates in a summary form. It was viewed by them that the environmental costs in India add up to about 4.53 percentage of GDP in 1992 prices.

Now we take up some methodological issues of natural resource accouting. Natural resources consist of two broad categories of resources, namely exhaustible and renewable. They are subjected to depletion (like any other capital resource) and depreciation. Accordingly two different questions arise: One, how to account depreciation and or degradation of exhaustible natural capital? Second, how to value changes in renewable resources?

Consider the case of exhaustible resources first. Extracting them now can in no way assure the constancy or improved welfare in the future (unless substitutes arrive). In a non-substituting society (e.g., cake-eating economy), therefore, the Hicksian measure of income from the extraction of an exhaustible resource is to subtract the value of all such extractions. This procedure however, would substantially reduce the incomes of the countries that are heavily dependent on extractive activities. For instance, if a country's income were originating only from crude oil extractions, then following the above guideline, the values of all current extractions will have to be subtracted from the national income of that country. It would imply that its national income would drop significantly, if not to be treated as zero! The only solution to this puzzle was given by the modified Hartwick rule (Hartwick, 1990), which suggests that along the equilibrium path of production and consumption, as long as the rental income from an

TABLE 11.2

Summary of Major Annual Environmental Costs in India

Problem	Impacts on health and/ or production	Low estimate (million US $)	High estimate (million US $)
Urban air pollution	Urban health impacts.	$ 517	$ 2102
Water pollution (health impacts)	Urban health impacts, esp. Diarrhoeal diseases.	$ 3076	$ 8344
Water pollution (production impacts)	Higher incremental costs for clean water supply.	Not estimated	Not estimated
Industrial hazardous waste	Long-term health impacts, esp. Cancer.	Not estimated	Not estimated
Soil degradation	Loss of agricultural output.	$ 1516	$ 2368
Rangeland degradation	Loss of livestock carrying capacity.	$ 238	$ 417
Deforestation	Loss of sustainable timber supply	$ 183	$ 244
Coastal and marine resources	Unsustainable harvesting of marine resources.	Not estimated	Not estimated
Loss of biodiversity	Loss of use, option, and existence values.	Not estimated	Not estimated
Tourism	Decline in tourism revenues.	$ 142	$ 283
Total costs of environmental degradation		$ 5672	$ 13,758
Total cost, per cent of GDP		2.64%	6.41%
Average cost – US $ % of GDP		$ 9715 4.53%	

Source: Brandon and Hommann (1995)

exhaustible resource is reinvested, the future income stream can be sustained. This also legitimizes expenditures on investments or capital formation and resource development for the welfare of society.

We now return to some more conceptual issues. How to value depletion or depreciation of exhaustible and also (to some extent) renewable resources within the framework of satellite accounting? Three major approaches for valuing exhaustible or depletable resources are briefly explained here. They are:

1. Present value method: The starting point is the assumption that exhaustible resources are natural resource stocks having long-term use values. In this method, a long-term view is taken for the resource. Accordingly, the present value of future expected returns PV_0 (i.e., the discounted sum of sale value minus the marginal costs of exploration, development, and extraction) from the use of the resources reflects the total value of the resource stock at time zero. If one takes the difference between the present value of the resource stock now (PV_1) and that in the previous period (PV_0), this difference accounts for the depletion cost of that resource. The only question then arises is about the appropriate discount rate for arriving at the present values. It is normally suggested to use a lower social discount rate.

2. Net Price Method: In this method, a concept of 'Hotelling' rent is used. Here again, the stock of the natural resource is taken into consideration. The net price of the resource is this rental on the stock of natural capital, equal to the difference between the market value of the resource and the unit cost of extraction, exploration and development. This rental itself will increase at the social discount rate.

3. User-cost Method: This method has been developed by El Serafy (1989). In the two methods mentioned above, it is crucial to estimate and recognize the stock of natural capital, along with an estimate of its depletion rate. Generally it is difficult and often impossible to get precise estimates of stocks of natural resources (as proven, inferred or indicated). Then, the computations of the rentals or present values can go wrong. Further, El Serafy argues that, instead of making the stock of natural resources as the starting point (with an argument of keeping natural resources intact, or investing on renewable and other resources at least at the rate of its depletion), it is important to follow the changes in the flows (or extractions) which alone are relevant for defining sustainable use patterns. He considers the rental on a stock of natural capital consisting of two components namely, a 'true' cost or value and another as 'user' cost. The true value itself is a measure of the net worth of the resource (for both the present and future generations), but the user cost is the value enjoyed by the present generation at the cost of the future generation or users. Therefore, this user cost is a capital consumption charge and is the relevant indicator of depreciation or depletion. Consider a stream of true income (X) from the use of a stock of natural resource but unknown, defined as a sustainable one. However, the society may be extracting it at an unsustainable

rate, earning a net income (net of extraction costs etc.,) (R), which is normally added to the GDP as a welfare measure. It is the difference between the net receipt (R), from extracting an exhaustible resource and its true income (X) that is called as the user cost that is to be interpreted as the capital consumption expenditure or an indicator of depreciation. It is only under this approach that a sustainability criterion is implied.

His formula for the ratio of true income to net income is deduced as:

$$X/R = 1 - 1/(1 + r)^{n+1} \tag{11.1}$$

where, 'r' is the discount rate and 'n' is the life expectancy of the resource. Then R–X is the user cost which is to be deducted from the estimates of income so as to arrive at the adjusted income. An application of this method of adjusting GDP will be presented as a case study later.

Now, consider the case of a renewable resource, say air quality—an environmental resource for sure. How does one value such a natural resource as air quality changes? A short cut to these actual accountings is to assume an optimal pollution abatement strategy and account for its costs. Figure 11.2 shows an analytical method of deriving the optimum pollution level and the 'polluter pay price' for it. MAB is the marginal benefit from abatement or savings in costs due to pollution accruing to both the polluting firm and the society, whereas MAC is the marginal cost of abatement, to be incurred by the polluting firm. The level of social tolerance of pollution is OW* whose social value is OC* to be charged as polluter pay charge. That will indicate the 'willingness to pay' by the polluting firm as well as its acceptability to the affected people. This estimate of 'willingness to pay' or 'polluter charges' is to be deducted from the conventional income to arrive at an adjusted income. A case study on water pollution abatement in 'Fiscal and Institutional Approaches to Pollution Abatement' by Murty illustrates this method. But, in actuality, it is difficult to measure either marginal abatement costs or the marginal abatement benefit. Therefore only second-best methods may have to be used. A mix of tax-standard approach or standards and controls approach may be more practical.

Next is the question about non-market values of natural and environmental goods and services in the accounting system. Various

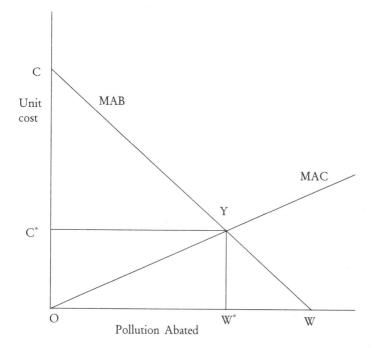

Fig. 11.2: Determining 'Pollution Pay' for Abatement

methods on this are mentioned in 'Environmental Economics Through Case Studies'. Specific methods of stated values are demonstrated in 'Economic Valuation of Biodiversity' and 'The Health Benefits of Improving the Household Environment' (Parikh and Ghose, 1995; Kadekodi and Ravindranath, 1997). This raises several additional questions on linking valuation of natural resources with income accounting (dealt by several chapters in this book).[2]

---

[2] Weitzman (1976) among others developed an analytical model linking valuation of capital and other resources with income accounting. In brief, his main result is that the 'Current value Hamiltonian' in an aggregate neo-classical growth model, i.e., the integral of utility over a period, is a welfare indicator. This Hamiltonian is shown to be equivalent to the Net National Product (NNP) of the economy. However, he dealt mainly with the proper valuation of man-made capital equivalent to present value of future stream of consumption and did not deal with valuation of natural resources. Since then, the basic issues associated with natural resources and linking them with income or welfare have attracted increasing interest among economists. Dasgupta, Kristrom and Maler (1994), Hartwick (1992), Howarth (1991), among others, have concentrated on dealing with specific issues such as valuation and inter-generational

Are There Any Estimates of Satellite or Integrated Environmental Accounts ?

As far as integrated income accounting is concerned, some marginal progress has been made mainly on the empirical side. Parikh et al. (1992), UN (1993), UNEP (1993), Peskin (1989), Parikh and Parikh (1997), among many others have suggested methods of correcting national income accounting by going back to the basic structure of the macro economy seen in terms of an Input-Output Transactions table. This basis for this approach comes from Leontief (1966) and Stone (1961). The approach starts with identifying all such sectors that are environmentally and natural resource-wise important. Then, each of these are divided into sub-blocks in terms of supply sectors/factors, as well as demand or receiving sectors/factors, isolating the natural resource and environmental factors. Flows of outputs or services from those natural and environmental resources (or factors) that are used as inputs by others are to be identified. Additional columns of consumption, to account for flows from natural and environmental resources directly in the form of final use, are also incorporated. The modified Input-Output table can be used to define the adjusted value added as well as final consumption, accounting for environmental and natural resource uses. In this manner, one would have accounted for the use of natural resources both as intermediate inputs as well as final-use consumption. The method is quite appealing, simple in description, but is equally complicated to implement. Economists need not be reminded about the complexities in estimating even the regular Input-Output tables of an economy.

Parikh and Parikh (1997) have further elaborated on the System of Environmental and Economic Accounting (SEEA) as developed by the United Nations (1993). Figure 11.3 illustrates their methodology of developing integrated stock and flow accounts within the framework of national income accountings. They provide a definition of Green net national product (NNP) shown in Box 11.3.

---

equity, depletion, degradation, defence against environmental degradation, labour in environmental management and so on. Most of these developments are in the neo-classical framework of optimizing welfare defined as the present value consumption. As argued by Maler (1991) and others, the main advantage of this approach, however, is its direct link with the system of national income accounting. Briefly, this method will be termed as the 'integrated approach'

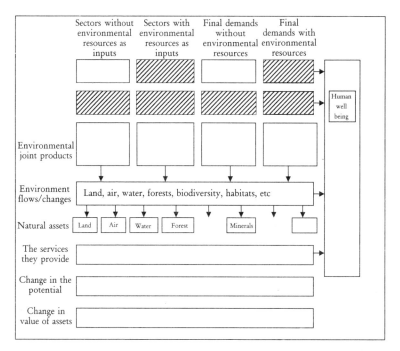

Source: Based on Parikh and Parikh (1997)

Fig. 11.3: Integrated Environmental and Economic Accounting

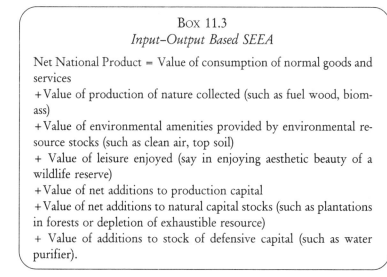

Box 11.3
Input–Output Based SEEA

Net National Product = Value of consumption of normal goods and services

+Value of production of nature collected (such as fuel wood, biomass)

+Value of environmental amenities provided by environmental resource stocks (such as clean air, top soil)

+ Value of leisure enjoyed (say in enjoying aesthetic beauty of a wildlife reserve)

+Value of net additions to production capital

+Value of net additions to natural capital stocks (such as plantations in forests or depletion of exhaustible resource)

+ Value of additions to stock of defensive capital (such as water purifier).

In doing these adjustments, the values of degradation, depletion or extraction and externalities are also to be accounted. Table 11.3 illustrates these computations based on an Input–Output (I–O) table for India. The conventional GDP in 1983–84 in current prices was Rs 2,15,580 crores. The production of this income required a number of natural and environmental resources. The likely effects are also listed under various categories of intermediate and final demands. For lack of comprehensive data and information, these could not be shown in value terms. Also, all the relevant causes and effects are not recorded either.

Very recently, one study at the state level has been completed to arrive at some of the components of the integrated accounts on the lines of Table 11.3. A study by TERI (2001) accounts for air (both indoor and outdoor), land, water, forests and minerals (mainly iron ore) for the environmental changes and their impacts. However, there are several other sectors, which are very sensitive to environment. The notable ones are tourism and fisheries. It is only hoped that such studies will enable the Central and state Statistical Organizations (CSOs) to develop and firm up the methodology, so as to compile green Gross National Product (GNP) on a regular basis.

What are the Major Issues in Sustainable Income Accounting?

In the context of sustainable income accounting, a number of issues, both at the theoretical and empirical levels, still remain to be addressed. Some of the major ones are to be noted.

The Case of Defensive Expenses against Environment Related Externalities

There is a category of expenses called defensive expenses that need to be carefully dealt with. These constitute such expenses that society incurs as precautionary, against facing the externality effects of environmental degradation. Defensive expenses are generally hidden as normal consumption expenses. Whereas it is that part of income, that is spent on goods, the consumption of which does not actually add to welfare but instead helps to maintain old levels of welfare by protecting against environmental hazards. A good example is the buying of health insurance against health problems likely to arise due to environmental degradation. Another example is the purchase of a water purifier to protect against deteriorating water quality.

TABLE 11.3

Towards Integrated Environmental and Economic Accounting for India: 1983–4

(Rs crore)

Production sectors	Total intermediate consumption	Private consumption	Govt. consumption	Gross investment	Stock changes	Exports	Imports	Gross output
			Conventional I-O Based Income Accounting					
1. Food agriculture	4473	33,904	215	–	–117	302	–760	38,017
2. Other agriculture	11,146	31,340	182	–	820	1628	–353	44,763
3. Basic industries	14,783	–	–	–	698	337	–1211	14,607
4. Other manufacturing industries and construction	46,772	27,030	3950	37,686	5109	7181	–5631	12,20,97
5. Petroleum refining	6879	1216	273	2000	40	–	–6830	3578
6. Coal	2523	193	27	200	159	–	–200	2902
7. Electricity, gas and water	6033	1078	106	500	–	–	–500	7217
8. Railways	3160	1359	470	281	–	–	–281	4989
9. Other transport	7878	6189	962	–	–	–	–	15,029
10. Rest of economy	40,185	33,004	5975	–	–	2482	–1576	80,070
11. Value added (GDP)	18,943,7	5433	17,402	–	–	3308	–	2,15,580
12. Gross output	3,332,69	1,407,46	29,562	40,667	6709	15,238	–17,342	3,33,269

(cont.)

351

Table 11.3 (cont.)

Production sectors	Total intermediate consumption	Private consumption	Govt. consumption	Gross investment	Stock changes	Exports	Imports	Gross output
		Natural and Environmental Resource Flows						
13. Air	ETP for industrial pollution	Health effects of indoor and outdoor pollution	ETP for industrial pollution	ETP for industrial pollution	–	ETP	–	
14. Soil	Fertilizer and pesticide use, overburden treatments in mining areas	–	–	–	–	–	–	
15. Water	ETP for industrial pollution	Health care against water borne diseases	ETP for industrial industrial	–	–	–	–	
16. Forest (area and biomass)	Depletion and degradation due to area conversion and industrial use	Fuelwood and biomass use, ecological services	Depletion and degradation due to area conversion and timber use	Depletion and degradation due to timber use and area conversion	–	Threat wildlife and medicinal plants		

(cont.)

352

Table 11.3 (cont.)

Production sectors	Total intermediate consumption	Private consumption	Govt. consumption	Gross investment	Stock changes	Exports	Imports	Gross output
17. Land (fodder, coastal and marine)	Degradation due to agricultural activity, mining and fishing	Urban habitat and encroachments	Degradation and land conversion	Degradation and land conversion	–	–	–	–
18. Biodiversity	Irreversible effects of industrial extraction of flora & fauna	Irreversible effects of floral and faunal extraction Tourism	Irreversible effects of industrial extraction of flora and fauna					
19. Solid waste	Industrial hazards and wastes	Kitchen and urban waste	Municipal waste					
20. Minerals	Depletion	–	Depletion			–	Depletion	

Source: Author's estimates

353

In what manner should the costs incurred as 'defensive expenses' by a society on abating environmental degradation be treated? How to distinguish consumption of normal goods from preventive and defensive goods? Even if such an estimate is made, how does one put it within the framework of SNA? For example, how does one account for expenditures to get clean air, which is made scarce due to forest degradation? If forest degradation is already accounted as depletion costs, will accounting for defensive expenses say, on air conditioners, not mean a double counting?

There are two methods to resolve these issues. The production of defensive goods and services require both labour and capital as in the production of any other normal good. From the demand side, there are two ways in which defensive expenses can be treated for valuation and accounting purposes. It can be considered as part of consumption expenditure. Alternatively, it can be treated as a negative regeneration, i.e., substitution instead of regeneration, which is only a special case of regeneration. Take the first case of treating defensive expenses as consumption. Consider an example of dealing with illness due to environmental degradation. Individuals then have two options. They can opt once and for all, to invest on defensive goods and services (such as buying a health insurance) as a precautionary measure, or incur medical and other expenses as and when they are affected by the exposure to the risk of environmental degradation. In the second instance, there is a chance factor associated with the individual falling sick or being affected by degradation. Considering the probability of an individual falling sick due to environmental degradation (in the absence of one-time defensive expenditures), the optimal investment on defensive expenditures can be deduced, which ought to be incorporated as part of the adjusted national income. The alternative method of treating defensive expenses as negative regeneration within the sustainable income accounting methodology can be useful in understanding implications of public investments on environment-related defensive expenses (e.g., urban solid waste incineration plant).

Income Accounting as a Balance Between Income and Expenditure

Like all accounts, income accounting is a balance between income and expenditure. It is not enough to account for externality only at the level of expenditures (e.g., defensive or unpaid). There has to be a balancing account at the income or value-added levels also. How does one deal with the income earned from working with environmental management programmes? For instance, a pollution abatement programme creates value-added in terms of wages and profits, but from the expenditure side, for the people paying for it, it does not improve their welfare. This disequilibrium impasse can be resolved by assuming a full employment situation, where labour deployed in pollution abatement is considered to be a transfer from normal goods production, with no change in welfare and value added.

Missing Data Problems

Stock and flow information on all natural and environmental resources are generally not available. As a starting point, depending upon data availability, generally a few of the natural resources are perhaps accountable. The question then is on the validity of dealing with only a select list of natural resources for accounting and integrating it with the SNA, when the natural resource endowments of an economy consist of many more such resources for examples, renewable resources such as sea corals, air quality and biodiversity. One can only hope that, as and when the methodology of valuation is improvized for practical applications, and when the actual data start flowing, some of these can be incorporated.

Problem of Long-term and Short-term Benefit/Use of
Natural Resources

System of National Accounts (SNA) is a flow income accounting system. Welfare benefits from preservation of natural resources have a long stream of benefits. In a strict theoretical sense, such benefits cannot be easily written off under current income or welfare streams. This issue gets more complicated particularly because of the fact that preservation can be costless. But it involves the sacrifice of current consumption from developmental use of natural resources. Therefore, care should be taken to spread preservation benefits over a long-time horizon and account for it accordingly.

Will there be a Problem of Double Counting?

Yes, there is also the usual problem of double counting, very common in income accounting. While talking of environmental services provided by environmental functions, one is not sure of being free from double counting. For instance, timber has a price reflecting its use or utility value after it is felled from the forest. But it has emerged out of the carbon sequestration function of the forest in the past, abating global climate change (i.e., having a non-use value). How does one segregate its use and non-use values? To complicate matters further, what is to be done if the security value of forests is also to be accounted along with the timber and non-timber values? A practical approach is to treat part of the use value as additional 'option value' or non-use value.

Problems of Aggregation

As an agreed system, SNA is based on one set of prices, commonly known either as 'producer prices', or 'purchaser prices'. Essentially, if the accounting is done in producer prices, the indirect taxes are shown separately, otherwise hidden in purchaser prices. In other words, all outputs, costs and values are in either of these two prices, and not in any mixed form. Do the values of natural resources reflect only the producer price or purchaser price or a mix? The task of aggregating the values of natural resources with national income accounting poses another theoretical problem. The values of environmental resources are elicited, broadly based on two methods, namely, 'revealed preference' values and 'stated preference' values. For some details of these concepts, see the chapter 'Environmental Economics Through Case Studies'. Values derived from market prices refer to revealed preferences. Many others are based on stated preferences (e.g., 'non-use' values or even 'use' values for non-marketed goods and services, say, deduced from a contingent valuation method). It is here that an inconsistency can arise when all such values are to be aggregated, knowing that different valuation methods follow different pricing systems. Only some empirical norms of adding such revealed and stated preference values have been developed (Carson et al., 1995). But the theoretical back-up is still missing.

Therefore, the task of bringing valuation of natural and environmental resources and income accounting closer is still far from complete. On a theoretical basis, there is no guarantee of an integration of these two, so as to arrive at a system of adjusted national income accounts (UN, 1993). Therefore, one may have to either resort to 'satellite accounting', or to the 'integrated approach' suggested by Weitzman and many others based on a certain shadow-price approach.

CASE STUDIES IN NATURAL RESOURCE ACCOUNTING

The purpose here is to present several case studies illustrating the methods of satellite or integrated income accounts for India. As an illustration, in 'Natural Resource Accounting', with the forest accounting for Himachal Pradesh (Table 11.1), most of the important ecosystem functions, their physical attributes or values and economic values are shown. Several other case studies are discussed with some details of methodology, data and methods of computations.

Accounting for Forest Resources under Integrated Environmental and Economic Accounting (IEEA): An Illustration

This is an illustration, not at the national level, but for a small region in India, from the Yamuna basin in north India. The Yamuna sub-basin is spread over four states—Haryana, Himachal Pradesh, Uttar Pradesh and Rajasthan (leaving out National Capital Region for its very insignificant forest resources). The details of this case study are available in Chopra and Kadekodi (1997).

Forests in these states are to be viewed both as a stock and as the source of a series of flows. The stocks are measurable in terms of forest area and growing stock rates. Biomass stock is, however, only one component of the stock measure. The other components are stock of forest knowledge (from which there is a flow of medicinal values, spiritual values, aesthetic values etc.), nutritional balance, bio-diversity or social security. What follows from the stock are the flows of forest services and goods. The forest flows are: timber of different kinds, fuel wood, fodder, hides, medicinal substances, roots, herbs, shoots, fruits, barks, flowers and other non-timber forest products (NTFP). Then, there are a large number of forest functions and services such as religious services, tourist flows, security, aesthetic beauty, carbon sequestration, nutritional cycling and so on. It is the flow accounting that is of immediate relevance for integrated income accounting.

In this illustration, four different aspects of a typical forest are accounted. They are extraction, regeneration, degradation and preservation of forest resources.

The starting point is the existing estimate of Net State Domestic Product (NSDP) for the states of Haryana, Himachal Pradesh, Uttar Pradesh and Rajasthan. The state domestic products for the four states (as upgraded for 1995-6, based on past data available up to 1988-9) are shown in Table 11.4. The following data and parametric estimates are made towards accounting for extraction, regeneration, degradation and preservation of forest resources.

1. Total dense forest area (TDA): This is an indicator of the stock of the forest as a natural capital. This information is available in the Forest Working Plans. This is the relevant forest area for which, perhaps, the regeneration and extraction features are applicable. On the other hand, in open forest areas, either the regeneration rate (mostly under plantation of fuel wood under joint forest management (JFM), social forestry (SF), etc.) just equals the extraction rate or their difference is very marginal. Therefore, there may not be any net change in biomass from such areas on account of regeneration and extraction.

2. Shadow price of stock of forest resource (ms): The true value of forest stock should be the ecological value of the biomass, which should include timber, NTFP, ecological function values, etc. Based on the field–level investigations and interviews with local communities, it is estimated that this value is about 1.5 times the market timber price, of which the estimated NTFP values are on average about 30 per cent of the timber values. Normally, the total value of all services and products that a well-stocked forest provides, can be much more than this factor of 1.5. But this factor of 1.5 reflects, the avoiding of double counting problems on account of multiple services that a dense forest area performs.

3. Annual forest degradation rate (å): Change in total dense forest area can be taken as an indicator of quality change of forests. Degradation rates can be estimated from the statistics recorded in reports of the Forest Working Plans.

4. Shadow value of degradation (ma): Corresponding to the area of degradation, a value for such forest area in rupees per unit area terms is required. This value should reflect the opportunity value of losing a well-stocked forest, such as a dense forest. One way of assessing this is by estimating the 'willingness to pay' (WTP) by the local communities to protect this forest area using a contingent valuation method.

5. Regeneration rate (H): Annual increments (m^3 per hectare) as recorded in Forest Working Plans can be used for this data.

TABLE 11.4

Forest-Related Data and Parameters for Integrated Environment and Economic Accounting in Yamuna Basin

State	Degradation = Annual change in dense forest area during 1995–6 å : sq km	Shadow value of degradation = WTP m_a : Rs/ sq km.	Regeneration rate = Annual increment H : m³/Ha	Extraction rate = Annual productivity R : m³/Ha	Total dense forest area in 1996 TDA : Ha	Shadow price of stock of forest = Timber price[b] 1.5 ms : Rs/m3	Preservation benefit = Tourist travel cost P : Rs lakhs/Year
(1)	(2)	(3)	(4)	(5)	(6)	(7)	(8)
Rajasthan	−36.04	1,07,232	0.22	0.555	39,388	18,540	576
UP	−18.74	32,006	1.71	2.690[a]	1,57,136	12,419	0
HP	107.40	17,600	1.28	1.745[a]	1,39,967	12,419	0
Haryana	−7.06	3,53,001	0.53	0.440	3882	27,810	0
Total Yamuna Basin	45.56		1.05	2.460	340373		

Note : [a] The actual extraction rates in the sample districts/villages were twice of these estimates. But keeping the entire of the forest range in the states, the extraction rates have been average to these estimates

[b] Stands for multiplication sign

Source: Kadekodi, Gopal K. and Agarwal, M.M: Integration of Preservation, Depletion, and Degradation of Natural Resources in Income Accounting, Institute of Economic Growth Working paper E/189/97

6. Extraction rate (R): This is taken to be the same as annual productivity m³ per hectare), again from the same sources as above.

7. The preservation value per year (P): There are a number of national parks and sancturies in the Yamuna basin. Data and information from all of them regarding the preservation benefits could not be collected. Hence, this is an instance of the problems of missing data as mentioned earlier. Based on a detailed survey data, only the Bharatpur National Park is considered here, as an illustration. The net contribution of the tourists per year for this park based on the travel-cost method can be taken as adding to the preservation benefits in Rajasthan. If such preservation values are added here, the corresponding value added by tourism will have to be subtracted from the usual estimates of SDP. The preservation value from the national park need not be equal to the tourism value as recorded in the national income accounts.

Kadekodi and Agarwal (1998) deduce a formula to derive the adjusted SDP as:

$$\text{SDP} = \text{Usual State Domestic Product} + 0.78 * m_a.\text{å} + m_s.\text{TDA}*(H-R)+P. \qquad (11.2)$$

Here, the adjustment terms stand for adjustment for forest quality degradation ($0.78 * m_a.$ å), adjustment for extraction and regeneration ($m_s.\text{TDA}*(H-R)$) and for preservation benefits P. Tables 11.4 and 11.5 show the estimated data, parameters and the computation of adjusted income in the states on account of changes in the forests of the Yamuna sub-basin.

Some comments on the database on SDP can be made. Data on SDP in Himachal Pradesh during 1980-1 to 1988-9 show that income from forestry and logging dominated the total SDP (77 per cent in 1980-1, 69 per cent in 1988-9). Because of such a dominance, any depletion of forests in this state will mean considerable impact on the SDP. This, precisely, is what is reflected in the estimates shown in Table 11.4. The adjusted SDP of Himachal Pradesh, on account of excessive extraction over and above regeneration can go down by as much as 21.64 per cent.

The estimates of SDP adjustments for other states are -0.73 per cent for Rajasthan, -2.53 per cent for Uttar Pradesh, and +0.04 per cent for Haryana. The positive adjustment in Haryana is perhaps attributable to recent JFM and other community programmes. The marginal

TABLE 11.5

Adjusted State Domestic Product in Yamuna Basin States

(Rs lakh)

State	Net SDP in 1995–96	SDP from forestry and logging currently accounted	Adjustment on account of forest flows [a]	Relative adjustment in SDP
	Projected from 1980–81 to 1988–89 data	Projected from 1980–81 to 1988–89 data	$0.78^{b} m_a \cdot \mathring{a}$ $+ m_s \cdot TDA^b (H- R) + P$	Ratio in Percentage
(1)	(2)	(3)	(4)	(5)
Rajasthan	2,59,216	8239(3.18)	−1900	−0.73
UP	7,55,378	13,334(1.77)	−19129	−2.53
HP	37,286	14,434(38.71)	−8068	−21.64
Haryana	1,75,162	2847(1.62)	+78	+0.04

Notes: [a] The adjustments shown in column 4 have the additional correction, of deducting SDP from forestry and logging sector. This is required to avoid double counting as extractions, depletion and regeneration are accounted separately. A factor of 0.78 is applied to WTP estimates to convert stated preference values. See Carson et al., (1995)

[b] Stands for multiplication sign. Figures in brackets are per cent of column (2)

Source: Kadekodi, Gopal K. and Agarwal, M.M: Integration of Preservation, Depletion, and Degradation of Natural Resources in Income Accounting, Institute of Economic Growth Working paper E/189/97

decline in Rajasthan is indicative of the stress on account of fuel-wood shortages. In the case of Uttar Pradesh (UP), it is a case of excessive extraction over and above the regeneration rate.

Accounting for Water Pollution in India: A Case Study

Water pollution is one of the major environmental problems as a result of industrialization. The other major related problems are air pollution, noise pollution, solid wastes and hazards, and climate-change effects. Water pollution may also occur from other economic activities such as agriculture and household use of water, but their magnitudes are not as alarming as those from industrial effluents.

Water pollution is measured by a number of indicators. The major ones are: Biological Oxygen Demand (BOD), Chemical Oxygen Demand (COD), pH, suspended solids, dissolved solids, variety of chemicals (e.g., oils, cyanides, sulphides), metals etc. See chapter 'Pollution Control in Tanneries' by Sankar for an account of these. There are several other indicators that are more relevant to determine quality of drinking water (e.g., toxicity, color, odour, coliforms and so on). There are no perfect estimates of the extent of water pollution for India as a whole. However, the Water (Prevention and Control of Pollution) Act of 1974 identifies 15 industries to be directly the most relevant ones responsible for water pollution in India. They are: ferrous metallurgical, non-ferrous metallurgical, mining, ore processing , petroleum, petro-chemicals, chemicals, ceramic, cement, textile, paper, fertilizer, coal, power generating, and processing of animal or vegetable products.

There are two alternative ways of valuing and accounting the impacts of water pollution. The first is to assess the health and other impacts of water pollution on human and animal life (may be plant life also). This information at the national scale is difficult to estimate. Only specifically designed 'dose-response' studies in water-polluted and water borne-disease infected areas can provide some magnitudes of the effects and costs. The second is to take account of the cost of water treatment before discharging the effluents into the rivers etc., following the principle of 'polluter pay'. In an economy-wide study, Brandon and Hommann (1995) attempted to provide an all-India-level estimate of urban and rural health effects due to water pollution (measured basically in terms of morbidity and mortality rates). Taking the estimates of reduction in Disability Adjusted Life Years (DALY) of the Indian population, they estimated the cost of water pollution in India to be anywhere between US $ 3076 to 8344 billion.

Murty et al., (1999) provide an alternative estimate based on the principle of 'polluter pay', in establishing Effluent Treatment Plants (ETP) as shown in Table 11.6. According to him, based on a sample survey of industries, not more than 25 per cent of Indian industries have been actually found to have set up ETPs in India. Using the cost norms from the survey data, and following a hypothetical situation of all industries having put up ETPs, he estimates the cost structures of ETPs in the major industries in India. The water pollution abatement costs as shown in Table 11.6 of computations are based on the assumption of a full employment economy, and all the industries

TABLE 11.6

Estimates of Capital Stock, Value-Added Foregone, and Total Annual Cost for Water Pollution Abatement in Major Water-Polluting Industries in India (Rs lakh): 1991–2

Industry	Cost structure of ETPs						
	Material cost	Power cost	Intermediate cost	Wage cost	Capital cost	Value-Added	Total ETP cost
1. Fertilizer	1038.90	378.60	1417.50	195.60	6211.10	6406.70	7824.20
2. Sugar	203.80	612.90	816.70	281.90	523.30	805.20	1621.90
3. Cement	0.00	13.60	13.60	09.10	75.50	84.60	98.20
4. Distillery	610.80	512.90	1123.70	219.10	3176.90	3396.00	4519.70
5. Chemical	1486.00	2002.90	3488.90	1111.80	1,32,769.70	1,33,881.50	1,37,370.40
6. Thermal power	15,025.60	1903.20	16,928.8	601.00	1279.20	1880.20	18,809.00
7. Refinery and petroleum products	483.20	268.80	752.00	217.2C	4272.80	4490.00	5242.00
8. Tannery	90.80	105.80	196.60	181.70	1117.50	1300.20	1496.80
9. Zinc	104.40	4.40	108.80	15.70	98.00	113.70	222.50
10. Iron and Steel	325.40	949.10	1274.50	542.40	399.30	941.70	2216.20
11. Paper	1170.70	2442.80	3613.50	545.80	7061.40	7607.20	11,220.70
12. Drugs	2624.80	2257.60	4882.40	1156.00	15,423.60	16,579.60	21,462.00

Note: Capital cost refers to the interest costs on capital stocks
Source: Murty et al., 1999

363

adhering to water quality standards. The total value added by the ETP activities are estimated to be Rs 64.10 lakh, as against the conventional GDP of Rs 5,98,964 crore in the Indian economy in 1991–2. This value-added components of the ETPs are indirect measures of 'value-added cost' from normal goods' productions for having diverted some resources such as capital and labour for the maintenance of ETPs (because of the assumption of full employment of capital and skilled labour involved in ETPs). However, since only about 25 per cent of the industries have actually put up the ETPs, the actual 'value added lost' in conventional GDP are of the order of Rs 16 crore. Assuming preservation of water quality to be a public good (or service), this 'value-added cost' gives an account of value of water quality preservation.

A Case Study of Mineral Accounting for the State of Goa

Goa is a rich iron ore mining region of India. In terms of its importance, this state produces about 33 per cent of the total iron ore in India, and about 40 per cent of iron-ore exports from India. The depletion of iron ore reserves in India in general, and in Goa state, in particular, has been of major concern for the nation (Kadekodi, 1982). Are we properly accounting this depleting resource?

In a recent study, by the Tata Energy Research Institute (TERI) estimated the adjusted income accounting for the state of Goa (2001). Among many other sectoral natural resource related adjustments, TERI has also incorporated the iron mining from Goa. Using the data on physical accounts from the TERI study, an estimate of iron-ore depletion and the corresponding adjustment in the SDP of Goa are shown in Table 11.7.

The present rate of extraction of iron ore from Goa in 1996 is about 7.04 per cent of the stocks. Following the 'Net Price Method', the per tonne rent or net price is Rs 109.33 per tonne of extracted ore (or Rs 15,066.24 lakh in total). With this net price, the adjusted state domestic product (ASDP) of Goa, i.e., net of this 'Net price', is Rs 2,56,295.70 lakh in 1996. Using the 'User Cost Method' (with expected life of the resource as 13.2 years, social discount rate of 6.00 per cent), the total user cost works out to Rs 6586.97 lakh, making the ASDP of Goa as Rs 2,50,802.03 lakh. As can be seen from the above computations, in both the methods, the adjustments have taken note of depletion of the iron-ore resource from Goa. The Net Price method would however, make the situation look very dismal. This is precisely because of basing depletion computations on a stock basis, and not on actual flow basis (as pointed out by El Serafy 1989).

A Case Study of Air Quality Accounting for India

There are four distinct characteristics of air quality that need to be noted before looking at its accountings. These are (i) Air quality is not one homogeneous concept. It involves a number of different and distinct parameters; (ii) Sources of air pollution are many, coming from production and consumption activities; (iii) Air quality is space dependent and (iv) Air quality is time dependent.

Air quality is definable in terms of a number of components or parameters. The major ones are: sulphur dioxide (SO_2), oxides of nitrogen (NO_x), suspended particulate materials (SPM), carbon monoxide (CO), hydrocarbons (HC), ammonia, ozone and volatile organic

TABLE 11.7

Adjusted Income for Goa on Account of Iron-ore Mining
(Depletion Accounting)

	Unit	1996
Physical Accounting		
Opening stock	000 tonnes	195663
Production	000 tonnes	13780
Closing stock	000 tonnes	181883
Income Accounting		
Production cost	Rs/tonne	248.40
Pithead price	Rs/tonne	477.00
Rent (net price)[a]	Rs/tonne	109.33
Total rent (net price)	Rs lakh	15,066.24
Lifetime	Years	13.2
SDP	Rs lakh	2,57,389
User Cost (at r = 6.00 per cent)	Rs lakh	6586.97
Adjusted SDP by User Cost method	Rs lakh	2,50,802.03
Adjusted SDP by Net Price method	Rs lakh	2,42,322.76

Note: [a] defined as Pithead price-production cost-profit margin
Source: TERI (2001)

compounds (VOC). Sometimes hazardous metals are also considered separately.

The major sources for these pollutants in India (specifically) are:

(i) The primary energy-producing sectors such as coal and petroleum refining etc.,
(ii) Secondary energy-producing sector, namely the power sector,
(iii) Industrial sectors (i.e., industries using chemicals and fossil fuel-based energy as inputs (e.g., petrol, diesel, coal etc.),
(iv) Transport sector (using fuels),
(v) Agriculture and livestock sector (producing methane),
(vi) Household sector (producing indoor air pollution).

The air quality varies from place to place, from time to time and from season to season, depending upon several ecological, economic social and demographic factors.

Because of such a mix of different components of air pollutants involved and the sources being a large number of production and consumption sectors, it is extremely difficult to arrive at a comprehensive information base of the physical accounts of air quality changes. Parikh and Parikh (1997) made an attempt to bring all these together in one accounting framework, using an input-output sectoral information at the all-India level, power and transport sector (in some detail) and household level emissions (including livestock sector). They have left out agriculture and mining sectors from their computations for lack of data and also for their marginal contributions. (see Table 11.8).

How to value air quality? How to arrive at integrated air quality accounts? Basically, there are two different approaches to value and account the air quality changes within an income accounting framework. They are: 'Maintenance cost or Avoidance cost Approach' and 'Impact Assessment Approach'. The first one is by following the supply channel, whereas the second is by following the demand or use channels. In either case, it is difficult to estimate the implied costs.

Ideally, the avoidance costs should be estimated by using the 'polluter pay' principle (discussed earlier). On an empirical basis, taking the data from efficient ETPs, some norms of air pollution abatement costs can be estimated. Based on such abatement costs, the corresponding value added by abatement technologies can be estimated. In so far as such abatement plants or treatment plants are not in place, the loss in value added from such non-existent abatement activities can be

TABLE 11.8

Summary Table of Physical Emission Accounts for India in 1989–90

('000 tonnes)

Sector	SO_2	NO_2	CO	VOC	SPM	Pb
Industrial	243.0	126.0	144	69.0	131	
	(4)	(4.9)	(6.6)	(1.0)	(1.5)	
Households	4898.1	992.5	425.6	5803.2	7770	
	(81.5)	(38.5)	(19.5)	(87.6)	(91.2)	
Transport	306.0	694.6	1616.7	751.4	206	15.9
	(5.1)	(27.0)	(74.0)	(11.3)	(2.4)	(100)
Power	565.0	765.0	–		410	–
	(9.4)	(29.7)			(4.8)	
Total	6012.1	2578.1	2186.3	6623.6	8517	15.9

Note: Numbers in brackets show percentages.
Source: Parikh and Parikh (1997)

considered as the value of air pollution (tolerated). Such value-added losses, if subtracted from the conventional GDP can give some indication of AGDP corresponding to air quality deterioration. Because of the complexity of this exercise, no comprehensive estimates exist in India based on this methodology.

The second method of assessing the damage due to air pollution has been attempted by a number researchers. Parikh and Parikh for the city of Mumbai (1997), Brandon and Hommann at the all-India level (1995), Parikh (2000) in this book itself, are some of the recent estimates. Basically the approach is to assess the health-damage effects. Brandon and Hommann (1995) arrive at the cost of premature deaths, costs of hospital admissions and sickness, and several minor sickness, all due to air quality deterioration in India to be in the range of US $ 517–2102 million. These estimates can be treated as first sets of satellite estimates for India.

SOME LESSONS FROM INDIAN INCOME ACCOUNTING

The methodology presented in this chapter is nothing new to economists. All resource flow accounts are to be reflected in income accounting, so also the natural resources. However, as far as natural resources are concerned, the database requirements are quite high. Therefore, instead of addressing all the components and aspects such as depletion, degradation, preservation, inter-generational values, dose-responses etc., together for each of the resource, efforts should be made to carry out more and more case studies and gain experience in applying different methods to different resources. Secondly, more theoretical researches are required to integrate the accounts, with an objective of arriving at an indicator of sustainable income of the economy. Some of the major national level parameters such as shadow prices of exhaustible resources or renewable resources should be developed by macro level development models (Howarth, 1991). Likewise, elasticities of air and water pollution on health, mortality and morbidity etc., can be developed by using national-level data. The National Sample Survey (NSS), having engaged in a survey of environmental status of the economy, together with demographic and health-status data from various other sources can be used to develop some of these parameters. Thirdly, environmental economists and statisticians should continue to demonstrate the possibilities of adjusting the domestic products for all the natural resource-related issues, some of which may not directly appear in the traditional income accountings (e.g., biodiversity). Certainly, a long way to go before a complete SEEA is available for policy planning for India.

The case studies presented are, by and large on individual resource-based levels, or at best at sectoral levels. They have been developed through studies by various scholars. They may be, in some instances, illustrative. But they have exposed the statistical possibilities to compute the adjusted income accounts for resources such as air, minerals, water and forests. The case studies, however, indicate that environmental accountings would substantially alter the usual income accounts. Such estimates, therefore, can become very useful for applying precautionary brakes in the use of natural resources.

REFERENCES

Alfsen, K.H. and B. Torstein (1990): 'Norwegian experience in natural resource accounting', *Development, Journal of SID*, 3(4):119–30.

Anderson, D. (1987): *The Economics of Afforestation: A Case Study in Africa*, John Hopkins University Press, London.

Bateman, I.J. and R.K. Turner (1993): 'Valuation of the environment methods and techniques: The contingent valuation method', in R.K. Turner (ed.), *Environmental Economics and Management: Principles and Practice*, Belhaven Press, London.

Brandon, Carter and Kirsten Hommann (1995): '*The cost of inaction: Valuing the economy-wide cost of environmental degradation in India*', The World Bank, Asia Environment Division, Washington, D.C.

Bromley, D.W. (1995): *Hand Book of Environmental Economics*, Blackwell, New York.

Carson, R.T., E.F. Nicholas, M.M. Kerry and J.L. Wright (1996): 'Contingent valuation and revealed preference methodologies: Comparing the estimates for quasi-public goods', *Land Economics*, 72 (1): 80–99.

Chopra, K. and Gopal Kadekodi (1997): Natural Resource Accounting in the Yamuna Basin: Accounting for Forest Resources, IEG Monograph, New Delhi.

Dasgupta, P.S. and G.M. Heal (1979): *Economic Theory and Exhaustible Resources*, Cambridge University Press, Cambridge.

Dasgupta, P., B. Kristrom and K–G Maler (1994): 'Current issues in resource accounting', Beijer Discussion Paper Series, No. 47, The Royal Swedish Academy of Sciences, Stockholm.

Dixit, A., P. Diamond and M. Hoel (1980): 'On Hartwick's rule for regular maximum paths of capital accumulation and resource depletion', *Review of Economic Studies*, 47: 551–56.

El Serafy, S. (1989): 'The proper calculation of income from depletable natural resources', in Y.J. Ahmed, et al., (eds.), *Environmental Accounting for Sustainable Development*, Washington, D.C., World Bank.

Fisher, A.C. and J.V. Krutilla (1985): 'The economics of nature preservation', in A.V. Kneese and J.L. Seeney (eds.), *Handbook of Natural Resources and Energy Economics*, vol. 1, North Holland Publication, Amsterdam, pp. 165–89.

Garrod, Guy and K.G. Smith (1999): *Economic Valuation of the Environment: Methods and Case Studies*, Edward Elgar Publications, Cheltanham.

Government of India (1996): Forestry Statistics—1996', Indian Council of Forestry Research and Education, Dehradun.

—— (1997): 'State of Forestry in India', Indian Council of Forestry Research and Education, Dehradun.

Grey, L.C. (19s14): 'Rent under the assumption of exhaustibility', *Quarterly Journal of Economics*, 28: 466–89.

Hartwick, J.M. (1990): 'Natural resources, national income accounting and economic depreciation', *Journal of Public Economics*, 43: 291–304.

—— (1992): 'Deforestation and national accounting', *Environmental and Resource Economics* 2(5): 513–22.

Hicks, J.R. (1940): 'The Valuation of Social Income', *Economica* VII: 105–24.

—— (1946): *Value and Capital*, 2nd Edition, Oxford University Press, Oxford.

Hicks, J.R. (1971): *The Social Framework: An introduction to economics*, 4th edition, Oxford University Press, Delhi.

Hoevenagel, R. (1996): 'The validity of the contingent valuation method: Perfect and regular embedding', *Environmental and Resource Economics*, 7(1): 57–78.

Hotelling, H. (1931): 'The Economics of Exhaustible Resources', *Journal of Political Economy*, 39: 137–75.

Howarth, R.B. (1991): 'Inter temporal equilibria and exhaustible resource: An overlapping generations approach', *Ecological Economics*, 5(3): 237–47.

Hueting, R. (1989): 'Correcting national income for environmental losses: Towards a practical solution', in Y.J. Ahmed, S. El Serafy, and E. Lutz, (eds.), *Environmental Accounting for Sustainable Development*, The World Bank, Washington D.C., 32–9.

Hultkrantz, L. (1991): 'National accounting of timber and forest environmental resources in Sweden', *Environmental and Resource Economics*, 2: 283–305.

International Institute of Environment and Development (IIED), (1994): Economic Evaluation of Tropical Forest Land Use Options: A review of methodology and applications, Environment Economic Programme, Monograph.

Kadekodi, G.K. (1982): *Economic Planning for Iron Ore Sector in India*, Hindustan Publishing House, New Delhi.

Kadekodi, Gopal and M.M. Agarwal (1998): 'Integration of Preservation, Depletion, and Degradation of Natural Resources in Income Accounting', Institute of Economic Growth, Working Paper Series, No. E/189/98, Delhi.

Kadekodi, Gopal and N.H. Ravindranath (1997): 'A macro-economic analysis of forestry options on carbon sequestration', *Ecological Economics* 23: 201–23.

Kulshreshtha, A.C. and Gulab Singh (1997): *1993 SNA Production and Assets Boundaries: Issues and Problems in Measurement in the Context of Indian National Accounts*, Paper presented at the Workshop on Contribution of Unorganized Sector: Administrative Arrangements, National Council of Applied Economic Research (NCAER), New Delhi, 31 March–2 April.

Leontief, W. (1966): *Input-Output Economics*, Oxford University Press, New York.

Maler, K-G. (1991): 'National accounts and environmental resources', *Environmental and Resource Economics* 1: 1–15.

Mitchell, R.C. and R.T. Carson (1989): *Using Surveys to Value Public Goods:*

The Contingent Valuation Method, The John Hopkins University Press for Resources for the Future, Washington, D.C.

Murty, M.N., A.J. James, and Smita Misra (1999): *The Economics of Water Pollution: The Indian Experience*, Oxford University Press, New Delhi.

Murty, M.N., B.N. Goldar, Gopal Kadekodi and S.N. Mishra (1992): National Parameters for Investment Project Appraisal in India, Monograph, Institute of Economic Growth, New Delhi.

National Environmental Engineering Research Institute (1997): Natural Resource Accounting in Yamuna river sub-basin, Draft interim report, Nagpur: Mimeograph, February.

Navrud, S. and E.D. Mungatana (1994): 'Environmental valuation in developing countries: The recreation value of wildlife viewing', *Ecological Economics*, 11: 135–151.

Netherlands Central Bureau of Statistics (NCBS) (1993): *Environmental Statistics of the Netherlands*, SDU Publications, The Hague.

O'Connor, Martin, L. Clive and S. Spash (eds.), (1998): *Valuation and the Environment: Theory, Method and Practice*, Edward Elgar Publications, Cheltanham.

Pandit, M.K. (1997): 'Ecological economics: Towards a synthesis of two disjunct disciplines', *Current Science* 72(2): 119–23.

Parikh, Kirit and Utpal Ghosh (1995): 'Natural Resource Accounting for Soils: Towards an empirical estimate of costs of soil degradation for India', IGIDR Discussion paper No. 48, Indira Gandhi Institute of Development Research, Mumbai.

Parikh, K.S. and Jyoti Parikh (1997): *Accounting and Valuation of Environment*: volume I: A premier for developing countries, Volume II: Case Studies from the ESCAP Region, United Nations, New York.

Parikh, K.S., J.K. Parikh, V.K. Sharma, and J.P. Painuly (1992): Natural Resource Accounting: A framework for India, Monograph, Indira Gandhi Institute of Development Research, Mumbai.

Penido-Vasquez, M. D. Zarin and P. Jipp (1992): Economic Returns from Forest Conversion in the Peruvian Amazon, *Ecological Economics*, 6: 163–174.

Peskin, H.M. (1989): 'Accounting for Natural Resource Depletion and Degradation in Developing Countries', Policy Planning Environment Department, Working paper No. 13, The World Bank.

Repetto, R., W. Magrath, M. Wells, C. Beer, and F. Rossini (1989): *Wasting Assets: Natural Resources in the National Income Accounts*, World Resources Institute, New York.

Samuelson, P.A. (1963): *Foundation of Economic Analysis*, Cambridge University Press, Harvard.

Smith, V.K. (1996): *Estimating Economic Values for Nature*, Edward Elgar Publications, Cheltanham.

Stone, R. (1961): *Input-Output and National Accounts*, OECD, Paris.

Tata Energy Research Institute (2001): Pilot Project on Natural Resource Accounting in Goa (Phase 1), TERI Project Report No. 99RD61.

Tobias, D. and R. Mendelson (1991): 'Valuing ecotourism in a tropical rain forest reserve', *Ambio*, 20(2).

Turner, R.K. (1993): *Sustainable Environmental Economics and Management: Principles and Practices*, Belhaven Press, New York.

United Nations (1968): *A System of National Accounts*, Publication E-69, XVII.3, New York.

—— (1993): *Integrated Environmental and Economic Accounting*, Interim version, Studies in Methods Series, F. No. 61, Department of Economic and Social Information and Policy Analysis, New York.

United Nations Environment Programme (1993): 'Environmental accounting: A review of the current debate', Environment and Economics Unit, Environmental Economics Series, Paper No. 8.

Verma, Madhu (2000): 'Economic Valuation of Forests of Himachal Pradesh', in Himachal Pradesh Forest Sector Review, International Institute for Environment and Development, London.

Weitzman, M.L. (1976): 'On the welfare significance of national product in a dynamic economy', *Quarterly Journal of Economics*, 90: 156–62.